THE PURSUIT OF ITALY

THE PURSUIT
OF ITALY

A HISTORY OF A LAND,

ITS REGIONS, AND THEIR PEOPLES

DAVID GILMOUR

FARRAR, STRAUS AND GIROUX

NEW YORK

Farrar, Straus and Giroux
18 West 18th Street, New York 10011

Copyright © 2011 by David Gilmour
Printed in the United States of America
Originally published in 2011 by Allen Lane, a division of
Penguin Books Ltd., Great Britain
Published in the United States by Farrar, Straus and Giroux
First American edition, 2011

Library of Congress Cataloging-in-Publication Data
Gilmour, David, 1952–
    The pursuit of Italy : a history of a land, its regions, and their
peoples / David Gilmour. — 1st American ed.
        p.   cm.
    Includes bibliographical references and index.
    ISBN 978-0-374-28316-2 (hardcover : alk. paper)   1. Italy—History.
2. Italy—Civilization.   I. Title.

DG467. G55 2011b
945—dc23

                                                        2011022110

                www.fsgbooks.com

            1   3   5   7   9   10   8   6   4   2

To Ming and Elspeth Campbell

'Italiam non sponte sequor'
'[It is by divine will] not my own that I pursue Italy.'
Virgil, *Aeneid*, Book 4

Contents

CONTENTS

List of Illustrations

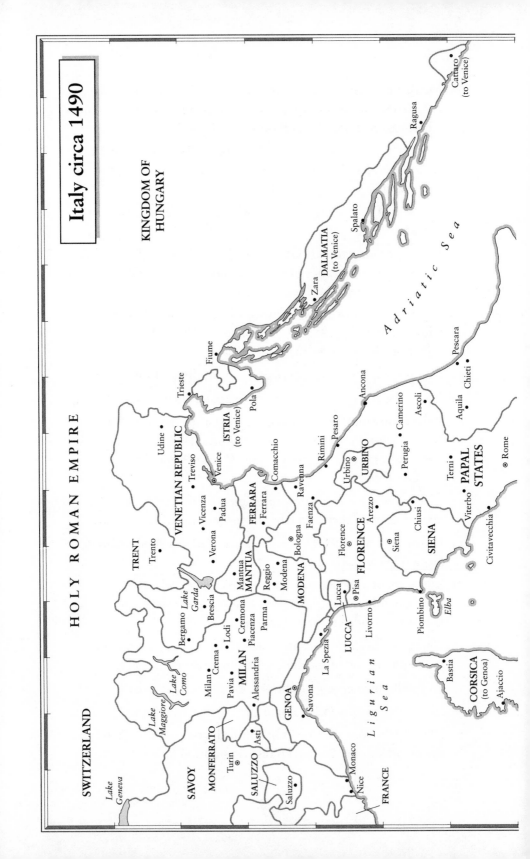

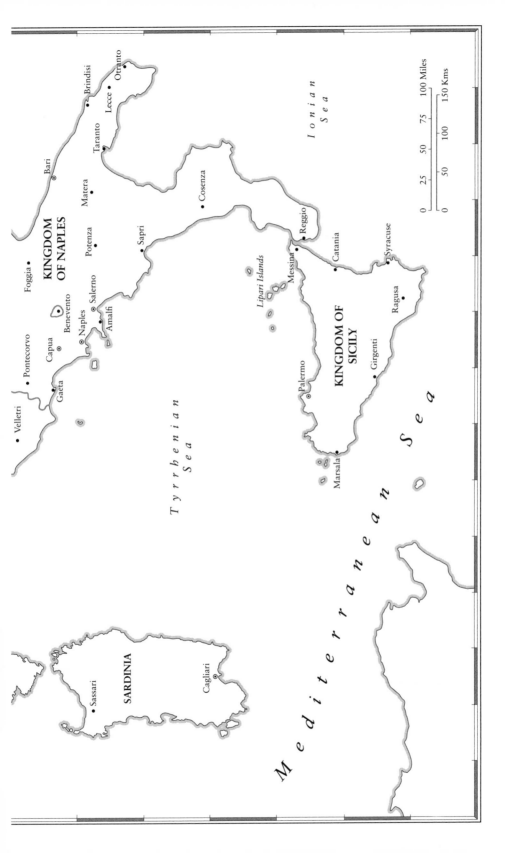

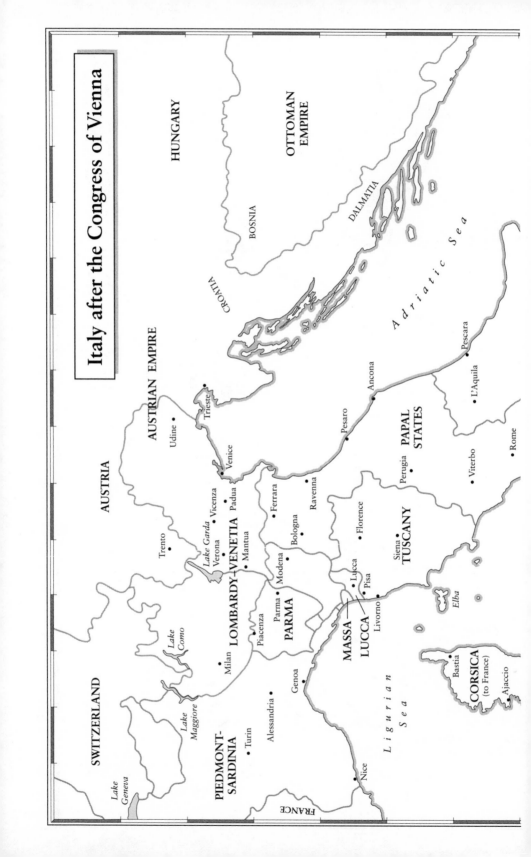

Italy after the Congress of Vienna

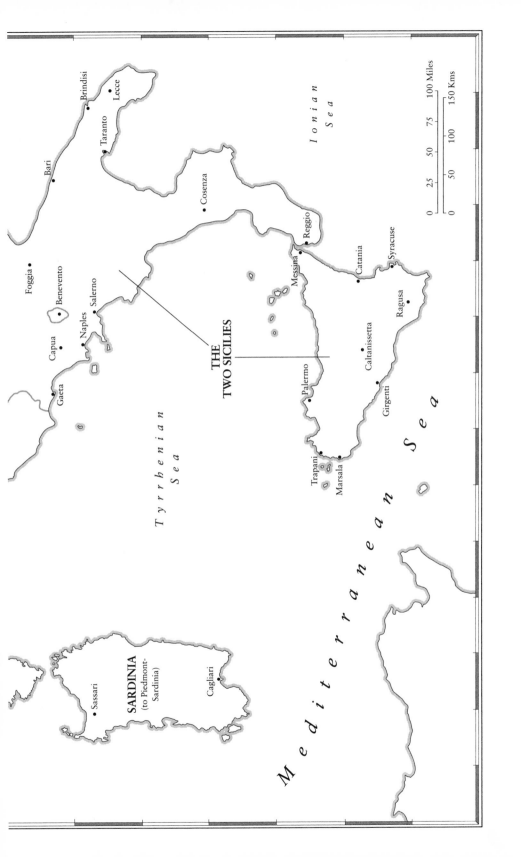

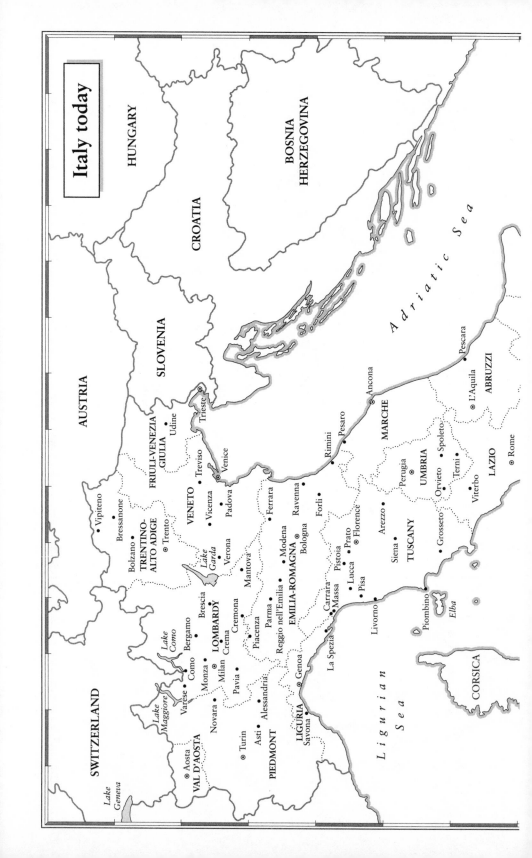

Italy today

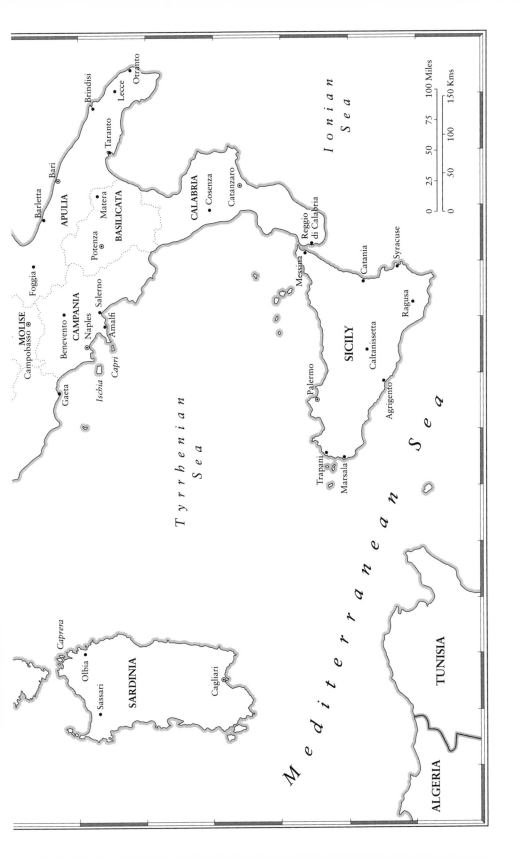

THE PURSUIT OF ITALY

Introduction

In the 1970s I visited a villa built in the fifteenth century by Lorenzo de' Medici, the Florentine ruler known as 'the Magnificent'. Shielded to the north by the wooded slopes of the Monti Pisani, it looked south over the Valley of the Arno; in the distance, beyond palm trees in the garden and olive groves a little farther off, you could see the Leaning Tower and the sea behind. The interior was of more recent decoration than the stark Renaissance façade: its enfilade of south-facing rooms breathed the nineteenth century, from their Empire furniture to the cluttered bric-à-brac of the fin-de-siècle. It was easy on later visits to imagine the house peopled with the noblemen of the Risorgimento, to envisage Count Cavour holding forth at the dining-room table with Baron Ricasoli or the Marquess d'Azeglio.

My host, Giovanni Tadini, was a dilettante of erudition and cosmopolitan tastes, an aristocrat of Piedmontese origin brought up in Siena. He remained a monarchist in republican Italy and stayed loyal to the Savoia, the exiled royal family; sometimes he talked, quite unpretentiously, about earlier Italian rulers such as the Medici as if they had been personal friends who had recently died. Showing me around his house, he might sigh at a portrait of Elisa Bonaparte, who had briefly ruled in Tuscany, or commend an etching of Santa Maria Novella, Alberti's Renaissance masterpiece in Florence. On the piano he would open a book of caricatures of customers at the Caffè Michelangiolo or show me his first edition of *The Struwwelpeter Alphabet*, an Edwardian children's book containing the immortally bad lines, 'When the Empire wants a stitch in her / Send for Kipling and for Kitchener.' As we wandered through rooms suffused with the scent of parma violets in brass jardinières, he would mix historical anecdotes

I

with personal memories, recounted in a deep orotund voice and interspersed with much rolling laughter. Sometimes treated as an informal ambassador in his own country, he was once called upon to escort Queen Elizabeth the Queen Mother to some of the great villas of Lucca and Florence as well as to Pisa cathedral at midnight. 'Wherever we went,' he recalled, 'her chief anxiety was to avoid the cups of tea that everyone offered and to seek out the gin.'

Giovanni had had a governess, Miss Ramage, and spoke English with better syntax and a wider vocabulary than most Britons. But the governess had been gone for four decades, and some of her sayings had been amended in her absence. 'As you can imagine,' he would remark gurgling, 'I felt like an elephant in a china shop' or, concluding a salacious story with a rich chuckle, would say, 'So I let them stew in their own gravy.' If he heard an interesting remark he would 'prop up' his ears; if I answered one of his questions accurately, he would beam and say, 'Hats off.'

After dinner I was examining a porcelain figurine of Cavour when a trim, elderly, silver-haired gentleman approached and introduced himself. He was Paolo Rossi, not the football player or the actor-musician but a distinguished politician and judge, a social democrat who in his youth had been an opponent of Mussolini. 'So,' he said, after seeing what I was looking at, 'you are interested in the unification, in the *Unità d'Italia*?' At the time I was a young journalist writing about Lebanon in the early years of its civil war, but I remembered enough from my schooldays to know what he was talking about.

My history teacher in the 1960s had been an old-fashioned liberal who, unfamiliar with the revisionist work of the great historian Denis Mack Smith, believed that Italy's Risorgimento had been an exemplary case of liberty triumphing over repression. In consequence I was astounded by the next words of Signor Rossi, who twenty years earlier had been minister of education. 'You know, Davide,' he said in a low conspiratorial voice, as if nervously uttering a heresy, 'Garibaldi did Italy a great disservice. If he had not invaded Sicily and Naples, we in the north would have the richest and most civilized state in Europe.' After looking round the room at the other guests, he added in an even lower voice, 'Of course to the south we would have a neighbour like Egypt.'

My work soon took me to Palestine, then back to Lebanon and next to post-Franco Spain, so it was several years before I could return to Italy and go to Palermo to write a biography of Giuseppe Tomasi di Lampedusa, the author of *The Leopard*. Yet the judge's words stayed in my mind, and I started to question whether the unification of Italy had been either a necessary or a successful enterprise. I never accepted his view that the Bourbon kingdom of Naples would have been like Egypt, but I sometimes wondered whether Italians might have been better off divided into three, four or even more states. Italians seemed to me to be internationalist and (in a good sense) provincial but not nationalist except when their leaders forced or cajoled them into being so. In any case nations are not inevitable, as the people of Kurdistan well know, and sometimes their creation is so artificial that, as with Yugoslavia, they simply fall apart. In today's Europe, which contains so many successful small nations, there surely would have been room for a flourishing Tuscany, perhaps the most civilized state of the eighteenth century, and a prosperous Venice, a once great republic with a thousand years of independent history.

Several years ago, I decided to stay in each of Italy's twenty regions and thus acquire some knowledge of them and their numerous diversities. Traditional histories of Italy had been written from a centripetal view, as if Italian unity had been pre-ordained. I wanted to look at the peninsula's centrifugal tendencies and inquire whether the lateness of unification and the troubles of the nation state had been not accidents of history but consequences of the peninsula's past and its geography, which may have made it unsuitable territory for nationalism. Were there not just too many Italies for a successful unity?

I thought at first of writing about the nineteenth and twentieth centuries, the periods of Lampedusa's novel and of his life, but I found myself always wanting to go further back, and then further still, to find what, if anything, earlier generations had felt about the concept of Italy, what the Enlightenment had thought, what Dante had believed, what Machiavelli had wanted, what the Emperors Augustus, Charlemagne, Frederick 'stupor mundi' and Napoleon had all made of it. When I told my editor, Stuart Proffitt, that Cicero had possessed an idea of Italy, he said, 'David, go back to Cicero.'

I have gone back to Cicero and to Virgil and to subsequent eras too, all of which thought of Italy in their own, often different fashions. The early chapters in this book do not pretend to be a history of the 2,000 years before Napoleon Bonaparte pounced on Italy and created havoc in 1796; rather they are a chronological sketch that attempts to identify the diversities and centrifugal inclinations in Italian history and to assess the way they influenced the course of the peninsula's more recent history.

Since this is not an academic work, I have allowed myself to be quirkily subjective in my selection of topics and to give perhaps disproportionate space to those that seem especially illustrative of various moments or eras: the medieval frescoes in Siena, for instance, and the commemorative statuary in Turin, the early operas of Giuseppe Verdi and a peculiar film by the marxist director Bernardo Bertolucci. This is the book of a modest traveller as well as of an historian – and of a listener too, because for many years I have enjoyed listening to Italians telling me about their lives and about their histories. The incomparable Richard Cobb, who taught me nearly forty years ago at Oxford, used to say that much of eighteenth- and nineteenth-century French history could be walked, seen, smelled and above all heard in cafés, buses and on park benches in Paris and Lyon, his favourite cities. Much the same is true of Italy, of eighteenth-century Naples, for example, or nineteenth-century Turin. I once visited a dismal café near the Porta Nuova station in the Piedmontese capital where the kind but gloomy *padrona* talked at length of the crimes of Neapolitans before ending with a sigh and the words, 'But while we know how to work, they know how to live.' Even today the differences between the two cities are so strong that I sometimes wonder that they belong to the same state. Was Naples, which 400 years ago was the second-largest city in Christendom, destined to become merely a regional capital with the status of Bari or Potenza?

I have encountered much kindness and inspiration in the thirty-five years since I first travelled to Italy. My earliest and perhaps most important debt is to my first friend there, Angelo Pardini, an elderly Tuscan *contadino* who farmed some scrappy acres of vines and olives owned by my parents in a village north-west of Lucca. His rent consisted of a few litres of murky oil and some demijohns of red and white wine, each of which was undrinkable in alternate years; in defence of his product he claimed, no doubt rightly, that it was pure and free of chemicals. He worked at other farms too and complained of *troppo lavoro*, too much work, yet he was often to be found in the early afternoon at the local trattoria, drinking a *caffè corretto*, coffee 'corrected' with a slug of grappa or Vecchia Romagna brandy, and he once admitted that he drank water only twice a year. His politics were a little confused: he voted christian democrat, he belonged to the communist trade union and he thought Mussolini had been a good chap, *molto bravo*.

Angelo was a man of great charm and much earthy wisdom. He took me to council meetings of the local *comune* in Pescaglia, introduced me to his fellow agricultural workers (mostly Sardinians) and occasionally drove me to his ancestral village, high in the hills above Camaiore, where his neighbour, a veteran of the First World War, sang songs celebrating the Battle of Vittorio Veneto against the Austrians in 1918. He had a lovely, vaguely Alsatian dog and gave me one of her puppies, but he had been careless about supervising its paternity, and a charming but very curious-looking creature was presented to me. La Giulia, as everyone called Angelo's wife, was a lady so large and formidable that she could only fit into his Fiat Cinquecento when the passenger seat had been removed. She was a wonderful cook of rustic dishes using a few local ingredients and made sublime polenta, served on linen and cut with a cotton thread. In the thirty years since her death I have been searching unsuccessfully for polenta of that quality, a quest which may explain some unappreciative remarks made about that yellow maize porridge later in this book.

I would like to be able to write similarly about other friends and acquaintances, Italian and British, who have helped me try to understand Italy, but must limit myself to making a list of those, many of them alas dead, to whom I am particularly indebted: Harold Acton, Giancarlo Aragona, Vernon Bartlett, Tina Battistoni, Boris Biancheri, Gerardo di Bugnano, Giancarlo Carofiglio, Franco Cassano, Cristina Celestini, Rosso Dante, Leglio Deghe' and his wife Susan, Deda Fezzi Price, Bona Frescobaldi, Dino Fruzza, Giuseppe Galasso, Michael Grant, Roberta Higgins, Carlo Knight, Denis Mack Smith, Donatella Manzottu, Roberto Martucci, Gabriele Pantucci, Emanuela Polo, Paolo

Rossi, Cintia Rucellai, Steven Runciman, Giuseppe di Sarzana, Ignacio Segorbe and his wife Gola, Gaia Servadio, Xan Smiley, Giovanni Tadini, Riccardo Tomacelli, Nichi Vendola, Dennis Walters, Giles Watson and his wife Mariagrazia Gerardi, Edoardo Winspeare and Francesco Winspeare.

I am especially thankful to those friends and relations who have read all or parts of the manuscript and who have given much useful advice on the text: Christopher Duggan, my brother Andrew Gilmour, my wife Sarah Gilmour, Ramachandra Guha, Richard Jenkyns, Robin Lane Fox, Gioacchino Lanza Tomasi, Nicoletta Polo, Maria Luisa Radighieri and Beppe Severgnini. The book has also had the good fortune to attract two great editors on either side of the Atlantic, Stuart Proffitt in London and Elisabeth Sifton in New York. I am immensely grateful to them both for their inspired, sustained and invariably good advice. Gillon Aitken, my literary agent, has been as generous as ever with soothing wisdom, and I am indebted also to those involved in the production of the book, especially Eugénie Aperghis van Nispen, Richard Duguid, Jenny Fry and David Watson. I owe special and perennial gratitude to my wife Sarah, who has at all times been reassuring, supportive and extraordinarily patient.

NOTE ON NAMES

I have usually retained people's Christian names in their original languages except for popes, kings and emperors whose anglicized forms are more familiar. I have, however, made the odd monarchical exception for the sake of clarity. In an era when Francis was a popular name for sovereigns, I have kept Francesco for the last King of the Two Sicilies and Franz-Josef for the penultimate Emperor of Austria. I have also decided not to inflict the name Humbert on those Kings of Italy baptized as Umberto.

I

Diverse Italies

FRACTURED GEOGRAPHY

Italy, complained Napoleon, is too long. It is indeed very long, the longest country in Europe outside Scandinavia and the Ukraine. It is also one of the thinnest, its peninsula about as narrow as Portugal and the Netherlands, broader only than Albania and Luxembourg. Ugo La Malfa, a republican politician of the twentieth century, liked to picture the country as a man with his feet in Africa and his hands clutching the Alps, trying to pull himself up into the middle of Europe.[1]

We think of Italy as a country with a north and a south, but actually its 720 miles run diagonally through different climatic and vegetation zones from the town of Aosta in the north-west, where French is an official language, to the Salentine Peninsula in the Apulian south-east, where Greek is still spoken. On the battlements of the Castle of Otranto you feel you are in the Balkans, and in a sense you are: you can see the mountains of Greece and Albania across the water; you are closer to Istanbul and the Ukraine than you are to Aosta; the Black Sea is nearer than the west coast of Sardinia. When Apulia joined the Kingdom of Italy in 1861, the new state's capital was Turin, a city so far away that Otranto is today closer to seventeen foreign capitals than it is to Turin. No wonder you sometimes hear Apulians refer to themselves as Greeks or Levantines. Sometimes they pretend that they are not also Italians.

In 1847 the Austrian chancellor, Prince Metternich, dismissed Italy as '*une expression géographique*', a remark that has subsequently succeeded in annoying many people, especially Italians and historians. At the time Italy may have been more than a geographical expression – though it was still divided into eight independent states – but Metternich was repeating a view widely held for more than 2,000 years: Italy, like Iberia, may have been a geographical unit with natural borders but it had not been united since Roman times and did not seem to require political unity now or in the future.

Italy seems to begin with the myth of Hercules, the Greek hero who rescued a stray calf that had wandered across southern Italy and swum the Straits of Messina. The land the animal crossed duly became known as Italia, from the word *ouitoulos* or bull-calf, a word that has also bequeathed us, via Oscan and Latin, the word *vitello* or veal. A related theory, recorded by the Greek historian Timaeus, held that the ancient Greeks had been so impressed by the cattle in Italy that they had rewarded the land with the same name.

This may be the explanation for the origin of the name 'Italia', but it does not seem quite convincing. For centuries northern visitors have been scathing about the skinny appearance of Italian cows, especially the small, white, wide-horned ones bred mainly for pulling carts and drawing ploughs. The arid south of the peninsula, bereft of pasture and hay fields, can hardly have seemed a herdsman's paradise even for the Greeks: the great Murge Plateau in Apulia cannot support cattle because it does not have streams. Italy today has to import more than half the milk it consumes and, if we associate the south with any kind of cattle now, it is with water buffaloes, producers of the milk used in making the soft white cheese *mozzarella di bùfala*. Yet the buffaloes are of Asian origin and were brought to Italy for ploughing in the early Middle Ages; later they went wild, roaming over Campania and the Pontine Marshes before they were domesticated once more in the eighteenth century. Used as draught animals rather than for milk and meat, the herds seemed to be dying out in the first half of the twenti-eth century. Their famous product did not become either famous or fashionable until the 1980s.

In the fifth century BC the word 'Italia' applied only to the Cala-brian toe of the Italian 'boot', which was inhabited by a people known as the Bruttians. Later it was extended to Lucania and Campania, and later still the term spread northwards to describe Rome's conquests in the peninsula. The Greek historians Herodotus and Thucydides did not regard the land beyond the River Po as a part of Italy, and indeed geographically the Po Valley belongs to the continental land-mass not the peninsula. But after the Romans had subdued its Gallic tribes and reached the Alps, that area too was added to Italia. By the second century BC another Greek historian, Polybius, confirmed that almost the whole of modern Italy was then Italia, though Roman poets of a later age sometimes called it by other names such as Hesperia, Ausonia, Saturnia terra and (appropriately for what is now the largest wine producer in the world) Oenotria, 'the land of wine'.

There was one sharp check to this progress. In 91 BC some of Rome's *socii* (subservient allies) rebelled and set up a state in the central Apennines called Italia, with a capital Corfinium (renamed Italica), administered by praetors, a senate and two consuls. The insurgents even produced coins showing the bull of Italia goring and about to rape the Roman wolf. They were defeated, however, in the ensuing Social War by Rome's traditional tactic of brutality plus concessions, and no further attempt was made to set up a state called Italy for many centuries to come.

Within a century of the war, the earlier version of Italia was organized as an administrative unit by Augustus, the first Roman emperor, who divided it into eleven districts; the Istrian Peninsula, which was joined to Venetia, was the only part that does not belong to the modern state of Italy.* A later emperor, Diocletian, expanded Italia to include Sicily, Sardinia, Corsica and Raetia, a district that contained parts of what are now Switzerland, Bavaria and the Tyrol.

Augustan Italy, lauded by Virgil and his fellow poets, remained an inspiration to the poets of the Middle Ages, to Petrarch who sang of 'the fair land / That the Apennines divide and the sea and the Alps surround',[2] and to many others later on. Yet until the end of the eighteenth century Italy remained a literary idea, an abstract concept, an imaginary homeland or simply a sentimental urge. If at times people used it to express resentment at foreign occupation, its independence and unity were not political aspirations. And for a large majority of the population it meant nothing at all. Even in 1861, at the time of unification, some Sicilians thought L'Italia – or rather la Talia – was their new queen. A full century later, the social reformer Danilo Dolci

*See map 3 on pp. xx–xxi.

encountered Sicilians who had never heard of Italy and asked him what it was.[3]

The geography we imbibe from school textbooks and atlases makes us think that Italy is peculiarly blessed in its position. According to the revolutionary patriot Giuseppe Mazzini, God had given Italians 'the most clearly demarcated fatherland in Europe'.[4] There it lies in the centre of the Mediterranean, protected in the north by its Alpine ramparts and everywhere else by its seas.

Italy is actually extremely unfortunate in its position, which has made it one of the most easily and frequently invaded places in the world. The Alps may look impressive but they have been penetrated without difficulty since the Bronze Age. In the twelfth century BC traders were bringing amber from the Baltic across the Alps to Etruria and Sardinia; by the Roman era seventeen of the twenty-three Alpine passes were being used. Few ramparts have been so consistently surmounted down the centuries. Hannibal brought his Carthaginian army over the Western Alps, while Alaric's Goths and Attila's Huns came from the east through the lower Julian and Carnic Alps. In 1796 General Bonaparte, as he then was, marched through the Maritime Alps between Nice and Genoa – allowing him to boast to his soldiers, '*Annibal a forcé les Alpes – nous, nous les avons tournés*' – but four years later, now as first consul, he descended on Italy through five more northerly passes. Afterwards he had himself painted riding a white charger through the snows of the Great St Bernard, though in fact he had been led through them on a little grey mule.

Many other aggressors have emulated these invaders of Italy. Once they had got through the passes and on to the plain, they could speed up across the Po Valley, which was flat, inviting and difficult to defend, unless they were attacking from the west, in which case they were hindered by tributaries of the Po flowing southwards in parallel from the northern lakes: Milan was simple to capture, and those other 'gateways' to Italy, Turin and Verona, were not much harder. One reason why the eastern Roman Empire (Byzantium) lasted for a thousand years longer than its western counterpart was that it was much easier to defend. The Goths and Huns might rampage around the Balkans but they were halted at Constantinople by the city walls and a fleet that prevented then from crossing the Bosphorus and ravaging Asia Minor. Later the Byzantines performed a similar feat in reverse, blocking the Arabs in the seventh century and thus preventing them from pouring into eastern Europe, reaching Italy and doubtless islamicizing Rome. At a time, a century before Charlemagne, when Europe was militarily weak, Byzantium saved it and made possible its later rise to dominance. Apart from the French Riviera, the Italian peninsula has the only Mediterranean coasts that (except around Bari) have never been Muslim.

Its seas made Italy even more vulnerable than its mountains. With 4,500 miles of coastline, the peninsula and its islands are almost impossible to patrol. They can be attacked from all directions by predators from three continents.

Boats were man's first means of transport, and by 5000 BC these had become sufficiently sturdy to undertake long sea voyages. In the fifth century BC Herodotus observed that a boat could sail 75 miles in twenty-four hours, a statistic suggesting that invaders of Italy from the Albanian shore could cross the 45 miles of the Strait of Otranto in summer daylight. The Adriatic was thus always a threat. To safeguard the Italian shore, one had to control the eastern shore with its useful harbours as well as Corfu, the island guarding the entrance to the strait. Venice could never have pretended to be the Queen (or Bride) of the Adriatic or the Lion of the Sea – let alone la Serenissima – if it had not bullied the Dalmatian city of Zara (now Zadar), if Trieste had become a serious rival or if Ragusa (later Dubrovnik) had developed a naval strength commensurate with its commercial power. During the great centuries of its republic, Venice was forced to construct its own integrated, protective world in the Adriatic, much of whose population was not Italian. No wonder that cartographers so often referred to the sea as the Gulf of Venice.

The islands were still more of a liability than the mainland coast. Despite its closeness to Tuscany, Elba in the sixteenth century was so frequently attacked by invaders from Africa (who were once known as the Barbary corsairs) that its inhabitants abandoned their homes along the shore and went to live in the hills. The same danger depopulated the coasts of Sardinia, whose forts and watchtowers did little to deter raiders questing for slaves; the island had already been an easy prey for invading Phoenicians, Carthaginians, Romans, Vandals, Byzantines, Arabs and Aragonese, as well as for more commercial colonialists in the form of Pisans and Genoese. Sicily had a similar problem on a grander scale, its position making it impossible for its inhabitants to control their destiny for the last two and a half thousand years. Syracuse's defeat of the Athenians during the Peloponnesian War in the fifth century BC was the island's most recent successful resistance against a serious invader. Since then, it has been too small and weak to defend itself, yet too large, too strategically important and (until the later Middle Ages) too fertile to escape invasions. It thus became a sort of prize for the dominant power in the western Mediterranean.

This Sicilian fate was in a less concentrated and continuous form the fate of the whole of Italy. Until the advent of Great Power diplomacy in the mid-nineteenth century, geography determined that for most of its history Italy had to conquer or be dominated by others. Its destinies could be those of either an imperial power or a type of colony but not those of a nation-state. A comparison with England, whose seas and navies have protected it, is illuminating. The Normans invaded Sicily in 1060 and England in 1066 and in both places established flourishing kingdoms, the Sicilian one being much the richer of the two. Over the subsequent millennium several English claimants crossed the Channel and seized the throne, but there has been only one successful invasion of England by a foreign army, the Dutch force in 1688, an event which was neither entirely foreign nor a typical invasion because William of Orange had been invited by powerful English politicians to overthrow the unpopular James II, his uncle and father-in-law. During the same nine centuries Italy was successfully invaded by Angevins, Aragonese, Germans (several times), French (many times), Spanish, Turks (briefly), Austrians (frequently), Russians, British and Americans.* None of them, however, was able to control the whole of the peninsula.

Whereas for England the North Sea is an obvious advantage, both

---

*An inexhaustive list of victorious invaders before 1060 would include Sicans, Elymians, Sicels, Greeks, Phoenicians, Carthaginians, Celts, Cimbri, Visigoths, Ostrogoths, Vandals, Alans, Huns, Lombards, Byzantines, Franks, Magyars, Vikings and Arabs.

economic and military, the virtues of the Mediterranean are less apparent to Italy. In fact the relationship of land and water around the peninsula is a complicated one. Despite its extensive coastline, Italy has only a few satisfactory ports, Genoa, La Spezia and Naples on the Tyrrhenian Sea, Taranto on the Ionian, Ancona, Brindisi and Venice in the Adriatic. Amalfi, which somehow managed to become a maritime power in the ninth century, has a very short beach and no proper harbour; it survived as a republic mainly by assisting Arab raiders attacking other parts of the Italian coast.* It did, however, have the advantages of Campanian hemp and flax for ropes and access to forests for building ships. Timber shortages in much of the rest of Italy hampered the construction of great navies. Although there were fine forests near the sea, especially in Tuscany and the Gargano Peninsula, the Mediterranean climate ensured that, once they had been cut down and the topsoil had been washed away, they did not regenerate properly, particularly in the south, where herds of goats roamed among the saplings. Much of the Sardinian coastline was thus covered by *màcchia*, the aromatic Mediterranean scrub that is good for the senses and perhaps for the soul but not for human welfare or the ecology of the zone.

The timber available in the peninsula was adequate during classical times, when deforestation had only just started, but it was not sufficient for Italians later on to compete with the Atlantic navies of England and Holland, which had access to Baltic forests, or the imperial fleets of Spain and Portugal. The shortage of oak, considered vital for ships' hulls, was a perennial problem. The Venetians felled the forests of Dalmatia for their vessels, for the millions of stakes required for the foundations of their buildings and for the thousands of *bricole*, the posts strapped together in wigwam shape that mark the navigable channels of the lagoon. Naturally the forests could not suffice for very long. In the epoch of its triumph against the Turks at the Battle of Lepanto (1571), Venice was having to buy not only hulls but whole ships made in Holland.

A popular recollection of Naples today is of its restaurants on the

---

*The flag of the Italian navy retains the blue ensign of Amalfi quartered with the red ensigns of the three other 'maritime republics', Venice, Genoa and Pisa.

seafront and its people merrily eating *frutti di mare*. Yet Italians have never been great fish-eaters, especially in the north, where they have usually preferred freshwater fish to the saltwater varieties. In classical times Roman plutocrats enjoyed the luxury of personal fishponds, while in the Middle Ages the people of Ferrara disdained the nearby Adriatic in favour of rivers and lakes where they could catch pike, tench and carp; the famous 'merchant of Prato', Francesco di Marco Datini, imported eels from the lagoons of Comacchio, near the sea north of Ravenna, bringing them over the Apennines to Tuscany.[5] After the economic boom of the 1960s, when the poor were able to afford food other than bread, polenta, pasta and home-made soup, they preferred to buy meat rather than fish. Between 1960 and 1975 they multiplied their carnivorous intake by a factor of three, a trend encouraged by the Vatican's relaxation of its rule forbidding meat to be eaten on Fridays. By the end of the century Italians were eating more meat than the British and less fish than the European average.

Fishing off the Italian coast has always been a seasonal and unpredictable occupation. Large numbers of tuna were traditionally slaughtered each year off Sardinia (as well as Sicily), but the 'fishing' (that is, channelling the victims into vast curtain nets) and the subsequent slaughter could only begin after the fish had swum into Sardinian waters in May, and could last for only a few weeks. A more general problem – though difficult to appreciate if you visit the thriving fish market in even a small port like Trani – is the scarcity of fish to catch: the only abundant species apart from tuna have been anchovies and sardines. In the mid-twentieth century – before the days of quotas – Italy had the largest fishing industry of those countries with a purely Mediterranean coastline, catching twenty times the tonnage of its nearest rival, Greece. Yet its total catch was only a sixth of that brought home by Britain's fishing fleet.

Fernand Braudel, the great French historian, has been criticized for the allegedly 'meaningless evolutionist terms' he used in describing the Mediterranean water as 'geologically too old' and 'biologically exhausted'. Yet he was right to stress the poverty of the Mediterranean compared to the Atlantic and to observe that 'the much-vaunted *frutti di mare* are only moderately abundant'.[6] The Mediterranean's narrow coastal shelf and its lack of real tides restrict the growth of nutrients for fish. By contrast, warm Atlantic currents from the Gulf of Mexico reaching the waters and continental shelf of western Europe provide a dense mass of plankton for vast shoals to feed on around Britain, Iceland and Newfoundland. One historical consequence of Italy's shortage of fish and fishermen was a shortage also of sailors. Venice had long been finding its crews in Dalmatia, and at the end of the sixteenth century Mediterranean states were recruiting sailors from northern Europe: following the failure of his Spanish Armada in 1588, Philip II apparently even tried to entice sailors from England.[7]

While Italy's frontier geography has done little to impede people trying to enter the peninsula, its interior has hindered invaders as well as inhabitants from moving around very easily. The Alps have several advantages over the Apennines, Italy's backbone which stretches in an arc for 870 miles down the peninsula and across to Sicily and the Egadi Islands. The northern mountains have rich summer pastures above the tree-line for sheep and cattle, their vegetation flourishes at a much higher altitude, and they have rivers and lakes that assist transport and commerce. They also contain the passes through which Italians can claim to have exported banking and capitalism to northern Europe in the Middle Ages. A mass of villages existed to supply their trade with guides and carts throughout the year: even in midwinter people and goods could come over the passes in sledges. While Milanese merchants of the thirteenth century built a route through the St Gotthard, from which they could penetrate Germany and the Low Countries via the Rhine, the Venetians preferred the Brenner, the lowest of the passes, which took them up to Innsbruck and thence to Nuremberg and Frankfurt. The size of the Transalpine trade – chiefly in fabrics, wine and spices – can be appreciated today by viewing the dimensions of the Fondaco dei Tedeschi, the vast square building by the Rialto on the Grand Canal (until recently the central post office), where the German merchants had to live and work when they were in Venice.

The Apennines, by contrast, are a multi-layered barrier of mountains, torrents and ravines that are difficult to traverse; neighbouring villages in the Calabrian Sila traditionally knew little about each other because they were separated by deep chasms. There were numerous paths across the northern mountains in the Middle Ages, but these were mostly suitable only for mules: you could not transport wagon-loads of wine over them as you could up the Brenner; as late as 1750 there were only two tracts adequate for carts across the whole of the Tuscan-Emilian range. The Apennines have thus created an east–west divide in Italy that has been historically almost as significant as that between north and south. Communications across them were so bad before railways and tunnels that travellers between Rome and Ancona found it easier and cheaper to go all the way by boat – across the Tyrrhenian, Ionian and Adriatic Seas – rather than go straight across the interior.

These mountains do have a few advantages for their inhabitants. Their height – the Gran Sasso in the Abruzzi reaches 9,554 feet – enables them to preserve ice and snow even in summer, a prerequisite for developing local skills in making ice creams and sorbets. This accounts for the otherwise surprising fact that in the middle of August 1860, just after they had conquered Sicily, Garibaldi's soldiers were seen climbing Aspromonte in the Calabrian toe to fetch snow for their refreshments.

A further advantage is the obstacles the mountainous interior has created for invading armies, which during the Second World War so benefited the Germans that British and American forces, despite their command of the air, took twenty-one months to fight their way from one end of Italy to the other. Mountains helped people retain their autonomy, as anyone who tried to rule the rugged interior of the Abruzzi soon learned. They also helped to preserve – and even create – cultural identities and variations for societies living only a couple of valleys apart. This again may seem a blessing to many of us: how fortunate we are to be able to contrast the Pisan-Lucchese Romanesque, dense and exquisite though internally sombre, with the sense of space and light in the Romanesque cathedrals of Bari and Trani. Yet a landscape which encourages cultural diversity is almost bound to promote political disunity. In the case of Italy it has done so since before Romulus founded Rome.

Few blessings, cultural or otherwise, come from the country's two great volcanoes, Etna in Sicily – the largest active volcano in Europe – and Vesuvius looming over Naples. Yet lethal though volcanic eruptions have often been, earthquakes are a more frequent danger.

There is scarcely a town in eastern Sicily or in the south-west of the peninsula that has not been devastated by them at least once. Since 1976 about 4,000 Italians have been killed in earthquakes in Friuli, Campania and Basilicata, Umbria and the Marches, Molise and Apulia, and in 2009 in the Abruzzi. In earlier periods the death toll was even higher. Three of the greatest southern writers of the twentieth century lost their closest relations in earthquakes: the novelist Ignazio Silone lost his mother in the Abruzzi in 1915, the philosopher Benedetto Croce lost his parents and only sister on Ischia in 1883, and the historian Gaetano Salvemini lost his wife, his sister and all five of his children at Messina in 1908, when an earthquake and the tsunami that followed it killed 70,000 people.

Rivers may be less destructive but, in the catalogue of geographical disadvantages that Italians must endure, they rank near the top. As classical writers attest, navigability in antiquity was better than it is now but it was never very good. In the first century BC the geographer Strabo wrote of the 'harmonious arrangement' of the rivers in France, which are today navigable for 4,000 miles. The navigable mileage of rivers in Italy is in the mid-hundreds: none of them has contributed to the growth in trade, industry and human movement comparable to that of the great rivers of northern Europe such as the Seine, the Rhône, the Rhine and the Elbe.

What benefits rivers bring to Italy are predictably in the north, which also enjoys summer rain, abundant springs and snow-fed Alpine streams. The Po is the only river in the country that is navigable for more than a fraction of its length; the waters of its delta contain high levels of plankton which support substantial numbers of fish; and together with its tributaries the river has created its great alluvial plain, Italy's largest and most fertile expanse of arable land. Human ingenuity in the fifteenth and sixteenth centuries also rearranged the area's waters for economic use. By building one canal from the Ticino to Milan and another to Milan from the River Adda, the wealthy capital of Lombardy was linked to the waters of Lakes Como and Maggiore as well as to the tributaries of the Po.

Even so, the river is only relatively useful. It does not serve the north of Italy as the Marne, the Seine and the Oise serve northern

France. Only one of its fourteen mouths on the Adriatic, the Po della Pila, can be used by boats. Although the Po itself is navigable for 300 miles, at least for small craft, seasonal fluctuations disrupt its flow; so does the enormous quantity of silt it carries to the sea. Some of its tributaries provide hydroelectricity and water for irrigation, as do the Piave and Adige rivers in the north-east. Yet none of them is navigable for more than a few miles – and even then only sporadically. The lower Adige is hampered by sandbanks at its mouth and in summer and early autumn it becomes, like the lower Piave, a small stream trickling between islands of dry pebbles.

The most hallowed river is Virgil's 'gentle Tiber', the second-longest in the country, whose relationship with Rome is as famous as that of the Seine flowing through Paris or the Thames progressing through London. The founders of the Eternal City chose their site well: it had defensible hills, the salt plains of Ostia and a water supply adequate for its needs until it became a great city requiring aqueducts. Yet perhaps they over-estimated the value of its river. Until the late nineteenth century the Tiber was anything but gentle and so prone to flooding that no other city had been built on it in antiquity. As late as 1875, in the last quixotic venture of his life, Giuseppe Garibaldi tried to have the river diverted to prevent it from flooding the capital.

Another problem, inevitably, was navigability. In classical times boats could ply between the port of Ostia and Rome and continue upstream for about 20 miles further. Now the Tiber is navigable only within the city itself. By contrast boats can go up the Thames to Lechlade – barely a dozen miles from its source – while the Seine, which flows slowly and majestically for nearly 500 miles, is so welcoming to vessels that it boasts a great port (Rouen) 75 miles from the sea.

The other rivers of the Apennines are no more useful than the Tiber. Even in the Middle Ages the Arno was either a torrent or a trickle, and transporting Carrara marble from Pisa to Florence sometimes required winching boats to trees along the river bank. Many rivers are virtually useless: while they cascade in winter, in summer they are too dry for irrigation; in Apulia some of them even fail to reach the sea. Torrents are the main agent of erosion in the Apennines, rushing down the mountain sides and bringing large quantities of silt and stones with them; on reaching the plain, some rivers merely replenish the coastal marshes. Deforestation has made the situation worse, hastening soil erosion and leading to floods, silting and the formation of malarial marshland. In the south this tree-clearing dates from classical times, even before the Romans reached the area, and has continued ever since, a process accelerated by the requirements of goats, dockyards, railway sleepers and telegraph poles. Sicily was once a land of forests, of hardwoods as well as pines, but by the late twentieth century less than 5 per cent of the island was covered by trees.

Garibaldi's campaign to divert the Tiber was motivated by the desire to prevent not only floods but also malaria. Rivers from the Volscian and Alban hills, to the east of Rome, poured so much water on to the coastal plain that they formed the Pontine Marshes, a long, stagnant expanse producing perfect conditions for the diffusion of malaria. Further north the Tuscan Maremma was a similar hazard; few people lived there until it was successfully drained in the 1950s. Only after Garibaldi's death were mosquitoes identified as the cause of malaria, which each year killed 15,000 people and debilitated many times that number. It was not until 1962 that Italy was officially declared a malaria-free country.

Stressing Italy's physical disadvantages helps explain the difficulties they have created for the cause of national unity. It is also useful to clarify why the country is not as rich as foreigners have often supposed it to be. There are many fertile parts of Italy, not just the Po Valley with its fields of maize and wheat but areas such as the lower Arno, the high Valtellina, the Capuan Plain (now controlled by the Camorra), the lemon groves of Palermo (recently destroyed by the Mafia) and the vineyards and olive groves of the Salentine Peninsula. Wine is grown in most areas except northern Veneto, western Piedmont, central Sicily and the Po Valley. Yet much of the peninsula is covered by mountains, which many Italians detest, seeing them as a cause of poverty and a waste of space. They are also an impediment to access and construction and in consequence encourage the building of endless *periferìa* over easier terrain. It sometimes seems there is barely a plain or a valley that has not been deemed a suitable site for development. Between 1950 and 2005 the Italian countryside lost to asphalt and concrete a total of 3.66 million hectares, a figure larger than the combined size of Tuscany and Umbria.[8]

Many foreigners, like me, have had the good fortune to sit watching the fireflies under a Tuscan pergola, drinking Chianti wine, pouring Lucchese olive oil over our rocket salads and feeling that the material life does not have much more to offer. There seems to be an abundance of good things, of *funghi porcini* and *bistecca fiorentina*, of figs and pulses and roasted vegetables, of hams hanging in the *cantina* awaiting the next visit. Tuscany enjoys a better climate, more fertile land and richer minerals than other parts of Italy; its share-cropping peasants, the ballad-singing *contadini*, were historically better off than agricultural workers elsewhere, and their traditional soup, *ribollita*, was a good deal more nutritious than polenta, the dismal and unhealthy staple of the north.

Yet even here, in one of the happiest and most civilized regions of the world, the land is not very productive. Even when Florence was the artistic and banking centre of the world, it was unable to survive on produce from its countryside for more than five months a year: in the four centuries after 1375 it experienced on average a famine in every fourth year, and in the sixteenth century the Medici grand duke had to import grain from as far away as England, Poland and Flanders. When Vernon Bartlett, a distinguished English journalist, settled in Tuscany after the Second World War, some of his neighbours, who had been prisoners in Britain, talked 'with envious affection of the rich English soil'.[9] Postcards and prosciutto, Capri and Chianti, gondolas and gorgonzola – such associations tell us and remind us of the Italy we want to remember.

ITALIAN PEOPLES

If you look through the telephone directory of Bari in Apulia you will be struck by the quantity of Italian surnames that indicate a foreign ancestry. There are some people named Greco, a good number called Spagnolo or Spagnuolo, and a great many with the name Albano or Albanese – not recent immigrants from Albania but people whose ancestors fled before the Turkish advances to the Adriatic in the fourteenth and fifteenth centuries. The names testify to what Italy has been for most of its history since the fall of Rome: a land of desire for settlers, immigrants and foreign conquerors. Its accessibility and wealth – in parts – still make it a goal for migrants, though these now come from somewhat further away. By 2009 Italy contained more than 600,000 migrants from a single country, Romania, as well as substantial numbers of Moroccans, Albanians, Chinese, South Americans and sub-Saharan Africans. The Tuscan town of Prato officially has 10,000 Chinese residents and unofficially double that number.[10] Perhaps it is their presence that has encouraged the arrival of a new type of immigrant, Manchurian prostitutes, who have annoyed their predecessors in the trade, mainly Brazilians and Africans, by charging less, working harder and doing their job in car-parks, alleyways and public conveniences. Many immigrants enter Italy illegally not because they have relations or good prospects there but because it is easier to reach than other countries.

If we agree with the French historian Lucien Febvre that the concept of prehistory is absurd, we should first acknowledge the Mesolithic people who were living in the Italian peninsula around 10,000 BC at the end of the Ice Age's last freezing spell. They were nomads who hunted and gathered fruit and moved north as the earth warmed up.

Around 7000 BC, before Britain became an island, another people, now known as Neolithic, began to arrive in Europe from south-west Asia. They penetrated Italy by sea and by land through the Balkans, absorbing their more primitive predecessors as they moved west. By 6000 BC they were in Apulia; soon afterwards they reached Calabria and Sicily; and from there they sent fresh expeditions to Corsica and Sardinia. They seem to have had a compulsion to go west, like Tennyson's Ulysses, 'to sail beyond the sunset and . . . may be . . . touch the Happy Isles'. Reflecting on their pioneering spirit, the archaeologist Barry Cunliffe suggests they had 'a desire to see what lies beyond, drawn on westwards, perhaps, by the fascination of the setting sun'.[11]

There was little diversity among the Neolithic people, who had reached and settled in northern Europe by 4000 BC. They cleared land with stone axes, they grew wheat and barley, kept sheep, cattle and pigs, and built themselves homes instead of living in caves. The differences that emerged among them were fashioned by climate, vegetation and resources. The inhabitants of Britain and Ireland could not have initiated what we call the Bronze Age without a supply of copper and tin needed for the alloy. Along the Mediterranean coasts people used olive oil for their food and their lamps; further north, where olives did not grow, they relied on animal fats for nourishment and tallow candles.

This north–south European divergence was replicated in Italy – and still is, as anyone who has compared Neapolitan cooking with butter-based Piedmontese dishes will know. While chestnuts, which have a nutritional value comparable to wheat, have hardly featured in southern diets, they have been an important resource in the north-west, where they grow well and where bread baked with their flour became a staple diet during the famished years after the Second World War. Yet the land is not simply divided between north and south or indeed between east and west but also partitioned, minutely and extensively, by the rugged limestone ridges of the Apennines. From the beginning, the Neolithic settlers lived in isolated territories, a segregation that fostered the development of distinctive languages, cultures and local customs.

Around 700 BC different groups were recognized as distinct entities and were later classified as such by Greek and Roman writers. In the north were the Ligurians, the Taurini (the 'bull-like' people of Turin) and the Veneti (who were famous, a thousand years before the foundation of Venice or the invention of gondolas, as warriors, feasters and breeders of chariot-horses); the central Apennines were inhabited by Umbrians, Sabines, Volscians and Samnites, and further south the mountains contained Lucanians and the Calabrian Bruttians; the Adriatic coast was divided south of Veneti territory among Picenes, Daunians, Peucetians and Messapians, while along the Tyrrhenian lived Etruscans, Latins, Faliscans and Campanians; the most recent arrivals were Greek colonists in the south. It was all very unlike Greece, whose inhabitants resembled each other, talked the same language and already thought of themselves as Greek. In Italy the population spoke about forty languages and did not consider themselves the same people, let alone as Italians.

Apart from the Greeks, the most distinctive and advanced people were the Etruscans, who were based in Etruria, where they built hill-top towns such as Volterra, and from where they spread north to the

Po Valley and south to the Bay of Naples. In his *Lays of Ancient Rome*, which drew on the work of the classical historian Livy, Thomas Babington Macaulay described the Roman hero Horatius Cocles holding a bridge over 'Father Tiber' and defying a mighty Etruscan army led by Lars Porsena of Clusium, who 'by the nine gods' had sworn to capture Rome and avenge its exiled dynasty. In fact the Etruscan leader probably did capture the city, some of whose kings had actually been Etruscans. At this stage, the middle of the first millennium BC, Rome had little identity separate from its Etruscan and Latin neighbours. Eventually Etruria was defeated and absorbed by the Romans, but by then its power had already been reduced by challenges from Gauls, Greeks, Phoenicians and the peoples of the interior.

Greek colonies appeared in Italy as early as the middle of the eighth century BC. Euboeans founded Cumae on the western promontory of the Bay of Naples, Achaeans settled in south-east Italy (where they seem to have made the connection between Italia and the bull-calf), Ionians went for south-west Italy and north-east Sicily, Dorians sailed for southern Sicily, and Spartans established a colony at Taranto, the best port south of Naples. They all set up city-states – an autonomous *polis*, consisting of a city and its hinterland – which were prosperous, cultured and toughly governed by rulers who have gone down in history as the original 'tyrants' – somewhat unfairly because the Greek *turannos* merely means autocrat. These colonies, precursors of the city-states of medieval Italy, nurtured Archimedes and Pythagoras but few democrats and no rulers capable of uniting them against threats from outside.

The classification of the other peoples of the peninsula is less scientific, partly because they spoke languages related to each other within the Italic group.* The tribes of Apulia were supposedly divided into Daunians, Peucetians and Messapians in the heel, but these names come from Greek writers and were adopted by Roman ones; perhaps the people themselves did not recognize such distinctions. As for the Samnites, highland tribes from Molise and the centre, they cannot rigorously be separated from the Lucanians and Bruttians whose ancestors they were.

*See p. 30.

The mountain communities, however separate and secure in their mountain enclaves, were not of course stationary. Since nowhere in the peninsula is more than seventy miles from a sea, their members were bound to meet the inhabitants of the coast – and to envy their prosperity. From the fifth century BC large numbers of Samnites migrated from the Apennines to Campania, where they ended Etruscan rule, and further south to the Ionian and Tyrrhenian coasts, the area known as Magna Graecia, where they clashed with the Greek colonies. Equally large changes were simultaneously taking place in the north. Huge waves of Gauls (also known as Celts) came from southern France across the Alps, their tribes settling in the Po Valley and ejecting the Etruscans who were living there. After founding Mediolanum (Milan), they surged south through Umbria and Etruria to Rome, which they sacked in 390 BC, forcing the priestesses known as the Vestal Virgins to flee from their temple; legend has it that the Capitoline Hill was saved by its sacred geese, who cackled at the approach of the Gallic infiltrators and woke up the guards. Eventually the invaders were paid an early form of danegeld to go away. Rome was not captured again for 800 years.

The so-called 'Romanization' of Italy* was carried out at an increasing pace in the final centuries BC. It imposed a political and a cultural identity on the peninsula but not an ethnic one; the Romans had no ethnic identity to impose. The satirist Juvenal even complained that the capital itself was multiracial because it had so many Greeks and Syrians living in it. During the imperial centuries millions of people travelled the great roads to settle or be stationed in provinces far from their birthplace. Yet there were no enormous changes to the ethnic composition of Italy in this long period except for a constant influx of foreign slaves: the great transformations took place before Rome's rise and after its collapse.

The barbarian invasions that had a significant impact on Italy's ethnic blending were those of the Ostrogoths, the first rulers after the last emperor had been deposed in AD 476, and the *langobardi*, another German people, who came over the eastern Alps in the following century. For two centuries the *langobardi* ('long-beards', later Lombards)

*See pp. 43–44.

ruled in most of Italy before succumbing to the Frankish army of the future Emperor Charlemagne.

By the ninth century AD Italy was inhabited by many people whose origins were in west Asia, north Africa, and northern and eastern Europe. Most northerners were Lombards and Romanized Italians. But in the south there were also Arabs, who established a brief emirate at Bari and ruled Sicily until they were displaced by the Normans; Greeks, some of them descendants from the colonies of Magna Graecia, others who had arrived more recently to administer Byzantium's territorial conquests of the sixth century; and a sizable Jewish population together with smaller numbers of Slavs, Armenians and Berbers.

All subsequent conquerors of areas of Italy brought people who settled in the country, mainly soldiers, merchants and officials. Yet none arrived in great numbers. More significant was the immigration of Albanians who in the later Middle Ages built themselves villages along the Adriatic coast and in the mountains of the Calabrian Sila, where towards the end of the twentieth century the inhabitants still spoke *arbëresh*, which they regarded as the purest form of Albanian.[12] They also settled in Sicily, where the town of Piana degli Albanesi south of Palermo still celebrates an Albanian Epiphany, commemorating the visit of the Magi to Bethlehem with flamboyant costumes and Greek Orthodox rites. Renowned as fighters, they served in the armies of Naples and Rome and also Venice, which was the most 'multicultural' and cosmopolitan of Italian cities. Apart from its Albanian minority, St Mark's lion presided over communities of Greeks, Jews, Turks, Germans, Persians, Armenians and Slavs. The last, who were mostly from Dalmatia, gave their name to the Riva degli Schiavoni (the long quayside outside the Doge's Palace) and to their Scuola di San Giorgio degli Schiavoni, which houses Carpaccio's most appealing paintings, episodes in the lives of St Jerome, St George and St Augustine.

The lengthy ethnic hybridization that produced modern Italians did not of course mean that they all now look similar. No one denies that Sardinians are easily recognizable or that the inhabitants of Parma do not resemble those of Palermo. Yet, however noticeable physical differences may often be, race has never been a serious factor in Italian history: there is no Italian race and there never has been one.

The arguments of those who claim otherwise, usually fascists or extreme nationalists, are ludicrous. So is the more recent boast by a leader of the Venetian League that, while Lombards are upstarts descended from the Gauls, his own people have a pure ethnic pedigree.[13] The truth was recognized long ago by the Risorgimento liberal Cesare Balbo, who observed that Italy was 'a multiracial community composed of successive waves of immigrants'; it had 'one of the most mixed bloodlines, one of the most eclectic civilizations and cultures which there has ever been'.[14]

The French president Charles de Gaulle famously asked how he could be expected to govern a country that had 246 different kinds of cheese. Italians may have fewer cheeses than the French but in other spheres of human accomplishment and behaviour there are more varieties in diverse and diffuse Italy than in highly centralized France. Both countries retain a predilection for stereotypes. In France Gascons are passionate, Bretons are hard-headed, Normans are stolid and sensible, while the male population of Perpignan has traditionally been ridiculed by other Frenchmen as people who do nothing apart from sitting in floppy berets sipping pastis or playing bowls and arguing under the plane trees.[15] Italians are also given eternal characteristics: the Tuscan temperament, for example, is apparently a blend of shrewdness, scepticism, individualism, enterprise, frugality, honesty, common sense and moderation in all things, especially religion, politics and pleasure.[16]

Italians have suffered from stereotyping both by foreigners and by their compatriots. In Renaissance Europe Italian merchants living abroad were often envied and despised by northerners, particularly Poles, who regarded them as feeble and effeminate, weedy luteplayers who preferred wine and salads to beer and roast meat. Italians also acquired a reputation for being Europe's worst soldiers, a reputation that endured. When the Stuart pretender, Bonnie Prince Charlie, turned to flee at the Battle of Culloden, his subordinate Lord Elcho chose to remember not the prince's Scottish ancestors or his Polish mother but his Roman childhood and Modenese grandmother when he allegedly shouted after him, 'Run then, you damned cowardly Italian!' Yet while the image of Italians was unmanly, it was often also violent and treacherous, linked to the stiletto, the stab in the back, or the craftily administered poison, especially in Elizabethan drama: in John Webster's tragedies *The White Divel* and *The Duchess of Malfi*, Italian characters find four different means of poisoning their victims.[17] Two centuries later, one of Walter Scott's characters is accused of behaving 'like a cowardly Italian' when he draws his 'fatal stiletto' and kills 'the man whom he dared not meet in manly encounter'.[18]

In Italy even books of high scholarship reinforce regional stereotypes. People are routinely referred to as 'typically Florentine' or 'typically Sicilian' in a way that perplexes those who would never write of someone as 'typically Lancastrian' or a 'typical Aberdonian'. In the introduction to one of his books, the distinguished Torinese philosopher Norberto Bobbio is described as 'typically Piedmontese', while in the book he himself used a similar technique to classify others. Writing of the historian Gaetano Salvemini and the economist Luigi Einaudi, two of the great figures of modern Italy, he described the second as 'the image of the reserved Piedmontese, a man of much good sense and few words, never eloquent, apparently cold, almost arid, precise as a clock', while the first became the archetypal southerner, 'the portrait of the combative southern Italian, generous and impetuous, incisive in his speech and penetrating in his gaze, inhabited by the demon of sincerity to the point of rudeness'.[19]

When intellectuals accept stereotypes, it is not surprising that other people do the same. I have several times heard Pisans disparaging the citizens of Lucca, alleging that the Lucchesi are narrow-minded and backward, although the latter like to think of themselves as reflective, religious, mild, acute, tenacious, ironic and creative[20] – a people understandably proud of their beautiful city and the independence that it maintained for so long. Yet despisers are often despised in turn: I have also witnessed astonished Pisans being told by Livornesi that they, citizens of a comparatively modern, cosmopolitan port, are more progressive and broad-minded than the guardians of the Leaning Tower.

Milan and Turin are great cities of the north-west with many things in common, including industry and southern immigrants who came north in the 1950s and 1960s to work in their factories. Yet citizens of one city often speak of the inhabitants of the other as if they were foreigners with characteristics peculiar to themselves. The Torinese may be honest but he is austere and aloof and too careful with his money; the Milanese may be generous but he is noisy and materialistic, obsessed about work and food and having a warm overcoat for winter. Italians sometimes claim they can distinguish between the two sets of citizens without hearing them speak. Taking an example of stereotyping nearer home, I have heard that the Genoese are supposed to be as stubborn as the Scots, have read that Sicilians are as taciturn as the Scots, and have listened to a Sardinian admiral telling me, without explication, that his fellow islanders are the Scots of Italy – possibly because both have remote highlands. Perhaps somebody somewhere has complained that the Torinese are as thrifty as the Picts.

We frown now on stereotypes, especially those that contain a tinge of truth. Yet all over Italy cities tenaciously conserve qualities and quirks that distinguish them from their neighbours in a fashion unimaginable to someone setting out to compare Nottingham with Northampton. Many of the ideas about rival places, 'the people over there', are nonsense, and few Italians really believe in them. Yet if you go to the Venetian lagoon, you might meet a man from the island of Murano who says the inhabitants of nearby Burano are savages, and if you go to Crema in Lombardy you might be told that the Cremonese, the residents of a neighbouring town, are untrustworthy because they supported the German emperor against the Lombard cities in the Middle Ages. All the same, real differences do exist, and, if you want to see for yourself, you could spend a day in Naples, with eyes, ears and nostrils open, followed by a night on the Palermo ferry and the next morning among Sicilians.

LINGUISTIC ITALY

In the spring of 2008 I was walking in the Apulian city of Bari with a friend, a film director from Lecce, a beautiful Baroque town of pale-yellow limestone some 90 miles to the south-east. After passing a group of young men talking loudly on the pavement, I told him I couldn't understand what they were saying, to which he replied that he couldn't either, adding only half in jest that the Leccesi were traditionally cultured and aristocratic while the Baresi were crafty and materialistic. A native of Apulia, a man who speaks both Italian and the *leccese* dialect of the Salentine Peninsula, he was defeated by the phonetic sounds and inflections of *barese*. Though the same foreign influences – mainly French and Spanish – have affected both cities, their dialects are spoken so differently that speakers of one find the language of the other almost incomprehensible. While today *barese* sounds similar to the dialects of Naples and Basilicata, *leccese* is more like Sicilian and Calabrian, even though Messina and Reggio are much further from Lecce than Bari.

Similar situations are found in other parts of Italy. Carrara is a town in north-west Tuscany whose inhabitants do not easily under-stand what other Tuscans are saying because their area once belonged to Modena – it was that duchy's 'outlet to the sea' – and they continue to speak in the *modenese* dialect. In fact they feel themselves to be psychologically so unTuscan that, when they go outside their town, they talk about 'going to Tuscany'.* In the same way inhabitants of the Giudecca talk about 'going to Venice' when they cross the half mile of water that separates them from the Doge's Palace. Even in provinces where everyone speaks in the local dialect, a person's geo-graphical upbringing can be located from accent, vocabulary and manner of speaking; the same is true of islands in the Venetian lagoon. A Tuscan *contadino* who taught me some of the *lucchese* dialect in the 1970s used to demonstrate how he could identify a man's village by the way he spoke. He also taught me words that were unintelligible beyond Lucca: when I used them recently in Lucca itself, I was told that my friends must have been very old peasants. Dialects, the most prominent manifestation of Italian diversity, have been so prevalent in the history of the peninsula that many people did not hear standard Italian being spoken until they first listened to the wireless.

Most of the tongues spoken in ancient Italy belonged to the Indo-European group of languages, whose precursors were brought thousands of years ago by Neolithic migrants from south-west Asia. Like the people themselves, two groups of these languages were soon

---

*In Tuscan-Italian 'The crow had stolen a piece of cheese from a window' is *il corvo aveva rubato da una finestra un pezzo di formaggio*, while in carrarese it is '*i corv i avev robat da 'na fnè 'n toc d'formai.*

formed, one going north, the other entering Italy from the Balkans and spreading west through the Mediterranean; two notable peoples who resisted the advance were the Basques and the Etruscans. Different Indo-European languages were spoken in Italy by Gauls in the north, Messapians in the Salento and Greeks on the coast, who introduced the alphabet to Europe and thereby encouraged everyone to start carving inscriptions. Most people, however, spoke one of the Indo-European languages that later became known as 'Italic'. Closely related forms of this were Oscan and Umbrian, used by the peoples of the interior and along the Adriatic; the populations of the west coast spoke more distant varieties such as Latin and Faliscan. The language of the Latins, who had their own cultural and linguistic identity by the sixth century BC, was used and later diffused across Italia by the Romans. In consequence, all the other languages, except Greek but including Etruscan, had died out in their written form by the time of Augustus; some may still have been spoken for a time but they were no longer used for inscriptions or other writing, which were now done in Latin. Most Sicilians remained Greek-speakers until the Arab conquest, though after the arrival of the Normans in the eleventh century both Greek and Arabic went into decline.

Modern Italian is derived from the spoken form of classical Latin, later known as 'vulgar' Latin, *volgare latino*, perhaps more happily translated as 'vernacular'. During its gradual evolution it accepted colloquialisms seldom found in literature together with diminutives, which allowed *frater* and *soror*, for example, to metamorphose into *fratello* and *sorella*. Yet the development of the language was hampered for centuries by the continued supremacy of Latin, the language of prose, of culture and of the Church. Apart from in Greek outposts in the south, Latin was the only written language until the thirteenth century and was used in schools for much longer. Italian was spoken in the vernacular with regional variations from the eighth century but was not written for another 500 years and then only occasionally, for poetry, in the Hohenstaufen court at Palermo and at Lucca and Pisa in western Tuscany. Poets writing in Italian had to contend not only with the dominance of Latin but also with the troubadours of Provence, who inspired writers in the north and whose language the Venetians briefly adopted for their literature.

The posthumous role of Dante Alighieri in the development of Italian has long been treated with reverence and solemnity. The great Florentine poet was, according to one scholar, not only 'the father of the Italian language' but also 'the father of the nation and the symbol of national greatness through the centuries'.[21] It is doubtful that Dante would have thought the second part of the description applicable to him, especially as he believed Italy should be part of the Holy Roman Empire and not a nation by itself. Yet he did write *The Divine Comedy* (or, as he himself called it, simply *La Commedia*) in Italian and extolled the virtues of the vernacular, the 'new sun' that would put Latin in the shade, in *De vulgari eloquentia*, a book he wrote in Latin.

The works of Dante, like those of his younger fellow Tuscans Petrarch and Boccaccio, advanced the cause of the Florentine vernacular in the later Middle Ages, even though Petrarch usually wrote in Latin and Dante thought *bolognese* a more beautiful language. By the sixteenth century it was widely felt that the peninsula's literary language should be close to theirs, a feeling which suggests that, if the great trio had been born in Sicily, the island's dialect would have been adopted as Italian, which foreigners would have had great difficulty in understanding.* Pietro Bembo, the Venetian scholar and cardinal, argued that, if writers in Latin imitated Cicero and Virgil, then writers in the vernacular should model themselves on Petrarch and Boccaccio. Although some people hoped for a more modern form of Tuscan, Bembo's arguments were persuasive, and several writers of the age decided to 'Tuscanize' their work. Latin scholars who scorned the vernacular as common and brutish – 'a language of the plebs is a plebeian language' – were defeated. There was even a sixteenth-century fashion for foreigners to study Tuscan in Italy in order to further their careers in diplomacy and commerce or sometimes simply to appreciate Dante and Ariosto.[22] Later, around 1600, another towering Tuscan, the Pisan astronomer Galileo, demanded that scientific work also should be conducted in the vernacular, arguing that more people

---

*The islanders' propensity to omit important consonants is reflected in the title of Giuseppe Tornatore's recent film *Baarìa*, which is how its citizens pronounce the name of their home town Bagheria.

would then be able to understand his work – an argument which the papacy failed to appreciate.

Tuscan had several advantages in its quest to become the Italian language: apart from its literary beauty, the spoken and written languages were similar, and its sounds as well as its grammatical rules made it closer to Latin than other dialects – the Latin *sanctus* and *bello* becoming Tuscan *santo* and *bello* but Sicilian *sando* and *beddu*. Furthermore, while in the rest of Italy Latin was the language of education until the eighteenth century, it had been replaced by the vernacular in Tuscany two centuries earlier. Florence is still regarded as the best place to learn Italian, though it is often claimed that in Siena (where people like to say *opara* instead of *opera*) the pronunciation is better. The inhabitants of Lucca are equally proud of the way they talk, though they tend to leave out the hard 'c' at the beginning of a word so that *mi casa* – my house – sounds like *mi hasa*. The Tuscan Count Sforza, who managed to be Italy's foreign minister before as well as after Mussolini, claimed that 'perfect pronunciation' would be 'Tuscan speech in a Roman mouth',[23] a slightly smug remark that unintentionally drew attention to the problem that in Italy the political and literary capitals were different.

Five centuries after Dante, Alessandro Manzoni, whose first language was *milanese* and his second French, promoted Tuscan as the language of Italian resurgence, even to the extent of studying in Florence so that he could write a new edition of his immense novel *The Betrothed* in the Tuscan vernacular, a process he called 'rinsing' his story in the Arno. Yet the attempts of Manzoni and others to impose a language spoken in only one region on a whole country were perhaps arrogant and certainly naive. How could you have a national language that was spoken in only one of the nation's chief cities? Nearly everyone outside Tuscany conducted their private and professional lives in dialect; for them literary Italian was a dead language or at best an official one, which sounded strange and artificial when they tried to speak it; moreover, unlike English and French, it had been scarcely enriched since the Middle Ages. This unsatisfactory state produced particular conundrums for literary folk. In the eighteenth century the Venetian Carlo Goldoni wrote his plays in three different languages – Venetian dialect, Tuscan and eventually French, the language of his memoirs. Two centuries later, Ignazio Silone wanted the peasants in his novel *Fontamara* to speak their own language – a dialect of the Abruzzi – but realized he had to make them speak a language they didn't know (Italian) so that his readership would understand what they were saying.

In any case the attempted imposition only partially and tardily succeeded. In 1861, the year the Kingdom of Italy was born, it has been calculated that one Italian in forty (2.5 per cent of the population of the peninsula) spoke Italian: just over 630,000 people – mainly Tuscans speaking what was after all their own dialect – out of a total of 25 million.[24] Even if we add others who had some familiarity with the language, such as those who had read it at secondary school, it is difficult to push the figure beyond 10 per cent. For the 80 per cent of the population classified as illiterate, Italian was a foreign language, not only in the south, where it was largely incomprehensible, but even in Venice, where lawyers and judges still talked in Venetian. Decades earlier, Byron had to speak dialect in Venice so as to be understood, and the friend who observed that it was like talking to an Irishman in brogue was quite wrong.[25]

Such problems were not unique to Italy in that era. Spain had four languages and a host of dialects; in France most of the south-western communes did not speak French, and few Parisians could understand what people were saying south of Lyon. Yet the situation was more critical in Italy. Over half the population spoke Castilian in Spain or French in France, and both languages had long been in use for administration and literature. In Italy nearly everyone spoke in dialect, not just peasants and artisans and the urban poor, but merchants, aristocrats and even monarchs. The Neapolitan King Ferdinand II spoke in Neapolitan, and so did his court. The Piedmontese King Victor Emanuel II (later King of Italy) spoke Piedmontese when he wasn't speaking French; so did his heirs, even after three generations of living in Rome. Most of the early statesmen of united Italy came from Piedmont and had to learn Italian as a new language: the best of them, Camillo Cavour, was happier speaking French and was so ignorant of how people talked in the south that he thought Sicilians still spoke Arabic. Francesco Crispi, a Sicilian who twice became prime minister, had an unusual linguistic ordeal to come through. Albanian was the language of his family, Greek the language of his church (he was baptized a Greek Orthodox) and Sicilian the language of his youth; in certain situations Italian may have been his fourth language.[26]

After unification Italian became more extensively spoken. Governments assisted the process with bureaucracy, school textbooks and the decision to enter the First World War, when millions of men drafted from all over the country were stationed together on the banks of the Isonzo River in Friuli. Yet there were other factors over which they had no control such as demographic movements and newspapers that wanted readers beyond the confines of their local town. Another instrument of dissemination was the country's favourite children's book, *The Adventures of Pinocchio*, whose author had family in the Tuscan village that gave him his pseudonym, Collodi.

Italians use an English word to describe these developments: they have been *standardizzando* their language for decades, and it is now more or less '*standard*'. English words have been infiltrating Italian for over a century: 'week-end' appeared in Panzini's *Dizionario moderno* in 1905 and was followed by 'pullover', 'smoking' (for dinner jacket) and similar novelties. *Va bene*, gentle and ubiquitous in the 1970s, has now been largely driven out by OK. English is increasingly used in journalism, even when the Italian equivalents are just as appropriate: companies do 'outsourcing', people are 'politically correct' (or more usually aren't), there is a ministry for 'Welfare' (though not yet a Treasury), and Silvio Berlusconi calls himself the '*recordman della persecuzione*', meaning he is more victimized than anyone else – which he isn't. Even a serious magazine like *L'Espresso* prefers 'Bye Bye' to *Addio* in giant lettering on its cover, while inside it will employ the words 'bluff', 'blackout', 'privacy', 'dynasty' and 'killer' all in the headlines of a single issue. The ugliest and most recent anglicism is the use of 'big' as a noun so that the leading figures of a political party, once referred to as *i leader*, are now known as *i big*.

Modern Italian has many foreign influences besides English. The Ostrogoths donated a few dozen words, usually rather ugly ones such as *stecca* (a stick) and *strappare* (to wrench). The Lombards were more generous, though theirs too are not beautiful: *gruccia* (a crutch), *guancia* (a cheek), *spaccare* (to cleave) and *schernire* (to sneer). Many words in dialects were introduced by the Arabs, who also furnished

Italian with much of its maritime vocabulary, for example *ammi-raglio, arsenale, tariffa* and *dogana* (customs). Catalan and Castilian influenced certain dialects during the periods of Spain's political dominance, but they were superseded in importance at the end of the seventeenth century by French, whose partisans regarded it as the true heir of Latin, a masculine language of logic and clarity in contrast with Italian, which they deemed feminine and emotional, suitable for opera and musical instructions.* French remained fashionable during the first half of the twentieth century, with *ragoût* taking a long time to become *ragù*. Until the Second World War foreign names were routinely pronounced in a French way, Churchill as Scürscill and Chamberlain as Sciamberlèn.[27]

However *standardizzato* Italian now is, the country retains its dialects as well as certain areas where foreign languages are spoken and protected. In the Val d'Aosta French has parity with Italian, as German has in the Alto Adige (the South Tyrol), where it is the mother tongue of most people and where churches celebrate mass alternately in both official languages. Italy's second language is *sardo*, which is spoken by a million people, though I have met Sardinians who have lived on the island for decades and have never understood a word of it. It has no literature except folk verse and it is subdivided into so many dialects that there are seven ways of saying Friday in *sardo*. Sounding more like Spanish than Italian, it has taken *rio* for river (*riu* in *sardo*) instead of *fiume*; in some areas it also retains Latin words such as *domus* for house instead of *casa*. On the island's west coast at Alghero people speak Catalan because they are of Catalan descent, settled there by a king of Aragon after he had expelled the local Sardinian population in the fourteenth century. Further south, on the little island of San Pietro, descendants of eighteenth-century settlers from the north talk in an old-fashioned form of the Piedmontese dialect.

Elsewhere Greek is still spoken in parts of Apulia and Calabria, Slovene is common in Udine, and pockets of Albanian survive in the provinces of Foggia, Taranto, Potenza, Cosenza, Catanzaro and also

---

*Charles V, the Habsburg emperor, is alleged to have said that he spoke French to men and Italian to women; he also revealed that he conversed with God in Spanish and with his horse in German.

in Sicily. In the Dolomites a few thousand people speak Ladin, a Rhaetian dialect close to Swiss Romansh, which in some Alpine valleys is taught in schools alongside German and Italian. Further east along the mountains, in the region of Friuli-Venezia Giulia, *friulano* (another Rhaetian dialect) is now an official language (thus joining Italian, Slovene and German in notices in government buildings), but most inhabitants of the regional capital, Trieste, do not speak it and stick to their own dialect, *triestino*.

The use of dialect is decreasing in most places but it does so slowly, partly because parents are usually proud of their roots and like to pass their ancestral speech on to another generation. The region of Emilia still has a dozen dialects, among them *modenese*, *ferrarese*, *bolognese* and *parmigiano*; many people in the Lombard town of Bergamo still refuse to speak anything other than *bergamasco*. As late as 1974 more than half the population of Italy spoke only in dialect within the family. Before the turn of the century that proportion had dropped, but still two-thirds of them either spoke solely in dialect or else in a mixture of dialect and Italian when at home; for them dialect is the maternal tongue, Italian the second language, the one they learn at school as what the Venetian actor, Lino Toffolo, calls 'our first foreign language'.[28]

If dialect is now spoken mainly by Venetians, southerners and the old, it will continue to decline, but there are and have been plenty of people on the alert to obstruct the process. After the Second World War the writer and film director Pier Paolo Pasolini set up the Academy for the Friulian Language despite the fact that he was born and educated in Bologna; he wrote his first volume of poetry in *friulano*, used the Roman dialect for his fiction and towards the end of his life denounced television as the destroyer of Italy's rich heritage of dialects. In the commune of Como, on the southern shore of the homonymous lake, people can now get married in *lumbard* rather than Italian; the newspaper *La Padania* recently appeared in Venetian; and at the festival of the Northern League speeches are simultaneously translated into the Milanese dialect known as *meneghino*. In much of the country Italians are eager to study their local dialect, and many people in Bologna enroll in a course called *Caurs ed Bulgnais*.[29]

The idea that a language is purer than a dialect is common but untrue: the relationship between the two is simply that of winner and loser. We talk of the Italian language and the Venetian dialect as if the second is a sort of deviant of the first whereas it is in fact much older, evolving from Latin centuries before the birth of Dante. Fortunately Venetian remains alive and is being constantly replenished: in the port of Marghera people today use four distinct types of slang. Over the years the language has given English (as well as Italian) essential words from its vocabulary, including ghetto, casino, lagoon, marzipan, quarantine and scampi. Outsiders, even Italians who have settled in Venice, find the dialect strange and hard to understand, partly because of the 'vanishing L' which means, for instance, that the pronoun 'he' (*lui* in Italian, *lu* in Venetian) is pronounced *yu*.[30]

A foreigner in Italy who walks about and eats in restaurants will quickly notice how extensively variations of language have been preserved. In Venice he will find that squares are called fields (*campi*) rather than *piazze*; the city has two *piazzette* next to its one *piazza*, San Marco. Meals and menus will invariably be a puzzle, even if he has a pocket dictionary. If he wants breakfast in Rome he should ask for *colazione* but if he uses the word in Turin or Milan he will get lunch; similarly *pranzo* in Rome is the midday meal while in the north it often means dinner, which elsewhere is *cena*. His phrasebook may tell him that *solo per il pranzo* means 'only open for lunch' but, if he sees the sign on a restaurant door in Vicenza, it will mean 'only open for dinner'. Even if he gets the word right, he has to be careful when ordering his breakfast: in the north a croissant is, confusingly, a *brioche*, while in Rome, even more confusingly, it is a *cornetto*, which can also be a musical instrument, a string-bean and a type of ice-cream.

When he goes out for his *pranzo/cena*, the tourist's confusion will increase. If he wants to start with anchovies, he would have to ask for *acciughe* when he is in the north and *alici* when he travels south; should he want to eat them with *focaccia*, it would be fine to ask for this in Tuscany and Liguria, but further north the word is *gnocco* and to the east in Modena it becomes *stria*; in Venice the word *focaccia* exists but means something different: a sweet cake rather than a savoury bread. The travelling carnivore is in a state of permanent confusion: lamb is *abbacchio* in Rome but *agnello* in Tuscany; a *bistecca* in Milan is a boneless slice of meat, but in Florence it is a giant T-bone steak, which the Milanese call a *bracciola al osso*. Yet the vegetarian too has a multitude of problems. Pasta is mysteriously transformed into *minestra* in the north, while *lattuga* (lettuce) becomes *insalata romana* in the capital. The Roman *carciofo* becomes *arcicioffo* and *arciciocco* in the north, *ardigioco* in Genoa and thence *artichaut* in France and artichoke in Britain. If a melon is desired at the end of dinner, the water variety (*cocomero*) is *melone d'acqua* in Naples and the ordinary *melone* becomes a *popone* in Tuscany.

Perhaps the restaurateur's son will offer to help the customer in his bewilderment. If he is still a boy, he is a *ragazzo* in Italian and a *ragasol* in *modenese*, but in most dialects he is something linguistically unrelated. Merely to take words for boy beginning with the letter 'p', he might be a *putel* in the Trentino, a *pischello* in Rome, a *putlet* in Mantua, a *piliso* in Piedmont, a *picciottu* or *picciutteddu* in Sicily, a *pizzinnu* or *piccioccu* in Sardinia, and a *picciriddu* in the Salento. Were he to travel across the north from Genoa to Friuli, he could be metamorphosed, not very mellifluously, from *garsùn* to *fànte*, *magatel*, *bagalt*, *redesòot*, *toso*, *butèl*, *mulo*, *fioo* and *frut*.

2

Imperial Italies

ROMAN ITALY

Italy's diversity was determined by its geography, its climate and its pattern of human settlement, all of which encouraged the growth of different cultures and customs. That diversity had been formed long before the Romans united the peninsula politically in the first century BC.

Mythology is also a part of that diversity. The family of Julius Caesar claimed it was descended from Aeneas, celebrated as the ancestor of the Roman people; in doing so it also added the goddess Venus, the mother of Aeneas, to the family tree. As Virgil recounts it in the *Aeneid*, this ancestor was a Trojan exile determined to follow his destiny despite the persecutions of gods and men and plagues and harpies. After spurning the love of Dido, Queen of Carthage, he sailed to Italy, killed the warrior Turnus and married Lavinia, his victim's fiancée. He then united his victorious Trojans with the defeated Latin natives and became subsequently revered as the founder of the Roman race.

Some 400 years later, in the early eighth century BC, a descendant of Aeneas was raped by the god Mars. The twin products of this violation, Romulus and Remus, were removed by their maternal grandfather and abandoned on the banks of the Tiber. Suckled by a she-wolf and nursed by a shepherdess, they grew up and bickered over which one should found a city. When his brother started building on the Capitoline Hill, Remus mocked him by jumping over his meagre walls. An enraged Romulus reacted by killing him and carried on building, appealing to outcasts and vagabonds to come and populate his new town. Realizing his dream could have no future without women, he then organized the kidnapping of the young women of a neighbouring tribe, an abduction known as 'the Rape of the Sabine Women'.

'Wolf's milk, exile and fratricide were an unusual ancestry', as the historian Robin Lane Fox has observed.[1] So, one might add, are a divine rape and a mass abduction, the latter episode acknowledged and recounted without embarrassment by descendants. The foundation myths of Rome are, obviously, just myths; so are Aeneas and Romulus. Yet they manage to tell us something about the city – and indeed the empire – that Rome later became. Romulus may have made his town an asylum for fugitives because he needed fighters, but later Romans also pursued hospitable policies on immigration and citizenship – to the amazement of the Greeks, who themselves refused to make citizens of freed slaves or former enemies. Such attitudes made it impossible to think of Romans as a race of their own. From the beginning their city was inhabited by Sabines, Albans and Etruscans as well as by Romulus and his outcasts. 'Romanness' was a political identity – and later a juridical term – but it had no racial connotation. You did not have to be born in Rome to be successful there. None of the great poets came from the city, and many of the emperors were born outside Italy.

In history, though not in myth, early Rome was ruled by several Etruscan kings, who were expelled at the end of the sixth century BC. In their place two Roman consuls were appointed to govern for one year at a time, and under them emerged a complex administrative structure of quaestors, praetors, censors, senators, aediles and tribunes. The early republic managed to produce a capable ruling class, its officials generally enjoying a reputation for high-mindedness and incorruptibility. All male citizens, including the 'plebs', had a vote in the assemblies that passed laws and elected officials, though in practice the voting was weighted in favour of the upper classes by a complicated system of block-voting. Besides, since elections had to take place in Rome, few of the poor outside the city turned up for the occasion. Nevertheless, by 69 BC there were nearly a million voters on the census, a suffrage numerically unsurpassed in any European country until the nineteenth century.

The proclaimed virtues of the Roman Republic are not ones that many later Italians have thought desirable to emulate. The senator

Cato the Elder, who successfully urged the destruction of Carthage, prided himself on his parsimony and austerity; for him luxury and Greek culture were abominations. His brand of rigid morality was shared by compatriots who delighted in being regarded as hardy and resolute and who exulted in the qualities of *gravitas, frugalitas, severitas* and *simplicitas*. In many ways the traits of the early Romans seem, superficially at least, to be the opposite of those belonging to the Italians of later eras: military prowess, political stability and respect for the law, combined with a lack of artistic originality, commercial enterprise, individualism and charm. The rare shared attributes include building and engineering – and a civic pride in the achievement.

One characteristic prefigured in the legends of Aeneas and Romulus was militarism. Rome's citizens were forced to serve in the army, and its consuls and other magistrates were ineligible for office until they had endured ten years of military service. Anyone in public life during the early republic was thus also a soldier. Historians used to claim that Rome was essentially a defensive power which became expansionist in circumstances not of its own deciding. Some of its conflicts that resulted in conquest may indeed have been forced upon it, but others, including all three of the Carthaginian Wars, were not. Inside the structure, innate and inbuilt, were a thirst to fight and a desire to dominate.

Within a span of only seventy years Rome transformed itself from middling city-state to supremacy in the Italian peninsula. In 338 BC the Romans defeated an alliance of Latin neighbours, Volscians and Campanians, and in 295 BC they reduced the Samnites and their coalition of Umbrians, Gauls and Etruscans. A few years later, they went south to the Greek cities, many of which welcomed them, before attacking recalcitrant Tarentum, which not even King Pyrrhus of Epirus, with his elephants and his pyrrhic victories, could save. By 272 BC they dominated Italy south of the Po but felt they needed something more: a few years later, they decided they needed an empire.

The wars within Italy seldom led to outright annexation. The defeated foes were usually absorbed within the Roman sphere by a system of treaties that turned them, sometimes willingly and sometimes not, into allies or *socii*. Rome's chief requirement of its allies was a supply of troops, which they had to raise and pay for, in times of war. However reluctant they may sometimes have been, the allies remained loyal even at moments when disloyalty might have led to the destruction of Rome. The Carthaginian general Hannibal spent fifteen years in Italy, defeating the legions, trying to persuade the *socii* to join him and finally sulking in Calabria. Yet except for the one with Capua in Campania, the second-largest city in Italy, most of Rome's alliances held, including all those with the Latin towns. In the north both the Ligurians and the Veneti remained faithful although they were the people most at risk when the Carthaginian army came over the Alps and was reinforced by Gallic tribesmen in the Po Valley.

The allies doubtless calculated that life under Rome was preferable to a future under north Africans and their uncouth Gallic associates. Yet there were advantages too in the relationship, including military aid in times of trouble. However brutal the Romans were in conquest and in retribution, they were often reasonable and lenient with their arrangements afterwards. In 381 BC they gave the Latin city of Tusculum all the privileges of Roman citizenship and allowed it to retain its government as well. Roman justice was not an oxymoron.

The favour the allies most desired was citizenship, the right to say in Cicero's phrase *civis romanus sum* and thus feel protected against any high-handed behaviour from Roman officials. Yet most of them had to put up with lesser rights until the lifetime of Caesar. While the inhabitants of certain Latin cities were granted citizenship in the fourth century BC, others had to make do with 'Latin status' for another two and a half centuries. Latin rights, later extended through much of the peninsula, accorded certain privileges, mainly social and legal, such as the right of Latins to marry Romans and of their children to become citizens. By the time of Hannibal's invasion towards the end of the third century, much of the peninsula enjoyed these rights. Thereafter the process stalled, and the goal of citizenship, which brought tax advantages as well as the right to stand for Roman office, remained elusive. In 122 BC, when Gaius Gracchus proposed giving Latins full citizenship, he was countered by people who claimed that in consequence there would be no room for Romans to attend games and festivals.[2]

For more than a century after Hannibal the resentments of the allies fermented: they had fought several wars for Rome and had received meagre consideration. Finally an explosion took place in 91 BC after the Senate had again rejected a proposal to extend citizenship. The ensuing Social War engulfed the peoples of the eastern centre, the Marsians and Picenes, and some in the south such as the Samnites and Lucanians; but it did not involve the colonies of Magna Graecia or the Etruscans and Umbrians in the north. The causes of the war are still disputed, historians traditionally claiming that the rebels were fighting for Roman citizenship while revisionist scholars argue that launching a savage war was an odd way of pursuing such a goal. According to the latter, the aim of the insurgents was quite the reverse: independence from Rome and a separate state called Italia.[3] Both views seem to discount the possibility that the various allies might have had different motives, different goals and different emotions. Yet the apparatus of the infant state, with its consuls, capital and senate, suggests that a good many rebels did want independence; so does the numismatic evidence, the quickly minted coins stamped with the name Italia and its Oscan equivalent *víteliú*.

Rome won with a combination of military suppression and political inducement: the moderate rebels were literally disarmed by the grant of citizenship to those who laid down their arms. Citizenship was also awarded to the Latins and other *socii*, most of whom had again remained loyal, but those north of the Po received only Latin rights until Caesar turned them into full citizens in 49 BC. All free Italians then received Roman citizenship. Two hundred and fifty years later, the whole population of the empire was given the same privilege by the Emperor Caracalla, the psychopathic fratricide and builder of the eponymous baths in Rome. Yet by then citizenship had lost much of its meaning: citizens no longer retained their exemptions from taxation and they had long lost their right to vote.

The incorporation of the allies into the body politic took place during a century of intensive 'Romanization', a process that included the absorption of a great deal of Hellenic culture. Roman architecture burgeoned in the Italian cities, Roman villas became ubiquitous in the countryside, Latin vanquished Etruscan and the Italic languages, and municipalities and their officials followed the Roman model. The chief agent of the process was the army, marching along straight Roman roads, living in legionary camps and communicating in Latin.

Its soldiers were also influential in retirement. Rome had long been placing settlements in strategic areas, especially the Po Valley, and it now constructed many more for the veterans of Pompey's and Caesar's huge armies.

In this, the last century before the birth of Christ, an idea of Italy did emerge, not the Italia of the Social War but the concept of a peaceful, united, Romanized Italy, a reconciliation of the peoples of the peninsula after centuries of warfare. A sense of harmony is projected by a coin depicting Roma in martial costume greeting Italia holding a cornucopia, roles and symbols that soon became familiar and persisted for centuries. In 1926, in commemoration of the 2,000th anniversary of his birth, the citizens of Mantua erected a big bronze statue of Virgil, their city's most famous son, gesticulating in midpiazza on a pedestal between marble statues representing Rome the ruler and Italy the mother. Mantua also has a much older statue, dating from the thirteenth century, which restricts Virgil's role to that of seated scholar with his book; evidently the medieval mind had been undistracted by the idea of Italy.[4]

Virgil was the laureate of this Italia. Perhaps he may be considered the first Italian and, if so, maybe the last (except perhaps for Machiavelli) for another 1,800 years. Mantua is a northern city surrounded by water and flat land and cloaked in fog for an average of seventy-one days a year, so it is not surprising that the poet was enraptured by the quality of light and the sylvan landscape of central Italy and Naples. Fortunate was the man, wrote Virgil, who had 'come to know the gods of the countryside, Pan and old Silvanus and the sisterhood of the nymphs'. Edward Fitzgerald's Omar Khayyam identified the essential ingredients of a good picnic as bread, wine, a book of verses, the bough of a tree and a lover who can sing, but the Persian poet had been anticipated a millennium before by the Roman who recommended 'elegant hampers'

> to condiment
> our meal with the delights of nature: a breeze
> touched with some blossom, a pattern of clouds, birdsong,
> and the babble of running water (in which wine jugs
> lie, waiting like sleeping mistresses).[5]

Mantua became formally part of Roman Italy only during Virgil's lifetime, so again it is easy to understand the poet's enthusiasm for the idea of fusion. In the *Aeneid* he had Aeneas tell tragic Dido '*italiam non sponte sequor*' – '[it is by divine will] not my own that I pursue Italy' – and in the narrative he fused Greek, Trojan and Italic peoples to create a Roman ancestry. Earlier, in the *Georgics*, he had united Rome and Italy in a natural partnership beneficial to both: 'the great mother of crops . . . the great mother of men' uniting with the great capital of the world. As Richard Jenkyns has observed, the poet illustrated the idea by evoking the Umbrian river Clitumnus mingling with the Tiber and then jointly flowing to Rome.[6] Virgil's poetry was a powerful influence on Dante and Milton, and his depiction of the Italian countryside has had an enduring visual impact. When we look at a painting by Claude, we may see a mythical or biblical scene transposed to the Roman *campagna*, but we also see an enchanted pastoral landscape, a mellow arcadia in the evening light, which the artist conjured both from his reading of Virgil and from his observations in the countryside. The poet can hardly be blamed if he also inspired the shepherdesses of Dresden china or Marie-Antoinette's *petit hameau* at Versailles.

Virgil's *laus italiae* ('praise of Italy') had a political purpose too. Accepting that the country was a place of extraordinary variety, he believed its strength and destiny lay in 'unity in diversity'. For him Roman Italy was not a glorified city-state but an entity that resembled a nation, a territory of shared values and experience. When he wrote of Actium, the naval action between the former allies Mark Antony and Octavian (the future Emperor Augustus), he described the battle not as part of a Roman civil war (which it was) but as a struggle between Octavian's Italians and their un-Roman oriental enemy personified by the decadent and sensuous Antony and his Egyptian lover, Cleopatra.

Augustus, who according to tradition preserved the *Aeneid* despite the dying wish of its author, was less lyrical about the idea of Italy. He used it for political ends, claiming that *tota italia* ('all Italy') had sworn an oath of allegiance and supported him in his war against Antony. But he did not put her on his coins or regard her as a nation. For him Italy was an administrative convenience not a cohesive unit, and when he divided it into eleven regions he was careful to preserve ethnic boundaries. Umbrians, Etruscans, Picenes and Ligurians each had their own regions; amalgamations of ethnic groups determined the shapes of all but two of the rest – Latins and Campanians, Sabines and Samnites, Lucanians and Bruttians.

Another man who had spoken of *totius italiae* – 'the whole of Italy' – was Cicero, the orator and statesman who after Caesar's death had argued that Octavian must free Italy from the tyranny of the drunk and debauched Antony – an argument that may have been just but was certainly premature (Octavian and Antony were then about to become allies) and led to his murder a few months later. As a minor aristocrat from Arpinum and a politician in need of votes, Cicero had seen like Virgil the advantages of diversity. He appreciated the place of his birth, its 'charming and health-giving' landscape, and he adored Rome, where he lived in grandeur on the Palatine. Yet he did not think of Italia as a whole as his homeland or *patria*. When his friend Atticus asked if he had two home cities or a single homeland, Cicero replied that he, like everyone born outside Rome, had two homelands, one by birth and one by citizenship: while Arpinum was his ancestral fatherland, Rome was his homeland as a citizen. The orator was content with a double identity. Ennius, a poet from Apulia, proclaimed a triple one, declaring he had three hearts, Greek, Oscan and Latin. It was romantic nationalism of the nineteenth century – and its more sinister successors – that insisted on a single heart.

While citizens generally had patriotic ties both to Rome and to their native city, they seldom thought of the rest of Italy as their homeland. The poet Catullus may have felt at home in both Rome and Verona but would not have had emotional links with places in between, other towns founded by the Romans such as Piacenza (Placentia – the pleasing) or Florence (Florentia – the flourishing). This dual but limited sense of patriotism was a product of the treaties of alliance between Rome and the various Italic peoples. These had been bilateral deals between the dominant power and the subject cities; the Romans did not encourage or even permit similar accords between the cities themselves. Roman Italy was thus not a federation of Italic territories but a kind of radial unit in which the political spokes, like the roads, all led to the capital.

The Romans of the first century BC were not nationalists and never had been; apart from other considerations, much of their culture was

foreign – Hellenic. Their Italy was essentially a land of city-states running themselves under the biggest city-state of all. The idea of Italy
had its moment with Virgil and his fellow Augustans, but it was being
superseded even at the time by imperial considerations. Rome transformed itself from city-state to empire so rapidly that there was no
room for nationalism, no time for an ethnic Italian identity to emerge.
In fact the Romans had chosen the imperial path long before they
controlled the whole of Italy.

The crucial year was 260 BC, when they decided to build a navy
from scratch with which to drive the Carthaginians out of Sicily. Since
the Romans had no nautical traditions while the Carthaginians (and
their Phoenician ancestors) had been sailing across the Mediterranean
for hundreds of years, this was an audacious move that achieved an
astonishing success: victory gave them not only their island goal but
Corsica and Sardinia as well. Sicily soon became a classic case of
imperial exploitation, an example to be imitated in other places by
European empires more than 2,000 years later. It became peaceful
and prosperous – its wheat yields were higher than in the twentieth
century – and provided wealth and a reliable supply of grain for
Rome. Cato described it as the 'republic's granary, the nurse at whose
breast the Roman people is fed'.[7] Most of the grain was produced by
slave labour.

The second Carthaginian War, the war against Hannibal between
218 and 201 BC, gave Rome much of Iberia and control of the western Mediterranean. It was followed by two Macedonian Wars, which
gave it Greece and supremacy in the eastern Mediterranean, and by
the third Carthaginian War, which expunged Carthage from the earth
and turned much of north Africa into a Roman province. Empire-
building rather than nation-building was always the priority.

There is much for the modern sensibility to dislike about the
Roman Empire, the crucifixions and the slavery, the gladiatorial contests, the corruption and degeneracy of its rulers. There can hardly be
a human contrast starker than that between the great men of the
republic – the Scipios, the Gracchi, the Catos, Cicero – and the collection of sadists, psychotics and delinquents – Caligula, Nero, Elagabalus
and others – who formed so large a proportion of the imperial leadership. The Roman republicans became consuls after serving in the

army and the government; the emperors' path to power was littered with the bodies of their murdered relations. Nero's victims included his first wife and his mother and perhaps his second wife also. Even the great Constantine – the first Christian emperor and the man responsible for the Roman Empire becoming a Christian state – ordered the killings of his second wife and his eldest son, the Deputy Emperor Crispus.

Yet the empire engendered prosperity, encouraged by free trade and a common currency, provided justice as well as law, and had a broad-mindedness about race and class that modern Europe has only recently striven to emulate. Senior officials did not have to be aristocrats or Romans or even Italians. Two of the best emperors, Trajan and Hadrian, came from Iberia, and some of their successors were from Gaul, Thrace, Illyria, Syria, Arabia and north Africa. What Roman history we learn at school seems to consist of conquests and murders and barbarian invasions, but the Mediterranean world enjoyed a far greater degree of peace during the first, second and fourth centuries of the Roman Empire than at any time since. Unlike cities of the Middle Ages, Roman towns did not need to build vast defensive walls; those of the capital were unnecessary until the fifth century. For most of the first century AD the long north African coast required only a solitary legion to keep it quiet; in the same period Spain needed none at all. The age of Augustus, like the age of the Antonines in the second century, was largely peaceful and broadly thriving – certainly in comparison with the subsequent millennium. Edward Gibbon, writing in the 1770s, may have been right to identify the years AD 98–180 as 'the period in the history of the world during which the condition of the human race was most happy and prosperous'.[8]

Unlike later imperialisms, the Roman Empire did not provoke quasi-nationalist feelings of resentment among subject peoples except in Judaea. There may have been ethnically coloured grievances in other places, such as Egypt and Britain, but the only sanguinary revolts – three of them – that might be regarded as nationalistic were Jewish. In the last one, in the 130s AD, Jewish rebels minted coins carrying such slogans as 'freedom', 'redemption' and 'Jerusalem'.[9] The man who suppressed this final revolt and turned Jerusalem into a Roman colony was Hadrian, in other respects among the most civilized of emperors.

An Iberian hellenophile of Roman descent, this sagacious politician spent his reign travelling the provinces, reforming government and erecting many lovely buildings as well as his wall across Britain; a proponent of peace, he halted the expansion of the frontiers and even withdrew the legions from Mesopotamia (now Iraq). For him the empire was a commonwealth, beneficial to all free people inside it, and he could not understand who would want to resist the prevailing Graeco-Roman culture; perhaps that explains his ferocity towards the Jews. He was not, of course, the only Roman who failed to understand the rebellions in Judaea. Elsewhere proto-nationalism had never been an issue during the rise of Rome, the domination of Italy and the extension of empire. And it did not become one later on. The empire collapsed in the fifth century for many reasons, both internal and external, but nationalistic opposition to Roman hegemony was not one of them. The subject peoples were not fighting for liberation or self-determination. Most of them, like the British, who had valued the *beata tranquillitas* of Roman peace, wanted the empire to survive.

BARBARIAN AND BYZANTINE ITALY

The great Italian historiographer Arnaldo Momigliano recounted that, when he wanted to understand Italian history, he caught a train and went to Ravenna. 'There, between the tomb of Theodoric and that of Dante, in the reassuring neighbourhood of the best manuscript of Aristophanes and in the less reassuring one of the best portrait of the Empress Theodora', he could begin to feel what Italian history had 'really been'.

> The presence of a foreign rule, the memory of an imperial pagan past, and the overwhelming force of the Catholic tradition have been three determining features of Italian history for many centuries. These three features first joined together when Ravenna became the capital of the Ostrogothic kingdom.[10]

It is an idiosyncratic passage but also an illuminating one so long as we remember that he was not really writing about 'Italian history' but about the history of what happened in the Italian peninsula. The

Goths, Lombards and Franks of the old 'Dark Ages' were fighting not about Italy but for territory they wanted to conquer and settle. As for the Byzantines, foes of the first two barbarian invaders, they fought because they, the Roman imperialists of the east, were ambitious to recover for themselves the western imperial heritage.

Historians have an everlasting desire to overturn the verdicts of their predecessors, and it has become customary to claim that the 'barbarian invasions' of the late Roman Empire were neither barbarian nor invasions but migrations of not very aggressive Germanic peoples. Similarly, the Dark Ages are no longer seen as especially dark: if they were a sort of twilight in some areas, in others, such as the Ravenna of the mosaics, they were positively bright. In the endless debates between change and continuity – as if all history, even for the briefest period, is not a combination of the two – continuity in this instance is triumphant, except in Italy, where historians have a long memory of intruders and can recognize an invasion when they see one. Yet although the cities may have survived in a diminished state, along with certain aspects of Roman administration, civilization was altered throughout the western empire, and people became poorer. Archaeological evidence indicates that in Britain after the withdrawal of the legions economic life reverted not to the preceding Iron Age but to the Bronze Age before that: at the beginning of the fifth century the craft of pottery became extinct, and the technique of making it on a wheel was not retrieved for three centuries.[11]

As rulers, the barbarians – if such they were – started well. Little is known of the origins of Odoacer, who in 476 overthrew the last emperor of the west (a child called Romulus Augustulus), except that his father was a notable at the court of Attila, King of the Huns. Odoacer made himself king, governed largely in accordance with Roman practice, and resided in the emperor's palace in Ravenna, which had been the imperial capital since the beginning of the century. Unfortunately he provoked the anger of the Byzantine emperor, Zeno, who persuaded Theodoric, chief of the Ostrogoths, to abandon his raids on the Balkans and instead invade Italy, where he would be permitted to make himself king as a vassal of Constantinople. Theodoric obliged with an invasion in 489, a long siege of Ravenna and the murder of Odoacer, his wife, his son and many of his followers.

The reign of the new king began with a bloodbath and ended soon after the execution of the philosopher Boethius, who wrote his celebrated *De consolatione philosophiae* while waiting in prison for his death. Yet for three decades in between Theodoric ruled wisely and peacefully. He insisted on religious tolerance, refusing to favour either side in the controversy over Arianism, the heresy which denied the full divinity of Christ, and he managed to dissuade his victorious Goths from bullying the Roman population. His was the last kingdom to extend over the whole of Italy for over 1,300 years, yet it was even more transient than other regimes of the age, disappearing shortly after his death and leaving little visible trace apart from his imposingly primitive mausoleum at Ravenna.

Theodoric had theoretically ruled Italy in the name of the Byzantine emperor on the Bosphorus, and it was one of Zeno's successors, Justinian, who intervened again in Italy when Theodoric's daughter was deposed and strangled by a cousin. The pretext was usurpation and murder, but the motive was the ambition of an emperor of the east to recover the empire of the west. Justinian ordered his general Belisarius to follow up his victories over the Sassanids in Persia and the Vandals in north Africa with an invasion of Sicily and the peninsula. The imperial army reached Ravenna in 540, thus making possible the creation of the great mosaic portrait which unsettled Momigliano: that of Justinian's tough and capable wife, the Empress Theodora, robed in imperial purple in the octagonal church of San Vitale, a long distance from her past as an actress, a dancer and a single mother.

Sporadically suspicious of his general, Justinian recalled Belisarius a few years later and left the rest of the 'reconquest' to be completed by Narses and his other commanders. After a war that lasted nearly twenty years, an emperor once again controlled Italy, this time through the exarchate (or viceroyalty) of Ravenna. Although the Byzantines were in fact Greeks and were phasing out Latin, they called themselves *rhomaioi* (Greek for Roman) and continued to do so for centuries to come; no one called anyone or anything Byzantine (derived from Buzas, Constantinople's first name) until the sixteenth century, after their empire had collapsed.[12] They regarded themselves as the heirs of classical and Christian Rome and believed that they had reversed the process of decline. Yet the war had been costly for the empire and ruinous for Italy, destroying the prosperity preserved by Odoacer and Theodoric. The genius of Belisarius may have given the illusion of a genuine imperial revival, but the Byzantines were not rich enough, strong enough or popular enough to keep the whole of Italy.

In 568 Alboino, King of the Lombards, brought his Germanic people from the Danube Valley over the Julian Alps and into north-east Italy. Their advance was almost unopposed, and by the end of the following year they had captured all the cities north of the Po apart from Pavia, which they took in 572 and later made their capital. From there bands of Lombards ventured further south, eventually establishing independent duchies at Spoleto and at Benevento. Between the Lombard kingdom in the north and a reduced Roman-Byzantine exarchate in Ravenna, an uneasy coexistence survived for nearly 200 years, long enough for the heartlands of both to become permanently known as Lombardy and Romagna. Yet the Lombard king seldom exercised the far-flung authority of Theodoric. He was king of his own people (*rex gentis langobardorum*) not King of Italy, and wide areas of the south remained outside his control. Even in the Lombard areas he was frequently opposed by the dukes, not only of Spoleto and Benevento but also several others who governed the duchies or city-territories of the kingdom. So influential were these magnates that towards the end of the sixth century the Lombards experimented for a disastrous, anarchic decade with rule by dukes only.

Byzantine power began to crumble in the north and centre of the peninsula early in the eighth century. In 727 Ravenna rebelled against the Byzantine prohibition of icons and killed the exarch; a generation later, it fell to the Lombards, thus ending its three and a half centuries of glory as the capital of the Roman Empire, of the Ostrogothic kingdom and of Byzantine Italy. Yet in the south the Byzantine Empire held on for longer than the Lombards in the north and even managed to expand its territory: at the beginning of the eleventh century its dominions in Italy included Apulia, Lucania and Calabria, all of them under the ecclesiastical control of Constantinople rather than Rome. Byzantium had possessed Sicily too, and Syracuse, one of the greatest cities of the Mediterranean, had briefly been its capital in the seventh century; but Arab invaders from north Africa had subsequently conquered the island, and Taormina, the last toehold, had capitulated in 902. Muslim armies also succeeded in seizing several cities in Apulia and in establishing an emirate based in Bari in 841. They were eventually driven out by Christian forces, and Bari became the imperial headquarters in Italy for a further two centuries. But in 1071 the Byzantines suffered two defeats at the extremities of their empire, in the east by the Seljuk Turks and in the west by Norman knights, who captured Bari and went on to build themselves a sturdy kingdom in southern Italy.

Thus a great empire left the western stage, though the duchy of Venice remained within its orbit. Centuries later, Byzantium was condemned by Gibbon, Montesquieu and other writers of the Enlightenment as corrupt, deceitful, ineffective and tortuously bureaucratic; even the adjective Byzantine was used pejoratively, though the noun itself was later rehabilitated in the poetry of W. B. Yeats along with the sages and spirits of Constantinople. Yet it seems unfair to apply such insulting attributes to an empire that lasted a thousand years longer than its western partner and which was forced to expend much of its stamina resisting invasions of, among others, Persians, Huns, Bulgars, Goths, Lombards, Arabs, Normans, Venetians, crusaders, and both the Seljuk and Ottoman Turks. By resisting the Arab armies in the seventh and eighth centuries, Byzantium had preserved not only itself but also Christendom and the future of Christian Europe.[13]

Lombard kings were still expanding their territories in the middle of the eighth century, yet within a generation they had lost everything, including their crown. Pushing southwards down the peninsula, they alarmed the papacy which, since the exclusion of the Byzantines from central Italy, now controlled Rome and its hinterland. Pope Stephen II thus travelled to France, where he crowned the Frankish ruler, Pepin the Short, and in return received military help against the Lombards. He thereby inaugurated one tradition – of papal appeals for foreign help – which lasted till the nineteenth century, and another – of French invasions of Italy – which enjoyed an equally long history. Pepin twice brought an army into Italy to defeat the pope's foes, but it was left to his son Charles, later known as Charlemagne, to descend upon Italy in 773, capture Pavia and sweep away the Lombard kingdom.

The following year Charles journeyed to Rome, where he received the title King of the Lombards to add to that of King of the Franks, and on a subsequent visit to the city he had his son, another Pepin, crowned King of Italy. He changed the name of the kingdom from *regnum langobardorum* to *regnum italiae* and he kept its administration separate from the rest of his empire. Yet he was less interested in Italy itself than in its role in his plan of *renovatio imperii* or 'the empire renewed'. The goal of his long, obsessive career as a warrior, which included eighteen battles just against the Saxons, was the recovery of the western Roman Empire, of which he considered himself the heir; and he did indeed conquer much of it, with the exceptions of Britain, most of Iberia and the Byzantine parts of south Italy. On Christmas Day 800 he returned to Rome to be crowned Emperor of the Romans, a title which greatly annoyed the other emperor in Constantinople.

The alliance between the Franks and the papacy stimulated two potent ideas that crystallized into two extremely powerful institutions: the idea of a universal power, whose embodiment, the Holy Roman Empire, was only extinguished by Napoleon 1,000 years later, and the idea of territorial dominion of the popes, a reality that survived for even longer. Although the relationship may have been conceived in need and amity, it developed into a contest with fluctuating fortunes for both sides that ended only when the Emperor Charles V emerged victorious more than seven centuries later. This lengthy struggle was one of the determining factors in the saga of Italian disunity.

The papacy owed its rise to a number of audacious claims: that St Peter was Bishop of Rome (for which there is little evidence), that Jesus had given him primacy over his other apostles (which is debatable – the apostles seem to have been unaware of it), and that Peter's successors – if they were his successors – had received divine authority for their claims to universal jurisdiction over the Church and to superiority over the monarchs of western Christendom. Fortune favoured pretensions to papal supremacy, especially after three rival patriarchates (Antioch, Jerusalem and Alexandria) came under Muslim rule in the seventh century, and a fourth (Constantinople) went into schism with the Roman Church in 1054. Yet while the pope's claims to be the 'Vicar of Christ' might conceivably be supported by a zealous interpretation of the New Testament, no one pretended that Jesus had said anything about Peter and his successors becoming rulers of earthly states. A fresh act of audacity was thus required to justify the papacy's temporal power.

In 754 the Frankish King Pepin had agreed to conquer and to give Pope Stephen territories in central Italy that had belonged to the exarchate of Ravenna. Known as the Donation of Pepin, the promise was confirmed and magnified (though largely unfulfilled) twenty years later by his son Charlemagne. Yet, as the Frankish kings had no rights in Italy at this time, it could be argued that their donations of former Byzantine land were invalid. An older and higher authority was needed, and thus the Donation of Constantine came into being, a document in which the formidable fourth-century Roman emperor, grateful for his recovery from leprosy, was supposed to have granted his papal contemporary temporal dominion as well as spiritual primacy over the Roman Empire of the west. Not until the Renaissance was this proved to be one of history's most spectacular forgeries. By that time the document (the work of a papal cleric in the eighth century) had served its purpose of justifying the formation of the Papal States, a thick band of territory stretching from the Adriatic to the Tyrrhenian that kept the Italian peninsula divided until the second half of the nineteenth century. The popes expanded their territories from Rome and its environs – the so-called 'Patrimony of St Peter' – to include the duchies of Perugia, Spoleto and Benevento, the March of Ancona and finally the Romagna and parts of Emilia. In the process Christ's differentiation between the realms of God and Caesar was forgotten; so was the sixth-century pope, Gregory the Great, who liked to be called 'the servant of the servants of God'. No one would have considered a Renaissance pope the servant of anyone, even God.

The strident struggles between the popes and the Holy Roman Empire date from the eleventh century. Before then both papacy and government descended into ages so dark that not even revisionists have been able to illuminate them. The empire of Charlemagne was divided between his grandsons and then his great-grandsons, and the dynasty's generally absentee rule in Italy petered out in the reigns of Charles the Bald (875–7) and Charles the Fat (880–7). The century closed with invasions by the Magyars from Hungary, who ravaged the north, and stability did not improve over the following sixty years. In the long history of Italian disunity these decades are in a league of their own, a period dominated by magnates claiming to be king – and sometimes emperor – fighting other equally implausible claimants.

One index of anarchy and upheaval is the list of claimants who succeeded in becoming kings of Italy between 888 and 962: one Marquess of Friuli, two Dukes of Spoleto, one Duke of Carinthia, one King of Provence, one Duke of Burgundy, two Kings of Arles, two Marquesses of Ivrea and one King of Germany.

ITALIA GERMANICA

A certain stability, or at least consistency, returned to Italy in the middle of the tenth century when Otto, the Saxon King of Germany, claimed the throne of Italy through his wife Adelaide (the daughter, widow and jilter of three previous kings of Italy) and made himself King of the Lombards. Following Charlemagne's example, he travelled to Rome in 962 and had the pope crown him emperor, thus inaugurating three centuries of rule over Italy by three dynasties of German emperors – Saxon, Salian and Swabian (usually known as Hohenstaufen) – with brief interludes supplied by members of the Welf and Supplinburger families. The gallery consisted of one Lothair, two Fredericks, three Conrads, four Ottos and seven Henrys.

The rulers styled themselves *rex romanorum et semper augustus* ('king of the Romans and ever emperor'), and the coronations that their realms required indicate both the complexity of their roles and the difficulty in fulfilling separate duties as kings of Germany, kings of Italy and Holy Roman emperors. After being elected by the German princes, they were crowned kings of Germany at Charlemagne's beloved Aachen (Aix-la-Chapelle) and became then also known as kings of the Romans. Later they crossed the Alps to receive the iron crown of the Lombards at Pavia, Monza or Milan. The last stage of the process was the journey to Rome, where they were crowned emperors by the pope.

The German Empire stretched from the Baltic and the North Sea to the Adriatic and the Tyrrhenian. Such a distance, with a lot of mountains in between, forced emperors to spend long periods on the road. An emperor might be in Italy, quarrelling with the pope over ecclesiastical appointments, when an outbreak of civil war in Germany made him hurry northwards; after settling that crisis, he might have to scuttle back across the Alps to confront the rebellious cities of

Lombardy or go even further south to deal with a military threat from Byzantium or the Norman kingdom of Sicily. Even so, emperors managed to find time for outside interests such as campaigning in Poland and participating in four of the Crusades. A predictable consequence of such frenetic activity was the neglect of Italy.

The emperors had their judicial and fiscal institutions in Italy; they also had their supporters among the magnates and bishops, whom they relied on for the administration of the cities. Yet the absence of their overlord enfeebled the institutions and the bishops and encouraged magnates to do what they liked to do anyway: plot and switch allegiances. Such a structure was ill-equipped to administer the new Italy of the eleventh century, in which agricultural wealth, the expansion of trade and a rise in population were transforming societies and economies. The growth and prosperity of the cities gave their citizens the desire and self-confidence to run the affairs of their own communes.* Unwilling to accept that they should remain loyal to an absentee foreigner with doubtful rights of sovereignty, they were soon electing their own leaders, running their own courts and raising their own militias. The emperors, distracted by incessant wars in Germany, made concessions that left the communes virtually autonomous. By the late eleventh century their rule over the Lombard and Tuscan cities had become almost nominal.

Frederick Barbarossa (Redbeard), the Duke of Swabia who became emperor in 1155, was determined to reverse the drift. A relentless warrior, with grandiose notions of his rights and his dignity, he later became renowned as a symbol of Teutonic unity, a hero to German romantics and an inspiration for Adolf Hitler, who code-named his invasion of Russia 'Operation Barbarossa'. He regarded the Ottos as successors to the Caesars and himself as successor to the Ottos. As he claimed his position to be equivalent to that of Augustus, he considered the kings of France and England to be inferior rulers. As for Italy, he was intent on reclaiming the so-called 'regalian rights' which lawyers in Bologna conveniently assured him he possessed. These included the rights to appoint officials in the cities, to receive taxes on fish and salt and to collect money from tolls and customs. He wanted

*See pp. 65–72.

the cash and was determined to get it; he also enjoyed the prestige acquired from the submission of others.

The defiance of Milan, the largest Italian city, inspired Barbarossa to invade Italy, which he did half a dozen times. His pretext – and perhaps it was a little more than a pretext – was that he was coming to the rescue of those pro-imperial towns, such as Como and Lodi, which earlier in the century had been devastated by the Milanese. He captured Milan in 1162 and destroyed it. He also obliterated the town of Crema, one of its allies, after besieging it with exceptional brutality: hostages from Crema were tied to the front of his siege towers so that the defendants could not avoid hitting their relatives and fellow citizens with arrows.

Barbarossa's actions led to the foundation of the Lombard League, formed by sixteen cities in 1167 to defend themselves against his imperial armies. An early confrontation was avoided, however, when more urgent matters forced the emperor to return to Germany, and he did not come back at the head of a new army for several years. Despite the defection of a couple of cities, the League won a great victory against him in 1176 at Legnano near Milan, its infantry forcing Barbarossa's German cavalry from the field. It was a historic moment for the peninsula, perhaps the most united moment between the death of Theodoric and the creation of modern Italy. When patriots of the nineteenth century scoured their history for heroic events to depict, Legnano was a popular choice for literature and painting; it also inspired one of Verdi's least memorable operas, *La battaglia di Legnano*, in which the chorus opens the evening with the words

> Long live Italy! A holy pact
> binds all her sons together.
> At last it has made of so many
> a single people of heroes!
> Unfurl the banners in the field,
> unconquered Lombard League!
> And may a shiver freeze the bones
> of fierce Barbarossa.[14]

His humiliating defeat forced Barbarossa to negotiate, and at the Treaty of Constance in 1183 he conceded the rights of the communes to elect their own leaders, make their own laws and administer their own territories. Concessions made by his opponents were nominal or unimportant: among them were an oath of allegiance and a promise to give a sum of money to future emperors as they proceeded to Rome for their coronations. As the historian Giuliano Procacci noted, 'the communes recognized the overall sovereignty of the emperor, but kept the sovereign rights they held'.[15] Barbarossa died seven years later, drowned in an Anatolian river on his way to join the Third Crusade, but his Italian ambitions lived on in the person of his grandson, the Emperor Frederick II, who made equally futile attempts to cow the cities of northern Italy.

The wars between Barbarossa and the communes were part of a longer and wider struggle between the Holy Roman emperor and the papacy, which had supported the Lombard League. As with so many conflicts on Italian soil, this one thus became internationalized, several popes calling in German and French princes to assist their cause. Competing factions in the Italian communes soon acquired labels of bewildering foreign origin. Papal supporters were known as Guelphs, called after the Bavarian Welf family that produced Otto IV, briefly an emperor in the early thirteenth century, as well as, later and less relevantly, the Hanoverian kings of Great Britain. Their opponents, the pro-imperial Ghibellines, took their appellation from an even more obscure source, the Salian and later Hohenstaufen town of Waiblingen, a name sometimes used to denote members of the house of Swabia. In their endless medieval struggles, however, Italian Guelphs and Ghibellines were motivated far more by local factors than by remote loyalties to popes and German emperors.

When Pope Leo III crowned Charlemagne, it was clear that the Franks, who had rescued the papacy from the Lombards, were the senior partners in the alliance. Yet Leo's successors tried to reverse the roles by claiming the right to choose who would be emperor. By the eleventh century they were insisting that the emperors acknowledge they received their thrones from the pope, who, as Christ's vicar on earth, was the highest authority in Christendom. Power was involved along with pride and prestige. Gregory VII, pope (1073–85) and later saint, insisted that only he had the right to invest the clergy with abbeys, bishoprics and other ecclesiastical offices: secular rulers who disobeyed him were excommunicated. The Emperor Henry IV, who planned to continue the policy of his father (Henry III) of appointing and dismissing popes as well as bishops, reacted by deposing Gregory and calling him 'a false monk'. In retaliation the pope excommunicated the emperor and encouraged his subjects to rebel. Alarmed by threats to his rule in Germany, a contrite Henry then apologized to the pope, waiting for three days in the snow outside the castle of Canossa until Gregory finally absolved him from excommunication. Within three years, however, they were again at odds, and Henry was deposed and excommunicated once more. This time he responded by seizing Rome and setting up an anti-pope who crowned him emperor, but he was soon expelled by the real pope's Norman allies, who burned much of the city. The feud between Henry and Gregory was not a unique one: these medieval centuries abound with examples of emperors dethroning popes and of popes deposing and excommunicating emperors as well as other monarchs.

Another ingredient in the dispute between pope and emperor was the status of the Norman kingdom of Sicily. The south of Italy was already very different from the north, more rural and feudal, more ethnically varied, its life determined by the Mediterranean and its peoples in a way unknown to the cities of the Po Valley with their ties to Europe beyond the Alps. Under authoritarian rulers, who liked to direct the economy themselves, and living uncomfortably beside a feudal baronage, the towns had little chance to prosper as their counterparts could do further north; the few that had recently flourished, such as the port of Amalfi with its merchants in Egypt and on the Bosphorus, soon withered. Like the north, the south had its Romans, Lombards and Franks, but it also contained large numbers of Byzantine Greeks and Muslim Arabs as well as a significant Jewish minority. This multicultural, multi-confessional amalgam was unexpectedly welded into a kingdom by a small band of knights from Normandy whose descendants ruled it, flamboyantly and on the whole successfully, for nearly 200 years.

Norman adventurers, seeking work as mercenary soldiers, had begun arriving in the south early in the eleventh century. Pope Benedict VIII hired some of them to fight the Byzantines in Apulia, and before long a few of the knights, notably the remarkable Hauteville brothers, were receiving lands from grateful employers. Fearing that these Normans were becoming too strong, a later pope led an army against them but was defeated and taken prisoner by one of the five Hautevilles, Robert Guiscard, in 1053. Making the best of it, the papacy agreed soon afterwards that, in return for recognizing papal sovereignty over the south, Robert Guiscard could call himself 'Duke of Apulia and Calabria and future Duke of Sicily'. The adjective 'future' soon became redundant when the new duke, assisted by his equally talented younger brother Roger, advanced down Calabria and invaded Sicily in 1061. Thereafter, Robert Guiscard concentrated on conquering the mainland north, capturing Bari and ending Byzantine rule there in 1071, while Roger (later known as 'the Great Count') overcame the Arabs of Sicily, taking Palermo in 1072 and completing his conquest of the island in 1090. After the deaths of the two brothers, the Great Count's son, another Roger, united the Hauteville territories and, following the capture of another pope, was recognized as Roger II, King of Sicily.

The new king was one of the finest rulers of the Middle Ages, a broadminded and farsighted man of wide culture and much administrative ability. He refused to join the Second Crusade because religious toleration was fundamental to his rule, and he insisted that the laws and customs of the peoples of his kingdom should be respected. Fluent in Greek and Arabic, he presided over the most intellectual and cosmopolitan court in Europe, and the architecture he loved – a blend of Saracen, Norman and Byzantine – is still visible in Palermo, in the Palatine chapel with its mosaics and in the red domes of the church of San Giovanni degli Eremiti. He returned Sicily to the prosperity and influence it had not enjoyed since the days of the ancient Greeks – and to which it would not return again. He made of the Mediterranean's largest island a microcosm of what the sea might be but very rarely is, a space where cultures, creeds and peoples meet in a climate of mutual tolerance and respect.

The popes treated the Normans much as they treated the emperors: cajoling and pleading when they needed them, fighting and trying to depose them when they did not. Robert Guiscard and Roger II both suffered excommunication. When the Hautevilles and the Hohenstaufen (Barbarossa's family) became dynastically united in 1186, the hostility became almost permanent. Roger was succeeded by his son

William I, another talented and successful Hauteville, unjustly known by his foes among the barons as William the Bad, and by his grandson, William II, called 'the Good' because he was more lenient to those perennially annoying subjects. Since Barbarossa after Legnano was no longer a threat to Italy, the second William decided to marry his aunt Constance to the emperor's heir, the future Henry VI; as his own marriage was childless, a son of this union might thus add the crown of Sicily to the titles of King of Germany, King of Italy and Holy Roman emperor. The prospect of an emperor ruling lands both north and south of the expanding papal states naturally alarmed Pope Celestine III, who first promoted a rival claimant (an Hauteville bastard) to the Sicilian throne and then tried to thwart Henry's plan to have his son Frederick elected King of Germany. He failed when Frederick was chosen by the electors at the age of two in 1196, but the deaths of the boy's parents before he was four, together with Constance's choice of the next pope (Innocent III) as her son's guardian, postponed an inevitable struggle.

The infant became the charismatic Frederick II, a monarch whose cultural range makes his fellow rulers of the period seem brutal, boorish and philistine in comparison. Hailed as *stupor mundi* ('the amazement of the world'), he was lauded in his time as a linguist, lawgiver, builder, soldier, administrator and scientist; as an ornithologist he wrote a masterly book on falconry and dismissed the notion that barnacle geese were hatched from barnacles in the sea – an example of deductive reasoning rather than observation because he had no opportunity of studying the breeding habits of the geese inside the Arctic Circle. Yet the adulation, like the appellation, was excessive. The comparison with contemporary kings may stand, but he was not as wise a ruler or as cultured a man as his maternal grandfather, Roger II. He was justly famous as a champion of religious tolerance, yet his skills as a builder, architect and linguist have been exaggerated. In any case, whatever his talents, he failed to solve the three great inherited problems of his position: relations with the papacy, relations with the Lombard cities, and the relationship between Sicily and the empire.

Frederick antagonized the papacy early in his reign by crowning his baby son King of Sicily and, a few years later, making sure he was elected King of Germany. When he himself was crowned emperor in

1220, at the age of twenty-five, he assured the papacy that the crowns would remain legally separated. Yet the assurance did not convince a subsequent pope, Gregory IX, once a friend of St Francis and St Dominic but now a dogmatic and irascible leader of the Church. In 1227 he excommunicated Frederick after an outbreak of plague had forced the emperor to abandon a crusade; when the expedition was resumed a year later, the pope was so enraged that an excommunicant was leading it that he launched an invasion of Sicily while its king and his army were away campaigning triumphantly for Christendom. Frederick soon returned from the Holy Land, where he had crowned himself King of Jerusalem, defeated the papal armies and forced Gregory to come to terms and absolve him from excommunication.

The truce between the two men lasted for almost a decade after 1230, but the pope did not relinquish his ambitions to remove the Hohenstaufen from Sicily and to promote a new dynasty for the empire. Frederick's invasion of Sardinia in 1239 gave him a pretext to excommunicate the emperor once again and build alliances with the pro-Guelph cities of the north. Gregory died in 1241, yet his vendetta was continued, with matching vindictiveness, by a successor, Innocent IV, who deposed Frederick, called him a precursor of the anti-Christ and urged the German electors to supply a new emperor.

Stupor mundi may have been unlucky in his relations with the papacy but he was unwise in his dealings with the Lombard cities. Claiming that northern Italy legally belonged to him, he was determined to succeed where Barbarossa, his paternal grandfather, had failed. In 1226 he summoned an imperial assembly to Cremona, most loyal of Ghibelline towns, and announced his intention 'to restore regalian rights'. His ambitions predictably led to a revival of the Lombard League, and most of the Po Valley cities banded together to resist him for the last quarter-century of his life. Frederick defeated the League at the Battle of Cortenuova in 1237 but then overplayed his hand by demanding an unconditional surrender, which the cities refused to give him; the following year he was humiliated by his failure to capture Brescia after a lengthy siege. Despite military successes in 1240–41, when he captured parts of the Papal States, and in 1246, when he suppressed a rebellion in the south, the campaigns achieved nothing durable. Even more humiliating than Brescia was the siege of Parma in 1248, when the apparently beleaguered garrison unexpectedly stole out of the town and ransacked Frederick's camp while he was out hunting.

The emperor died in 1250 and, after the brief reign of his son Conrad, his southern territories were claimed by his bastard child Manfred. Another talented descendant of the Hautevilles, Manfred was a poet, a scientist and a diplomat wiser than his father in his dealings with northern Italy. Yet Frederick's death had not halted the papacy's efforts to eliminate the house of Hohenstaufen and to find a new monarch for the kingdom of Sicily. In 1266, after the entreaties of several popes, Charles of Anjou, a brother of the French king, victoriously invaded: Manfred was killed in battle, and the last male Hohenstaufen, Conrad's teenage son Conradin, was executed.

Charles made himself unpopular in Sicily, chiefly by transferring his capital from Palermo to Naples, and he was ejected by the islanders following the uprising in 1282 known as the Sicilian Vespers. In his place the throne was offered to King Peter of Aragon, whose wife was a daughter of Manfred. Peter's acceptance and reign may have given some solace to supporters of the Hohenstaufen, but Aragonese rule presaged the long decline of the island. Already cut off from north Africa and the Arab world, it was now detached from France and Italy, although over the centuries the southern mainland – known as 'continental Sicily' – was from time to time reunited with island Sicily to be called eventually the Kingdom of the Two Sicilies. Yet from the end of the thirteenth century the island was effectively an outpost of Spain, tied torpidly to Iberia for over 400 years. Like Sardinia, it received viceroys but little attention from its Hispanic rulers.

Frederick's rule had resulted in the extinction of his dynasty and the impoverishment of Sicily, which had to pay for his wars. Another casualty was the idea of uniting Italy under a single ruler, which is what he wanted and which no one tried to make a reality again for another six centuries. The beneficiaries of his failure were the cities of Tuscany and the north, which could now pursue their cultural and communal development – as well as their local rivalries – without much external interference. The defeat of a cultured monarch of the south thus led to a cultural efflorescence of the north.

3

Cities and Powers

COMMUNAL DREAMS

If you were a petitioner to the government of Siena in the later Middle Ages, you would enter the Sala della Pace, a painted room in the city's great Gothic town hall, the Palazzo Pubblico. There you would face the nine governing councillors, known as the *noveschi*, seated on a dais beneath a large fresco representing Good Government. The fresco would be encouraging because it depicts the winged figures of Faith, Hope and Charity flying above the six female virtues, who include Peace and Magnanimity. The figure of Justice is especially reassuring: her scales are even, and each one carries an angel. Standing there, you might feel you were before a just and more or less ideal government, which is what the *noveschi* thought they were.

If you glanced at the walls to the right and left, you would quickly understand the difference between good government and bad government and thus be in a position to select the sensible path to follow. The fresco to the right, *The Well-Governed City*, illustrates the benefits you would expect from such a title. The elegant city is inhabited by happy dancers, industrious artisans, people with good food and fine garments and leisure to chat and read and play board-games. Outside the city gate their rustic compatriots are also merry, usefully employed threshing corn and gathering the harvest, and prosperous as well, owning chickens and donkeys and saddlebacked pigs. Such joys are absent in the fresco to the left, *The Ill-Governed City*, where a horned Tyranny presides over a dark, spectral landscape beyond the walls and scenes of violence and insecurity within: a dagger is drawn, a woman is seized by soldiers, a corpse lies on the ground. Fear stalks the countryside with a sword, while Justice is vanquished, hands bound and scales broken.[1]

The frescoes were painted between 1337 and 1340 by Ambrogio Lorenzetti, late products of the golden age of Sienese painting that was begun sixty years earlier by Duccio di Buoninsegna, continued with Simone Martini and terminated by the Black Death in 1348 that carried off Lorenzetti, his brother Piero and every established Sienese artist except Lippo Memmi. Whereas Duccio's rich, translucent works were painted in the service of religion, and the town hall's most famous painting, the *Guidoriccio*, portrays a Sienese general, Lorenzetti's most celebrated works are the mesmerizing political allegories that cover the walls of the Sala della Pace. In *The Well-Governed City* everyday scenes of rural and urban life were depicted with a skill and love of detail unmatched by anyone until Pieter Brueghel, who must surely have seen them when he visited Siena 200 years later. Guided by the city's rulers, Lorenzetti's role was less the contemporary chronicler than the propagandist of communal government and advocate of a civil life unsubordinated to religion. Symbolism in such matters was important. When the councillors constructed the tower of the Palazzo Pubblico in 1338, they ensured that, although it was built at the bottom of a slope, it would be higher than the tower of the cathedral, which is on a hill.

Siena still seems one of the blessed places of the Earth, a town whose beauty alone might justify the claim inscribed on the Camollia Gate: *cor magis tibi Sena pandit* – 'Siena opens her heart wide to you'. From the shell-shaped Piazza del Campo, the three *terzi* (districts) spread along the town's three curving ridges, their harmonious buildings constructed in the bricks of that warm hue known to artists as 'burnt sienna'. In the prosperous years before the Black Death, 'the city of the Virgin', as it was called, had a population of over 50,000 in addition to another 50,000 in its *contado*, the country districts and small towns it controlled to its south and west. By the time of Lorenzetti's frescoes, Siena had added Grosseto and Massa Marittima to its domains.

The city owed much of its wealth to bankers: the Bonsignori were the papacy's principal money men in the thirteenth century, and the Monte dei Paschi has claims to be the oldest bank in the world, functioning without interruption since 1472. Its chief disadvantages – common to most hill-towns founded by the Etruscans – were its distance from a river and a water supply too meagre to support manufacturing and the labour it required: Siena could thus never hope to compete with the great woollen industries of Lucca and Prato, towns built next to rivers on the plains of northern Tuscany. Yet the Sienese – whom Dante dismissed as vain and derided for their expensive search for an underground stream that did not exist[2] – were unable to grasp there might be a limit to the size of their population. By the 1330s Florence had twice as many inhabitants as Siena, yet it was at this time that the smaller city, already possessor of the striking zebra-striped cathedral we see today, decided to erect the largest church in Christendom. The project was halted by the Black Death, which killed half the town's population, and was abandoned soon afterwards, but some of its pillars and arches still stand as testament to monumental ambition. The existing cathedral, which is pretty large itself, would have become merely the transept of the greater glory.

Siena's rulers, whom their subjects might meet beneath Lorenzetti's frescoes, were titled 'the Nine Governors and Defenders of the Commune', whose regime, buttressed by councils and committees, lasted from 1287 to 1355. Although the Nine themselves were a self-perpetuating oligarchy, choosing their successors from some sixty families, they were supported by a wide coalition of classes and interests and directed one of the most stable city-states of the Middle Ages.

On taking office, the Nine swore to provide 'a good peace and concord' to the people of 'the magnificent city of Siena'. The wording of the oath was laudable, and so was the constitution of 1309 which enforced planning permission. Serious and resolute about their cultural duties, the Nine ordered the building of the Palazzo Pubblico and later its huge tower; they paved the Piazza del Campo in roseate brick in a herringbone pattern; and they commissioned Duccio's great *Maestà* as an altarpiece for the cathedral. They also compelled citizens to embellish their city: houses required building permits and final inspections, they had to be built with loam with façades of brick, and they were supposed to have columns and arches – though evidently many did not.[3]

Harmony and uniformity were priorities. Streets were widened and straightened, thoroughfares paved, overhanging buildings forbidden. The Nine employed officials 'in charge of the beauty of the city' as well as firemen and night-watchmen to preserve it. They were strict also about rubbish, requiring shopkeepers to sweep the street in front of their shops on Saturdays and sending out enforcers to ensure that this was done. Less civic-minded citizens may sometimes have been irked by the regulations. Prostitutes were excluded from certain areas, especially around the cathedral, while in the Campo no one was allowed to carry weapons, feed babies or even eat figs.[4] The Nine would evidently not have tolerated the gum-chewers of today.

Siena with its commune, its culture and its civic pride resembled other city-states that speckled northern and central Italy in the Middle Ages. The inhabitants of these places shared both a loyalty to their cities and a pride in their achievements that helped define who they were and how they behaved. They might fight and riot with their fellow townsfolk but they revered their cities. In his *Purgatorio* Dante stresses the personal identification with a city when one character declares 'Siena made me' and another embraces a stranger on discovering he is a fellow Mantuan.[5] The Florentine Boccaccio, the literary colourist of his age, demonstrated his loyalty in the *Decameron* by disparaging citizens of nearly all Italian cities except his own and Bologna. The Sienese are credulous and the Venetians untrustworthy, Pisan women are ugly and Perugian men are sodomites, in the Marches the males are uncouth and mean-hearted, like those from Pistoia, who are also rogues. The south contributes its share of wickedness with assassins from Sicily and thieves and grave-robbers from Naples, but no people rival the 'rapacious and money-grubbing' Genoese, who are depicted as pirates, misers and murderers. Boccaccio's happy fornicators and shameless adulterers come from all over Italy, but the only consistently good people live in Florence, where the women are all beautiful and the men are noble, chivalrous, agreeable and wise.

Life was communal; there was not much of a barrier between public and private lives. People identified themselves with the commune and its symbols, above all with the local patron saints such as St Nicholas in Bari, St Ambrose in Milan and St Januarius (the blood-liquefying San Gennaro) in Naples. The patron saints of Venice (St Mark) and Siena (St Catherine) had devotional parity with the Virgin. Other symbols were the *campanile*, the bell-tower with magnetic appeal, and the *carroccio*, the ox-drawn wagon carrying flags and a cross into battle. It was embarrassing and humiliating to be unable to defend your *carroccio* and lose it to the enemy. The Milanese lost theirs in 1150 to the Cremonese and again in 1237 to the emperor, when it got stuck in the mud at the Battle of Cortenuova.

Medieval Italians talked of their city as if it were a kind of paradise, its life regulated by sublime statutes framed by lawyers at the new University of Bologna. They were proud of its appearance, especially as culture was then chiefly civic and communal; the great age of individual patronage, both noble and ecclesiastic, came later. Entire populations would turn out with trumpets and pipes to celebrate an artistic event, as the people of Siena did in 1311 when they escorted Duccio's *Maestà* from the painter's workshop outside the city through the gate in the walls and up to the cathedral. Since things were constructed in their name – and not, as later, in that of the Medici in Florence or the Gonzaga in Mantua – they could take a proprietorial interest in the paving of streets, the laying out of squares, the building of stone bridges.

Nine centuries after their emergence, the city-states remain embedded in Italy's psyche, the crucial component of its people's identity and of their social and cultural inheritance. Modern inhabitants of these cities are still proud of their heritage and feel responsibility for its retention. That is why the town centres – though not unfortunately much of the country outside them – are so well preserved today.

Yet for all their culture and prosperity and the participation of their citizens, the city-states were predestined to fall. Their failure was inherent in the circumstances of their formation and development, scores of little towns living close together, anxious about spies and plotters inside the walls, nervous of large and predatory neighbours without. Fear and suspicion led to alliances and pre-emptive moves and an endless succession of little wars. The cities needed a benign protector such as Rome had once been and the Holy Roman emperors never were – until the eighteenth century, when it was too late. It was the endemic factionalism and violence in Italy that made Dante plead not for a state or a nation but for a strong and universal empire. Nationalist historians later hailed the Florentine poet as the 'father of the nation', but Dante cannot objectively be seen as a proto-nationalist. He never visited the south nor indeed much of the north but, even in the central areas that he knew, he noticed little that the Italians had in common, acknowledging (in Latin) only that they shared 'certain very simple standards of customs and manners and speech'. As he wandered about in his exile, the great Florentine decided there were just two possible forms of government, the communal and the imperial, and, much as his work was imbued with a municipal spirit, he recommended the latter because it was more likely to establish peace and order. He did not consider Italian unification as a conceivable third way. Sovereignty and secular authority, he believed, should belong exclusively to the Holy Roman emperor, who derived his powers not from the pope but from God. Dante wanted rulers who were 'illustrious heroes' like Frederick II and his son Manfred, and towards the end of his life he put his faith in the Emperor Henry VII, whom he acclaimed as the 'lieutenant of God', 'the consolation of the world', a modern Augustus to whom the Almighty had entrusted 'the governance of human affairs so that mankind might have peace under the cloudless sky that such a protection affords'.[6]

COMMUNAL REALITIES

Italy's self-governing communes had their origins in the ancient *polis*, in the cities that the Greeks had established in Sicily in the middle of the eighth century BC. Such entities also existed under Rome, autonomous though not independent, and it has been estimated that in the age of Hadrian there were 1,500 of them, containing about half the population of the empire.[7]

Italy's communes emerged in the late eleventh century into the vacuum left by absentee emperors which bishops and imperial officials were unable to fill. By 1150 all the larger towns of Tuscany and Lombardy had communes, though there were few in feudal Piedmont and none in the south. The empire's delegates were replaced by elected consuls, laws were made by councils, and administration was directed by committees. Communes differed over the details of elections – secret ballots, terms of office, eligibility and so on – but their institutions, like their ethos, corresponded. They governed their cities through similar sets of officials and they all set out to control their surrounding countryside, establishing their *contadi* by conquest or purchase and ensuring that their nobles lived in towers or palaces in the city rather than in threatening castles outside.

As populations grew and city walls were extended during the twelfth century, defects in communal government began to show. Power struggles among the elites, feuds among the nobility and civil strife among all classes brought problems that were seldom solved by part-time amateur governments. Short terms of office and complicated balloting procedures seemed admirable in theory, but they led to inexperienced officials and administrative inefficiency. People were loyal to their commune but not on the whole to its leaders, whom they regarded as simply the chiefs of the faction currently in power. As the absence of impartiality became more blatant and more critical, communes of the late twelfth century began appointing a new official, the *podestà*, to deal with problems of justice, civil disorder and fractious aristocrats. The significance of this figure was that he was neutral, a nobleman usually from another city who might be expected to stay impartial and above faction. For some decades in some cities the system worked up to a point, but the innate instability of the city-state, which the Greeks themselves had been unable to stabilize, left the role of the *podestà* increasingly irrelevant and eventually redundant.

In the early days the communes had been run largely by aristocratic alliances, yet their expansion and growing wealth seemed to require the participation of other classes, especially the cities' merchants and bankers. These were after all the chief generators of wealth, important figures not only in the communes but also in the panorama of European trade, which they dominated. Risking piracy or shipwreck at sea or robbery on land, they were the men who supplied such needs and luxuries of the material life as leather from Córdoba, wool from the Cotswolds, sugar from Damascus, spices from the Levant, tuna from Sardinia, ceramics from Majorca, sword-blades from Toledo, almonds from Valencia and raisins from Màlaga. Not surprisingly, they felt entitled to some say in government and resented their exclusion from office.

Merchants, bankers and the rest of the middle classes – from lawyers and doctors to shopkeepers and artisans – were grouped in the city's guilds. The 12,000 citizens of Prato had fifteen guilds, of which the most important, representing the town's chief industry, was the Arte della lana, the wool merchants' guild. In the hierarchy of Florentine guilds of the period the most influential were those of judges, bankers, doctors, dealers in silk, traders in wool and furriers, who were much in demand in winter because pelts were cheaper than cloth. Florence's Arte dei medici e speziali, which included doctors, surgeons, dentists and opticians, had over a thousand members: after passing their exams doctors had to promise to refrain from taverns and brothels and in return they were rewarded by the city with a horse, an attendant and exemption from paying taxes.[8] Surviving Florentine guildhalls, such as those of the silk makers and the wool merchants, are among the city's loveliest buildings.

From the beginning of the thirteenth century associations between members of various guilds were formed under the term the *popolo*, though the word itself is misleading because people later regarded as 'the people' – the poor, the peasants and the unskilled workers – were excluded from it. The *popolo* consisted of many different types of guildsmen pressing for political concessions from the nobles; its richer members, such as merchants and lawyers (known as the *popolo grasso*), aspired to office, while its poorer members, such as shopkeepers and artisans (the *popolo minuto*), demanded equitable justice and taxation, matters in which nobles often had an unfair advantage. Class distinctions, however, were seldom precise, and the factions that fought and rioted in the cities were rarely homogeneous. Nobles sometimes joined the *popolo*, guildsmen often sided with the aristocracy, and men of the *popolo minuto* frequently fought against the adherents of the *popolo grasso*.

Urban conflicts increased at the beginning of the thirteenth century. Armed bands of the *popolo* managed to expel the nobles of Lucca in 1203, and the *popolo* took power in that city again in 1250 and shortly afterwards in Bologna and Genoa as well. Even Siena, more peaceful than most cities, suffered sporadic riots, risings and coups in the three decades after the overthrow of the Nine in 1355: the *popolo* were in power from that year to 1368, when an uprising put leaders of the *popolo minuto* into government. Yet the triumphs of the *popolo* were really limited to Tuscany, especially Florence, where the *popolo minuto* shared power for much of the fourteenth century; in only a handful of towns in Lombardy, Emilia and the Veneto did it enjoy more than a transient success.

Urban violence was not only between classes or economic interests. Aristocratic factionalism – too many nobles competing for too few offices – often developed into warfare. As the magnates lived in cities rather than castles in the country, they felt the need to build urban strongholds in the form of medieval skyscrapers, towers sometimes 200 feet high, a phenomenon now best represented in the small town of San Gimignano and in the city of Bologna, where twenty-two of its more than eighty towers are still fully or partially standing; Florence in its heyday contained even more, perhaps as many as 150. Such structures were clearly designed for military purposes, to serve as watchtower and refuge and defensive bastion, but they were also objects of prestige value, of ostentation and arrogance and the desire to intimidate. They answered to man's perennial yearning to build higher than his neighbours, to 'tower over' others.

Class, competition and vendettas all contributed to factionalism; so did distant loyalties to the empire and the papacy. Yet the victory of one faction over another seldom resulted in peace. Once they had expelled or exterminated their opponents, triumphant Guelphs could be relied upon to turn against each other in town after town – Parma, Florence, Reggio, Piacenza, Imola, Modena and indeed others. The feud in Florence between the strongly pro-papal 'Black Guelphs' and the more conciliatory 'White Guelphs' forced Dante into permanent exile.

Looking back from the foreign invasions of the sixteenth century to the medieval experience of the city-states, Francesco Guicciardini, the great Florentine historian and statesman, admitted that the 'calamities' that Italy was enduring might have been avoided if the country had been united. Nevertheless, there would not have been such wealth, such merchandise, such a 'splendour of innumerable noble and beautiful cities', under a single power; thus he was glad that neither Frederick nor anyone else had emerged as king of all Italy.[9] In any case rivalry between communes had certain healthy aspects: it assisted civic patriotism and loyalty to a city, and it promoted artistic competition between neighbours. Furthermore, rivalry did not invariably degenerate into violence. Communes were sometimes able to cooperate – as they demonstrated in the various incarnations of the Lombard League. They might have no desire for unity or federalism but they were prepared to form tactical, temporary alliances to ward off a threatening outsider.

Left to themselves, however, the communes had a natural tendency to expand – to strengthen a border, thwart a rival, acquire more agricultural land – and expansion was inevitably achieved at the expense of weaker neighbours. From the beginning of the fourteenth century it was clear that Florence, which had once lagged behind Lucca and Pisa, would become the dominant power in Tuscany and thus a city to be feared and even hated by other cities. Poor Prato, only eleven miles from Florence, never had a chance. It was absorbed in 1350, soon followed by Arezzo, Pisa and eventually Siena; only Lucca remained permanently beyond the Florentine reach. Other cities were as predatory and successful, notably Milan and Venice, which between them came to control most of the north and the north-east. Wars between the cities continued for a hundred years from the Black Death until the Peace of Lodi in 1454, which established the Lega Italica (Italian League), whose members pledged to come to each other's defence. By that time power in the peninsula was effectively divided among Venice, Milan, Florence, Naples and the Papal States.

The internal factionalism of the cities, so incessant a feature of the thirteenth century, raised doubts about the viability of communal government. Decades of anarchy and violence left people yearning for strong leadership even if they lost some of their liberties as a result. Communes thus began to welcome dictators in the Roman sense, men who would lead their cities in a crisis and retire soon afterwards. As it turned out, however, the most successful 'temporary' leaders refused to retire and instead became 'signori' and founders of dynasties. It would be simplistic to describe this process as a descent from democracy to tyranny, but the change was significant: decisions were now made by one man, whose successors were his descendants. Not many people, it seems, reacted to this development by weeping for lost liberty or sighing for a return to the commune.

Signorial rule was more common in the north, where feudalism was invigorated as a result, than in Tuscany, on the other side of the Apennines. By the middle of the thirteenth century it had come to Verona, Vicenza, Padua, Cremona, Pavia and Piacenza. Some cities, such as Genoa, Bologna and Perugia, oscillated between old and new regimes before opting for one, Genoa eventually returning to republicanism and Bologna and Perugia becoming signorial. Others succumbed quickly to powerful and enduring dynasties such as the Gonzaga in Mantua, the Malatesta in Rimini, the Montefeltro in Urbino, and the Visconti and Sforza in Milan. The heads of the Estensi family became lords of Ferrara, Modena and Reggio in the thirteenth century and, though later deprived of Ferrara by the pope, they carried on as dukes of Modena (one of their daughters marrying the Stuart King James II) until overthrown by nationalists in 1859.

The *signori* would not have got where they did without being clever, ruthless, rich and intimidating. Yet few of them were as cruel as Ezzelino da Romano, aptly placed by Dante boiling in blood in the seventh circle of the *Inferno*. He was one of the monsters of Italian history, who called himself 'Vicar of the [Trevisan] March' and terrorized the cities of Verona, Vicenza, Treviso and Padua in the first half of the thirteenth century. Some of the others were generous and up to a point civilized, such as Oberto Pallavicini, Ezzelino's counterpart in the west, or Luchino Visconti in Milan, the most talented and sympathetic of all, a man whose family ruled over much of Lombardy and the north until 1447.

Signorial rule was neither inevitable nor always successful in the cities where it was imposed. Venice and Siena escaped it altogether, and others rejected it after experimental periods. Cities with a weak landed nobility and a strong urban economy were less susceptible than others to the ambitions of aspiring *signori*. Pisa was the only great Tuscan city that was signorial for long. Florence had a republic on and off until 1530, nearly 300 years after signorial government had become established in some cities of the north. Lucca had *signori* at the beginning of the thirteenth and fourteenth centuries – with a period of Pisan rule in between – but thereafter re-established a republic that lasted until the end of the eighteenth century, when it was captured by a French revolutionary army. Napoleon Bonaparte later gave it to his sister Elisa.

REPUBLICAN ITALY

Leon Battista Alberti (1404–72) seems almost too good to have been true. The illegitimate son of an exiled Florentine, this generous and attractive figure was one of the great intellectuals of his age. He was a priest and a secretary at the papal chancery, yet he managed to exclude religion from nearly all his writing. At school in Padua he had studied classical Latin literature and he quickly grasped how the lessons of ancient Rome were pertinent to the republics of contemporary Italy. Writing as an adult in both Latin and Tuscan, Alberti produced books that included poetry, biographies, a comedy, treatises on philosophy, one work on diplomatic ciphers and another one on mathematics. He wrote the first Italian grammar, which promoted the use of the Tuscan vernacular, and the first book of geography in Europe since the classical era; in his work *On Painting* he established the rules for achieving perspective in art.

As the pope's architectural adviser, Alberti wrote a survey of architecture in ten volumes, the most important work on the subject during the Renaissance. Yet, like other scholars of his time, he was eager to be a useful citizen and to put his theories into practice; he thus became an outstanding architect, as the churches of Sant' Andrea in Mantua and Santa Maria Novella in Florence demonstrate. His talents were diverse but they were also complementary. He was the archetypal 'universal man' of the Renaissance, one of a band of remarkable humanists who in their range were the intellectual counterparts of Michelangelo and Leonardo da Vinci.

Humanist thought owed much to republican Rome and much also to the republican communes of the twelfth and thirteenth centuries, the period when patriotism and active citizenship were encouraged, when the bishops and imperial agents lost power and people recognized each other as fellow citizens rather than as fellow subjects of a remote sovereign. To civic pride, an inheritance of communal Italy, the humanists added the aim of a secular intellectual life and a spirit of scientific inquiry. They attacked superstition and the corruption of the Church, they insisted on research uncontaminated by religion or politics, and they promoted the revival of classical learning, finding and preserving Greek and Latin texts and arguing that these contained instructive and relevant material that could not be found in the Bible. Their work was supported by nobles, rulers and sometimes even a pope, men who were eager to become patrons of scholarship as well as of art. Several of these humanists were given posts in government, especially in Florence, the capital of humanism from around 1375 to 1450.

The inspiration for the humanists was the Tuscan Petrarch, who died in 1374; for them he had something of Virgil as a poet, of Seneca as a stoic and of Cicero as a stylist; he was revered too as the discoverer of Cicero's letters to his friend Atticus. Yet the humanists of succeeding generations were not inclined to limit themselves to his precept of study and solitude. They wanted a life of service also, to be administrators as well as scholars, to advance the cause of republicanism through example and education, training citizens to strive for the ideal republic through a knowledge of history, philosophy, the classical texts and to some extent science. Coluccio Salutati was a bibliophile and chancellor of Florence, in charge of the republic's official correspondence, while Leonardo Bruni followed him as chancellor and was in addition an historian. The combative Lorenzo Valla was a philosopher, historian and secretary to the King of Naples; he was also the man who punctured the temporal pretensions of the papacy by revealing that the 'Donation of Constantine' was a forgery.*

The humanists were not the first people to look to ancient Rome as their exemplar. The political instability of their commune had left medieval Florentines sighing for a new Caesar, while Rome's populist dictator in the fourteenth century, Cola di Rienzo, had declared himself tribune, proclaimed Roman rule over the world and granted Roman citizenship to the Italian cities.† Yet Bruni and the humanists were inspired by the Roman Republic rather than by Caesar, Augus-

---

*See p. 55.

†Caesar and Cola di Rienzo remained sources of inspiration for many years. Rienzo inspired a novel by Bulwer-Lytton and an opera by Wagner, the latter much admired in Stalin's Russia and in Hitler's Germany. The title Caesar mutated to Tsar in 1547, when Ivan the Terrible assumed the role in Russia. In the German-speaking territories the emperor of Austria was a Kaiser (a Caesar), but to the rest of the world that title has referred to the Prussian Hohenzollerns who became emperors of Germany in 1871.

tus and their heirs. Cicero was their hero, Virgil their poetic inspiration. The Florentines now saw themselves as defenders of liberty against the encroachments of tyranny, though they tended to exaggerate the resemblances with Rome, even thinking of their citizens as 'true Roman people and descendants of Romulus'.[10] Exaltation of the ancient republic sometimes had unforeseen and even undesirable consequences: several aspiring assassins of the ruling Medici in the early sixteenth century – one of them successful – were hoping to emulate Brutus, the most notorious of Caesar's killers. Remarkable though the humanists were, their constant identification with the classical world seems sometimes naive. Italians of their time did not actually lead lives very similar to those of the ancients, except perhaps for those with villas in the countryside, and they found pageants and dancing more entertaining than gladiators and oratory. Nor did their architecture have as much in common as they seemed to think. Just as Romanesque buildings are not Roman except for their rounded arches, so Renaissance churches, even those by Alberti, do not closely resemble the pillared temples of the classical world.

The Florentines were a proud people with much to be proud about, though they did not always see their projects through to completion: most of their principal churches were left without façades.* After the Black Death their economy revived rapidly, and by the end of the fourteenth century they had acquired a silk industry and a new set of bankers, among them the Medici. Their city-state had also expanded by 1433 to absorb nearly the whole of Tuscany except for Siena and Lucca. Venice may have been a more successful republic† but – in the fifteenth century at least – Florence was the more intellectual and cultured one. Florentine painters, sculptors and architects were innovators, encouraged by the humanists and by their own study of classical forms. Several of them were scientists as well. Filippo Brunelleschi's dome for Florence cathedral is not only an artistic masterpiece but an engineering triumph as well. With its 4 million bricks, it remains

---

*While Santa Croce was given a neo-Gothic west front in the nineteenth century, San Lorenzo, Santo Spirito and Santa Maria del Carmine remain without façades to this day.
†See chapter 4.

the largest masonry dome ever built, larger than St Peter's in Rome, St Paul's in London and the Capitol in Washington.

Another reason for Florentine self-congratulation was the system of government, the Signoria and two consultative bodies (the executive branch), the Council of the People and the Council of the Commune (the legislature), and a fairly effective civil service. The Signoria consisted of eight chief magistrates (known as priors) chosen by the four districts of the city, and a ninth, the gonfalonier of justice. As they were elected for terms of two months only and prevented from being immediately re-elected, it was difficult for priors to accumulate power or aspire to tyranny. By 1400 some 6,000 citizens were eligible for the chief magistracies, a figure that gave Florence a degree of political participation larger than anywhere else in Europe: during the 120 years before that date members from 1,350 families became priors. The spirit of the communes and the example of Rome seemed to have helped forge a just and plausible system.[11]

Yet the republic never managed to solve the problem of factionalism, endemic to all city-states except Venice. Ideal theoretical systems were incapable of preventing feuding between groups of powerful families. Thus the republic was usually in a precarious position, and in the 1430s it effectively succumbed to the Medici, as later republics did in 1512 and again in 1530. The humanists despaired at the extinction of their hopes for what seemed so irrational a reason as factionalism. Leonardo Bruni remained chancellor under Cosimo de' Medici but he no longer aspired to change his world; as a solace he read Plato in his spare time while pondering on what might have been.

One reason for the republic's failure was its military incompetence. While its various wars against Milan may have been defensive ones, the campaigns against its Tuscan rivals were aggressive and, as it turned out, often farcical. Humiliated repeatedly on medieval battlefields by armies from Pisa, Siena and Lucca, the republic later employed its artist-scientists to combine with its soldiers to defeat the enemy by means of ingenious engineering. Already famous for his as yet uncompleted dome, Brunelleschi was dispatched in 1430 to Lucca, where he began to divert the River Serchio so as to flood the land around the city and force it to surrender. The still more ingenious Lucchesi, however, sallied out and breached Brunelleschi's new canal, flooding the plain in an unexpected way so that it demolished a dam built by the architect and swamped the Florentine camp. Seventy years later, a new republic tried a similar tactic, although this time the plan was to divert the River Arno away from Pisa so as to leave that city without water. The engineer employed to design the project was Leonardo da Vinci, an even more versatile figure than Brunelleschi, but his miscalculations with his canal were as embarrassing as his predecessor's. On this occasion the waterway was destroyed not by the defenders but by a storm which collapsed its walls.[12]

Whatever they might say about being the heirs of Romulus, the Florentines knew they were not very good at warfare. They were too prosperous to want to fight and perhaps too individualistic to form a disciplined militia of citizens. As a result they entrusted their defence to foreign protectors (usually Neapolitan) or hired mercenaries, who were mostly brutal, expensive and unreliable. The Florentine hierarchy had a different explanation for the city's lack of virility – the rifeness of sodomy which, it claimed, corrupted and enfeebled its manhood and resulted in a low birth rate. Florence was indeed so notorious for this propensity that Florenzer became a German word for pederast. In response, the government encouraged anonymous denunciations of suspected pederasts and created special magistrates, 'Officials of the Night', to enforce new laws against the vice. Niccolò Machiavelli was one of those accused of sodomy, though in his case with a woman, a prostitute known as 'Curly'.

Less questionable explanations for the instability of the republic might be sought in its constitutional flaws – electing a new executive every two months was an inept interpretation of democracy – and in the city's ethos, which encouraged the belief that in Florence (unlike Venice or Siena) the public good should give way to private interest. Despairing of its politicals, Dante had earlier castigated Florentines as 'the most empty-headed' of all Tuscans and compared their city to a 'sick woman who can find no rest on her downy bed but tosses and turns to try to ease her pain'.[13] Even more frustrated by Florentine fractiousness was Machiavelli, a great Renaissance figure who has been much vilified by posterity: since Shakespeare referred to him as 'the murderous Machiavel', his name has been such a byword for political duplicity that it is still used to describe behaviour that he himself would never have countenanced. Machiavelli's republican convictions have been somewhat obscured by his most famous book, *The Prince*, in which he explained how an authoritarian ruler could secure power and advised princes that it was safer for them to be feared than be loved – advice closely followed by hundreds of rulers of numerous nations over subsequent centuries. Yet he was a genuine republican, much influenced by his study of Cicero, and he urged Florentines to emulate the ancient Romans' patriotism and sense of responsibility; had they been able to do so, he believed they could have built the finest republic of all time. He was also perhaps the only real Italian of his age, a man who did not simply shout 'Italia!' as a rallying cry for expelling invaders but seems to have believed that a unified Italy was a potential entity whose emergence had hitherto been thwarted by the papacy. The last chapter of *The Prince* is an 'Exhortation to liberate Italy from the barbarian yoke' and a plea for someone to lead the way.

In the middle third of the fifteenth century the effective ruler of Florence was Cosimo de' Medici, a great European banker with branches as distant as London, Bruges and Lyon. He had opposed the war against Lucca and had been exiled for his wisdom. After the debacle and the resulting chaos in Florence, he was invited home to govern behind the façade of republican institutions. A learned and conscientious man, he understood the inherent strength of Florentine republicanism and never tried to make himself a *signore*. The Signoria and the councils remained, their composition subtly influenced by Medici's supporters. Cosimo himself was seldom an official: prudently, he limited himself to three brief periods as gonfalonier of justice.

His talents were inherited not by his son Piero 'the Gouty' but by his grandson Lorenzo 'the Magnificent', a man of multiple accomplishments. Cultured and intellectual, Lorenzo was the most charismatic exemplar of a Renaissance ruler, a statesman whose diplomatic skills preserved peace in Italy for most of his 'reign' between 1469 and his death in 1492. After the 'Pazzi Conspiracy' of 1478 – an assassination attempt that missed him but killed his brother – he found ways of excluding his family's opponents from office although, like his grandfather, he refused to become an official with a title himself. His position was never legally defined and, apart from being known as '*il ma-gnifico*', he held no rank. After he died, an official decree referred to him merely as 'the leading citizen of Florence'.[14]

If one obstacle to a republican revival was the quality of the Medici rulers, another was the ineptitude of the republicans themselves. A second Piero de' Medici, Lorenzo's son and successor, lacked his father's negotiating skills and during the King of France's invasion of 1494 he blundered so deeply that he was forced into exile. Yet the new republican regime, led initially by Girolamo Savonarola, the radical priest and demagogue, had learned none of the lessons of the old: its constitution enlarged popular participation and made Florence both more democratic and more difficult to govern than before. Furthermore, it wasted most of its short lifetime trying to recover Pisa, a city which, though Florence had conquered it in 1406, had been independent since the arrival of the French. As Pisa's harbour had silted up, the city was now of little use to the Florentines, and their obsessive, fifteen-year-old war to recover it, which included the fiasco of Leonardo's canal, almost bankrupted them.

The diplomatic power of the Medici was another problem because the family was no longer limited to Florence, even if it was not until later in the sixteenth century that it supplied two famous queens of France. Giovanni, the cardinal son of Lorenzo, became papal legate to Bologna and the Romagna in 1511, a position he used the following year to organize an army of Spanish and papal troops to overthrow the Florentine Republic and bring his family, headed by his brother Giuliano, back to power. Another year on, Giovanni became Pope Leo X and immediately made his illegitimate cousin Giulio the Cardinal-Archbishop of Florence. Leo died in 1521 and was succeeded by the only Dutch pope, Adrian VI, who lasted barely a year and was followed by Giulio, who as Clement VII directed the papacy for eleven turbulent years from 1523. After a last spasm of radical republicanism chased the Medici out of Florence again in 1527, Clement devoted his time to defeating the new regime and securing his family's return. Although the city's new fortifications, built partly by Michelangelo, held out well, forces belonging to the pope and the Emperor Charles V starved the last republic into submission in 1530.

There had been dozens of republics in Italy in the thirteenth and fourteenth centuries. A number survived into the next century but were then extinguished by *signori* or absorbed by neighbours. After oscillating between republican and signorial rule, Bologna and Perugia were incorporated into the Papal States in the sixteenth century. Milan, the most successful signory of all, demonstrated that the old communal spirit was still alive when, in the middle of the fifteenth century, between the end of the Visconti and the beginning of the Sforza dynasties, it threw up a short-lived regime, the Ambrosian republic, known after its patron saint. Yet it fell because, as with most Italian republics, it was divided into factions, because its leadership became unrealistically radical and because ultimately most of its merchants and nobles did not want it. Signorial Milan had been the model for people who sought an alternative to communal instability.

In the early sixteenth century only five republics were left, Venice, Genoa and three in Tuscany. Florence's went in 1530 followed by Siena's a generation later, leaving Lucca the sole survivor of the inland republics. Like the Venetians and the Genoese, the Lucchesi had realized that republicanism was safer in the hands of a select oligarchy than in a system such as the Florentine that opened government office to thousands of unqualified people.[15]

Although Siena remained intact until it was absorbed by Florence in 1557, its economic power had vanished long before. So, unfortunately, had its cultural identity. By the early fifteenth century its population had declined to 20,000 – less than half of what it had been before the Black Death – though the influence of its great artistic age was still visible, exemplified by the exquisite paintings of Sassetta, a late follower of Ambrogio Lorenzetti. Yet that age was soon gone, along with the city's communal culture and Gothic architecture, vernacular brick losing out to classical stone and marble; even Duccio's *Maestà* was removed from the altar of the cathedral. The shadow of the Florentine Renaissance was partly responsible. So was the Piccolomini family, which produced the two Sienese popes, Pius II and Pius III. The first of these had an interesting pre-priestly life as an excommunicate, secretary to an anti-pope, poet laureate at the Habsburg court in Vienna, talented humanist scholar and begetter of numerous illegitimate children. When he became pope in 1458, he directed his humanism towards the rebuilding in Renaissance style of his home town Corsignano, which was rechristened Pienza in commemoration. He also made his nephew, the future Pius III, Archbishop of Siena, an appointment that led to the construction of a series of classical white palaces for the Piccolomini clan amidst the burnt sienna bricks of communal Siena.

After it had lost its cultural identity, Siena also lost its artistic reputation. Here too the Florentines made a contribution. As the art historian John White noted, 'the patent on the history of art was taken out in Florence'.[16] The chief culprit was Giorgio Vasari, a poor painter, a pedantic architect and the wrecker of Florentine Gothic, but celebrated for being the author of a hugely influential work celebrating the supremacy of Florentine art, *Lives of the Most Eminent Italian Architects, Painters and Sculptors*, published in 1550. For Vasari and his myriad followers, art had been rescued from its dismal medieval abyss by the talents of Florence. The age of the 'primitives', wooden and lifeless, had been vanquished by the Florentine Renaissance, an extended miracle begun by Giotto, continued by Masaccio and completed by Michelangelo. In such a narrative there was no room for Duccio, Simone Martini or the Lorenzetti brothers; forgotten – or, if remembered, mocked – they were only rescued and revived in the 1930s by the English art critic John Pope-Hennessy. The reputation of Florentine art is of course unassailable, but its supremacy can nowadays be somewhat qualified. It was 'rather an exciting experience', said a director of the Rijksmuseum in Amsterdam, to witness the end of the oldest tradition in art history: 'Vasari's Florentinocentrism'.[17]

PRINCELY ITALY

Power in Italy in the late fifteenth century was effectively shared among five states: a genuine republic (Venice), a nominal republic (Florence), a duchy (Milan), a kingdom (Naples) and the Papal States, a monarchy without a fixed dynasty, although several families were soon competing to supply more than one pontiff.* The variance in

---

*In the seventy years after 1455 the Borgia, Piccolomini, della Rovere and Medici each provided two popes.

title was more than nominal: it reflected real differences in ethos between the states.

European society in the late Middle Ages was being happily seduced by aristocratic values and monarchical glamour. In Italy the world of communes and citizens was disappearing beneath a panoply of princes and their courts; aristocratic pomp and competitive extravagance had almost everywhere become the fashion. Government officials were now being selected by rulers instead of being balloted or chosen directly by voters. In the monarchies – as in the smaller lordships – the life of the state was being conflated with the life of the court, and the officials of the two became effectively indistinguishable.

Civic patronage survived in the republics though on a smaller scale than in the fourteenth century, when the communes of Florence and Siena built their glorious palaces of government. Yet elsewhere in Italy patronage was now in the hands of princes and, to a lesser extent, the Church and wealthy noblemen. The versatile craftsmen of the Middle Ages – humble men toiling in teams in their workshops – gave way to flamboyant and temperamental artists who preferred to work at a court. Some of the best, such as the Venetians Tintoretto and Giovanni Bellini, stayed at home – Tintoretto apparently only once left Venice, for a brief business visit to Mantua with his wife – but others were attracted to princely courts by the allure of sophistication, the promise of riches, an abundance of good food and frequent theatrical entertainments. Leonardo, Raphael and Michelangelo all worked for long periods for powerful patrons. So did Titian, who spent much time depicting the Emperor Charles V at the imperial courts in Bologna and Augsburg, painting for the emperor's son, Philip II of Spain (who never paid him), and accepting commissions from the Farnese pope, Paul III. In 1533 Charles rewarded him with a noble title.

The first real court painter was Andrea Mantegna, employed by the Gonzaga marquesses of Mantua from 1459 until his death fortyseven years later. He was a clever choice for a dynasty with such political and cultural pretensions. With his talents, his knowledge of the classical world and his understanding of perspective, Mantegna managed to glorify his subjects, making his nobles seem like saints or ancient heroes as well as contemporary men. Viewers of his powerful series *The Triumph of Julius Caesar* (now at Hampton Court) can sense the implied connection between his patrons and the conquering Caesar, who is depicted parading through Rome preceded by his soldiers, trumpeters, prisoners and booty. Both parties to this business arrangement were satisfied. Mantegna, the son of a woodworker, acquired an income, a house and the noble title he craved; the Gonzaga got their propaganda and the reputation they still enjoy, that of being great and generous patrons of the arts.

In the fifteenth century Milan was the most aggressive and successful of the mainland states. It was also one of the richest, its prosperity extended into its *contado* by canals and irrigation, the introduction of rice and the planting of mulberry trees for the nascent silk industry. The Sforza's Milan seemed the leading candidate for princely preeminence in Italy until the French invasions of the late fifteenth century which led eventually to the city's absorption by the Spanish.

South-east along the Po Valley, uncomfortably close to Milan and Venice, were two small but vigorous principalities, the duchy of Ferrara and the marquessate of Mantua. Further away in the hills of the Marches was another one, the remarkable realm of Urbino. In each case the ruling princely family remained in power for centuries – until the main branch died out. Given the nature of Renaissance politics and the fickleness of allies, this was an astonishing achievement and one that would have been impossible had the families been less ruthless and opportunistic. The success of the Gonzaga owed much to their notorious skill in identifying and then siding with the likely winner in any war. It owed even more to the political and military talents of Isabella d'Este, a daughter of the Duke of Ferrara who became regent of Mantua after the death of her husband (the marquess) in 1519 and so enhanced the prestige of her domain that her first son became a duke and her second a cardinal. Yet the finances of these high-spending states were always a problem, especially in Mantua and Urbino, cities that at the end of the fifteenth century were challenging the cultural primacy of Florence. The Duke of Urbino, Federigo da Montefeltro (Piero della Francesco's sitter in the most famous of Renaissance profiles), was the archetypal Renaissance prince, a scholar, bibliophile and builder on a colossal scale. Yet he was unable to sit back and enjoy his pictures and his vast ducal palace. Financial needs forced him to exercise another talent – fighting – in the service of wealthier rulers; the employers he fought for as a *condottiere* or mercenary commander included kings of Naples, dukes of Milan and three popes.

Historians encourage us to remember that the Renaissance in Italy was not confined to Tuscany, the north and the Papal States. Yet the variation in its cultural impact on different parts of the peninsula illustrates as well as anything the contrasts between southern Italy and the centre-north. In the middle years of the fifteenth century Alfonso V of Aragon also became King of Naples and Sicily and transferred his court to the Campanian city, where he did indeed preside over a culture that blended the Italian Renaissance with Spanish Gothic.* Yet his influence did not last. On his death in 1458 the kingdom was divided, Sicily and Aragon going to his brother while Naples was left to endure the cruel and incompetent rule of his son Ferrante. Although Naples became the largest city in Italy, it failed to retain its cultural influence.†

Outside the southern capital there was little sign of the Renaissance. The south lacked the small courts and independent cities that stimulated cultural and economic life further north. In Apulia the town of Lecce later enjoyed an efflorescence in its own style of Baroque and today revels in its reputation as 'the Florence of the south' – not a very apt sobriquet because the glories of Florence come from the Middle Ages and the Renaissance and not from the city's imitative Baroque moment. Churches in Basilicata in the town of Matera, where many citizens in the twentieth century still lived in caves, may be Romanesque or Baroque or a mixture of the two, but they are not classical. This is often the pattern in other towns of the south except where natural calamities occurred that required a total rebuilding. Like Messina across the Straits, Reggio di Calabria is today an entirely twentieth-century city dating from the 1908 earthquake. In south-eastern Sicily the towns of Noto and Ragusa were more handsomely rebuilt, in golden Baroque, after the earthquake

---

*The Renaissance arrived very late in Spain. A century after Brunelleschi had built his dome in Florence, the Spanish were still building Gothic cathedrals.
†It also became the second largest in Europe after Paris. At the end of the sixteenth century it had a population of 280,000, twice the size of Venice and more than three times the size of Florence.

of 1693. What was left of Catania after Mount Etna's most savage eruption in 1669 was destroyed by an earthquake a generation later – disasters to which the city's inhabitants responded by erecting one of the densest and most imposing concentrations of Baroque churches in the world.

Since the thirteenth century, the south had been impoverished by rivalry between the Angevin and Aragonese dynasties and by incessant struggles between monarchs and their barons. Matters did not improve much when the Spanish crown took over at the beginning of the sixteenth century. Apart from keeping the peace in Sicily, the new rulers seemed to think the island did not need governance; no Spanish king went near the place except the Emperor Charles V, who was also Charles I of Spain, and who went everywhere. Perhaps they had a point. The Sicilian nobles seemed to be happy idling in Palermo, spending the rents from their estates on building palaces and buying titles from the Spanish – a brilliant scheme for raising money for the government: in the seventeenth century over a hundred princedoms were created in a population of about a million.* Palermo thus acquired plenty of grand buildings but it lacked the kind of intellectual life it had enjoyed under King Roger and the Emperor Frederick. The Renaissance largely passed it by; so, later, did the Enlightenment.

At the beginning of the sixteenth century Rome became the centre of the High Renaissance, but not long before that, at a time when Masaccio and Donatello were transforming art in Florence, the ancient centre of the world was a small town with ruins. For most of the thirteenth century the papacy had resided in Avignon, directed by seven consecutive French popes and 111 French cardinals; returning to Rome in 1377, it suffered the Great Schism, a period of forty years during which there were always two – and sometimes three – rival popes, each with his own set of cardinals and each claiming to be the legitimate pontiff. Only when the confusion was over and the papacy was in the hands of one man, the Colonna Pope Martin V (1417–31), could the rebuilding of Rome begin.

The pace of growth was brisk. In little more than a century Rome

---

*By the end of the following century this figure had increased to 148. The island also contained 788 marquesses and about 1,500 dukes and other barons.[18]

became a city of palaces, fountains, paved streets and new churches; as it did so, the population increased from 17,000 to 115,000, making it the third-largest city in Italy after Naples and Venice. The building of the new was accompanied by much pillaging and destruction of the old: Egyptian granite from the Baths of Caracalla was taken for the fountains in the Piazza Farnese, and the Colosseum proved to be a handy quarry for the Ponte Sisto. No one could accuse the Renaissance popes of having a sentimental concern for conservation. They were intent on building monuments in the Eternal City that would emblazon their names for eternity: the della Rovere, Medici and Farnese, and later the Borghese, Barberini, Pamphilj and Chigi.

The papacy's greatest patron of the arts was also its most bellicose warrior, the della Rovere Pope Julius II, an impetuous and irascible pontiff devoid of spiritual tendencies who persuaded a reluctant Michelangelo to paint the ceiling of the Sistine Chapel, even though the artist grumbled that his profession was sculpture not painting – just as he grumbled later that he was not an architect when Pope Paul III cajoled him into taking over the building of the new St Peter's. Julius did, however, recognize Michelangelo's true vocation by commissioning him to sculpt two monuments to the della Rovere personal glory: the papal tomb, which he did not complete, and a papal bronze statue that was installed in a church in Bologna but removed a few years later and melted down for cannon for the Duke of Ferrara.

Invariable priorities for Renaissance popes were the embellishment of Rome, the success and enrichment of their families, and the preservation – and, when possible, the extension – of the Papal States. Few pontiffs bothered much about religion until the Reformation except to employ interdicts and excommunication against their enemies. It is indeed difficult to understand these men without ignoring their religious roles and treating them instead as typical Renaissance princes, more brutal and rapacious than many, but similarly passionate about riches, art, power and their dynasties. Corruption in Rome was worse than anywhere else in Italy, perhaps because popes had more means to corrupt and more desire to be corrupted than other princes: people were prepared to pay a lot of money for a benefice and a fortune for a cardinal's hat. Sometimes, however, cash was sacrificed to the principle of nepotism, relations being advanced to positions where they could be trusted to promote the interests of the pope and the rest of the family. Sixtus IV (1471–84), the first della Rovere pope, started the fashion by making three of his nephews cardinals (including the future Julius II) and awarding six bishoprics to one of them who died in his twenties. The Spanish Borgia pope, Alexander VI (1492–1503), was even worse, appointing his monstrous son Cesare Archbishop of Valencia at the age of sixteen and a cardinal the following year; later he made him Duke of Romagna and encouraged him to set up a Borgia state in the north that was mercifully short-lived.

A more successful and somewhat more attractive dynasty was the Farnese, whose pontiff, Paul III (1534–49), was the brother of the Borgia pope's mistress. Paul saw his son established as Duke of Parma and Piacenza, an independent duchy which his descendants ruled for the next 260 years (latterly through the female line) and then for a decade in the middle of the nineteenth century. He was also the grandfather of Alessandro Farnese, known as 'the Great Cardinal' for his charity and his political skills, and great-grandfather of another Alessandro, the renowned soldier who retained the southern Netherlands for Spain and might therefore be regarded – for better or worse – as the father of modern Belgium.

Nepotism remained a compulsive papal habit for 200 years – except during the brief reign of the Dutch pontiff Adrian VI (1522–3) – until the Neapolitan pope, Innocent XII, put a stop to it late in the seventeenth century. Even so, it enjoyed a revival when the Braschi pope, Pius VI (1775–99), made one of his nephews a duke and another a cardinal shortly before the French Revolution. Corrupt and lamentable as it was in principle, nepotism also encouraged papal fantasies and military adventures: the Farnese in Parma, the Borgia in the Romagna, the Medici against the republicans of their native city – these families' papal representatives were fighting primarily for their relations. In addition, nepotism damaged the reputation of the Church since it was hard for Christians to see much of a connection between the lives of Jesus and his disciples and those of the Renaissance popes and their courts. Many people in southern as well as northern Europe wanted the Church to be reformed, bishops forced to live in their dioceses and abuses such as selling indulgences ended. Yet the papacy wanted money a lot more than it wanted reform: as Pope Martin V is alleged to have said in the early fifteenth century, 'Without reform the Church has been advancing for fourteen centuries; without money it might not last a week.'[19]

At the Lateran Council of 1513–17 the reformers were decisively defeated. Assisted by Spain, the Church then retrenched, dogmatic and authoritarian, rejecting humanism and rejoicing in the eventual triumph of the Counter-Reformation over the classical values of the Renaissance. Paul IV, the elderly pope elected in 1555, burned books by the thousands, confined the Jews of Rome to ghettoes and ordered fig-leaves to be painted on to Michelangelo's figures on the ceiling of the Sistine Chapel. Most of his successors and their cardinals insisted upon a strict observation of the decrees of the Council of Trent (1545–63), the doctrinal essentials of the Counter-Reformation. The dynamic and influential Cardinal-Archbishop of Milan, Carlo Borromeo (1538–84 and canonized in 1610), ordered the prohibition of dances and carnivals and forced his priests to interrogate their parishioners for information about heretics and banned books. Although the papacy did make a few concessions to reformers at Trent – bishops were told to reside in their bishoprics – its refusal to compromise with Protestantism made the division of Europe inevitable and lost it England, Scotland, Zurich and Geneva, the Netherlands, most of Germany and Scandinavia. The Protestants in Italy soon emigrated, mainly to Geneva, but most Italians remained faithful to the Church, their devotion to the Virgin and the saints outweighing their dismay at the behaviour of the popes.

As successful as the Farnese in the pursuit of family interest were the Medici popes, who twice succeeded in bringing their exiled family home to Florence and back to power. After 1530 Pope Clement VII and his recent foe and current ally, the Emperor Charles V, agreed that the Medici should become hereditary rulers of Florence and decided the line would begin with Alessandro, an illegitimate teenage great-nephew of the first Medici pope. When, a few years later, the newly anointed Duke Alessandro was murdered by a jealous cousin, no suitable descendants of Lorenzo the Magnificent could be found to succeed him, yet such was the magic of the family name that another Medici teenager was found to step in, a relation (luckily called Cosimo) so remote that he could not even claim as his ancestor the great Cosimo, the first member of the family to rule Florence.

The new Cosimo proved to be as patient and skilful as the old one, dealing diplomatically with the most powerful of all emperors, from whose son he obtained – after a siege – the long-desired Siena, whose Palazzo Pubblico was soon decorated with the Medici coat of arms. He employed spies and confined political opponents, yet he succeeded in creating a stable administrative system that endured almost unopposed for 200 years. As befitted the age and its aristocracy, the Medici moved out of the family's palace in the old city and crossed the Arno, installing themselves in the vast and ponderous Pitti Palace, where they had plenty of space to lay out the Boboli Gardens. More significantly, Cosimo came to regard his realm as the state not the city, a departure from the instincts and habits of previous Medici. He acknowledged he had a duty to develop the economy in the whole of his dominions, not just in the capital and its old *contado*. When the pope promoted him in 1569, Cosimo chose to take the title of Grand Duke of Tuscany; henceforth the Medici were not so much Florentines as Tuscans.

Cosimo and his successors were able rulers and enlightened economists; some of them were also scientists. They developed Livorno (which for centuries the British insisted on calling Leghorn) as a free port and encouraged merchants from anywhere to settle there, including the Jewish ancestors of Benjamin Disraeli. They also tirelessly promoted agriculture, notably with energetic but largely unsuccessful attempts to drain the coastal marshes of the Maremma. The line died out, however, in an ambience of archetypal decadence. The penultimate grand duke, Cosimo III, who ruled longer than any Medici (1670–1723), was a bigot, a prude and a collector of holy relics. Under him the Tuscan navy was reduced to a total of three galleys while the army contained soldiers who were senile, lame and half-blind.[20] His successor, Gian Gastone, achieved decadence in a different way: often drunk in public, he was a slothful homosexual with little chance of producing children with his frightening German wife. Widely mocked though he was, Gian Gastone was nevertheless a more sensible and tolerant ruler than his father. He reversed the Church's encroachments in Tuscany and revoked anti-Semitic edicts; he also reduced taxes on the peasantry and abolished those levied on beasts of burden. Following his death in 1737, the family became extinct, though the duchy lived on under a new dynasty until, through no fault of its own, it was engulfed by the hysteria of the Risorgimento.

The Medici's last act encapsulated attitudes they had held for centuries towards their rights, duties and the importance of public relations. Gian Gastone's sister, Anna Maria Ludovica, decreed that after her death (1743) all the family properties, all the paintings and statues and jewellery, should remain 'for the ornament of the state, for the benefit of the people and for an inducement to the curiosity of foreigners'. Although this treasure was left to the next line of grand dukes, it was never 'to be alienated or taken away from the capital or from the territories of the grand duchy'.[21] It is still in Tuscany.

4

Adriatic Venice

People have seldom felt neutral about Venice, a city that has provoked an abundance of contrasting emotions, love and hostility, envy and admiration, grief and gratitude. Since it ceased to be an independent state in 1797, most visitors have succumbed to its enchantment, to the beauty of its buildings, the appeal of its canals and the blending of light and stone and water. John Ruskin, who pronounced himself a 'foster-child of Venice', was its most vigorous and effective champion, the author of *The Stones of Venice*, a three-volume, mid-Victorian work of insight, polemic, fine writing and occasional silliness. His book might have deterred attempts at emulation, but it didn't: as James Morris, one of the most evocative writers on the city, has remarked, Venice is 'paved with purple passages' – including some good ones of his own. Admitting it was 'a great pleasure to write the word' Venice, Henry James thought there might be 'a certain impudence' in writing any more. 'There is notoriously nothing more to be said on the subject,' he wrote; but he said it all the same, at length.[1]

The enduring success of the Venetian Republic aroused the admiration of intellectuals from other Italian states where the republican experiment had failed. In the early sixteenth century the Florentine Guicciardini opined that Venice had the best government of all time, while his fellow Tuscan, the poet and satirist Pietro Aretino, lauded the city as a 'universal fatherland', a 'refuge of displaced peoples' and a 'freedom common to all'.[2] Subsequent writers extolled the tolerance and stability, the tradition of public service, the wealth and art and manners of this vigorous maritime republic. In his epitaph for the city William Wordsworth lamented the passing of 'the eldest child of liberty', a power that had held 'the gorgeous East in fee' and had subsequently acted as 'the safeguard of the West'.* A later poetic sensibility suspired in Venice when Robert Browning came to live and die in the Ca' Rezzonico, the sumptuous Baroque palace on the Grand Canal. He had already penned his personal epitaph: 'Open my heart and you will see / Graved inside of it, Italy.'†

Not all Victorians held such views. Many of them believed that Venice had been iniquitous, a decadent and corrupt state that had survived by means of prisons, spies and tyranny. The city was also considered backward and stuck in the past: radical Tory MPs in Westminster in the 1880s used 'Venetian' as an adjective to describe reactionary colleagues they considered elitist and oligarchic.[3] Earlier Lord Byron had contributed to the myth of sinister Venice in his play *The Two Foscari*, in which the condemned man denounces the state for its spies, slaves and dungeons, its Bridge of Sighs, its 'strangling chamber' and its 'torturing instruments'. A generation later, Giuseppe Verdi thought of turning the drama into an opera for his Venetian debut at the Fenice theatre; when it was pointed out that Venice was not the most appropriate venue for the work – descendants of the 'villains' still lived there – the composer substituted *Ernani* and took *I due Foscari* to be performed in Rome.

Many of the state's critics were French. Jean-Jacques Rousseau mocked its decadence, called its republic a sham and condemned the Council of Ten (which had charge of the state's security) as 'a tribunal of blood', '*horrible également*' to both patricians and people[4] – a judgement so misguided it makes one wish its author had lived long enough to witness real tribunals of blood directed by his apostle Robespierre. Napoleon Bonaparte followed this deluded philosopher, tormenting dejected Venetian delegates in 1797 with his ignorant views on their state's alleged tyranny. The first modern historian of Venice was Pierre Daru, previously Napoleon's minister of war, whose eight-volume work depicts the republic as a hidebound and decadent oligarchy. While Daru (like his master) presumably took this line to justify the invasion and destruction of a neutral state, the motives of later historians are less obvious. Critics have zealously examined

*'On the Extinction of the Venetian Republic' (1807).
†'De Gustibus' (1855).

Venice's blemishes, such as its slave-trading and its colonial rule – defects not unique to Venice – and its diversion of the Fourth Crusade in order to sack Constantinople in 1204. The historian Steven Runciman may have been right to describe this last event as one of the greatest of all crimes against humanity, yet 1204 was a single year in a 1,100-year history.[5]

Everyone agrees that Venice is different from anywhere else. Visitors immediately see that it has no hills and that its streets are full of water; soon they also notice that it has neither ramparts nor a castle; the Doge's Palace, the headquarters of the Venetian Empire, is unfortified. As they wander about, they will observe that there are no fountains, no ruins and not many statues in public places; since it was founded after the fall of Rome, it has no amphitheatres, no triumphal arches and no classical archaeologists. Nor does it have noblemen's towers – those sinister structures that abounded elsewhere in the north – which accurately suggests a lack of murderous factions. The patricians had palaces, but these too are different. The external decoration – the harmonious arrangement of windows, pillars, balconies and arches – is concentrated on the façade, while the unadorned brick sides usually look at other brick sides across narrow lanes. While the patricians could do as they pleased with their façades, they were prevented by law from putting statues and balustrades on their roofs: all they were allowed were chimneys and – provided they were senior figures in the admiralty – a pair of small obelisks.[6]

Most city centres in northern Italy are a mixture of architectural styles since the Romanesque, but in Venice the emphases are different and the proportions often inverted. The influence of Byzantium on the lagoon is obvious: St Mark's is modelled on a church in Constantinople, and a number of Veneto-Byzantine palaces survive near the Rialto. Yet Venice is fundamentally Gothic, one of the few Italian cities to be thus blessed; it was still constructing in the Gothic style after the others had given up. The city has some great Renaissance buildings, especially those by Jacopo Sansovino and Andrea Palladio, but they – like the churches and palaces in elaborate Baroque – do not always seem to belong to Venice. Sansovino's library, across the Piazzetta from the Doge's Palace, is a beautiful structure yet it is unrelated to any earlier Venetian building; it is not even similar to the one adjoining it, the rusticated, practical Mint built at the same time by the same architect. One might say similar things – as Ruskin did*[7] – about Palladio's great churches, whose geometrical harmonies are spread out across the water from St Mark's: San Giorgio Maggiore, the Zitelle, the Redentore. In the mid-sixteenth century, when the wooden bridge on the Rialto was in danger of falling down, the Venetian authorities organized a competition to design an alternative in stone. Several famous architects, including Palladio and Michelangelo, put forward proposals, but the prize was awarded to the virtually unknown Antonio da Ponte because his plan showed an understanding of local topography. Palladio's scheme, which only small boats could have passed under, would have been more appropriate in the spacious park of a country house in England.

Venice is said to have been founded in AD 421 by refugees from the mainland fleeing Vandal invaders; in the following century they were joined by others escaping the Lombards. They settled on the islets, mudflats and sandbanks of the lagoon, initially at Torcello and at Malamocco on the Lido, but in the early ninth century they established their capital on the safer central islands of the Rialto. Bleak and inhospitable though the lagoon must have seemed, it provided a secure sanctuary. The problem was less how to defend than how to inhabit what was largely a swamp. For centuries the inhabitants drained and dredged, diverting silt-carrying rivers from the lagoon and converting sandbanks into islands which they could build upon. The construction of a building required long wooden stakes driven into the mud covered first by clay and then by wood planking upon which a brick wall base was laid – all below the high water mark; upon these foundations the building was then completed in brick, often with stone too and sometimes with marble as well.[8]

In its early years Venice was governed from the exarchate of Ravenna, and its '*dux*' (later doge) was a vassal duke of the Byzantine Empire. Later it became autonomous, but the link between Venice and Constantinople remained strong until the thirteenth century. For

---

*In one of his more intemperate moments Ruskin declared of San Giorgio Maggiore that it was 'impossible to conceive a design more gross, more barbarous, more childish in conception, more servile in plagiarism, more insipid in result, more contemptible under every point of rational regard'.

an empire with little commercial nous, the trade and shipping of the islanders made Venice a very useful ally; the lagoon also benefited from Byzantium's cultural influence and from trading links with different parts of the empire. Another boon was Charlemagne's decision, after two failed assaults on the Lido, to let Venice remain tied to the Byzantines, thereby excluding it from his kingdom of Italy and from the Holy Roman Empire. This spared the city's inhabitants from having to choose between Guelphs and Ghibellines and, though they gave money to the Lombard League, from fighting in Italy's interminable medieval wars. Venice had plenty of enemies in the Adriatic – Arabs, Slavs, Normans and later Turks – but its only lasting Italian foe was Genoa, and the wars between them were a result of commercial rivalry in the Levant.

Until the early fifteenth century Venice turned its back on the peninsula and concentrated initially on the eastern shores of the Adriatic. Needing Istria for its stone and Dalmatia for its timber, it gained control of their coasts and, around the turn of the millennium, its doge proclaimed himself *Dux Dalmatiae et Chroatiae*, a title with implications that the kings of Hungary resented. In the twelfth century the Venetian fleet enabled the city to have a strong trading presence in the crusader kingdom of Jerusalem, but it was not until the next century that circumstances allowed it the opportunity to acquire an empire at the expense of Byzantium. Providing the knights of the Fourth Crusade with ships in 1202, Enrico Dandolo – an old, blind and ferocious doge – persuaded the crusaders (who had planned to invade Muslim Egypt) to attack and loot the Christian town of Zara and thence to capture and plunder Constantinople, the greatest city of Christendom, overthrowing the emperor in the process and transforming his empire of the east from a Greek entity into a Latin one. Although the Greeks were back in control half a century later, Byzantium was by then irretrievably weakened and in no shape to defend itself against the advance of the Ottoman Turks.

After the Crusade and the pillaging of Byzantium, Venice ceased to be simply a maritime republic with trading posts scattered across the eastern Mediterranean. It became a colonial power that acquired, together with many smaller places, Crete in the thirteenth century, Corfu and parts of the Morea in the fourteenth, Cyprus and Salonika in the fifteenth, and Cephalonia in 1500. The island of Crete was divided into six districts named after the six *sestieri* of Venice: San Marco, Castello, Cannaregio, Dorsoduro, San Polo and Santa Croce. Yet the empire remained essentially mercantile, one of the colonies' main purposes being to provide friendly harbours all the way home from the Black Sea. Its total population of some 400,000 people (including Venice itself) meant that it could never have been a true colonizing enterprise. The empire was less a place of settlement and plantation than a world of ships and quays, wharves and warehouses, populated mainly by shipwrights, sailors, fishermen, merchants, dockers, consuls and customs officers.

Until the later fourteenth century Venice's chief enemies were not the Arabs or the Turks but the Genoese, who, after subduing Pisa in 1284, dominated the Tyrrhenian coast and much of the western Mediterranean. Genoa was as great a maritime power as Venice, maintaining trading posts as far away as Syria and the Black Sea. Although the navies of the two republics were well matched, the Genoese unexpectedly lost the most crucial of their battles, at Chioggia in 1380, when their ships besieging Venice were blockaded by a returning Venetian fleet and destroyed. Genoa's main disadvantage as a state was its chronic factionalism, the most persistent in all Italy: the city suffered fourteen revolutionary outbreaks in the first half of the fourteenth century. Yet political weakness did not prevent the Genoese from becoming the world's principal bankers in the late sixteenth century, taking over from Lyon and Antwerp as the financial centre of western Europe.

It was the lagoon that saved Venice from the Genoese, as it had protected the city from earlier invaders. In the ninth century Charlemagne's son Pepin ran aground on the sandbanks and lost his ships, an Arab fleet proved incapable of negotiating the currents, and a Magyar army that was invincible on land launched a disastrous attack in coracles. Innocuous though it may seem to visitors, the lagoon is a labyrinth of currents and shoals, of mudflats and sandbanks, of narrow channels and unexpected shallows, both a haven for its occupants and a hazard for outsiders. One of the smallest islands is called Buel del Lovo ('wolf-gut' in Venetian) because its navigable channel is so tortuous.

A trip down the lagoon to the fishing ports of Chioggia and Pellestrina takes you away from the touristic isles of Burano and Torcello and shows you how human settlement has changed over the centuries and in some cases disappeared altogether. The earliest buildings on most of the smaller islands are convents and monasteries, and many ruins remain, much vandalized since the suppression of the religious orders. One island was set aside for plague victims, another for lunatics, a third for quarantine. Many others were appropriated for military purposes, usually by the French and Austrian occupiers of the nineteenth century: then they were used for barracks, hospitals, munitions factories and gunpowder magazines. More recently, some have acquired new roles such as a fish cannery, a university, an archaeological school and a sailing marina.[9]

The voyage also reminds you how real and important the maritime life still is to the economy and livelihood of the lagoon. Among the lines of fishing vessels, the boats of pilots and coastguards are constantly busy; beyond the island fortresses, oil tankers ply their way to and from the refinery at Porto Marghera (destroying as they do so the delicate ecological balance of the lagoon). Everywhere you notice the maintenance operations, the boatyards and the dry-docks, the incessant dredging, the re-siting and replacing of the *bricole* and other posts. You become aware of how the lagoon is defended against the Adriatic when you see the great sea-walls of Pellestrina, erected to stop the waves from breaking in, sweeping away the port and swamping the other islands.

Knowledge of the lagoon allied to supreme nautical skills enabled Venice to become a great sea-power. Its galleys, rowed very largely by free men not slaves, were the Mediterranean's most effective fighting ships until the sixteenth century. By contrast with Genoa, where business was an affair of individuals, the Venetian state directed much of the city's economic life: it regulated trade, organized convoys for its merchant marine and ran the great shipbuilding yards of the Arsenale, which was the largest factory in the west, capable in a crisis of constructing several galleys a week. The yards' workforce of about 1,500 men, the *arsenalotti*, were well rewarded for their skills, each receiving annually, among other benefits, 500 litres of wine. In the early sixteenth century Venice was the richest and most splendid city in Christian Europe, its wealth generated by trade and the production of vast quantities of silk and glass: its largest employer, with a thousand looms, was the silk industry.

By that time Venice had already acquired its reputation as a state offering its citizens political stability and personal freedom. It never experienced a successful revolt or conspiracy, although in the fourteenth century there had been one failed plot and one insane attempt by a doge to set up a monarchy. The Venetian political system was convoluted but, as Italians from the mainland admitted, it functioned. Power was diffused, its concentration prevented by councils and committees and electoral procedures so obscure and complicated that it is hard to see how they were dreamed up. The head of state was an elected leader, the doge, the most fettered ruler in Italy. Beneath him and his six councillors (the *minor consiglio*) were the body of ministers (the *collegio*), which formed the executive, and the largely autonomous, often maligned Council of Ten (*consiglio dei dieci*), responsible for the security of the state. A senate of some 200 mainly old men provided the legislature and below that was the Great Council (the *maggior consiglio*), which effectively contained the ruling class, consisting eventually of more than 2,000 patricians. Often criticized as a narrow oligarchy that closed its membership in 1297, the Great Council did in fact continue to admit newcomers, though fewer than before. It was in any case the largest elective body in Italy, and its meetings required the construction of the vast Sala in the Doge's Palace decorated with the largest oil painting in the world – Tintoretto's version of paradise – and a host of lesser works depicting the acmatic moments of Venetian glory.

The factionalism of medieval Italy had forced communes to appoint a *podestà*, a nobleman from outside, to act as an impartial administrator. Yet as the historian Mario Ascheri has pointed out, Venice did not need a *podestà* because centuries earlier it had created a tradition for its head of state that guaranteed impartiality.[10] The doges lived grandly, housed in splendour in the palace that people often choose as their favourite building in the world. Yet most of them were figureheads who could do little without the consent of their councillors and their law-officers. Moreover, the post required numerous sacrifices: its holders could not trade or accept gifts or own property outside the republic; nor could they abdicate or leave Venice if they wanted to; they were not even allowed to talk to foreign ambassadors on their own. As for their relations, Venice was so unlike the rest of Italy that a doge's son, far from being able to succeed his father, was not allowed to vote or hold office – or even marry a foreigner without the permission of the Great Council.

The doges were nearly always old men – when he started the job in 1521 Antonio Grimani was eighty-seven – elected for life in the most labyrinthine of processes. The youngest member of the Great Council would go out into the Piazza San Marco and choose the first lad he saw as a ballot boy. The boy would then pick thirty names of the council from an urn, a number which would be reduced by lot to nine members who now went into conclave to vote for forty, again reduced by lot, this time to twelve, who had to choose twenty-five, brought back down by lot to nine, who each had seven votes to choose forty-five, who were then reduced to the eleven who finally chose the forty-five who elected the doge.[11] Even at the end of all this, matters might not be straightforward. The election of Marino, the second Grimani doge, required seventy-one ballots.

Venice possessed the most harmonious society in Italy. Outsiders noticed that its citizens were more united than in other places and that they shared a community spirit, a belief in the common good, that was absent in Florence or Genoa. There was little violence or street-fighting, which would have been difficult in any case because of the canals. Venice had class but not class conflict. Aristocrats did not parade about with armed retinues, and fishermen and *arsenalotti* did not riot in the streets. Men of the middle classes did not agitate strenuously to become part of the ruling oligarchy: they made their fortunes and spent much of them on the buildings of their confraternities, the magnificent *scuole* which they adorned with cycles of paintings by such artists as Carpaccio, Tintoretto and the elder Tiepolo. In Venice political discontent was defused by the opportunities of sea trade in which all classes participated. At home the patrician and the gondolier lived in very different conditions but they were judged by the same system: there were no legal privileges for nobles. Civil and criminal jurisdiction were regarded as on the whole fair, and women came to enjoy legal rights rarely found elsewhere: husbands were prevented from being in the same room when their wives were making their wills.[12] As for the foreign propaganda about dungeons groaning with political prisoners, this was a libel. Despite Bonaparte's taunts about tyranny, his occupying army was unable to find a single political prisoner in the whole of the republic.

Patricians liked to think that, of Venice's twenty-four founding families, half of them were descended from early Christians and could thus call themselves 'apostolic'.[13] Yet, pretentious though they may have been about their status, they seldom behaved like patricians in the rest of Europe. Since they did not own country estates before their city acquired a mainland, they did not have a tradition of living in castles or hunting in forests. Nor did they despise trade or administration: they happily accepted their roles as shippers, merchants and councillors. Portraits in other states show nobles wearing bright and sometimes garish costumes, but in Venice patricians wore plain black robes except when they held office. Ostentation was largely confined to the façades of their *palazzi*, whether on the Grand Canal or in humbler districts where many of them lived; sumptuary laws limited the amount of silk, brocade or tapestries they could use for interior decoration.

Venice had the least feudal of aristocracies: no baronial courts or feudal contracts, no private armies, no pompous coats of arms and no primogeniture. The patricians did not even have titles, although in the nineteenth century the Austrian rulers invited them to become counts; their only official distinction was the initials NH and ND (*Nobil Homo* and *Nobile Donna*) after their names. Renowned for its tradition of public service and conscientious paternalism, the patriciate identified itself with the state to an extent not easy to find among the baronage of European monarchies. It saw itself not as a collection of individuals but as a body administering a state that actively discouraged individualism; indeed, Venetian history reveals a shorter list of charismatic figures than anywhere else except perhaps Siena. In their lifetimes doges were seldom painted in heroic manner, and their deaths went uncommemorated by the state: the great tombs in Santi Giovanni e Paolo had to be erected at the expense of their families. The cult of the individual was so weak in Venice that before 1866, when the city was joined to Italy, it contained only one statue in a public place – and then only because its erection was the condition of a legacy from a wealthy *condottiere*, Bartolemeo Colleoni.*

*In fact the condition was not strictly obeyed. Although Colleoni had stipulated the Piazza San Marco as the location, the state decided to erect Verrocchio's great equestrian statue in a lesser place with a similar name, outside the Scuola di San Marco in the *sestiere* of Castello.

Venice was celebrated for religious and racial tolerance, though its citizens were not of course devoid of religious fervour: they stole the body of St Mark from Alexandria and the relics of other saints as well; they were serious about the cause of church reform; and they reacted to plagues by building the great churches of the Salute and the Redentore. They even had the unusual habit of canonizing Old Testament figures by naming such churches as San Giobbe (Job) and San Moisè (Moses) in their honour. Yet, as James Morris has observed, there is 'no sense of priestly power' in Venice.[14] Religion was important, but its position was subordinate to the state: the doges, not the bishops, were its protectors. The people, as they put it themselves, were Venetians first and Christians afterwards, an attitude that naturally provoked the anger of various popes, who periodically placed the city under an interdict. Yet the Venetians were rarely cowed by such actions and in 1606 they simply ignored an excommunication of their senate and an interdict imposed upon their state because the republic had decided that no property could be given to the clergy and no churches or monasteries could be founded without its consent. They had also had the temerity to arrest two priests and charge them with common crimes without handing them over to an ecclesiastical court. Upon receiving the interdict, Venice ordered its priests to carry on their work as normal, which they did, thereby forcing the Borghese pope, Paul V, to back down and lift the ban. The pontiff was not greatly consoled by his opponents' concession over the clerical miscreants, who were handed over to the French ambassador.

People of different faiths were permitted to celebrate their religion in Venice, and Protestantism too was regarded for a while with sympathy; a considerable number of patricians were potential converts in the sixteenth century. For a few years the republic managed to resist papal demands to set up a local inquisition but in 1547 it acquiesced. As inquisitions go, the Venetian version was relatively relaxed, partly because the state insisted that the inquisitors should include one of its own nobles. When Paolo Veronese completed his enormous picture of *The Last Supper*, the Inquisition summoned him to explain how he could have depicted so sacred an event in such a gaudy and materialistic manner: the diners, clad in velvet, silk and ermine, are feasting in an ambience of table cloths, marble floors and Corinthian pillars;

decanters, jugs and wineskins testify that a lot of drinking is going on – as does the presence of two drunk German halberdiers – and the pagan, hedonistic note is reinforced by the presence of dogs, a cat, a jester with a parrot, and women leaning out of a nearby house to enjoy the spectacle. Tolerant though they were prepared to be, the inquisitors were unimpressed by Veronese's claim that painters could take the same liberties as poets and madmen and they ordered him to make alterations. In the event the artist made no changes at all except to change the title by inscribing on two pilasters a line from St Luke's Gospel: 'And Levi made him [Jesus] a great feast in his own house' – the event that provoked the Pharisees to admonish Jesus for eating and drinking with publicans and sinners. Veronese's Renaissance diners do not look very like publicans but they look even less like disciples.

The inquisitors might allow Veronese to outwit them but they felt they could not be so lenient with heretics. Some Protestants came to Venice in the belief that it was a sanctuary: one unfortunate Savoyard Calvinist, who settled there in the 1570s, thought he was safe because Venice 'was a free country where each could live as he wished'. He soon wished he had opted for another refuge because he was one of the heretics who were executed, though not in the manner of inquisitions elsewhere – on bonfires in front of vast crowds – but by being rowed out at night, bound to a heavy stone and dropped in the lagoon. Some twenty-five heretics perished in this way, not a huge number by the standards of Spain or Rome or of the England of Mary Tudor, which burned nearly 300 men and women for remaining loyal to the Protestantism of the queen's deceased brother. Perhaps there would have been more victims in Venice if class and communal solidarity had not discouraged the exposure of other deviants.[15]

In *The Merchant of Venice* Shakespeare's Antonio accepts the likelihood of his death at the hands of Shylock with the words:

> The Duke [doge] cannot deny the course of law:
> For the commodity that strangers have
> With us in Venice, if it be denied,
> Will much impeach the justice of the state,
> Since that the trade and profit of the city
> Consisteth of all nations.[16]

Although Shakespeare never went to Venice, he encapsulated in this short speech much of what its citizens thought about the republic: that its ruler was not a tyrant and could not ignore the law; that the system of justice was evenhanded and inviolate; that Venice was a generally broadminded, multi-ethnic city; and that its prosperity depended on trade and good relations with other countries.

Visitors in the sixteenth century were so struck by the population's diversity that they believed Venetians were outnumbered by foreigners. The state welcomed several foreign communities and allowed them to build their synagogues and their orthodox churches in the city; nevertheless, always wary of disorder, it felt safer if they lived together in single-ethnic allocations. The Venetians were a suspicious and secretive people, perennially worried about the possibility of plots, and so they designated areas in various *sestieri* of the city for the foreigners to inhabit: Greeks and Slavs lived in Castello, Armenians were divided between Santa Croce and their monastery on the island of San Lazzaro; the Germans had their quarters next to the Rialto Bridge, while further up the Grand Canal the Turks had theirs, the Fondaco dei Turchi, where they were moved for their own safety after the Battle of Lepanto in 1571. From the early sixteenth century the Jewish community resided in an area called the Ghetto, a word which then had none of its later connotations: it was simply the name of the district, surrounded by a canal, called after the brass foundry that used to exist close by. The Venetians were not anti-Semites, and their ghetto was not intended as a place of banishment for an unpopular community. The Jews were forced to wear distinguishing clothes but they were seldom persecuted in other ways; many of them flourished as bankers, merchants and doctors. As the historian of Venice Peter Lauritzen has written, 'the Jews were no more segregated or ill-treated than were the Turks, the Persians and the Germans, or even the foreign ambassadors, all of whom lived a restricted life in their own compounds'. If they were not treated as well as they had been during the Arab caliphate of Córdoba – or as they were in Salonika under the Ottomans – Jews nevertheless found in Venice one of their safest havens in Christian Europe. The prestige and prosperity of its Semitic community encouraged Benjamin Disraeli to claim, quite fancifully, that his ancestors were Venetian Jews.[17]

For almost a thousand years after the first settlers arrived in the lagoon, Venice had ignored the mainland. It had evolved into an Adriatic and Mediterranean power, not a peninsular one; it possessed islands off Turkey and the Levant but not Padua, a day's ride to its west. Shortly after 1400, however, Venice turned around. Some patricians opposed the reversal, arguing that expansion on the mainland could lead to a costly embroilment in Italian affairs. They were right. Venice inevitably became involved in the peninsula's wars, its economic interests shifted from the maritime towards the terrestrial, and many of its noblemen preferred to live as rent-receiving landowners than as risk-taking merchants. Venetians now became more Italian, more receptive to humanism and the Renaissance, even if in this sphere they lagged far behind Florence. Yet the proponents of expansion had good arguments too. The acquisition of land would safeguard their overland trade routes and allow them control of the rivers dumping silt into the lagoon; it would provide them with supplies of timber and food, an important consideration now that Ottoman expansion was hindering the import of grain from the Black Sea; and it would give them the opportunity to check the eastward expansion of Milan, which, under the leadership of Giangaleazzo Visconti, had become the most powerful city on the mainland.

Giangaleazzo seemed on the verge of conquering the whole of northern Italy when he died unexpectedly in 1402. Venice took the opportunity of his demise to go on the offensive and quickly acquire Vicenza, Verona, Padua, the Trevisan March as well as, a few years later, Friuli. The advantage in the fighting with Milan itself oscillated between the combatants, but when the wars ended, concluded by the Peace of Lodi in 1454, the Venetian mainland (known as the *terraferma*) was larger than the duchy of Milan and included the Lombard cities of Bergamo, Brescia and Crema.

The Venetians were not as generous as the ancient Romans in extending their citizenship to subject cities on the *terraferma*; few nobles from outside were ever admitted to the governing patriciate. Yet on the whole they kept their promises to respect the laws and customs of their new territories. Peasants and artisans on the mainland were certainly grateful that Venetian courts protected their rights from the exactions of local landlords; and it was the cities, not the

aristocrats of the *terraferma*, that supported Venice in its most peril-
ous moment, the War of the League of Cambrai at the beginning of
the sixteenth century. Nearly 300 years later, cities of the mainland
again rose in defence of themselves and of Venice, this time against
Bonaparte during the French conquest and occupation of the region.

Venetian success was too much for the rest of Europe; it was simply
too blatant and too glittering for jealous rivals to stomach. Reproached
for greed, the republic was also accused of treachery because it continued to trade with the Ottomans between wars. In 1503 Venice
finally went too far by seizing and absorbing some of Cesare Borgia's
conquests in the Romagna. Although the new pope, Julius II, hated
the Borgias, he was determined to collect the territories himself and he
insisted on their surrender. When the Venetians yielded only a fraction
of their gains, the enraged pontiff put together an alliance which had
as its objective the capture of the whole of the *terraferma* and its division among the victors. Known as the League of Cambrai (1508), it
was headed by the four most powerful men in Europe: King Ferdinand of Aragon, King Louis XII of France, the Emperor Maximilian
and Julius. It also had the backing of several lesser allies including the
Duke of Savoy, the Duke of Milan and the King of Hungary; only the
dying King of England, Henry VII, and his son, Henry VIII, refused
to take part in the dismemberment of the republic.

Venice soon suffered a catastrophic defeat at the Battle of Agnadello
(1509) and lost most of the *terraferma*. Restricted to little more than
the lagoon, it was saved unexpectedly by the mercurial Julius, who
suddenly identified France as the chief danger to the peninsula.
Switching sides and joining Venice, the pope also managed to persuade Spain and the emperor to enter his new coalition, the Holy
League of 1511; now that the enemy was France, Henry VIII joined
in too. When the French were driven out of Milan a year later, the
Venetians bizarrely selected the moment to abandon the league and
join the losing side. As a result they lost in 1513 what they had
regained a year earlier although, by the end of these wars in 1516,
they again possessed the *terraferma*. The constant changing of sides
by all the main players makes this one of the most cynical as well as
most frivolous periods of European diplomacy. It certainly forced the
Venetians to realize they were no longer a fully independent power:

for survival they now needed France as an ally or else Spain, which from 1519 was joined to the empire under Charles V, the heir of the imperial, Castilian and Aragonese thrones.

The beginning of Venetian decline has been a subject long debated by historians. It has sometimes been dated as early as the fifteenth century, starting with the adventures on the mainland; more frequently it has been identified with the war against the League of Cambrai; occasionally it is placed later still, after the Battle of Lepanto in 1571.[18] Yet perhaps the moment of truth came in 1529 after a Spanish victory in another war against another coalition, the League of Cognac formed by France, the papacy, Venice, Florence and Milan. The Venetians were ignored in the subsequent peace treaty between France and Spain and were later forced to give Charles V tribute as well as three ports in Apulia which they had acquired to bolster their defence of the Adriatic.

Venice's downhill slide was neither uniform nor consistent. In the fifteenth century, at a time when the republic was expanding in northern Italy, it was losing islands in the Aegean to the Ottoman Empire. Forty years after its humiliation by Charles V, it was instrumental in defeating the Turks at Lepanto, and for a century afterwards it controlled much of the central Mediterranean with a fleet of increasingly obsolete ships. In the first half of the seventeenth century Venice sensibly stayed clear of further wars between France and Spain and, although it lost Crete to the Turks in 1669, it enjoyed a brief resurgence, even conquering the Peloponnese from the Ottoman enemy at the end of the century. Yet the success was transient, and within a generation Venice's maritime empire had been reduced to the Dalmatian coast and the island of Corfu.

Even as Venetian power declined in the early sixteenth century, the republic itself was growing in wealth and population. By 1565 the city had some 170,000 inhabitants with another 2 million on its *terraferma*. The number of citizens was diminished by a terrible plague in 1576–7 and an even worse one in 1630, which left the city with barely 100,000 inhabitants. The economy began to shrink, but the wealth of the upper classes did not altogether evaporate. In the seventeenth century the city's merchants and patricians continued the tradition of the previous century by building hundreds of villas on the *terraferma*, often along the Brenta Canal, graceful summer retreats with columned porticoes and statues in the garden.

Venetian art flourished even at times when Venice seemed about to lose all its possessions outside the lagoon. In Florence the Renaissance emerged in a period of comparative republican tranquillity; by the time it had installed itself in Venice – as Titian was beginning his career – the armies of the League of Cambrai were threatening the city. Yet as one appreciates the work of the Venetian masters, from the light and gentle storytelling of Carpaccio to the dark religious passion of Tintoretto, who painted at least nine versions of *The Last Supper*, one finds scant suggestion that their city was often in great peril. As they revel in colour and light and texture, they seem almost unaware of the violence engulfing northern Italy. Painting declined after the dangers were over, in the seventeenth century – as people who go to see Tintoretto at San Rocco can judge as they climb the stairs and glance at Antonio Zanchi's embarrassing painting of *Venice Delivered from the Plague*; one cannot help wondering whether Zanchi himself felt a bit ashamed to be in such proximity to the masterpieces of the older artist. Architecture accompanied painting in a joint decline. One may not agree with Ruskin that the Renaissance was a disaster for Venice, but it's easy to regret some of the city's Baroque, the grandiloquent palaces, the florid statuary, the overloaded façades of certain ostentatious churches. In Italy the best Baroque belongs to Rome and to the south.

Venice in its decadence remained a civilized place. It kept out of the War of the Austrian Succession (1740–48) and was at peace for most of the eighteenth century, until the arrival of Napoleon Bonaparte. Its women began to enjoy greater freedoms than before: fewer of them were forced into convents and those in unhappy unions found marriages easier to dissolve. Venice enjoyed a theatrical golden age with Goldoni's realistic comedies and a reputation as a great centre for music, possessing four conservatoires and a large number of theatres where opera could be performed. Its most talented musician was the violinist and composer Antonio Vivaldi, whose job at a local orphanage for girls, the Conservatorio della Pietà, obliged him to provide his employers with two concertos a month. Yet the city was undeniably decadent. Giambattista Tiepolo was a highly talented painter but a victim of the decorative taste of his period: his luminous ceiling frescoes, with light blues and pinks, angels and clouds and impossibly white-skinned women, suggest neither passions nor anguish nor even dilemmas of the mind; he owed very little to Tintoretto or to that great later master, the tormented Caravaggio. Venetian patricians had long been considered an enlightened class and, perhaps as a result, they did not bother much about the ideas of the European Enlightenment. Having lost their purpose as merchants and colonial governors, many of them sighed and resigned themselves to a perpetual quest for pleasure. As Andrea di Robilant explained to his friend Giacomo Casanova, 'since I do not gamble and there is nothing I want to buy for myself and I cannot stand trying to reason with our politicians and having nothing more to read . . . I spend my time with the ladies'.[19]

After losing its empire, its power and much of its productive wealth, Venice turned to tourism, a move much sneered at by outsiders – as if it were unique for a city with a great past to sell itself to foreign visitors, as if Florence, Rome and Naples did not all do the same. Venice had long welcomed tourists, even stealing the bones and bodies of saints to entice medieval pilgrims to stay in its dozens of *alberghi*. Yet in catering to the pleasures of the eighteenth century its very name became a byword for venal sin, mocked and laughed at as if the city were a permanent carnival and its people were all gamblers playing faro or baccarat continuously in the casinos when they weren't idling in other ways, wearing masks, dancing at balls and lounging in gondolas. The men were typecast as libertines like Casanova, while the women – even those who were not courtesans – were thought to enjoy a routine of unbroken frivolity, drinking chocolate, watching puppet shows, languidly fanning themselves and sometimes playing a spinet decorated with rustic scenes or floral patterns. Ladies were believed to exist in a world draped with damask and chinoiserie and frescoed by one of the Tiepolos, a world of mirrors and mandolins, of lapdogs and lacquer furniture, of the latest toilette set made in Augsburg, a decor perhaps including a slight hint of undemanding piety such as a scene of the Holy Family painted on the headboard of a bed.

Venice naturally exploited the myth and made money from it: if an Englishman hired a gondola for an innocent ride, he was liable to be rowed to a courtesan's door. The paintings of Canaletto (1697–1768) reveal a combination of commercial and patriotic motives: he wanted foreigners to pay him to take home canvases of his personal Venice, a city that was sunny, happy and golden, its serenity symbolized by the thousands of tiny artificial waves – simply joined-up 'u's – with which he depicted unruffled water. His younger rival Francesco Guardi was very different. A more romantic and more poetic artist, he liked to portray the often tempestuous atmosphere of the lagoon; by contrast with Canaletto, his paintings seem to suggest that the end of Venetian glory was near, as indeed it was, the republic dying shortly after his own death in 1793.

Musing on the past from the formal chastity of the Victorian age, Browning evoked the myth of decadent Venice with the 'balls and masks begun at midnight, burning ever to mid-day', 'the breast's superb abundance where a man might base his head' and the final unkind question, 'What of soul was left, I wonder, when the kissing had to stop?'[20] Yet the kissing would not have stopped of its own accord: like the casinos and the carnival, it stopped because Bonaparte was determined to inflict his own version of liberty upon a famously free people. The Corsican general stole Venice, gave it to Austria and then took it back again; Austria retrieved it at Napoleon's fall and then lost it in a war with Prussia in circumstances that allowed France to present it to the new kingdom of Italy in 1866.

None of this was destined to happen: Venice had endured too long to be ranked as one with Nineveh and Tyre. Ancient Rome had had a great history: between its capture by the Gauls and its sacking by the Goths it lasted for 800 years in spite of frequent coups and overthrows of governments. The Republic of Venice survived 1,100 years with no pillaging and no capture until it succumbed to Bonaparte; at no time had its government been overthrown. In 1797 it was a state in decline, certainly, but it need not have fallen much further. It might have recovered (like the Netherlands), it should have regained its independence in 1814 (again like the Netherlands) and today Venice could have been (like The Hague) the capital of a successful small country inside the European Union. Its incorporation into the kingdom of Italy – which its people did not want – was almost as much an aberration in its history as its forced membership of the Habsburg and napoleonic empires.

5

Disputed Italies

FOREIGN RULERS

'Since the Roman zenith,' wrote Guicciardini in the sixteenth century, 'Italy had never known such prosperity or such a desirable condition as that which it enjoyed in all tranquillity in the year of Our Lord 1490 and the years immediately before and after.'[1] While the Italian states were enjoying a period of unprecedented amity – the larger ones finally realizing they could not dominate all the others – the peninsula had been spared a full-scale foreign invasion from the north for over 200 years. All this changed in 1494 when Charles VIII became the first of three consecutive French kings to lead a huge army into Italy.

As a relation of the Angevins, Charles had a weak and generally dormant claim to the throne of Naples. But he was encouraged to revive it by Ludovico Sforza, the cultured and crafty ruler of Milan, and so the young king marched down the peninsula almost unopposed and occupied Naples. After an enthusiastic welcome from his new subjects, he enjoyed himself in the city, throwing banquets and tournaments. Yet Charles was too impatient and unintelligent for his popularity to last. As a French army sickened from its first experience of syphilis, he suddenly found himself opposed by a powerful coalition that included Venice, Mantua, Florence, the pope and Ludovico of Milan, who had changed sides. Charles made a run for the north in July 1495 but he was caught at Fornovo by an army of Venetians and Mantuans who outnumbered his diseased and decimated force by three to one. Since the French continued to retreat after the battle, the Italian forces contrived to claim a victory: their commander, the

Gonzaga Lord of Mantua, even celebrated the event by building a 'victory' church in his capital and commissioning Mantegna to paint the *Madonna della Vittoria*. Yet everyone else realized that it had been a defeat, that the Italian casualties had been enormous and that the French had been allowed to escape almost unscathed when they should have been crushed.

Luigi Barzini, a perceptive writer and journalist of the twentieth century, considered Fornovo a crucial moment in his country's history:

> If the Italians had won, they would probably have discovered then the pride of being a united people, the self-confidence born of defending their common liberty and independence. Italy would have emerged as a reasonably respectable nation, capable of determining her own future, a country which adventurous foreigners would think twice before attacking. Nobody would have ventured lightly across the Alps, for fear of being destroyed. The European powers would have been discouraged from endlessly quarrelling over Italian politics and from cutting slices of Italian soil, with their defenceless and laborious inhabitants, in order to placate dynastic rivalries and satisfy everybody's greed. The history of Italy, Europe, and the world would probably have taken different tacks. The Italian national character would have developed along different lines.[2]

This is, of course, speculation, and it is difficult to agree with all of it. If the Battle of Legnano had not made a nation, why would a victory at Fornovo have done so? And who, apart perhaps from Machiavelli, wanted a nation anyway? Yet, as Barzini suggested, the annihilation of the French army might have discouraged later invasions. Charles's uncontested march to Naples demonstrated, in the recent words of Giordano Bruno Guerri, that Italy 'was a very easy land to conquer'.[3] Certainly it encouraged the next French king, Louis XII, to emulate his predecessor in 1499, an invasion which, since he had a claim to the Milanese duchy, led to the overthrow and lasting incarceration of the unscrupulous Ludovico. It also spurred his successor, Francis I, to do the same, though his adventures in Italy ended in disaster when he was defeated and captured by the Emperor Charles V at the Battle of Pavia in 1525.

The French invasions brought Spain into the northern half of the peninsula to engage in what was essentially a struggle for supremacy in western Europe. While the peoples of Italy naturally would have preferred this rivalry to have been contested across the Pyrenees, strategic considerations determined that the main battleground would be Lombardy because it lay between Naples, which the Emperor Charles had inherited through his Spanish mother, and the Low Countries and Germany, which had come to him through his Habsburg grandfather. The chief prize in the conflict was Milan, which oscillated between rule by the French and the Sforza until 1535, when, following the death of the last Sforza duke, Charles took control and gave it to his son Philip, the future Spanish king. Thus was the political and cultural independence of Milan extinguished as a consequence of Ludovico's encouragement of Charles VIII's aggression in Italy. The rest of the peninsula also suffered as a result of the French invasions: Venice had to fight its Cambrai War; Naples was seized by both the French and the Spanish; Florence went backwards and forwards between republicans and the Medici; and in 1527 Rome was sacked by an imperial army.

As the historian Richard Mackenney has noted, the savage wars fought in Italy mainly by foreigners between 1494 and 1530 were the 'one truly "Italian" experience' of the age.[4] Yet, like other foreign invasions over the following three centuries, they stimulated no Italian national response. Charles VIII may have been chased out of Italy in 1495, but many Italians had applauded and supported him the year before. Venetians and Mantuans may have fought together at Fornovo but at other times they were on opposing sides. Soldiers from Venice and elsewhere may have shouted 'Italia! Italia!' as they went into battle against a foreign enemy, but many Italians fought as allies of the foreigners without feeling guilty about betraying any *'patria'*. This was a phenomenon that survived into the 1860s.

Scholars who have searched for signs of a nascent nationalism in the later Middle Ages have not been very successful: people in the peninsula may have thought of themselves as culturally Italian because they were wealthier and more artistic than anyone else, but they had no notion of a political or united Italy. Numerous historians of the nineteenth and twentieth centuries, both foreign and Italian, found it more rewarding to speculate about who had been the peninsula's chief enemies, invariably awarding the prizes to Spain and Austria while remaining oblivious to the claims of France which, with its thousand-year history of invasion, was at least a plausible candidate. Writers lamented 'the dead hand of Spain' in the sixteenth and seventeenth centuries just as they regretted 'the dead hand of Austria' in subsequent eras. Yet the governments of the Austrian Habsburgs were seldom inert, while the record of their Spanish cousins has been often distorted.

Spanish hegemony on the Italian peninsula was confirmed in 1559 at the Treaty of Cateau-Cambrésis, at which the French renounced their claim to Milan, subsequently left Italy and spent the rest of the century fighting their religious wars. The native peoples were more forgiving towards their new Hispanic overlords than historians have been: they did not particularly resent their arrival and subsequently they welcomed the peace and stability that came with them. Prosperous times continued, and Italians remained the richest people in Europe. The most visible reminder of Spanish rule today is the centre of Naples, where Spanish viceroys built palaces, churches, a castle, the hillside district known as the Quartieri Spagnoli and the Via Toledo, which Stendhal considered to be 'the busiest, most joyous thoroughfare in the entire universe'.[5]

Italy in the seventeenth century has traditionally been regarded as weak, poor, decadent and oppressed. The view is partly true and partly exaggerated, but in any case these defects were not always the fault of the Spaniards. If the peninsula became increasingly rural, it was not because its rulers decreed so. Merchants could not be prevented from investing profits in land rather than trade; it was a trend in much of Europe in that era – and in other eras as well. Nor was Spain responsible for the war that broke out in 1613 and spawned other wars that lasted till 1659: the culpability lay with the Duke of Savoy, Charles Emanuel I, who like many of his lineage was intent on territorial aggrandizement. Perhaps Spain may be blamed more justly for supporting the intolerance and rigidity of the Church and the atrocities of the Inquisition, but popes not Spaniards prosecuted Galileo and burned the remarkable scientist and free-thinker Giordano Bruno.

The Spanish have often been accused of 'corrupting', 'provincializing' and 'hispanicizing' southern Italy, introducing duelling and bullfighting and inciting local nobles to become obsessed with matters of status and protocol. Yet since the Lombards under Spanish rule were seldom attracted to these customs, the explanation may be that Sicilians and Neapolitans willingly embraced them. According to the historian Denis Mack Smith, '*spagnolismo* sometimes seemed to characterize the Sicilian ruled more than the Spanish rulers'.[6] Sicilians often blamed Spain for their poverty and they rightly objected to the hated *macinato*, an inequitable tax on the grinding of corn. Yet they made little effort themselves to become richer. Palermo was a parasite city where most of the nobles lived, far from their lands and farther from the desire to develop them. Spanish rulers were surprised by their laziness, their lack of interest in improving their *latifondi*, their failure to build provincial roads so that, as a result, the wheat their agents planned to export had to be transported on mules to the coasts. Yet the Spaniards, especially those from Castile and Andalusia, must have seen something of themselves in their Sicilian subjects. They also thought it more prestigious to acquire new estates than to improve existing ones; they too liked to petrify their incomes in palaces and religious buildings.

ENLIGHTENED ITALY

Naples and Sicily belonged to the Spanish Habsburgs until 1700, when the last member of that branch of the family died without choosing between French and Austrian claimants to his throne until the last moment, when he opted for Philip of Anjou, grandson of Louis XIV. During the consequent War of the Spanish Succession, armies of both the Austrian emperor and the French prince occupied Sicily. At its end the Treaties of Utrecht (1713–14) confirmed the Bourbon contender as Philip V of Spain, but France's military defeats by the Duke of Marlborough forced it to cede territory in North America to the British and to abandon those interests in Italy it might have inherited from the Spanish crown.

After Utrecht Austria hoped to return to Sicily, but the British, illogically and incomprehensibly, persuaded its ally that the island should go to another friend in the recent war, Victor Amadeus, the ambitious ruler of Piedmont and Savoy, who now assumed the title King of Sicily. This was an unwise arrangement because no part of

Italy is so unlike Sicily as Piedmont. Victor Amadeus sailed to Palermo in a British ship, the first monarch to visit the island since 1535 and the last to do so till the Bourbon Ferdinand IV fled there to escape the armies of revolutionary France. Coming from Piedmont, where the nobility had a tradition of military and state service, the new king could not understand why Sicilian aristocrats were so unwilling to be soldiers or administrators. He called their assembly in Palermo an 'ice-cream parliament' because eating ice-cream seemed to be its members' most conspicuous activity. The nobles were equally contemptuous of this rustic-looking northerner and regretted the disappearance of Spain's elegant and elaborate viceregal court. After attempting a few reforms, Victor Amadeus soon tired of trying to rule an ungrateful island from Turin and offered it to Austria provided he was compensated by somewhere else where he could be called a king; eventually he managed to get himself made King of Sardinia. Meanwhile a large Spanish force invaded Sicily, but its navy was destroyed by a British fleet while its army was defeated by Austrian troops coming across the Straits of Messina. The Treaty of The Hague in 1720 confirmed Sicily as a possession of the Austrians, who soon made themselves unpopular on the island by trying to reform institutions which the islanders did not wish to see reformed. In 1734 another Spanish attempt to seize Sicily succeeded, and the Bourbons thereafter ruled it until they were defeated by Garibaldi in 1860.

Each change of Sicilian ruler between 1700 and 1734 was a consequence of a wider European conflict, of the contest between Habsburg emperors (Spanish and Austrian) and French monarchs (first Valois, then – in Spain as well as France – Bourbon) that had been dragging on for 200 years. In the process the chief antagonists altered Italian boundaries and dynasties, usually at treaties negotiated in the Netherlands, with no regard for the wishes or interests of the inhabitants. Sicilians could watch Spanish, Austrian or Piedmontese armies tramping over their island just as they could spy the British navy supporting one force or another off their coasts, yet they had no say in what might happen when the fighting was over.

The rest of Italy was also affected by mysterious decisions taken in the north. Like the Medici in Tuscany, the Farnese in Parma died out in the 1730s through the failure of its last males to procreate. The succession correctly went to the last duke's acquisitive niece, Elizabeth Farnese, although, as she was living in Madrid as Queen of Spain, the duchy was assigned to her son, Don Carlos, whom the European states had simultaneously selected to be the next Grand Duke of Tuscany. Rushing to Florence with an army ready to take over, the young Spanish prince displayed his life-long obsession with hunting by shooting arrows at the birds woven into the tapestries in the Pitti Palace. But Gian Gastone de' Medici failed to die as soon as everyone expected, and, by the time he did expire, the War of the Polish Succession (1733–5) had upset all plans and altered Don Carlos's ambitions. Now, at a moment of Austrian military weakness, Elizabeth Farnese revived Spanish claims to the crowns of Naples and Sicily and told her son to overrun those kingdoms, which he soon did. As Charles VII, he ruled in Naples from 1734 to 1759, when he succeeded his half-brother as Charles III of Spain, the nation he ruled until his death in 1788.

After Charles had taken Naples from Austria, the vanquished power annexed Parma but was soon forced to return it to a Bourbon-Farnese ruler, Philip, a younger brother of the new Neapolitan king. A condition of European acceptance of Charles in Naples was the separation of the southern crowns from Spain, a proviso that later allowed his younger son Ferdinand to create his own dynasty in Naples. A similar condition was attached to the succession in Tuscany that finally settled on Francis Stephen, Duke of Lorraine, who had to be recompensed for the loss of his own duchy, given to ex-King Stanislaw of Poland, the loser in the War of the Polish Succession and the father-in-law of the French monarch Louis XV. Shortly before his death in 1737, the last Medici insisted that Tuscany must never form part of the Habsburg Empire whose heiress, Maria Theresa, was the wife of Francis Stephen. After yet another war over another succession (this time the Austrian), the long game of musical thrones was finally stopped in 1748 at the Treaty of Aix-la-Chapelle. The peninsula remained dominated by foreign dynasties – the Bourbons in Parma and the south, the Habsburgs in Milan (since the War of the Spanish Succession) as well as Tuscany – but it had now achieved a certain equilibrium of power. A half-century of war was giving way to a half-century of peace.

Aix-la-Chapelle was signed at a time when the ideas of the French *philosophes* and other writers of the Enlightenment were just beginning to percolate through the minds of Italian rulers and some of their subjects. People were coming to expect more from their monarch, not that he should share power with them but that he should act wisely, as a philosopher-king, educating his subjects, reining in the Church and the nobility, taking a leading part in promoting agriculture and trade. Thus arrived the era of 'enlightened despotism', a term applied to an age during which, at least in retrospect, the sovereigns of Europe are made to appear as if they had been competing hard to personify the notion: digging canals and draining marshes, constructing roads and abolishing tolls, reading Voltaire and Montesquieu before expelling the Jesuits and dissolving the monasteries – and all the time building an enlightened paradise with schools, hospitals, universities and academies.

The prince most closely resembling the stereotype in Italy was the second son of Maria Theresa, Peter Leopold, the Grand Duke of Tuscany from 1765 to 1790. Intelligent and energetic, he was driven by the desire for reform in both economic and humanitarian affairs. He attacked monopolies and encouraged free trade, built roads and bridges, made taxes both lower and fairer, and reduced the public debt; he also made a valiant attempt to drain the Maremma's marshes. In consultation with the Milanese writer Cesare Beccaria he drew up a penal code that made Tuscany the first state in Europe to abolish the death penalty and burn the gallows – a measure so audacious and encouraging to the cause of enlightenment that a Spanish reformer implored his own progressive sovereign to turn his eyes to Tuscany, to 'reflect upon the mildness of the penalties', upon 'the small number of crimes' committed there, and to 'read over and over again the penal code' of its prince.[7] Among his other merits, Peter Leopold was conscientious and loyal to a state that had had no connection to either of his parents' families before 1734. Although from 1770 he was heir to the imperial throne in Vienna, the grand duke kept his father's promise to defend the rights and maintain the autonomy of his duchy. In 1790 he became the penultimate Holy Roman emperor after the death of his brother, Joseph II, who was the greatest and most innovative of all enlightened monarchs, an emancipator of serfs as well as Jews, although unlike Catherine of Russia and Frederick of Prussia he has not been known as 'the Great' – perhaps because at the end of his life he was defeated by the forces of Belgian conservatism. During his brief reign in Vienna, Leopold II (as Peter Leopold became) retained his reforming zeal, abolishing various punishments and ordering the police to be kind to prisoners; he even gave his subjects 'something of the principle of *habeas corpus*'.[8]

Enlightened despotism would not have lasted even without the French Revolution. The phrase is after all an oxymoron, though it seemed to make sense for half a century; ultimately, the ideas of the Enlightenment were bound to lead to demands for constitutional reform and the abolition of despots. Besides, however enlightened the rulers were, there was a limit to how despotic their behaviour could be, even without parliaments. Wherever reforms were attempted – in Florence, Milan, Naples or elsewhere – there were nobles and clerics always ready to dilute, delay and otherwise obstruct them.

The first half of the eighteenth century had been a great age for Italian scholarship, a time when the peninsula housed some of Europe's finest philosophers and historians, men of the stature of Giambattista Vico, Lodovico Muratori and Pietro Giannone. Later in the century, their followers flocked to the enlightened courts, especially to Florence, the favourite rallying-point for reformers from Spain as well as Italy. They were eager to advise and cooperate with rulers on practical projects and simultaneously to establish a peninsular intelligentsia that could function across Italy's many boundaries, creating in the process what they hoped would be 'a republic of letters'. This was a flourishing era for cultural and scientific academies and also for journals, which could disseminate ideas and discoveries beyond the frontiers.

Contemporary intellectuals sometimes talked of a cultural Italy but not of a political *patria*: nationalism did not exist before the French Revolution. Most of them accepted what the despots gave in the way of reforms and did not ask for much more. Like the Piedmontese writer Vittorio Alfieri, they might write plays attacking tyranny but they did not criticize the enlightened despots. As Guicciardini had done in the sixteenth century, some accepted and even revered the political disunity and consequent diversity and cosmopolitanism of their country. When one intellectual suggested the possibility of a single Italy, another remarked that he did not want 'love of country to affect our impartiality as good cosmopolites'.[9]

After Florence and Austrian-ruled Milan, Naples was the best place for intellectuals to be, living under the sympathetic eyes of its new Bourbon monarchs and their talented ministers. Rome or Turin would not have tolerated the presence of Antonio Genovesi, who inspired many people with his advocacy of radical economic and humanitarian reforms. Yet in the tolerant atmosphere of Bourbon Naples he could enjoy a successful public career as a professor of metaphysics and a professor of ethics before becoming in 1754 the first professor of political economy in Europe.

Charles of Naples was an unusual enlightened despot. He promoted learning, so long as it did not affect himself or his children. He constructed a great opera house, although he disliked music and slept or chatted during performances. He was a keen builder, but mostly of palaces in places convenient for the hunting which he did every afternoon regardless of the weather. Yet however unread and unlearned he was, Charles was an intelligent and conscientious ruler – at least in the mornings – with the knack of picking able ministers to carry out sensible policies. Although he was not greatly interested in economics or legislation, his rule oversaw a doubling in revenue and a decrease in taxation; and he made Naples one of the great capitals of Europe.

As the king's eldest son was an imbecile and his second was heir to the Spanish crown, the Neapolitan throne went to the third brother, Ferdinand, who was left alone at the age of eight when his parents went to Madrid. While a Council of Regents directed his realm, Ferdinand emerged as a boisterous, bonhomous, rough-edged youth who loved hunting as much as his father and hated reading, writing and even signing his own name. His first complaint about his wife, a Habsburg princess, was that she liked books. His rustic manners and earthy vocabulary may have been ill-suited to the palace of Caserta – 'the Italian Versailles' – but they made him popular; he was called the *lazzarone* king because he empathized with the city's famous underclass known as *lazzaroni*, and like them he enjoyed eating *maccheroni* with his fingers. As in the time of his father, intelligent advisers carried out reforms that the monarch often cared little about. 'If he remained ignorant,' observed the aesthete and historian Harold Acton, 'at least his subjects were becoming enlightened.'[10]

Ferdinand presided over a huge capital city, containing perhaps half a million people, most of whom lived precariously in the shadow of famine, earthquakes and of course Vesuvius. Its poorest inhabitants were famous for *l'arte di arrangiarsi*, the skill of getting by, somehow acquiring enough coins for a bowl of *maccheroni* without worrying too much about where the next one was coming from. Northern Italians have seldom liked Naples, but northern Europeans have usually been more generous. Goethe admired *l'arte di arrangiarsi* and denied that its practitioners were idlers; Naples was 'a happy country', he thought, a 'paradise' where everyone lived 'in a state of intoxicated self-forgetfulness', himself included.[11] The eighteenth-century city teemed with beggars and vagrants but it was not a violent place. As witnesses and statistics testify, the Neapolitans seldom got drunk or rioted, and the murder rate was low.

For the German poet, Palermo was also a paradise, and Sicily as a whole was 'the clue to everything'. 'To have seen Italy without having seen Sicily,' he bizarrely warned, was 'not to have seen Italy at all.'[12] Yet to see Sicily in the eighteenth century was to see a place with no trace of that epoch except in the profusion of its buildings, for the island was immune to the spirit of the Enlightenment. As the Sicilian historian Rosario Romeo observed, the only European development that the island welcomed was the Counter-Reformation; the Protestant Reformation, the Renaissance and the Enlightenment had virtually no impact. Unlike Naples, Sicily contained only a handful of reformers, and even they were too timid and tepid to advocate the abolition of feudalism.[13] King Ferdinand had outstanding ministers in Naples who were unable to do anything with an island where the landed classes wanted nothing to change: if the Prince of Palagonia accepted the abolition of his *droit du seigneur* (which was nominal in most places anyway), he felt justified in imposing a marriage tax on his vassals for having made an apparent sacrifice. Aristocrats in other parts of Italy were showing increasing interest in visiting their estates and making them more productive, but in Sicily landowners did not follow the trend. Instead of riding from time to time over their *latifondi*, seeing what was happening on their farms, they stayed in Palermo, trundling up and down the marine front each afternoon in their carriages, attended by their liveried footmen.[14] When the great Neapolitan viceroy, the Marquess of Caracciolo, arrived in Palermo in 1781, the nobles united to impede his reforms, especially those that might have led to a reduction of their feudal powers.

Italians may have been dejected by the survival of foreign dynasties in the peninsula, but most of them would have recognized that the eighteenth-century representatives of the Habsburgs and Bourbons were superior to native rulers. Travellers usually identified the pope's domains as the most misgoverned region of Italy. Goethe contrasted the public buildings in Tuscany, 'beautiful and imposing . . . combining usefulness with grace', with the squalor and disorder in the Papal States, which seemed 'to keep alive only because the earth refuses to swallow them'.[15] The countryside was neglected, agriculture was stagnant, and internal trade was obstructed by endless tolls; it was difficult to find signs of any real economic activity except in Ancona, which had been a free port since 1732. Rome was the most violent city in the whole of Italy, with far more murders than in Naples, which was three times the size. The French scholar and traveller Charles de Brosses considered its government 'the worst imaginable', exactly the opposite of what Machiavelli and Thomas More had 'envisaged in their Utopias'. Its population of 150,000 was divided, according to him, into three portions, one-third of them being clergy, another third doing a little work, and the last third doing nothing at all.[16] Yet neither popes nor cardinals made a serious attempt to improve matters except one, Benedict IV, an intelligent man who had read Voltaire and the *philosophes* and knew that the art of government required something beyond an attitude of rigid obscurantism. Yet despite his efforts to improve agriculture and reduce taxation, his reforms had achieved little by the time of his death in 1758.

A hundred years later, the Papal States retained their reputation for bad government and were often contrasted with Piedmont, hailed in the mid-nineteenth century as the most progressive of the peninsular states, prosperous and liberal, the only one capable of welding and leading a brave new Italy. Yet in the seventeenth and eighteenth (and early part of the nineteenth) centuries Piedmont was a very backward and reactionary place. To many Italians it seemed primitive and rather foreign; its people, including its monarchs and aristocrats, spoke in French or in local dialect. Compared to the cities of Lombardy and Emilia, those in Piedmont were culturally meagre and so out of touch with the rest of the Po Valley that even the Renaissance had had little influence; Turin itself has no true Renaissance churches except its cathedral. In many parts of northern and central Italy nobles were happy to be merchants and bankers. In Piedmont their career options were limited to three: the army (the most popular), the Church and public service.

The ruling dynasty was the house of Savoy, the Savoyards or, in Italian, Savoia or Sabaudi. They had been counts and later dukes of Savoy in the Middle Ages, ruling Nice and Savoy on one side of the Alps and parts of Piedmont on the other. In 1563 they shifted their capital from Chambéry to Turin because it was clear that the Po Valley offered more room for expansion than Savoy, which was perennially threatened and frequently invaded by France. That military expansion was the dynasty's principal ambition can be perceived today by anyone wandering around Turin and looking at the many statues of kings, princes and generals waving their swords from the saddle. One of the most martial is in the Piazza San Carlo, where the bronze figure of Emanuel Philibert, mounted on a prancing horse, is pushing his sword back in its scabbard after the Battle of Saint-Quentin, a victory for him and his Spanish allies against the French in 1557. A century later, his successors' persecution of the Waldensian Protestants in western Piedmont incited John Milton to ask God to avenge his

> slaughtered saints, whose bones
> Lie scattered on the Alpine mountains cold . . .
> Slain by the bloody Piedmontese that rolled
> Mother with infant down the rocks . . .*

When writing of the Savoia in Piedmont, historians have found it difficult to avoid using adjectives such as wily, unscrupulous, ruthless and opportunistic to describe rulers who merited their reputation for choosing the winning side in a conflict. All those adjectives apply to Emanuel Philibert's son, Charles Emanuel I, who started several wars

*'On the Late Massacre in Piedmont' (1655).

during his long reign between 1580 and 1630 and swapped sides between France and Spain depending on which seemed likely to reward him with the most territory. In his even longer reign a century later, Victor Amadeus II too played France off against Spain, and both he and his son, Charles Emanuel III, managed to snaffle large slices of Lombardy. Victor Amadeus was also the duke who, without any claim to either island, had himself made King of Sicily and then King of Sardinia, after which his territories were generally known as the Kingdom of Piedmont-Sardinia.*

Such reforms as the government undertook in the early eighteenth century owed little to the Enlightenment: they were inspired by the absolutist example of Louis XIV rather than by any ideas of the *philosophes*. Thus the armed forces were strengthened and the tax system made more efficient for the purpose of increasing state power. Censorship and political repression were so heavy that several of Piedmont's small number of intellectuals decided to emigrate. Vittorio Alfieri, the distinguished poet and dramatist, was one who chose to escape, preferring to write in France or Florence where he lived happily with the Countess of Albany, the wife of the Stuart pretender, Bonnie Prince Charlie. Others, less fortunate, were prevented from leaving and confined for long periods in prison. Pietro Giannone, the great anti-papal historian who inspired Gibbon, was kidnapped by Piedmontese agents working with the Inquisition and died in gaol in 1748 after a captivity of twelve years.

NAPOLEONIC ITALY

'Peoples of Italy!' the young General Bonaparte proclaimed in April 1796, 'the French army is coming to break your chains ... We shall respect your property, your religion and your customs.' His words doubtless sounded encouraging to people in Italy who had not heard

---

*Through a dynastic connection with Guy de Lusignan, a crusader who was briefly King of Jerusalem and then King of Cyprus in the twelfth century, the Savoia also claimed to be titular kings of Cyprus and Jerusalem. Official documents carried the title after that of Sardinia until they became Kings of Italy in 1861. The Habsburgs and Bourbons made similar claims.

another speech made by the same officer a month earlier. 'Soldiers!' he had told his army, 'you are hungry and naked; the government [the Directory in Paris] owes you much but can give you nothing . . . I will lead you into the most fertile plains on earth. Rich provinces, opulent towns, all shall be at your disposal; there you will find honour, glory and riches.' Here was the voice not of the liberator but of Alaric and Attila, of the eternal barbarian coming through the Alps in search of plunder. For all his Italian and Corsican ancestry, Napoleon would not have been outraged by the comparison; the following year he warned the Venetians he would indeed be their Attila – and he kept his word.

The two speeches reveal some of the ambiguity in Napoleon's attitudes to Italy. There was another strand as well, not fully formed as yet but apparent in a question he asked subordinates after his Italian victories in 1796. 'Do you suppose that I triumph in Italy to make the reputations of the lawyers of the Directory?'[17] It was not difficult to guess the answer. Of all his many conquests, Italy was his favourite, the territory he regarded as his special domain. As first consul, and even more as emperor, he thought increasingly of Italy not as a French interest or a nation to be liberated but as a possession of his own, a fief to be exploited for the aggrandizement of himself and his acquisitive family.

In 1793 Georges Danton had persuaded the revolutionary government in Paris that France's borders should be its 'natural frontiers' – the Rhine, the Alps and the Pyrenees – even though these contained the whole of the Austrian Netherlands (the future Belgium) as well as other Habsburg territories and Savoy. For France the most important of the natural frontiers was the Rhine because beyond the river lay the heartland of the Austrian Empire, its most powerful continental enemy. In 1796 the Directory resolved that Bonaparte should defeat the Austrian and Piedmontese armies in Italy and occupy Milan so that it could use the resulting gains as a bargaining counter, to be offered back to Vienna in exchange for concessions in the Rhineland.

Aged twenty-six, the commander of the Army of Italy possessed little martial experience except for his dogged performance as an artillery officer at the Siege of Toulon in 1793. Yet he came through the Maritime Alps with magnificent self-assurance, brushed aside the Piedmontese in a few days and defeated the Austrians in a series of battles with names still resonant for students of military history: Lodi, Castiglione, Arcola, Rivoli. As he moved eastwards along the Po Valley, Bonaparte offered Venice an alliance against Austria, but the republic – perhaps honourably, certainly foolishly – insisted on remaining neutral. Furious at this defiance, the general declared war, ranting in Italian at the Venetian delegates, 'I want no more senate, I want no more inquisitors, I shall be an Attila for the Venetian state.' The state was duly destroyed and replaced by a 'democratic' republic, which Bonaparte quickly and brazenly betrayed. He had conquered so much territory that he no longer needed to think of equations between Lombardy and the Rhineland. France could have both, he realized, if he gave Venice and eastern Venetia to Austria. The Treaty of Campoformio in October 1797 formally and conclusively destroyed the Venetian Republic and divided it along the line of the River Adige; its western areas were incorporated into Lombardy and became, under napoleonic rule, successively part of the Cisalpine Republic, the French Republic and the Kingdom of Italy.

One of the goals of the Directory's foreign policy was the accumulation of foreign wealth. Foreigners, the government decided, should pay for the privilege of being liberated by France and not protest if liberty was accompanied by high taxes, conscription and the theft of their best paintings. Curiously, neither napoleonic nor revolutionary leaders seemed to realize how unpopular this policy would make them. Sometimes they even tried to delude themselves and others about what they were doing: eighteen months after Bonaparte had occupied Milan, his army's newspaper addressed the people of the Cisalpine Republic: 'You are the first example in history of a people who became free without sacrifice, without revolution, without torment. We gave you liberty, know how to conserve it.'[18] By then the actual sacrifices of the republic's capital, Milan, included the extortion of 20 million francs, the city itself looted by French soldiery, and the removal of many art treasures, though Bonaparte had a tender moment when he saw the poor condition of Leonardo's *Last Supper* and gave orders that its convent home should not be used as a billet for his troops.

Two types of pillage were favoured by the occupying forces. One was the immediate sacking of a town after its capture, a practice often condoned by the generals. Bonaparte himself permitted the sacking of the Piedmontese town of Mondovi and the Lombard city of Pavia. One of his divisional commanders, General Masséna, was a notorious looter who did not discourage his soldiers from following his example: after one victory they had gone off plundering when they were surprised by some Austrian battalions, who routed them and captured their guns. Masséna, it was reported, had to flee from a woman's bed in his nightshirt.[19]

The second form of plunder was more official. French armies would occupy a city, seize its banks and munitions, and demand food and clothing for their soldiers. In their wake officials arrived to collect indemnities and take away paintings. The great treasures of Italy were not stolen and sold to buy provisions for the army: they were stolen to embellish Paris and furnish the Louvre. When the Duke of Parma pleaded with Bonaparte to let him keep a painting by Correggio – and even offered to pay him its value in cash – the general ignored him, insisting that it should adorn the French 'capital for ages, and give birth to similar exertions of genius'.[20] In Venice the French commander was both greedy and vindictive. Apart from looting numerous works by Titian, Veronese and Tintoretto, he ordered officials to destroy the Venetian emblem – the Lion of St Mark – wherever they found it on the *terraferma*, and in the city itself he took down the lion from its pillar in the Piazzetta and sent it with the famous bronze horses of St Mark's to Paris. Even his 'improvements', such as the Public Gardens and the west side of the Piazza, required a spate of demolitions.

After the conquest of so much territory, the French government's goal of 'natural frontiers' was superseded by the idea of 'sister republics', which led later, under the empire, to the concept of satellite states. In Italy Bonaparte set up sister republics in the north but frequently changed their borders and sometimes abolished them altogether. After eighteen months in the peninsula he tired of his Italian work and became eager to find somewhere to fight England, the country that had captured so many of France's overseas possessions over the previous half-century. Realizing that an attempt to cross the English Channel might end in catastrophe, he encouraged the Directory to give him an army to take to Egypt with the aim of cutting communications between Britain and its expanding empire in India. As always with Bonaparte, however, personal ambition was the prime determinant of action. 'We must go to the Orient,' this aspiring Alexander told his secretary, Bourrienne, 'all great glory has always been acquired there.'*[21] Although he won a number of battles against Mamelukes and Turkish forces, the expedition to Egypt was a failure. Bonaparte's fleet was destroyed by Admiral Nelson at the Battle of the Nile in 1798, and his army was repulsed by a Turkish garrison assisted by British ships at the city of Acre. After a year in Egypt he felt stranded and frustrated with nothing much to do. Yearning to be in Paris and to be part of the next power struggle there, he sneaked away by boat, abandoning his soldiers without even telling them he was going.

Meanwhile the Directory was helping his career by its foolhardy aggression in Italy. Dispatching its armies to the south, it drove one ruling Ferdinand out of Naples and the other one (Peter Leopold's son) out of Tuscany. By early 1799 it controlled nearly all the peninsula and had set up another brace of republics, the Parthenopean in Naples and a Roman sister to the north. The naivety in establishing such regimes in places where few people wanted them was confirmed by their brisk collapse. While a British force arrived in Naples, Russian and Austrian armies overran the north, destroying the Cisalpine Republic and occupying Turin. Within a few months, the Directory had lost the whole of peninsular Italy except for Genoa.

France itself was saved from invasion not by Bonaparte's return from Egypt in October 1799 but by Masséna's victory the previous month against a Russian army at Zurich. Although the Directory thus seemed to have been saved, Bonaparte was nevertheless determined to overthrow it and in November he staged the *coup d'état* of 18 Brumaire that established him as first consul. One of his first actions was to send Masséna to Italy, where a starving Genoa had to be defended against an Austrian siege, while he himself organized a fresh army to lead through the Alpine snows into Lombardy. In June 1800, at the

---

*Bonaparte failed, however, to convince his underling that he also would win glory. 'Well, Bourrienne, you too will be immortal.' 'How, general?' 'Are you not my secretary?' 'Tell me the name of Alexander's.'[22]

Piedmontese village of Marengo, Bonaparte was losing the battle until French reinforcements unexpectedly arrived in the afternoon and reversed the fortunes of the contest. Marengo turned out to be the most decisive victory of his career. Had he lost the battle, he would have lost the war and probably the consulship; his narrow win secured his job and won him Italy.

Marengo gave Bonaparte another chance to indulge his passion for changing the names and boundaries of Italian states. Whimsically he transformed the Grand Duchy of Tuscany into the kingdom of Etruria and gave it to the heir of the Bourbon Duke of Parma, whose own duchy he planned to annex. Further north he also annexed Piedmont and reinstated the Cisalpine Republic, enlarging it with Novara, Verona and papal Romagna. Soon he decided also to change the name of the republic, informing cheering Italian delegates whom he had summoned to Lyon that 'Cisalpine' would be substituted by 'Italian'. Bonaparte made himself president of the republic and chose as his deputy Count Francesco Melzi d'Eril, an intelligent Lombard aristocrat. Melzi's diplomatic skills managed to secure a certain autonomy for the republic, whose president was usually absent, but he made the mistake of believing in his chief's occasional, insincere talk about Italy and liberty. He hoped that Bonaparte's presidency would be temporary and that it would give way to a united and independent state in the north. Yet there was never any chance of this happening because, for personal as well as strategic reasons, the first consul refused to relinquish Italy. As he told the Prussian ambassador in Paris, 'she is a mistress whose favours I refuse to share with anybody else'.

The Italian Republic became redundant when Bonaparte decided he should be the new Charlemagne rather than the new Alexander and that France should be the heart of a new Roman Empire of the West. He loved the idea of a millennial 'succession' and promoted it with remarks about his 'illustrious predecessor' and a visit to Charlemagne's Aachen before his coronation as emperor in 1804 – the occasion when in the cathedral of Notre Dame he snatched the crown from the pope's hands and placed it upon his own head. The relationship between the papacy and the empire was back to where it had been a thousand years earlier. 'Your Holiness is sovereign of Rome,' Napoleon told Pius VII, 'but I am its emperor.'[23]

In the empire there was no room for republics: its territories were to be ruled by monarchs and viceroys who were relations of the emperor. If Napoleon had Charlemagne's imperial crown, it was logical for him to have the Italian crown as well, just as it was historically logical for his son (though he did not have one until 1811) to become King of the Romans. Napoleon established the kingdom of Italy in 1805, with his stepson Eugène as viceroy, a move that prompted a further rearrangement of borders. To the territory of the old Italian Republic were added eastern Venetia, the Papal Marches and the Trentino, creating a conglomeration which gave the kingdom some 7 million people, a third of the population of the peninsula.

The rest of the north and centre was annexed to the French Empire, usually on the grounds that Italian rulers could not be trusted to enforce the 'Continental System', a policy designed to ruin Britain's trade. Napoleon had already taken Piedmont and now added Liguria, followed by Etruria (and the deposition of its king), then by Parma and Piacenza, and finally by the rest of the Papal States, whose spiritual and temporal leader was imprisoned and kept in France until the empire collapsed. Only in the south did the borders remain much the same, though the rulers were changed. In December 1805 the emperor decreed that 'the dynasty of Naples has ceased to reign' and decided its replacement would be the Bonaparte family. His elder brother Joseph, who called himself head of the family and considered himself next in line to the imperial throne, was duly given the crown of Naples. This rather idle, vaguely liberal man enjoyed life in his Mediterranean capital, where he enriched himself, but after two years he was forced to exchange it for the forbidding task of upholding bonapartist rule in Spain. He was replaced by his sister Caroline's husband, Marshal Murat.

By 1810 all of peninsular Italy – all the territories of the communes, the popes, the republics, the duchies and the sovereign monarchs – had been reduced to three napoleonic blocks, imperial, Italian and Neapolitan. Only from the islands, protected by the British navy, were the Bonapartes excluded. In Sicily, where the Bourbon royal family had fled, power was in the hands of Lord William Bentinck, the commander of a British force. He persuaded Sicilians to accept a constitution and a parliament, though a more enduring consequence of the English presence was the establishment of the Marsala wine industry. As the Continental System had robbed Britain of its usual wine supplies, the country had to promote the cultivation of vines in territories it controlled. In doing so, British entrepreneurs created an abiding affection back home for the fortified wines of Portugal, Madeira, Jerez and Sicily.

Avid republican though he had once been, Napoleon loved the pomp and glamour of monarchy. As much of a nepotist as any Renaissance pope, he offered titles and courts to all his siblings; even Jérôme, the youngest and most frivolous brother, was made King of Westphalia at the age of twenty-two. Italy offered Napoleon several opportunities to park his relations in useful places, opportunities that he took and which later inspired the opening lines of Tolstoy's *War and Peace*: 'Eh bien, mon prince,' observes the francophone Anna Pávlovna, 'so Genoa and Lucca are now no more than estates of the Bonaparte family.' Not only did Napoleon appoint one brother (Joseph) and one brother-in-law (Murat) kings, but one sister (Caroline) became a queen, his stepson (Eugène) a viceroy, and another brother-in-law (Prince Borghese) governor-general of the departments beyond the Alps (Piedmont, Parma and Liguria). One sister (Pauline) was given the small duchy of Guastalla, which she happily sold back to its donor for 6 million francs, while another (Elisa) became Princess of Piombino, Princess of Lucca and Grand Duchess of Tuscany. Neither of the two most independent-minded brothers ruled in Italy, Lucien because he thought Napoleon a megalomaniac, and Louis because he ruled Holland until 1810, when he was sacked for trying to rule as a Dutch king rather than as a French viceroy. The emperor subsequently annexed Holland.

Napoleon gave his relations the lustrous trimmings of monarchy. Eugène's court in Milan was very grand, its household containing thirty-five chamberlains and twenty-six ladies-in-waiting; in Naples Murat was even grander, employing forty-four chamberlains, among whom were eighteen dukes and sixteen princes.[24] Yet the siblings were treated by their powerful brother more as errant subordinates than as dignified heads of state. Theoretically independent, they were effectively vassals, forced to suffix 'Napoleon' to their names so that Elisa became Princess Elisa-Napoleon and Murat was known as King

Joachim-Napoleon. Like the others, Joseph was repeatedly admonished, ordered about and reminded that he owed everything to the emperor. Yearning to establish a lasting Bonaparte dynasty, Napoleon tried to improve his family's status and prospects by marrying his brothers to European royal families. He forced Jérôme to accept an annulment of his first marriage in order to marry a German princess and he exiled Lucien for refusing to divorce his second wife so that he could marry a Spanish infanta. Napoleon left his own wife, Josephine, to espouse the daughter of his defeated foe the Austrian emperor, but he would not allow Louis to leave Hortense, Josephine's daughter, to whom he was miserably and jealously married.

Eugène had the most difficult job in Italy because his stepfather was always interfering in the affairs of a state with which he was well acquainted and of which he was the official head. The viceroy had to ensure that the kingdom was well defended because the Po Valley was still the most popular battleground in southern Europe, and he also had to provide large numbers of soldiers for service outside Italy. From 1809 the Peninsular War required three Italian divisions, which were forced to fight a merciless and unfamiliar guerrilla war in conditions so bad that the men sometimes had to live off grass soup and bread made from acorns and crushed olive stones; of the 30,000 Italians the kingdom sent to Spain, only 9,000 returned, many of them wounded. The casualties in Russia were even higher: 27,000 men marched with the Grande Armée in 1812, but only 1,000 struggled back through the snows to their homes in northern Italy.[25]

In 1810 Eugène reported that 40,000 men in the kingdom had either deserted or avoided conscription. Naples and the annexed Papal States, which also had to supply troops for Spain and Russia, had a similar problem plus the additional one that their deserters fled and joined bands of brigands in the hills. Napoleon told Joseph to be tougher with his subjects and to execute more *lazzaroni*, but both kings of Naples managed to achieve a greater degree of autonomy than Eugène. Murat even preferred Neapolitan ministers to French ones and showed sufficient independence of spirit for Napoleon to consider replacing him.

The happiest place in napoleonic Italy was Lucca, which the emperor treated with untypical indulgence. He awarded it, with

Piombino, to Elisa, the sister who most resembled him and the one he was least fond of. Energetic and ambitious, she was so commanding a figure she was nicknamed la Sémiramis de Lucques after the legendary Queen of Assyria who is supposed to have founded Babylon. In her principality, with a population of only 150,000, she behaved like an enlightened despot, encouraging industry, carrying out public works and patronizing the arts, including appointing Niccolò Paganini, the greatest violinist in Europe, her director of music and – so it was rumoured – one of her lovers. Gratifyingly for her brother, she renovated the Carrara marble industry so that it was able to provide the municipalities of the empire with 12,000 busts of their emperor. Napoleon, however, was not sufficiently grateful to reward Elisa with the real state and the real power that she craved. Although she was made Grand Duchess of Tuscany in 1809, she ruled from the Pitti Palace not as an independent sovereign but as an unpopular administrator of a department of the French Empire.

Murat, like Eugène, fought with Napoleon in Russia but afterwards, with the French in retreat, he hurried back to Naples to try to save his throne. He quickly made a pact with the Austrians, who, like the Prussians and Russians, were moving westwards towards France, and he brought an army up from Naples to confront – or pretend to confront – Eugène. At the beginning of 1814, three months before Napoleon's abdication and exile to Elba, Elisa warned her brother that, although the Tuscans did not like the Neapolitans, 'the ideas of independence had spread so widely in Italy in the last two months' that she believed they would submit to them if they could 'finish up being ruled by a prince of their own'.[26] Her subjects did not, however, have the chance to do so because the allies decided that they wanted the Bourbons back in Naples. In March 1815, on hearing that Napoleon had abandoned planting olives in Elba to have another stab at being emperor, a desperate Murat offered his services to his brother-in-law. Rebuffed, perhaps fatally – Napoleon later recognized that Murat's skills as a cavalry commander might have changed the result at Waterloo – he made a passionate appeal to patriotism, exhorting Italians to follow him towards his unexpected new goal of independence: 'From the Alps to the Straits of Sicily can be heard a single cry: Italian independence!'[27] Yet few people followed him, and his forces were defeated by the Austrians; later, as the defeated Napoleon was sailing into exile at St Helena, he launched a crazy attack on the Calabrian coast, where he was captured and shot. His fate demonstrated that Elisa had been wrong: the cry – if it existed – had not been heard, and the 'ideas of independence' had not spread far. A Russian patriotism had resisted Napoleon and driven him out of the tsar's dominions; in Spain also patriotism had made a significant contribution to the French defeat. Yet in Italy there was no patriotic uprising even when it was clear that Napoleon was done for.

The debit side of napoleonic rule in Italy is easy to catalogue: the loss of life in the endless wars, the taxes and indemnities, the looting of art, the decline of foreign trade, the executions of men unwilling to be conscripted to fight wars they had no interest in. Yet there were some credits too, outweighed though they may have been. Napoleon was seen by many, however mistakenly, as a protector of nationalities and a liberator of the oppressed. The Genoese artist Felice Guascone refused to criticize him and painted a series of pictures celebrating his rule and deploring the return of reaction afterwards.[28] Many people benefited from the introduction of divorce, the improvement in roads, the new and fairer system of inheritance, the religious liberty that demolished ghetto walls, the opportunities provided by *la carrière ouverte aux talents*. Later some of them realized that the introduction of the napoleonic codes of law, together with fiscal and institutional reforms, were essential foundations for a modern state.

Less easy to quantify than the debits and credits is the effect of French rule on the future of Italy. Revolutionary France had a huge impact on the peninsula for it overturned much of the Ancien Régime, but the republics it imposed south of the Po were disliked by nearly everyone except lawyers and professors. The French made few jacobins in Italy and hardly any in places with traditions of reform such as Tuscany, where the reintroduction of the death penalty in the annexed duchy caused resentment. In the imperial decade Napoleon was no more popular and he ended up being hated by those Italians who believed he had betrayed their hopes of an independent Italy – a state he had never had any intention of creating. Yet he did help indirectly to foster a sense of nation. Italians suffered terribly in his armies, but survivors retained a certain loyalty to their new *tricolore* flag – the

green, white and red adopted in various shapes in the different muta-
tions of napoleonic north Italy – and to its implied recognition of a
patria. One veteran of the Russian campaign fought half a century
later with Garibaldi.[29]

Napoleon's influence on the future of Italy was real if uninten-
tional. He encouraged a nationalist mentality with his talk, his armies
and his demolition of ancient duchies; and he stimulated a form of
adversarial though seldom violent nationalism with his oppression,
his arrogance, his exactions and his art thefts. Above all, he showed
Italy that it did not need to carry on with its old ways and its old systems; he let it glimpse the possibility of a different future. If the
peninsula's myriad entities could be reduced to three, might they not
one day end up as one? In 1805 Napoleon had made himself King of
Italy; he did not make himself king of a geographical expression.

ITALY AND THE RESTORATION

In September 1814 Napoleon's opponents gathered in Vienna to
restore the Europe with which their enemy had so compulsively tam-
pered. Although their work was interrupted by the bogeyman's return
and the Battle of Waterloo, they completed their task quickly and
without acrimony. They had set out to restore the 'legitimist' pre-
1789 order but soon understood the need to be flexible about borders
and dynasties. In Italy the three territorial units of Napoleon's reign
were transformed into nine states, two fewer than in 1789.

Some Italians, chiefly in Milan, lobbied against the new arrangements. One of them told the British foreign secretary, Lord Castlereagh,
that Italians were no longer the same people who twenty years earlier
had been 'happy and lethargic under the paternal rule of Austria';
they had now acquired 'a greater love' of their country and, furthermore, they had 'learned to fight'.[30] Castlereagh was not interested,
and nor were his allies from Russia, Prussia and Austria. As in the
eighteenth century, the European powers saw Italy as a diplomatic
games board, a lucky resource for compensating and rewarding allies.
If the Habsburgs renounced the Austrian Netherlands (which were
briefly united to Holland before choosing to disunite to become

Belgium), then they had to be allowed back into Italy. Since none of the powers wanted to see nationalism, independence or jacobinism in the peninsula, they were happy to let Austria keep control and act as a barrier to the infiltration of French influence and ideas. Piedmont was awarded the republic of Genoa for a similar reason – the need to strengthen a state on the French border.

From the congress the Austrian emperor received the new kingdom of Lombardy-Venetia, which he ruled through a viceroy. His brother Ferdinand was returned to the Grand Duchy of Tuscany, while his daughter Marie-Louise (Napoleon's second wife) became Duchess of Parma, a move that required compensation for the Bourbons of Parma in the shape of the former republic of Lucca, a city with which they had no connection. The rest of the peninsula was rearranged along more traditional lines. The papacy got the Papal States, the Habsburg-Este family was back in Modena, and the Bourbon King of Naples returned from Sicily to his mainland capital. In 1815 all the Italian states except Piedmont were ruled by Habsburgs and their relations or by their close and dependent allies.

Its conclusions demonstrated that the congress was more concerned with security and balance of power than with a strict interpretation of legitimacy. The two entirely 'legitimate' states missing from the post-napoleonic map were the ancient republics of Venice and Genoa, while the republic of Lucca had been converted into a duchy. No doubt the French example had made the powers wary of the word 'republic', but European leaders were surely able to differentiate between Robespierre's gory regime and the Venetian state that had predated it by 1,100 years. Genoa did not want to become part of reactionary Piedmont any more than Venice wished to be ruled by Frenchmen, Austrians or mainland Italians. Yet since they possessed no former dynasties to clamour for restoration, both were considered disposable and so were sacrificed unsentimentally to the territorial ambitions of neighbours.

The 'Restoration' has traditionally been seen as the Dark Age of modern Italy, a backward-looking era of clerical control and unenlightened authoritarianism. The word soon became synonymous with 'reaction' and 'repression' and later also with 'foreign oppression', since the Habsburg satellites could (and did) call on Austria to send troops if insurrections threatened them. Yet the picture is only true of certain places. The Duke of Modena may have refused all change and any reform – like his father-in-law, the King of Piedmont – but his neighbour the Duchess of Parma had different views: although she was evidently not pining for her husband, imprisoned on St Helena, she retained his system of administration in her duchy.

The restoration of the pope's temporal power was indeed a return to a Dark Age, literally so at night because street lighting was regarded as the work of the devil. So were vaccination and railways: Gregory XVI, who was pope from 1831 to 1846, made the equation '*Chemin de fer, Chemin d'Enfer*' and banned railway construction in the Papal States. Even the conservative Austrian chancellor Metternich, the chief architect of post-napoleonic Europe, was appalled by a 'detested and detestable' government that had no idea how to govern. The inhabitants of the Romagna, accustomed to the administrative efficiency of Eugène's Italian kingdom, were dismayed to be returned to the rule of cardinal-legates. They had never had much affection for Rome on the other side of the Apennines, where the roads were so bad that they found it quicker to reach their capital by sea. As Christopher Duggan has drily observed, 'While all roads may once have led to Rome, in the 1820s only two did, and neither was very safe.'[31]

No state was more proudly and profoundly reactionary than Piedmont. Its king, Victor Emanuel I, demonstrated his attitude by returning with his courtiers to Turin coiffured with powder and pigtails and wearing hats that had gone out of fashion with Frederick the Great. He then officially turned the clock back with a royal edict abolishing all laws made by Napoleon and returning his state to its unenlightened eighteenth century. His politics were almost a caricature of obscurantism: noble privileges came back along with guilds, internal customs barriers and the persecution of Jews and Protestants. Virtually nothing of the napoleonic system was retained except an effective police force.

The successors of Victor Emanuel, his brother Charles Felix and his cousin Charles Albert, shared his conservative and intransigent instincts. Although the belated reintroduction of parts of the napoleonic codes helped modernize the administration, Piedmont remained a benighted state until the middle of the century. Ecclesiastical courts survived, education was controlled by the Jesuits, and the government insisted on both civil and religious censorship. Newspapers were banned from printing words such as 'nation', 'revolution' and even 'Italy'; you could use the word 'liberty' only if you were attacking it.[32] Such a stultifying regime understandably encouraged writers and artists to abandon Turin for the freer and more cosmopolitan cities of Florence and Milan.

The restoration in Naples might have been an equally reactionary affair. In 1799 Ferdinand IV had sailed from Sicily intent on retribution and punishment for the defeated supporters of the Parthenopean Republic. Primitive feelings of vengeance overcame the monarch's more usual good nature and, in violation of the terms of the surrender, he had ordered swift and drastic justice. Although often referred to as the Bourbon 'Terror', the repression was not quite on the scale that the dynasty's enemies later claimed; about 200 people were executed. Yet the cost to the king's reputation was high and enduring. One of his victims was Eleonora Pimentel, who had once written rhapsodies to the benevolence of Ferdinand's government and who was hanged for subsequently writing in praise of liberty and equality in the republican newspaper. More dangerously for the future of his dynasty, the king alienated members of his aristocracy by executing several idealistic young noblemen. Most serious of all, his revenge was a propaganda gift for republicans and patriots because it helped to start and later sustain the myth that Italian unification was a saga of heroism and self-sacrifice.

In 1815 Ferdinand returned to Naples in a more restrained mood. He did not feel very grateful to the British, whose navy had protected him in Sicily, because they had bullied him, removed his queen from the court, appointed his more liberal son as regent and insisted on a constitution in Palermo providing for a free press and a bicameral parliament. Yet he was reluctant to antagonize the winning nations of the napoleonic wars, some of which had flirted with the idea of retaining Murat. In any case he wanted a quieter life and no more enforced sojourns in Sicily. The process of government interested him even less than before, and he entrusted the administration to his minister Luigi Medici so that he could devote his time to the pleasures of eating, hunting and his children's company. Sometimes he railed against the napoleonic codes and wanted them to be abolished, as they had been in Piedmont, but he was too weak and too indifferent to overrule the astute Medici and his other ministers. The result was that feudal privileges were not brought back, the civil code was not abrogated, and Naples retained the political and institutional reforms of Murat and Joseph Bonaparte. Ferdinand derived some consolation, however, by disregarding the Sicilians and abolishing their British-inspired constitution. At Vienna it had been decided at last to unite the crowns of Naples and Sicily, and as a result he gave up his old titles (Ferdinand IV of Naples and Ferdinand III of Sicily) to become Ferdinand I of the Two Sicilies. He now had a constitutional excuse not to permit a separate arrangement for Sicily.

The king died in 1825, sixty-six years after he had ascended the throne left to him on his father's departure for Madrid. In his final decade he had presided over a reasonably tolerant regime and had stirred himself to combat smallpox, ordering clinics to be built in every village in Sicily and making vaccination compulsory for all (himself included). A perceptive Irish woman, Lady Blessington, who lived in Naples in his final years, described Ferdinand as 'not a sovereign of superior mental requirements' but 'assuredly a good-natured man'. Although she herself was anti-Bourbon and preferred the circle that had supported Murat, she admitted that the people of Naples were not oppressed by their government. 'We are told that Italians writhe under the despotism of their rulers,' she wrote, 'but nowhere have I seen such happy faces.'[33]

The king was succeeded by his son Francis, who abandoned his liberalism at the start of his short reign, and then by his grandson Ferdinand II, who was also for some time a liberal. Like his recent ancestors, the young Ferdinand was ill-educated but on the whole humane and well-meaning, a prince who dutifully toured his dominions and renounced some of the crown's hunting reserves. He also encouraged science, deciding to hold a Congress of Italian Scientists in Naples in 1845. Yet in the second half of his reign he became a conservative and was lambasted by liberals and later historians as a stupid, cruel and despotic tyrant. After the Sicilian revolution in 1848 he was nicknamed King 'Bomba' for briefly bombarding the walls of Messina, while conditions in Neapolitan prisons, which an outraged

William Gladstone (at the time a Tory MP) visited in 1850 and denounced a year later, led to his ostracization by much of Europe, especially France and Britain which accepted Gladstone's resounding though meaningless judgement of the regime as 'the negation of God erected into a system of government'. Much of this was unfair or at least one-sided. Victor Emanuel II, King of Piedmont and later King of Italy, was not known as 'Bomba' although he had bombarded his own city of Genoa in the same revolutionary period; nor was his government condemned as the negation of God even though prison conditions in Piedmont were as terrible as they were in Naples. But in the 1850s Piedmont was emerging as the great European hope of British liberals, and the fate of Naples was to be cast as its antagonist.

The Kingdom of the Two Sicilies was widely regarded, in Italy as in the rest of Europe, as a place of sloth and squalor, of grandeur and poverty, a place where landless labourers kept themselves just alive by scratching the parched soil of distant noblemen, where street urchins in the city picked the pockets of wealthy tourists and bands of brigands roamed with impunity in the hills outside, a land exploited and oppressed by an indolent monarchy, a frivolous aristocracy and a swarm of grasping clergy.

This picture was inherited and preserved by generations of historians until recently the stereotype was re-examined. Then it transpired that the kingdom was not just a land of *latifondi*, of vast desiccated estates in the interior that contained little except scrub for goats and some thin soil for wheat. Naples may not have had the irrigation or the natural advantages of Lombardy, but it was not an entirely backward place; wheat yields there were higher than in the Papal States. As for the *latifondisti*, it emerged that they were not all absentee landlords frittering away the produce of their workers by living in luxury in the capital. The *latifondo* was part feudal and part capitalist, part social structure and part business enterprise. Owners used their lands to feed themselves and the people who lived there, but they often grew food for foreign markets as well. The exported produce of the Barracco family, *latifondisti* from Calabria, included liquorice, olive oil, fine wool and cacciacavallo cheese.[34]

The state of industry in Naples has been similarly disparaged: travel accounts of the period leave the impression that the inhabitants had never heard of the spinning jenny or the steam engine. Yet a modernized textile industry, aided by a sensible tariff policy, existed in the Apennine foothills in the early nineteenth century; not much later, an engineering industry was established around the capital. Naples in fact enjoyed a number of industrial 'firsts'. It possessed the largest shipyards in Italy, it launched the first peninsular steamboat (1818) and it enjoyed the largest merchant marine in the Mediterranean; it also built the first iron suspension bridge in Italy, constructed the first Italian railway and was among the first Italian cities to use gas for street lighting. Admittedly, not all these achievements were as impressive as they sound. Naples may have built the first railway, but it was a short one, and its construction did not lead to a rapid expansion of the network. Most of the other states soon caught up and overtook it: by 1860, when the whole of southern Italy had only 125 miles of track, Lombardy had 360 and Piedmont, after a slow start, possessed over 500.

A glance at its economic statistics reveals how separate Naples as a trading partner was from the rest of Italy. In 1855 85 per cent of its exports were sent to Britain, France and Austria, while only 3 per cent crossed the border into the Papal States; Neapolitan trade with Britain was three times greater than that with all the other Italian states added together.[35] Feelings of separateness were not confined to commerce; Naples possessed its own remarkable legal system, widely regarded as superior to any other in the peninsula. Outsiders noticed that the place was different, a distinct, cosmopolitan entity, a kingdom (with or without Sicily) with an ancient history and borders which, almost uniquely in Italy, were not subjected to rearrangement after every war. Moreover, Naples itself was still by far the largest city in Italy – indeed the third-largest in Europe after London and Paris – and had been a capital since Charles of Anjou had established himself there 600 years earlier. It was the only Italian city, thought Stendhal, that had 'the true makings of a capital'; the rest were 'glorified provincial towns like Lyon'.[36] Before 1860 hardly anyone contemplated the idea that the kingdom might be destroyed and its territory annexed by an all-Italian state; and little in the subsequent history of that state indicates that the Neapolitans would have been unhappier if they had been left to govern themselves.

In their propaganda Italian patriots of the nineteenth century identified the Neapolitan Bourbons as the chief home-grown tyrants and Austrian Habsburgs as their foreign equivalents. Yet even they were unable to convince themselves that the Grand Duchy of Tuscany was an oppressive state. It was governed by Ferdinand III, son of the great Peter Leopold and brother of the Austrian emperor whose armies had lost four wars against Napoleon and whose daughter had been sacrificed to the French emperor's desire to beget an heir. Ferdinand's return to Florence in 1814 did not lead to a persecution of bonapartists or to the abolition of reforms. As in the eighteenth century, Tuscany was a tolerant and civilized place that preferred Jews to Jesuits and welcomed exiles from Piedmont and from other states. Tariffs were low, censorship was feeble, and the armed forces were almost non-existent, though in an emergency the state could call for Austrian troops. Ferdinand was succeeded in 1824 by his son Leopold II, another benevolent ruler until the revolutions of 1848 converted him – along with Pope Pius IX and the King of Naples – to conservatism. In the early part of his reign he reduced taxes, carried out liberal reforms, encouraged science and returned to that perennially elusive project of Tuscan rulers, the draining of the Maremma marshlands on the Tyrrhenian coast. Under Habsburg rule neither Mazzini nor Garibaldi nor anyone else could muster revolutionary support in Tuscany. Even at the time of the 1848 revolution few of their followers were found outside Florence and Livorno.

An easier target for nationalistic passion was Lombardy-Venetia, which, unlike Tuscany, was part of a foreign empire. Patriotic intellectuals fulminated against Austria not because it was a bad ruler but because it was an occupier, though for propaganda purposes they had to claim that it was both. They needed to label Austria as the oppressor to justify their title to be considered liberators. Thus a regime that matched Tuscany in providing the best government in the peninsula became the victim of myths and traducers.

The Emperor Francis had spent his childhood in Florence and retained his affection for Italy despite the repeated defeats of his armies there at the hands of Napoleon. Having no desire to revive the Ancien Régime, he presided distantly over a stable and generally peaceful state served by an efficient bureaucracy and an uncorrupted police force. Under Austrian rule Lombardy possessed the most productive agriculture and the most prosperous industry in Italy. Its inhabitants grumbled about taxation and conscription, but only a minority grumbled about the nature of the regime. The emperor's chief error was to insist that his mentally deficient son Ferdinand should succeed him after his death in 1835.

Insurrections broke out and conspiracies were discovered in much of Italy (including Lombardy) in the 1820s and 1830s, but the Venetians showed little desire to remove a benign government and take part in them. While disappointed that they had been denied the chance to govern themselves, they were pleased that their city was the joint capital of the kingdom of Lombardy-Venetia and relieved that they were no longer governed by the French. Napoleon had stolen the bronze horses of St Mark's and displayed them in Paris, but Austria brought them back and, with due ceremony, reinstated them on the cathedral's façade.

The most engaging witness of French and Austrian rule in northern Italy was Henri Beyle, the charming and irrepressible Frenchman who wrote books as Stendhal and called himself Brulard in his memoirs. As a youth of seventeen, he came over the Great St Bernard in 1800, intent on joining General Bonaparte's army as a subaltern of dragoons. Within weeks of his arrival in Lombardy, he had encountered the three great passions of his adult life: music, love and Italy. One evening he saw Cimarosa's *Il matrimonio segreto* and was overwhelmed by the experience. 'To live in Italy and hear such music,' he recalled in his autobiography, 'became the basis of all my reasoning.'[37] In Milan he went to La Scala several times a week; he also became addicted to falling in love with difficult and sometimes unattainable women.

Stendhal spent Napoleon's imperial years in the army, stationed in Brunswick and later serving on the quartermaster's staff in the Russian campaign of 1812. Throughout this time he dreamed of returning to his 'dear Italy', which was his 'true country' and 'in harmony' with his nature. A print of Milan cathedral made him feel so nostalgic that he could not bear to look at it; the smell of veal cutlets cooked in breadcrumbs *alla milanese* made his yearning still more acute. He wanted his epitaph to begin with the words '*Arrigo Beyle, milanese*'.

After the emperor's abdication in 1814, Stendhal returned, unemployed but delighted, to Italy, where he lived for seven years and acquired a second identity, one that was less cynical and more enthusiastic than the one he had left behind in France. A romantic, though an untypically unlyrical one, he sympathized with the nascent patriotic feelings he found in the salons of Milan. But he did not greatly admire the patriotic intellectuals or believe that their aspirations for a united Italy were practical: for him even Naples was hardly Italian while Florence had no more in common with Otranto than it did with Le Havre.[38] He knew there was much wrong with contemporary Italy but he could not bring himself to be harsh about the land of love and music even when he tried: *The Charterhouse of Parma*, apparently a novel about conspiracy, despotism and imprisonment, is really a love letter to Italy.

Stendhal was a bonapartist who ensured that the style of *The Charterhouse* was plain and unromantic by reading a few pages of Napoleon's civil code each morning before writing. He claimed the emperor had 'rudely transformed' Milan, turning a city 'hitherto renowned for nothing save over-eating into the intellectual capital of Italy'; he also claimed, in 1818, that Milan and Florence were mourning Napoleon, though feelings of bereavement were seldom evident outside the liberal circles he frequented. Yet although he was in the anti-Austrian camp, he did not pretend that Italians were suffering under rule from Vienna, and he admitted that people were happier and freer in Milan than they were in Rome or papal Bologna. Novels and operas that would have been banned in Turin could be published and performed in the Habsburg capitals of Venice and Milan. At La Scala in 1845 Giuseppe Verdi encountered no problems with his opera *Giovanna d'Arco*, but in Rome the censors stripped poor Joan of Arc of her name and even of her nationality so that eventually she appeared before audiences as Orietta of Lesbos, a Genoese heroine leading Greek islanders against the Turks.

Generations of European schoolchildren were taught that Napoleon had brought the idea of unity to Italy, that his defeat had led to a dismal interlude of oppression and reaction, and that Italy's destiny had finally been fulfilled by the heroic endeavours of its patriots. Yet the determinist theory is completely unhistorical. Italy was no more preordained to unite than Scandinavia, Yugoslavia or North America. Equally mistaken are the ideas that Naples was a foul despotism deserving of destruction, that Lombardy-Venetia was a monument to foreign tyranny and that Piedmont was the liberal knight predestined to rescue Italy and lead her to glory and to unity. Two of the most distinguished Piedmontese of the era – both of them future prime ministers in Turin – realized that the propaganda was all nonsense. Count Cavour knew the truth about Habsburg rule in Lombardy but admitted that in his journalism of the 1840s he was 'obliged to be over-patriotic and cry out against Austria along with everyone else'. As for the Marquess d'Azeglio, a more genuine patriot than Cavour, the propaganda seemed to him grotesque. 'To call the present rulers of Italy tyrants,' he wrote in 1846, 'would be a childish absurdity.'[39]

6

Revolutionary Italies

ROMANTIC ITALY

Massimo d'Azeglio might have been a character from *The Charter-house of Parma*. He was a romantic figure, tall and handsome and blue-eyed, and he possessed the aristocratic charm and sexual appeal of the novel's protagonist, Fabrizio del Dongo. Irreverent and unreserved (unusual qualities in Piedmont), he could talk to anyone from dancing girls to countesses, from bandits and wagoners to colonels and cardinals. A painter and a writer by profession, his amateur skills included music, swimming, riding and fencing. Perhaps his talents were too diffuse for him to be really good at anything, even politics, although in 1849, at the age of fifty, he became prime minister of Piedmont. Azeglio seldom bothered to conceal his rather frequent boredom, and in old age he regretted the invention of *l'homme sérieux* in France. He also deplored the fact that 'the most tedious of the seven [deadly] sins – pride, envy and avarice – [had] got the better of the other four': a Friend of Pleasure (another rare species in Piedmont), he saw nothing very reprehensible about sex, eating, laziness and occasional wrath. He enjoyed a good number of love affairs and tolerated two bad marriages.

Massimo was born in 1798, the fourth son of a noble Piedmontese family, the Taparelli d'Azeglio. After an agreeable childhood in Florence, he studied painting in Rome, leaving the city each summer to paint in the hill villages of the Castelli Romani, staying in carters' inns and finding himself on easy terms with peasants and local brigands. Later he lived in Milan, where he exhibited his pictures at the Brera. He never liked Turin, which he found boring and oppressive, a philistine capital without art galleries or a good opera, a city permeated with a religious atmosphere that gave him a feeling of 'moral suffocation'. Florence was a far more congenial abode; so was Milan where, in the capital of the Austrian 'oppressors', this Italian patriot could 'breathe freely' and publish his books.[1]

Apart from his matrimonial misfortunes, the only blight on Azeglio's life was the sense of shame he felt at being an Italian in that era. He admitted he was so 'morbidly sensitive' about the condition of Italy and felt so humiliated that part of it remained under a 'foreign yoke' that he chose not to make friends with foreigners in case they mocked him.[2] For him the only cure for this national and personal inferiority complex was independence for the whole peninsula – independence, but not unity. Azeglio knew mid-century Italy, its land and its peoples, better than other politicians, and he was more realistic than they about the potential difficulties of unification. His priorities were the expulsion of the Austrians, the reform of native governments and some kind of unity for the north.

As an artist and writer, Azeglio nursed his 'feeling of humiliation' by trawling the past in search of heroic episodes which he could then transform and publicize through his art. One glorious subject for a canvas was the Battle of Legnano, Barbarossa's defeat by the Lombard League in 1176. Another was the so-called Challenge of Barletta, a much mythologized event from the early sixteenth century at which thirteen Italian knights in Apulia, outraged by a slur on the Italian character, challenged thirteen French knights to a duel and were victorious. While working on this canvas, Azeglio realized the subject could also be used for a patriotic novel, one that might 'be understood in the streets and marketplaces'. He duly wrote *Ettore Fieramosca* and got it past the Austrian censor even though the hero (Ettore) declares that foreigners are the obstacle to Italian unity. Encouraged by its success, both financial and patriotic, he wrote a second novel, this time about the siege that destroyed the Florentine Republic in 1530, and began a third on the Lombard League, which he did not complete. By then, the mid-1840s, this many-sided man had decided that his patriotism required two new professions, that of soldier (in his youth he had served briefly in the Piedmontese army) and that of politician. Presumably he had realized by this time that as a novelist he was not in the same league as his father-in-law, Alessandro Manzoni.

Other Italians were equally ashamed of Italy's decline. Although the composer Gioacchino Rossini was not much of a patriot, he liked to thank God for the Spanish: 'If there were no Spaniards,' he once observed, 'the Italians would be the last people in Europe.'[3] What made decadence so galling was the consciousness that, while Italians had for centuries been recognized as the most prosperous and civilized people on the continent, they were now regarded by foreigners as lazy, effeminate and rather comical. Italians were and are frequently rude about Italy – Dante called it a 'brothel' in *Inferno* and a 'desert' in *Purgatorio* – but they weren't and aren't happy when foreigners say similar things. Goethe described Italy as 'the shadow of a nation' while the French poet Alphonse de Lamartine termed it a 'land of the past . . . where everything sleeps', its people too fond of 'sensual pleasures' to be able to fight properly. Disparaged as a 'trivial poet' for these opinions, Lamartine made the mistake of challenging his Italian detractor and was badly wounded in a duel.

Italians could hate both the condescension of foreigners and the reasons why visitors wanted to come to Italy. Some of them could even resent Stendhal because he adored what they detested, the Italy of love and music and hospitality, Italy the giant antique shop and innkeeper of the world, Italy the land of limitless ruins and the domicile of effete dilettanti. Many Italians were convinced that their dignity could not be restored without the recovery of masculinity and martial ardour. Vittorio Alfieri, the Piedmontese poet-prophet of unity who wrote 'An exhortation to free Italy from the barbarians', was especially concerned with the question of virility, a recurrent concern for future builders or rebuilders of the nation up to and including Mussolini. When, according to Alfieri, Italians recovered the virility of their ancient ancestors and discarded the manners of the cosmopolitan present, they would again be able to lead Europe.

Numerous patriots joined Azeglio in quest of a past to be proud of. They also searched for heroes who had fought valiantly against invaders and who had been prepared to sacrifice their lives for the sake of Italy. As they could not find such figures in recent centuries, they had to rummage through the more distant past. Ancient Rome was not an ideal model partly because it had not been a nation and partly because Napoleon had very recently appropriated its glory, making himself a Caesar and his son the King of Rome. The idea of Italian Davids standing up to northern Goliaths seemed a more promising source, yet it became so difficult to unearth suitable examples that patriotic artists often found themselves writing, painting and composing music about the same event: *I lombardi alla prima crociata* (*The Lombards on the First Crusade*) was an epic poem by Tommaso Grossi, an early opera by Verdi and the subject of several pictures by Francesco Hayez. Another drawback was that certain selected episodes, the Battle of Legnano excepted, were not fully appropriate: while the Sicilian Vespers of 1282 (exalted by the historian Michele Amari and again painted by Hayez and set to music by Verdi) might conceivably be portrayed as an uprising against a foreign invader, the incident – in which thousands of Frenchmen in Palermo were slaughtered after one of them pestered a Sicilian woman – might also be regarded as a grotesque reprisal. A third defect was that the paintings of these events – huge, hideous, sub-Delacroix expanses – belong to the most unfortunate period in the history of Italian art. A dispiriting though representative sample of this genre can be examined today in the Museo Civico of the Tuscan town of Pistoia. The walls are covered by canvases depicting scenes such as 'the Pazzi Conspiracy' and 'other rebellions against tyranny', the murder of Francesco Ferruccio (a hero of the Florentine Republic) and the riot instigated by Balilla, the Genoese boy who inspired a mob to chase the Austrians out of his city in 1746. The most ghastly exhibit of all is another vast painting of the Sicilian Vespers, this time by Giulio Piatti, an infernal and almost lunatic composition of people brandishing knives and staring insanely.

The literary equivalents of this art were the books of Azeglio and the poetry of Giovanni Berchet, but the only novel of the era that has truly lasted is Alessandro Manzoni's *I promessi sposi* (*The Betrothed*), a work that acquired the status of a monument soon after its publication and transformed its author into a national prophet, a patriarchal fount of moral and patriotic wisdom. In fact the Milanese Manzoni, who was a poet as well as a novelist, deserved this reputation less for his masterpiece than for his contribution to the making of the language* and perhaps also for the nationalistic sentiments of a patriotic ode claiming that the Italians were a single people between the Alps and the sea, a people united by blood, heart, arms, language, memories and Catholicism. Of course he knew this was an exaggeration, that at the time of writing (1821) Italians shared little of these things except the same Church, but he used poetic licence to attack the idea of 'diversity', a word he believed was insulting to Italy because it summed 'up a long history of misfortune and humiliation'.[4]

Yet Manzoni had his defects as both a patriot and a prophet. Indifferent to the medieval past of the communes, he defended the papacy's historic role and believed in its contemporary national relevance. *The Betrothed*, a saga of tyranny eventually vanquished, may have become a canonical text for the patriotic movement, but the idea that it foreshadowed a struggle for national liberation is far-fetched. Its seventeeth-century heroes are not heroic – they display Christian resignation; the villains are not foreign – Don Rodrigo is a home-grown tyrant with a Spanish name, not a recognizable caricature of a Bourbon or Habsburg overlord; and the plot is melodramatic and Manichaean. The pervading aura of divine providence at work certainly seems at odds with the patriotic belief that Italians could only become free if they themselves removed their shackles. Perhaps the success of the novel owed something to the fact that there were few Italian competitors at the time.

The figure who most closely combined romantic culture with revolutionary politics was Giuseppe Mazzini, the sad-eyed ascetic who in the early 1830s appealed for a revival or resurgence of Italy, a '*risorgimento*', and connected this idea to the project of unifying the peninsula politically. For him a nation was a 'universality of citizens speaking the same tongue', a definition that was not of course applicable to Italy. Yet Mazzini pretended that it was. Born in Genoa in 1805, his sense of mission was fixed early in life, and he dressed always in black in mourning for what he regarded as his lost fatherland. He read widely in literature and history, and from his reading he absorbed ideas that he adapted and exploited to further his cause. Inspired by the works of Dante, by the history of Rome and by the example of the Lombard League, he appropriated suitable passages

*See p. 32.

and details and incorporated them into a programme that was obviously neither communal nor imperial. For the goal that he and his democratic followers aimed for was simply an Italy that would be both independent and undivided. Only a unitary state, they believed, would liberate Italy from its age-old rivalries.

Other ideologues believed the opposite, that only regard for those rivalries would allow Italians to respect each other's differences and live together in harmony: a unitary state could never conceivably work in so diverse a country. The foremost federalist was the brilliant Milanese intellectual Carlo Cattaneo, who considered 'the ancient love of liberty in Italy' to be more important than 'the cult of unity'. Like Guicciardini 300 years earlier, he believed that Italy had prospered from competition between the cities and argued that a political system that failed to take the communal spirit into account would not succeed. In his eyes this spirit was far from being a medieval irrelevance: it was alive – as it still is, remaining a vital component of the national identity even today. Cattaneo did not greatly exaggerate when he claimed, 'The communes are the nation: they are the nation in the most innermost sanctuary of its liberty.'[5]

Cattaneo was no romantic nationalist. Indeed he believed that nationalism was essentially illiberal – an unusual credence in those days – and he suspected with some reason that this would be the case with Piedmont. As a Milanese historian, he was aware of the old Piedmontese custom of grabbing and annexing bits of Lombardy, and he was rightly apprehensive about the ambitions of the Savoia monarchs in his own time. As a Lombard, he was also aware of his region's ancient trading relationships beyond the Alps and recognized that there could be advantages, administrative and economic, in becoming a self-governing part of the Habsburg Empire. Such advantages would obviously disappear if Lombardy were to be annexed by Piedmont.

Piedmontese patriots understandably disagreed. In 1843 Vincenzo Gioberti, a theologian from Turin, published a book called *Del primato morale e civile degli Italiani* (*Of the Moral and Civil Pre-eminence of the Italians*), a work whose title alone was calculated to improve morale. Earnestly and verbosely, Gioberti told Italians that pre-eminence had been theirs and would be so again if only they could stand up and seize it. Readers, who had been led to believe that they were actually inferior to other nations, were naturally pleased by the message, although few of them were enthusiastic about the formula Gioberti suggested for their salvation: a federation of Italian states under the presidency of the pope (currently the elderly and reactionary Gregory XVI), who would be allowed to retain his temporal power over the Papal States. This was an even more dramatic divergence from Mazzini's ideology than the views of Cattaneo. Mazzini and his supporters followed Machiavelli in believing that the papacy had been one of the chief obstacles to Italian unity in the past; no Italy of their dreams would concede to the pope an ounce of political power.

After the appearance of *Primato*, Azeglio persuaded his cousin, Cesare Balbo, to write another book on Italian possibilities, *Delle speranze d'Italia* (*On the Hopes of Italy*), another anti-Mazzinian work with another optimistic title written by another prominent Piedmontese. Balbo agreed with Gioberti that a federal solution was essential, but he argued that a confederation under the Piedmontese monarchy would be preferable to one under the pope. Independence from Austria (or any other power) was also vital: one couldn't achieve pre-eminence without first attaining parity, and the way to achieve parity with independent nations was to gain independence for oneself. Political unity, by contrast, was unimportant, indeed a 'childish' idea because a confederation was clearly the system 'most suited to Italy's nature and history'.[6]

In the mid-1840s Piedmont did not seem a very promising candidate for leadership of a pan-Italian confederation. It was still governed by a conservative, authoritarian monarch, Charles Albert, who had savagely crushed an attempted coup in 1833. Yet the king was also a member of the Savoia dynasty who had inherited ancestral urges to continue the expansion of the realm. As the obstacle to the fulfilment of such desires was now Austria, it seemed logical for him to give at least tacit support to moderates in the national movement, to those at any rate who were not republican or democratic or in any way radical. As his country possessed the best army in the peninsula, he believed he would without difficulty dominate the patriotic side in any war against Austria.

One of the king's abettors in this matter was Massimo d'Azeglio, whose picaresque career was showing no sign of flagging. In 1845 he abandoned fiction and began his unexpected involvement in politics. Equally unforeseen was the energy he displayed during a surreptitious tour of the Romagna, where he spoke to a number of patriots hoping for an end to papal rule there. On informing Charles Albert of their hopes for Piedmontese assistance, the king replied with doubtful sincerity that, when the time was right, everything he had – even his life – would be dedicated to the Italian cause.

INSURGENT ITALY

Italian conspirators did not enjoy a good reputation. If 'treacherous' was the adjective most often applied to the archetypal plotter of the Renaissance, 'incompetence' and 'fiasco' are appropriate nouns to describe the actions and consequences of many nineteenth-century schemers. Conspirators came in several guises, including the bomb-thrower who missed his target, the youth who achieved nothing except his own death, and the *carbonaro*, the member of a secret society of masonic inspiration who moved in a shadowy world of passwords, secret cells, police informers and hidden weapons. Their conspiracies tended to have brief lives and dramatic endings: in some cases they were betrayed before anything happened; in others a group of young men reached a southern shore where, after shouting *Viva Italia!* at an astonished populace, they were arrested and taken before a firing squad, some of them singing as they died an operatic chorus about how wonderful it was to die for one's country.

Not all conspiracies ended like that. If the plotters happened to be soldiers, they sometimes enjoyed a brief success. In 1820, inspired by the proclamation of a constitution in Spain, *carbonari* in the Bourbon army, allied with former followers of Murat, joined an uprising outside Naples. Although they persuaded the aged King Ferdinand to grant a constitution, they had little popular support and were soon suppressed by Austrian troops. A similar rising with a similar conclusion occurred the same year in Piedmont. Army officers rebelled, the Spanish constitution was proclaimed, and an Austrian force was called in to restore absolute rule.

Revolutions in other parts of Europe twice heralded rebellions in Italy. In 1820 the catalyst was Spain, but in 1830 it was France, where the July Revolution expelled the most reactionary of all Bourbon rulers. In the following year a spate of insurrections broke out in the Po Valley – in Modena, Parma and Bologna – which as usual the Austrians easily extinguished. None of these or the earlier revolts were inspired by the goal of Italian independence. Nor did they enjoy significant local support or indeed much sympathy from other parts of Italy.

After the failures of 1831, the *carbonari* began to fade from the revolutionary stage. Their place was occupied by Mazzini, who had been exiled from Italy in 1830 and had gone to live in Marseille. There the young Genoese patriot founded Giovine Italia (Young Italy), a society that later had as many as 50,000 members, becoming in effect the first Italian political party. Mazzini's organization had the advantage over the *carbonari* of possessing a clear programme whose objectives for Italy included democracy, unification and, ideally, a republic, though this last was not essential and could be jettisoned if a decent monarchical candidate emerged. Politics, however, were only a part of Mazzini's campaign. Other ingredients he regarded as crucial for success were education, insurrection and violence.*

From France Mazzini began plotting conspiracies, some of which were discovered by the authorities at the planning stage. In 1833 he helped organize a plot in Turin which the Piedmontese government quashed with public executions in a repression far harsher than Ferdinand's in Naples or Austria's in Lombardy in 1821–3 (when the Austrians had commuted all the death sentences). Mazzini was among those condemned to death in absentia. The following year another of his coups failed in Genoa, which resulted in a death sentence for another young revolutionary, Giuseppe Garibaldi, who fled to South America and did not return to Italy for fourteen years.

After the failed coups in Piedmont, Mazzini was expelled from France and took refuge in Switzerland, where he set up Young Europe,

*Young Italy inspired the creation of numerous organizations around the world, including in the early twentieth century the Hindu nationalist Young India, whose members were taught to make bombs to blow up the British by a Russian revolutionary in Paris. Young India in turn inspired Nathuram Godse, the Hindu extremist who assassinated Gandhi in 1948.

an organization that promoted self-determination, freedom for the oppressed and a Europe of cooperating nation-states. In 1837, after another expulsion, he emigrated to England, where he spent most of the rest of his life, safe from the threat of eviction. In London he lived frugally and alone, seeming to survive on coffee, working obsessively into the night, tirelessly writing letters, articles and propaganda. He liked the English, and they liked him, regarding this rather mournful man, with his gaunt face and large eyes, as the romantic figure he undoubtedly was, an aspiring liberator dedicated to his cause.

A united Italy was achieved in Mazzini's lifetime not by his team but by opponents of theirs led by Cavour, who had not believed in unification until just before it happened. Subsequently the winners wrote the history, or most of it, and they edited Mazzini out of the glory, maligning him personally and denying his contribution to the great epic of unity. For them Mazzini was simply a terrorist and a revolutionary, an enemy of Italy, although actually he was in many ways an admirable person, a generous and uncorrupt individual, an internationalist rather than a chauvinist, a man who condemned the death penalty and held progressive views on women's rights and social justice. Undeniably he possessed an unfeeling and unappealing side, for he schemed from the safety of London to send young idealists on fatal expeditions in Italy because, as he all too bluntly put it, 'ideas ripen quickly when they are nourished by the blood of martyrs'. He was sure that Italians had to fight and be killed in order to win their nation: it was 'better to act and fail than do absolutely nothing'.[7]

These sentiments were shared by two followers of Mazzini from Venice, the brothers Bandiera, who in 1844 embarked upon the most foolish, futile and unorganized insurrection of all. They were officers in the Austrian navy (in which their father was a vice-admiral) but also anti-Habsburg plotters who, on becoming aware they were under suspicion, managed to evade arrest and flee to the Ionian Islands. There they learned that a revolt had broken out in Calabria and decided to assist it, prompting their mother to track them down in Corfu and tell them they were madmen. 'What kind of foolishness is yours,' she asked her elder son, 'on a mere frenzied impulse to cast aside your parents, your wife, your rank, name and family, for the sake of nothing at all?'[8]

Ignoring their wretched mother, the Bandieras set off with a hand-ful of companions and in midsummer landed on the coast of Calabria, where they kissed the sand and were surprised to find the weather too hot to march about in the daytime. Disappointingly, they attracted no local support and soon discovered that the revolt they had read about in the newspapers had been a small one extinguished some weeks earlier. Eventually they took refuge in an inn, where they were caught off-guard by local militiamen, who captured them and carried them off for trial in Cosenza. The brothers' subsequent executions – and those of seven of their companions – were blamed on Mazzini, whose exhortations incited many such escapades but who on this occasion had discouraged the expedition. Yet predictably the London plotter found consolation in their 'martyrdom'. It did not matter, he wrote, that the Bandieras had not succeeded because they were 'apostles' and 'martyrs': 'the Appeal of Martyrdom is brother to the Angel of Victory.'[9]

1848 was the year of European revolutions and the year of the fall of Prince Metternich, who a year before had made his celebrated description of Italy as 'a geographical expression'. Yet this time it was Italy that set the continental pace, ahead of Orleanist France, the German Confederation and the Habsburg Empire. A popular uprising broke out in Sicily in early January and forced Ferdinand II to grant his kingdom a constitution three weeks later. Within two months, constitutions had also been proclaimed in Tuscany, Piedmont and Rome, and further insurrections had erupted in Venice, Milan, Parma and Modena.

In Italy these outbursts had a multiplicity of causes, motives and objectives. They were not coordinated and they were seldom inspired by similar grievances or even similar ideologies. The Sicilian revolt owed little to Mazzini: it was a popular movement driven by hostility to the government in Naples and supported by local aristocrats who wanted autonomy for their island. Encouraged by its early success to aim for detachment from the Bourbons, the new parliament soon declared Sicilian independence. Yet only a small number of islanders were eager to exchange the partnership with Naples for membership of an Italian federation.

The citizens of some Italian states had little desire to change their rulers. A constitution in Rome seemed merely a logical step after the 1846 election of a charismatic and apparently liberal pope, Pius IX, who had relaxed censorship and declared an amnesty, and who seemed to be demonstrating that Gioberti's programme might have a future after all. In Tuscany there was equally scant zeal to change the regime except in that most untypical Tuscan town, the port of Livorno. There was little patriotic inclination to rise against Grand Duke Leopold II, a moderate and enlightened leader who had encouraged an Italian customs union and was even prepared to join a federation of Italian princes.

The most Mazzinian insurrection took place in Milan, where the populace rose in March and, after five days of street-fighting, forced the Austrian commander, Marshal Radetzky, to withdraw his troops from the city. The revolt spread to other Lombard towns, which were all captured by revolutionary insurgents except for the fortress city of Mantua, and also to the countryside among peasants distressed by the recent agricultural crisis and the consequent fall in living standards. Yet in Milan's sister capital of Venice, where Mazzini had found it difficult to recruit members for Young Italy, Italian nationalist fervour was almost non-existent. When Venetians rose in March, they did so not as aspirant Italians but as Venetian patriots eager to regain their independence fifty years after Bonaparte had destroyed it. Almost alone among Italians, they were proud of their pre-napoleonic past and wished to return to it. After forcing the Austrian garrison into an unexpectedly rapid surrender, they set up their own government and, to great enthusiasm, proclaimed the restoration of their republic.

In any Italian conflict with Austria the protagonist had to be Piedmont, a state with a strong army and a long military tradition. Seizing his opportunity to take control of the situation, King Charles Albert thus moved quickly to support the Milanese insurgents, and in late March he declared war on the Austrian Empire. His troops then advanced and won a number of small engagements, while his government set out to annex Parma and Modena, whose ducal rulers had fled. The patriotic cause in the north rapidly acquired so much momentum that even the pope and the king in Naples dispatched forces in support. Much has been made of popular participation in the struggle, of the thousands of volunteers joining up, of the titled lady who raised her own battalion, of the city women who fought on the barricades in Brescia and Milan. Yet the great majority of volunteers came not from the south or the countryside but from the educated middle classes of the north. In any case, there were not very many even of these. Azeglio observed that an Italian population of 25 million could muster fewer than 50,000 volunteers – an unimpressive figure for a struggle of national liberation.

Things began to go wrong when the pope decided they were going too quickly. Azeglio, who had written an excoriating criticism of the previous pope, was now such an admirer of Pius IX that at the age of forty-nine he volunteered as a staff officer in the papal army marching north under the command of General Durando. Pius intended his troops to play a defensive role, stationed on the northern borders of his dominions to deter an Austrian attack, but Durando and his staff officer were set on a more ambitious strategy. Placed in charge of the army's proclamations, which were published in the press, Azeglio tried to push Pius into pursuing an aggressive war of independence in alliance with Piedmont. Thus he told the world that the pope would fight a crusade for God and Italy and would, together with Charles Albert, expel the Austrians from the peninsula. This proclamation inflamed the pope who, when forced to choose between his mildly patriotic feelings for Italy and his international obligations as leader of the Catholic Church, found no difficulty in selecting the latter. In late April, in a document known as the Allocution, he therefore declared that he had been misrepresented, that fighting a war against Catholic Austria was far from his thoughts and that, even if Italy were one day united, he never wished to be its president. By then, however, Durando had crossed without orders into Habsburg territory and was now in Venetia, where Austria twice defeated his troops: in the second battle, outside Vicenza, Azeglio received a bullet in his knee, an injury that caused him trouble for many years to come.

After their early victories in the spring, the Piedmontese had been busy organizing plebiscites, persuading voters in Milan, Parma and Modena to vote for annexation to their kingdom. The task was not a difficult one because everybody knew that getting military assistance from the Piedmontese against Austria was dependent on an affirmative vote. Even Venice, which had no desire to be annexed, submitted as approaching Habsburg armies began the reconquest of the *terra-ferma*. Yet Piedmont's behaviour antagonized many people. King Ferdinand II quickly withdrew his Neapolitan force when he realized that Turin was aiming for expansion. Carlo Cattaneo, a leader of the revolution in Milan, concluded sadly that his Lombard suspicion of Piedmont had proved to be accurate. And in England Queen Victoria wrote a cross letter to her foreign secretary, Lord Palmerston: 'Why Charles Albert ought to get any additional territory, the Queen cannot in the least see.'[10]

Unfortunately for the Piedmontese king, annexation was quickly followed by military defeat. At the head of his army, Charles Albert was beaten in July by Radetzky's Austrians at Custoza near Verona, a small reverse which he turned into a big one by retreating all the way to Milan in case the Lombards exploited his discomfiture by proclaiming a republic. Although he had promised to defend the city, he decided to discard his pledge as soon as he reached Lombardy. Then, abandoning his newly acquired territories, he accepted an armistice with Austria and publicly put the blame for his defeat on the Milanese. The Venetians refused to accept the armistice and carried on fighting.

Revolution was also defeated in the south. In May Ferdinand was able to dispense with the constitution he had granted in February and turn his attention to Sicily, whose government spurned the offer of autonomy under the Bourbon crown and even invited a surprised Piedmontese prince to become its sovereign. In July Ferdinand invaded the island, bombarding the fortifications of Messina and angering Britain and France so much that they stepped in and forced him to accept an armistice for six months. The Sicilian government failed to take advantage of the respite to prepare a defensive plan or even procure weapons for its soldiers, yet at the same time it rejected a fresh offer from Ferdinand of a separate parliament and a viceroy. The combination of arrogance and incompetence led, predictably, to a swift and humiliating collapse. Neapolitan forces recaptured Palermo without a fight.

In other parts of Italy revolutionary sentiment was still alive. Pope Pius found it so strong in Rome that in November, following the assassination of his chief minister, he fled in disguise across the

Neapolitan border to the fortress port of Gaeta. In Tuscany Grand Duke Leopold stayed longer, presiding nervously over an increasingly radical government until February 1849, when, with the assembly in newly constitutional Florence debating the possibility of his removal, he also left for Gaeta.

The following month, the Piedmontese government returned to the offensive, repudiating the armistice and ordering its army to attack the Austrians. The campaign was short and catastrophic: the commander-in-chief never received the government's order to attack, and his army was routed by the formidable Radetzky. On the day of the defeat the king abdicated and commenced a sorrowful journey to Portuguese exile and death. Although the Piedmontese had again been the aggressors, Austria was again generous with its armistice, demanding little beyond a modest indemnity. In the same period its troops captured the city of Brescia, which had risen in support of Piedmont, and shortly afterwards brought the grand duke back to Tuscany. Such an outcome was naturally humiliating for Piedmont, which had fought two embarrassingly inept campaigns. Especially galling for the monarchy in Turin was the knowledge that, while a royalist army had twice been defeated by an octogenarian field marshal, the republican revolutions in Venice and Rome were still being defended with valour.

The Venetian president, Daniele Manin, was not a romantic hero of the type that Risorgimento propaganda liked to extol. A middle-aged lawyer, he was short and bespectacled, rational and pragmatic, an undashing and even accidental leader of a revolt. Nor were his priorities congenial to later ideologues. He put Venice before Italy, regarding the restoration of the republic as more desirable for Venetians than unification with Piedmont and other parts of Italy. Aware that they had something solid to fight for – a land rather than a set of ideas – the Venetians supported Manin from the initial insurrection at the Arsenale in March 1848 through the establishment of the republic and its military defiance to the last grinding weeks of an inexorable siege. Decimated by cholera, bombarded by the Austrians and abandoned by the Piedmontese, they resisted until August 1849. If they did not quite fulfil their pledge to resist until the last slice of polenta – and watch their city smashed to pieces – we can all be grateful for that.

The Venetians have been largely neglected in nationalist mythology because, however heroically they resisted the Habsburg Empire, they never – either then or later – showed much desire to join the rest of Italy. Besides, the memory of Mazzini and Garibaldi fighting in Rome for a future nation made more inspiring propaganda than the memory of Manin's efforts to re-establish an ancient republic.

In February 1849, after the pope had fled and refused to come back, a constituent assembly in Rome proclaimed a republic and invited Mazzini, who had been in exile for seventeen years, to join its government, effectively as its leader. During the only three months of his life when he exercised political power, this much-traduced revolutionary proved to be a wise and tolerant statesman. He abolished clerical censorship but did not attack religion; he repealed the death penalty and refused to countenance political repression. Having always insisted that Rome should become the capital of a united Italy, Mazzini briefly had the chance to demonstrate how it might be governed.

The Roman Republic was also aided by another former exile, Giuseppe Garibaldi, who had worked for thirteen years as a sailor and soldier in South America. Returning to Europe in the revolutionary spring of 1848, he had led without special distinction a volunteer force against the Austrians in the foothills of the Alps. Surprised to find that the local population was unwilling to join his irregular troops, he had been outmanoeuvred by the enemy and forced to take refuge in Switzerland. The following year he went to Rome, where the republic was being besieged at the request of the pope by French, Austrian and Neapolitan troops. Against the odds, Garibaldi managed to defeat both an army from Naples and an over-confident force from France, but in the summer, at the Battle of the Villa Corsini, his tactic of ordering repeated frontal attacks left the French victorious. His eternal instincts – 'Never retreat' and 'When in doubt, charge with the bayonet' – on this occasion failed him.

The outcome of the siege was, of course, as inevitable as that of Venice. With Rome on the verge of capitulation, Garibaldi refused to surrender and marched out of the city to continue the struggle in the hills of central Italy. The republican defeat was greeted with much joy by Piedmontese politicians such as Gioberti and Cavour, who had even advocated dispatching troops from Turin to assist in the denouement. For them, Mazzini and Garibaldi were as much the enemies of Italy as the Austrian Empire. Even Azeglio compared the Roman Republic to a comic interlude in an opera whereas in fact – together with the siege of Venice and the insurrections in Lombardy – it was one of the most serious episodes of 1848–9, a subject that might have been worthy of an opera by Verdi.

OPERATIC ITALY

By 1848 Italian opera had gained a reputation that few people could have predicted two generations earlier. In the early years of the century the musical form, invented by Florentine composers over 200 years before, had appeared to be dying: Domenico Cimarosa was dead, Giovanni Paisiello had stopped composing, the eighteenth-century tradition of *opera seria* – with its dazzling arias, its skimpy drama and its invariable happy endings – seemed to have passed away as terminally as the royal courts that had sustained it. At the time of Cimarosa's death in 1801 the glories to come could not have been anticipated. Gioacchino Rossini was eight, Gaetano Donizetti was only three, Vincenzo Bellini had not quite been conceived, and the parents of Giuseppe Verdi were still children.

The resurgence of Italian opera was accomplished almost single-handedly by Rossini, a sparkling composer with a talent for comedy who became famous with two operas produced in Venice in 1813, *Tancredi* and *L'italiana in Algeri* (*The Italian Girl in Algiers*). He dominated opera in the peninsula for the next decade and for several years afterwards, even when he was living abroad as a French composer writing for the Paris Opéra. Although his Romanticism was reluctant and even alien to his nature, Rossini became acknowledged as the father of Italian Romantic opera. At the age of thirty-seven, after he had produced *Guillaume Tell*, he stopped writing operas, but by then his reputation was unassailable.

At the time of Rossini's retirement, two younger and more naturally Romantic composers were waiting to take over. One was Donizetti, who wrote with a grace and a facility to rival the master: while Rossini had taken sixteen days to write *Il barbiere di Siviglia*, he allegedly needed only fourteen days to compose *L'elisir d'amore*. The other was the Sicilian, Bellini, who made audiences swoon with his plangent melodies and his melancholy lyricism. Both men triumphed soon after *Guillaume Tell*, Donizetti with *Anna Bolena* in 1830, Bellini a year later with *Norma*, although he had to wait until the second night for acclamation: at the première at La Scala in Milan the Druid priestess flopped, thus inaugurating an unhappy tradition for tragic women on first nights that went on to engulf *La traviata* in Venice in 1853 and *Madama Butterfly* in 1904. In his final opera, *I puritani*, Bellini created the character Elvira, the role that a century later ensured the fame of the great Greek-American soprano Maria Callas.

The works of these three – and of several lesser composers such as Giovanni Pacini and Saverio Mercadante – transformed Italian opera from a courtly entertainment with mythological figures such as Orpheus into a middle-class passion that demanded historical and romantic tragedies. All of Verdi's operas end in tragedy (except of course for his two comedies); even in *Simon Boccanegra*, in which the lovers – almost uniquely – remain united and alive, the heroine is forced to witness the murder of her father in the final scene.

Foreign observers were astonished by the passion for opera in the peninsula: Italians used theatres as Englishmen used clubs, as places where they could meet each other and chat; the fashionable ladies of Milan were thus reduced to opening their salons only on Friday, when La Scala was closed. The energy and enthusiasm of operatic culture reinforced the northern European view that Italian was the language of passion, pleasure and melodrama. Many Italians were doubtless content with this, but some wondered whether the obsession with musical melodrama was injuring their sensibility to art and the subtlety of fine writing. The Sicilian aristocrat Giuseppe di Lampedusa, who was born in the year of *La bohème* (1896), claimed that 'opera mania' had for a century 'absorbed all the artistic energies of the nation'. There could be no symphonies and no successful plays because 'music was opera, drama was opera', even painters had abandoned their canvases to design Don Carlos's prison and the sacred groves of *Norma*. By 1910, when the frenzy diminished, Italian intellectual life resembled 'a field which locusts had visited for a hundred consecutive years'.[11]

The popularity of opera prompted a wave of theatre construction. In the half-century after the fall of Napoleon, over 600 playhouses were built in Italy, half of which were large enough to put on operas.[12] Cities such as Venice and Milan had several theatres where opera could be performed, and most towns of the north and centre had at least one, however small: the orchestra pit in Lucca's Teatro Giglio is so narrow that the harpist and percussionists have to play from adjacent boxes. Yet it was easier to build opera houses than to people them with adequate musicians. In the heyday of Donizetti and Bellini, Italy possessed some great singers yet its orchestras were so poor that they sometimes broke down during performances; the madcap overture of *Guillaume Tell* was apparently never played correctly in the peninsula because no orchestra had enough cellists. The most successful composers were thus eager to have their premières only in the finest opera houses – the San Carlo in Naples, La Fenice in Venice and La Scala – before they earned enough renown to have them in Paris. In spite of La Scala's claims to sempiternal pre-eminence, the best opera house before 1860 was usually the San Carlo. While the Bourbons did not personally enjoy going to the opera, they spent a lot of money on their theatre, providing the best orchestra and many of the best singers. It was the favourite Italian venue for both Rossini and Donizetti.

Around 1840 the great operatic revival seemed in danger of petering out. Bellini, perhaps the most talented of the composers (and the one most admired by Wagner), had died in 1835 at the age of thirty-three. Rossini had another three decades of life but he was depressed and overweight, composing nothing except an occasional *bolero* or *canzone* and refusing to write anything of note until the *Petite messe solennelle* in 1863. Donizetti was just still going, and in 1842 he produced an opera in Vienna and accepted the post of court composer to the Austrian emperor. But this kind and attractive man was already dying from the effects of syphilis; in 1844 he was declared insane and four years later he died in his home town of Bergamo. Italy was plainly in need of a new star.

Giuseppe Verdi was born in 1813 in the hamlet of Roncole, close to the River Po and to the town of Busseto. As France had annexed the region, he began life as a French citizen and was christened Joseph; the following year, after Napoleon's abdication, he became a subject of the Austrian grand duchess who ruled Parma. In middle age he enjoyed calling himself 'a peasant from Roncole' although actually he was the son of an innkeeper wealthy enough to employ labourers on his land and to purchase a second-hand spinet for his musical off-spring. Giuseppe's infant life was subjected to a further myth that he never bothered to refute. His so-called birthplace, his *casa natale*, was declared a national monument in 1901 and is today a museum, yet he was not in fact born in it. His parents moved to the '*casa natale*' when he was a teenager.

The boy went to school in Busseto, found a patron who sponsored his music studies in Milan and began a career that was almost over-whelmed at its start by family tragedies. After losing his only sibling at the age of nineteen, Giuseppe married his patron's daughter when he was twenty-two but had lost through illness his entire young family – daughter, son and wife – by the time he was twenty-six, the age when his first opera (*Oberto*) was performed at La Scala. After his wife's death, he tried to get out of composing his second, a comedy, but the impresario insisted – perhaps out of kindness – that the contract should be fulfilled, and *Un giorno di regno* (*King for a Day*) was duly staged in Milan. Considering the misery Verdi was going through, and the fact that he had little sense of humour anyway, it is a surprisingly attractive and light-hearted piece which owes much to the work and spirit of Rossini. Unfortunately, the audience at La Scala did not agree. The première was such a fiasco (the word then favoured to denote a first-night flop) that it was taken off next day. The composer did not write another comedy for over fifty years.

Verdi's career was rescued by *Nabucco*, which was performed seventy-five times at La Scala in 1842, produced at nineteen other playhouses the year after, and repeated at twenty-five more in 1844.[13] This was later proclaimed the first of Verdi's 'Risorgimento operas', since Italian nationalists asserted that audiences living under the Austrian 'yoke' identified themselves with the Hebrew slaves sighing for freedom from the Babylonian king, Nebuchadnezzar (Nabucco), who had removed them from Jerusalem. There is not much contemporary evidence, however, to suggest that audiences made this connection or that the composer intended them to do so. The opera became popular chiefly because it was a strong and moving work by a striking new talent.

Nabucco was followed by another so-called 'Risorgimento opera', *I lombardi alla prima crociata* (*The Lombards on the First Crusade*), the spectators of which were allegedly persuaded to think of themselves as crusaders and the Austrians as their Saracen foes. After that, Verdi composed his most beautiful early opera, *Ernani*, succeeded by three others (*I due Foscari*, *Giovanna d'Arco* and *Alzira*) which were written hurriedly and carelessly and are among his least memorable works. Next came the third 'Risorgimento opera', *Attila*, in which the audience is supposed to have considered itself Roman and even to have joined in with encouraging shouts when the Roman general tells the King of the Huns, 'You will have the world, leave Italy to me.' Early in 1847 Verdi returned to form with *Macbeth*, enjoyed some success with *I masnadieri* (*The Bandits*) at Covent Garden in the presence of Queen Victoria, and followed them up with *Il corsaro* (*The Corsair*), one of the weakest of all his works.

Verdi was subsequently acclaimed as '*il maestro della rivoluzione italiana*', the great patriot whose music inspired people to man the barricades or rush to Garibaldi's banner in 1848 and 1849. Yet the only opera he produced in 'the Year of Revolutions' was an apolitical drama about pirates performed in Trieste, a city of the Austrian Empire. He himself did not go to Trieste but nor did he spend much of 1848 in Italy. Since August of the previous year, he had been living in Paris, converting (not very successfully) *I lombardi* into *Jérusalem* for the Opéra. Although the work had its première in November, Verdi remained in Paris even after the risings in Sicily and elsewhere, apparently preferring to witness a revolution in France rather than one in his homeland. Not until after the 'Five Days' in Milan that ejected Radetzky did he travel to the Lombard capital.

The composer was of course a patriot with strong sentimental feelings about an independent Italy. At stirring moments he himself could be stirred. From Milan he wrote to Francesco Piave, the librettist of *Ernani* and *Macbeth*, regretting that he had missed the fighting and willing to honour the heroes who had driven out the Austrians. 'The hour of liberation' was nigh, he proclaimed, as if writing a portentous libretto, no power could resist the people's wish, and within a few years, perhaps only a few months, Italy would be 'free, united and republican'. Piave, he sternly told his correspondent, must not again talk to him about writing music.

> What has got into you? Do you think that I want to bother myself now with notes, with sounds? There cannot be any music welcome to Italian ears in 1848 except the music of cannon! I would not write a note for all the money in the world: I would feel an immense remorse, using music-paper, which is so good for making shells.[14]

Later in the letter, after noting that Piave had become a national guard in Manin's Venetian Republic, Verdi confided that, if he had been able to enlist, he would have been a common soldier rather than a 'wretched tribune', but he did not explain why he had been unable to enlist; he was only thirty-four, fifteen years younger than Azeglio, who had managed the transition from artist to officer without difficulty. The real explanation doubtless came in the next paragraph when he told Piave he had 'to go back to France because of obligations and business', which he clarified as meaning two operas to write and a lot of money to collect. Verdi was thus a patriot so long as patriotism did not interfere with work or business. Subsequently it transpired that the chief purpose of his Italian visit had been not to applaud the revolution or tour the barricades but to buy a farm near Roncole, which later became his home. By the middle of May, he was safely back in France, after just over a month in Italy and just before the battle for Lombardy began.

From Paris Verdi wailed at the armistice that followed the Piedmontese defeat in the first Battle of Custoza. 'What a wretched time we live in! What a pygmy time! Nothing great: not even great crimes!' He himself composed the music for a battle hymn, '*Suona la tromba*' ('Sound the Trumpet'), which had been written by the young poet Goffredo Mameli and which Verdi sent to Mazzini in the hope that it would 'soon be sung on the Lombard plains, to the music of cannon'.[15] Mazzini had requested the hymn in May, but the composer did not send it until the autumn, by which time both Lombardy and the Italian cannons had been silenced. Although it might have been used in later campaigns, the work never caught on, and a different poem by Mameli, 'Fratelli d'Italia' ('Brothers of Italy'), set to music by Michele Novaro, eventually became the Italian national anthem. Mameli himself was killed in 1849, at the age of twenty-one, fighting with Garibaldi's forces in Rome.

While he was in Paris, Verdi wrote his one indisputable 'Risorgimento opera', *La battaglia di Legnano*, a work that celebrated what his librettist called 'the most glorious epoch of Italian history' – the twelfth century. Staged in January 1849 in the Rome of Mazzini's republic, its composer left France with reluctance to conduct the opening performances; again he stayed in Italy for just over a month and again he left before the real fighting – Garibaldi's defence of the city – took place. In the circumstances of the moment, the opera could hardly have failed to be a success. From the opening chorus, which declared that Italy was 'at last . . . a single people of heroes', to the final act ('To Die for the Fatherland'), for which an encore became obligatory, the applause was so loud that the music could hardly be heard.

Verdi was evidently the composer laureate in Rome at the beginning of 1849, but he does not appear to have been regarded as such in other parts of Italy during the revolutions. Some patriots wondered why his previous three operas had been about brigands, pirates and a Scottish usurper married to a murderess. Others were puzzled that, at such a critical time, he had chosen to write about a medieval battle instead of a more recent event such as the 'Five Days' of Milan. Following the proclamations of the new constitutions early in 1848, a few towns staged *Attila* and *Ernani*, but elsewhere Verdi's name on the posters was absent. As the musicologist Roger Parker has shown, patriots had little appetite for the 'Risorgimento operas' even in the most important year of the Risorgimento. The people of Bologna, one theatrical journal observed, preferred to sing nationalist songs themselves rather than watch *I lombardi*, while the arrival of *Nabucco* in Naples was a disappointment because audiences were not at that moment interested in 'the traditions . . . of the ancient Orient'. Considering a production of *Attila* in Ferrara, the author of another article wondered why it was necessary to 'recall an epoch so humiliating for Italy' rather than stage an opera 'more suitable to the current times' that would 'recall only those facts that lend glory to our most dear homeland'. Parker also discovered that Verdi's music did not feature in the concerts performed in liberated Milan between the 'Five Days' and the return of Radetzky four months later. Instead of listening to the most talented Italian still composing, the Milanese preferred choruses from lesser musicians that urged 'Italians into the fray' and told them not to sleep 'until Italy belongs to us'.[16]

None of this would have surprised Verdi, who never thought of himself as the '*maestro della rivoluzione*'. He had patriotic and republican instincts, he had given his children names from ancient Rome (Virginia and Icilio Romano) that seemed to reflect this, he considered himself to be Italian and he wanted Italy to be free. Yet he had no passionate animus against Austria. In 1836 he had composed a cantata for the Habsburg emperor's birthday, and his first visit abroad was to Vienna, where he conducted *Nabucco*, a work that evidently did not upset the Austrians. On his return to Parma, he conducted the same opera before the Austrian archduchess, Marie-Louise, who granted him an audience and gave him a present. Subsequently she became the dedicatee of his next work, *I lombardi*.

If Verdi felt comfortable with the Austrians, they were similarly untroubled by him. Their censorship was generally light before 1848, and even afterwards they allowed revivals of *Attila* and *Nabucco* at La Scala. A few alterations were demanded for *Ernani* but none for *Nabucco* or indeed *Attila*, and only one, an esoteric change, for *I lombardi*, where the words 'Ave Maria' were substituted by 'Salve Maria'. Censors in Lombardy-Venetia, and in other parts of Italy, were at the time less concerned with politics than with questions of religion and morals. The Austrians were more perturbed a little later by Verdi's *Stiffelio*, in which a Protestant minister, quoting the New Testament, forgives his adulterous wife, than by a Roman general telling Attila to leave Italy to him.

The Habsburg authorities did not regard Verdi as politically dangerous before 1848 because they had no reason to do so. The composer was a man of range as well as talent, and he had no intention of limiting his settings to his time or his country. In fact he preferred to base his works on the dramas of foreign writers: only five of his twenty-six operas have an Italian provenance. Among the dramatists he used were Byron, Voltaire, Eugène Scribe and Alexandre Dumas *fils*, but his favourites were Schiller, Victor Hugo and, above all, Shakespeare. Apart from *Macbeth*, the English playwright provided Verdi with the material for his two last and perhaps greatest operas, *Otello* and the incomparable *Falstaff*; he also inspired him with the idea of *King Lear*, which Verdi hoped for years to turn into a huge, magnificent, unconventional opera.

Since the era of the Risorgimento coincided with that of Romantic opera, subsequent generations have spent much time searching for connections between the two. Doubtless they would have liked to make them with Rossini, Bellini and Donizetti, but the last two had died too soon, and the first was politically unacceptable. Rossini's operas contain the odd suggestively patriotic phrase. The soprano in *Tancredi*, for example, has to sing of '*cara Italia*', while the protagonist in *L'italiana in Algeri* exhorts her listeners to 'think of the fatherland' and do their duty; the composer had even written a hymn for Murat that began with the line, 'Italy, arise; the time has come'. Yet such occasional sentiments could not rescue Rossini from his well-known transgressions: that he had been a conservative happily working for the Bourbons, that he was a friend of Metternich for over forty years, that he had written embarrassing cantatas for the reactionary Holy Alliance,* and that in April 1848 he had been so frightened by the situation in Bologna that he had run away to Florence.

Scourers of Verdi's librettos were able to affirm their hero's patriotic credentials without having to deal with encumbrances like these. The connections they made were, nevertheless, often tenuous: no reading of *Macbeth*'s libretto can convince one that Verdi was thinking of Italy when he made his Scottish exiles sing of their 'oppressed homeland'. Similar connections were also made by foreign writers who, though often sceptical about other claims of united Italy, propagated the Verdian myth without investigating how much of it was true. A typical example is the Oxford philosopher Isaiah Berlin, who claimed that Verdi 'lived near the centre of gravity of his nation, and spoke to his countrymen and for them, as no one else did, not even Manzoni or Garibaldi'. The composer, he alleged, was tireless in his work for the cause. 'The hymn which Verdi wrote for Mazzini is only an episode in a single great campaign.' The patriot 'responded deeply and personally to every twist and turn in the Italian struggle for unity and freedom. The Hebrews of *Nabucco*,' Berlin added, piling up the

---

*Formed in September 1815 by the sovereigns of Russia, Prussia and Austria.

mistakes in the space of half a paragraph, 'were Italians in captivity', and their famous chorus was 'the national prayer for resurrection'.[17]

On glancing at Verdi's librettos, one quickly becomes aware of the complex and intimate nature of his stories. The typical Verdian plot has the tenor and soprano falling in love and being thwarted by the baritone, sometimes with the assistance of the mezzo. Even *Legnano* is based on a love triangle: the soprano had loved the tenor but, believing him to be dead, had married the baritone, who swears vengeance on realizing that his wife and the resurrected tenor still love each other. Any political messages in the works are subordinate to the amorous problems of the leading characters and are further obscured by the difficulty in the 'Risorgimento operas' of identifying the true villains. If the crusaders in *I lombardi* are the good guys, why are they trying to kill each other, and why is the Saracen Orontes the opera's most appealing figure? Why does Attila, the archetypal barbarian invader, become the most sympathetic character in the eponymous opera? Why in *Legnano* is another ferocious aggressor, Barbarossa, treated so gently, and why do audiences need to be reminded that Italy's historic divisions were so deep that the citizens of Como had fought on the emperor's side against the Lombard League?

The myth most frequently repeated is that audiences at *Nabucco* identified themselves with the Hebrew slaves, regarded their chorus ('*Va pensiero*') as a kind of secret national anthem, and demanded encores of it at every performance. A glance at the words, by Temistocle Solera, makes one wonder how such a myth could ever have gained credence.

> Go thoughts on golden wings,
> Go rest upon the slopes, the hills,
> Where, soft and mild, the sweet breezes
> Of our homeland smell so sweet!
> Greet the banks of the Jordan,
> The ruined towers of Zion.
> Oh my homeland so beautiful and lost!
> Oh, remembrance so dear and fateful!
> Golden harp of the prophetic bards:
> Why hang mute upon the willow?
> Rekindle the memories in our breast,
> Tell us of times past.[18]

The words and music are beautiful, but they are a lament for the past rather than a martial call for action; not until the end of the scene, and only after Zechariah has told them to 'rise up' and stop behaving like 'timorous women', do the slaves think of breaking their chains. The chorus itself contains nothing relevant to the current situation in Italy. Contemporary Italians could still smell the 'sweet breezes' of their homeland, they could still see such towers as they had not demolished and they could still enjoy the banks of the River Po, even with an Austrian viceroy in Milan. They had no need of 'so dear and fateful' a 'remembrance'.

While investigating *Nabucco*, Roger Parker was puzzled to find that, although contemporary journals often wrote about other scenes of the opera, they made few references to '*Va pensiero*' and no mention of spectators demanding encores. Later he discovered that the tale of the encores had been constructed by Franco Abbiati, the author of a four-volume biography of Verdi published as recently as 1959. In his support Abbiati had cited one particular review, which had made no mention of the encores, but had evidently taken the idea from a different review in a different journal reporting a different performance in which an encore had been given to a different chorus, '*Immenso Jehova*', which concludes the opera and contains not the slightest hint of aspirational nationalism.[19]

Music can, of course, stir people and encourage them to have noble and heroic sentiments even if that had not been the composer's intention. There are moments in Beethoven's symphonies that can make one feel one is leading a cavalry charge. Donizetti had had no propaganda project in mind when he wrote *Gemma di Vergy* in 1834, but its performance in the revolutionary atmosphere of Palermo at the end of 1847 led to shouts of 'Long live Italy!', 'Long live the pope!' and even 'Long live the king!' *Norma* had a similar effect, equally unintended by its long-dead composer, at La Scala in 1859. Some of Verdi's operas, performed in the feverish ambience of certain Risorgimento years, also inspired people to see unintended patriotism in the works and to shout their approval at them. Yet with the sole exception of *Legnano* in Rome, the evidence for political shouting – as opposed to the usual baying of claques – is weak. Verdi was popular outside as well as inside the opera house because he wrote melodies which people could sing in taverns or whistle on street corners, tunes that could be performed by town bands, on barrel-organs and later on the accordion. His music and plots inspired many people and doubtless incited some of them to take up arms or make other sacrifices for Italy. Yet the operas of other composers had a similar effect, Bellini's *I puritani*, for example, or Donizetti's *Marino Faliero*.

Nearly all of Verdi's early operas – the fifteen he wrote before 1849 – soon went out of fashion, though a few enjoyed a revival in the twentieth century and then joined the international repertoire. Most of them share defects seldom found in the later works, including an over-hearty boisterousness and noise levels so much higher than those of his predecessors that Verdi seems to belong to a special category of loudness beside Beethoven; Queen Victoria was at least half right when she complained that *I masnadieri* was 'very noisy and trivial'. In addition, Verdi's orchestration in the early works is often primitive, sometimes repetitious and on occasion little more than an accompaniment, the equivalent of strumming, when all the strings are playing in unison. As Verdi rarely began to orchestrate before he started rehearsals, this is not altogether surprising. Critics have accused him of composing 'barrel-organ music', which is an unfair charge, but he did make excessive use of stage-bands, and some of his instrumental music carries a whiff of the fairground.

Artistic evaluation is fraught with the problems of subjectivity and in Verdi's case by the knowledge of how great a composer he became later, from *Rigoletto* (1851) onwards. Yet it is clear that, just as he was not a national patriotic figure in 1848, neither was he the Italians' favourite operatic composer at that time. Donizetti's operas were performed far more frequently. If Verdi had died after *Legnano*, at the age of thirty-five, his legacy would have looked poor compared to Bellini's, who had died at thirty-three. Without the knowledge that they had preceded *Il trovatore* and *La traviata*, it is unlikely that many of the early operas would be performed today; some of them, such as *Oberto*, *Alzira* and *Giovanna d'Arco*, might have disappeared altogether. Perhaps only *Nabucco*, *Ernani* and *Macbeth* would now be in the repertoire.

7

The Making of Italy

If the Austrian Empire had been defeated in 1848, the victorious new Italy would have been very different from the one that emerged a decade later. Like the Germany born in 1871, it would have become a confederation of states, each of them retaining its own government and parliament.* Even if Piedmont had been dominant in the north, it would not have been in a position to 'piedmontize' the rest of the peninsula. All the main rulers further south – the pope, the grand duke and the Neapolitan king – had accepted parliaments early in 1848, and they could surely have remained as constitutional monarchs within a confederation. Ferdinand of Naples and Leopold of Tuscany would then have had a status comparable to the Kings of Württemberg and Bavaria in 1871.

The chief loser in 1849 seemed to be Piedmont, yet the real victims of Austria's success in Italy were revolution and federalism. For all the passion of Mazzini and the heroics of Garibaldi, many of their patriotic contemporaries came to accept that independence would not be won by conspiracies and guerrilla warfare. Nor did an Italian confederation now seem a system sufficiently strong to confront the armies of the Austrian Empire. What Italy needed, patriots now argued, was a powerful dynasty – one like the Hohenzollern in Prussia – around which it could coalesce. And once Naples and Tuscany had revoked their constitutions and joined the Austrian side, the only possible can-

---

*Germany in 1871 contained four kingdoms, five grand duchies, twelve other duchies or principalities and the free cities of Hamburg, Lübeck and Bremen.

didate for the role was the Savoia, now represented by Charles Albert's son, Victor Emanuel II. Despite a war so disastrous that it had led to an abdication, the Savoia managed to shrug off the embarrassment of defeat and emerge as the standard-bearers of Italy, kings of the only constitutional and anti-Austrian state in the peninsula.

A significant figure in the rehabilitation of Piedmont was that improbable statesman, Massimo d'Azeglio, who in the spring of 1849 was close to despair. 'The people of Italy,' he had decided, were 'twenty per cent stupid, rascally and bold, eighty per cent stupid, honest and timid, and such a people has the government it deserves.' It was the Italians rather than the Austrians who were the real problem for Italy. 'Even if the Austrians went away of their own accord we should not be a nation as a result of that ... We have to give thought to forming Italians if we wish to have an Italy.'[1]

Azeglio was chosen as prime minister of Piedmont in May 1849 despite his lack of parliamentary and administrative experience; even since his election to the parliament in Turin the previous June, he had usually been absent from Piedmont, recuperating from his Vicenza wound. He appeared to have neither the enthusiasm nor the qualifications needed for high office, and he had already turned down offers of ministerial positions. Even as premier he did not hide his impatience or his boredom with debates in which he seldom participated. Yet unexpectedly he proved to be a success. An honest and clear-sighted politician, admired both at home and abroad, his wisdom and his moderation were crucial for the consolidation of the parliamentary system.

Azeglio's success in persuading the new king to accept the constitution was perhaps his most notable achievement. Victor Emanuel would have preferred to abolish parliament altogether, but Azeglio persuaded his bluff and uncouth new sovereign to retain a system which gave him the powers he most coveted: the supreme command of the armed forces and the authority to make war or peace without consulting parliament. The statesman also did his master a service by promoting his image as '*il re galantuomo*' ('the gentleman king'), a sobriquet that caught on and is still sometimes used to describe him. Later Azeglio came to regret this favour, realizing it was an unsuitable nickname for a boorish individual whose chief passions were hunting, philandering and posturing as a great commander.

Other priorities for Azeglio were the conclusion of a peace treaty with Austria and a reduction in the enormous power of the Church in Piedmont. During his premiership, legislation known as the Siccardi Laws introduced freedom of worship, abolished religious censorship, tackled the Church's control of education and ensured that civil and criminal cases involving priests would now be tried in state courts. Yet he remained unenthusiastic about the job and in the autumn of 1852, after three and a half years, he was happy to let it go. By then he was contending with difficulties with parliamentary opponents, who thought his anti-clericalism too weak, difficulties with the king who thought it too strong and refused to sign further laws 'that might displease the pope', and difficulties with a minister he had brought into government, the arrogant and assertive Cavour, who lorded it over cabinet meetings and even announced policy in parliament without consulting his colleagues.

On his resignation Azeglio refused a pension and honours, even an offer of the Order of the Annunziata, which would have given him the privilege of calling the king 'cousin'; as he himself informed Victor Emanuel, he was returning to the profession of painter, and it would hardly be fitting for the king's cousin to be a seller of pictures. Yet he remained involved in politics, and his letters of the period reveal him to have been Italy's shrewdest and most knowledgeable commentator on political affairs, a man who should have been consulted more often over the next decade both by Cavour, his successor, and by Victor Emanuel. One service he was persuaded to perform was to chaperone the king during a royal visit to London and Paris in 1855: his principal English duties were to prevent Victor Emanuel from making gaffes and coarse jokes at court and to read out the official speeches in Italian, a language which the monarch spoke badly. Cavour joined the party at the last moment and persuaded Victor Emanuel to trim his huge moustache, but neither he nor Azeglio could prevent him from gossiping maliciously in both capitals or telling a startled Queen Victoria that he hoped to execute Mazzini and exterminate the Austrians.

Camillo Benso, Count of Cavour, was a very different character from his predecessor. Assiduous and energetic, he was a natural parliamentarian who spoke clearly and intervened often in debates. He dominated the small 'Subalpine Parliament' in Turin, an oval hall in the Palazzo Carignano decorated with gilt and upholstered in red velvet so that it looked more like a theatre or a stage-set than a debating chamber. He also dominated his cabinets, frequently doing the work of colleagues whose abilities seemed to him inadequate. In 1855, in addition to his role as prime minister, he was foreign minister, finance minister and supervisor of the army and the navy.

Another way in which Cavour differed from Azeglio was in his lack of patriotic feeling. His instinct had always been to go north, to travel to Britain and France and see what was going on in the countries he most admired. In Italy he preferred to stay in Piedmont and seldom showed interest in the rest of the peninsula; never in his life did he go south of Pisa. Until his final years, he pooh-poohed the idea of unification and complained as late as 1856 that Manin, the Venetian patriot who now favoured Italian independence, was too preoccupied with 'the idea of Italian unity and other such nonsense'.[2] Yet the events of 1848–9 and his experience under Azeglio made him eager for a further fight with Austria. Were he able to obtain the support of Britain and France, he believed he could expel the Austrians from Italy and create an enlarged Piedmont spread across the whole of the north.

Ingratiation of these potential allies thus became an early goal in his premiership. One possible way of achieving it was to offer military support to both in their Crimean War against Russia, a curious proposal opposed by his colleagues and by the public, who did not see what Piedmont could conceivably gain from interfering in the Eastern Question. Cavour persisted, however, hoping that his new allies would be grateful and believing that the war would redeem Piedmont's military reputation; like later Italian leaders, he yearned for his country to be taken seriously by the powers of northern Europe. In 1855 a small army was duly dispatched to the Black Sea, where its men did nothing except die of cholera until they played a small role in a French victory near the end. Piedmont did not gain anything from the subsequent peace treaty in Paris.

Two years later, Cavour suggested to the British that they might like one of his navy's frigates to help their 'heroic soldiers' overcome the Indian Mutiny. This was another bizarre offer – especially as those heroes were fighting at Delhi, Kanpur and Lucknow, all of them more than 500 miles from the sea – and an interesting illustration of the anglophilia of the Risorgimento leaders. Garibaldi too supported the British against the 'mutineers' and together with both Cavour and Mazzini he also opposed independence for the Irish. In addition, he flattered the British by comparing them to the ancient Romans and telling them their country was the 'foremost in human progress, [the] enemy of despotism, the only safe refuge of the exile [and the] friend of the oppressed', adding theatrically that his sword was ever ready if England should need it. Azeglio was another gusher, judging 'the organization of English civilization' to be 'the finest that man [had] so far managed to evolve'. In return, the English loved Garibaldi, admired Azeglio and both liked and respected Mazzini. Those who had to deal with Cavour appreciated his abilities but found him untrustworthy and unscrupulous: in the words of the foreign secretary, Lord John Russell, he was just 'too French & too tricky'.[3]

Cavour's foreign policy of gestures co-existed with a wiser and more practical guidance of internal matters. The 1850s were the great decade of Piedmontese history, a time when tariffs went down, prosperity went up, railways multiplied and the textile industry became competitive. Much of this was owed to Cavour, who understood business and the economy. So was a healthy gust of liberalism. Piedmont became a freer and more relaxed place in which even Mazzini's works could be found in bookshops (though not Mazzini himself, who was back in exile in England). Censorship was not, however, abolished, and anomalies survived. The Sicilian setting of Verdi's *I vespri siciliani*, an opera which had had its première in Paris, needed to be changed to Portugal before it could be performed in Turin. Doubtless its subject matter was deemed too exciting for patriots absorbed by the possibilities of a Franco-Piedmontese alliance. The resulting *Giovanna de Guzman* appalled the critic of the *Gazzetta Piemontese*, who ridiculed the drama, a bad translation of a French libretto so poor that Verdi had even tried to cancel his contract with the Paris Opéra.[4]

The improvement in Piedmont's image led to a striking reversal of roles. Instead of Piedmontese dissidents scurrying across the border to the freer cities of Florence or Milan, Turin now attracted patriots from Lombardy, Venetia and the duchies of the Po Valley. Azeglio had welcomed thousands of immigrants on condition they renounced politics, and the state had benefited as a result; Piedmont received a new intelligentsia and became more Italian in its outlook. This hospitality was not, however, extended to Garibaldi until 1854; Mazzini remained out in the cold for ever.

Most patriot exiles came to believe that Italian independence could be achieved only under the Savoyard banner, and other options were gradually disregarded. Gioberti's hope of a federation under the pope was extinguished by political repression in Rome, while Mazzini discredited his own cause with a further series of futile plots and hopeless expeditions. Many republican supporters, who found their leader increasingly unrealistic and inflexible, moved over to the Piedmontese camp. Garibaldi was one of those who understood that in any war of independence Piedmont and its army would be essential. On refusing to become the leader of a Mazzinian insurrection, he explained that he would 'not risk making Italians a laughing stock by supporting an utterly useless rebellion'.[5]

Another convert was Daniele Manin who by 1856 was prepared to abandon republicanism and accept conditionally the House of Savoy as the monarchy of Italy. In a declaration in the London *Times*, he clarified his conditions.

> Convinced that above all Italy must be made, that this is the first and most important question, we say to the Monarchy of Savoy: 'Make Italy and we are with you. – If not, not.'
>
> And to the constitutionalists we say: 'Think about making Italy and not of enlarging Piedmont; be Italians and not municipalists, and we are with you. – If not, not.'[6]

Manin died the following year, but these late ideas of his inspired the new National Society, an organization dedicated to the goal of Italian independence. Garibaldi joined it and brought a number of Mazzinians with him, but the society never generated much popular enthusiasm. In fact it ended up as little more than a tool for Cavour and a propagandist for Piedmont. During the conflicts of 1859–60 it promised to organize insurrections in various parts of Italy, but these never quite came off. Its members were incapable of grasping how few people really shared their aspirations.

LOMBARDY AND THE DUCHIES, 1859

The great international hope of the Italian patriots was Louis Napoleon Bonaparte, Emperor of the French. Known as Napoleon III (though Napoleon II, like the boy Louis XVII, had never been crowned), his credentials were promising. His paternal uncle (Napoleon) had been King of Italy, his maternal uncle (Eugène) had been Viceroy of Italy, and he himself had spent childhood winters in Rome, where his mother had taken her sons after separating from their father, the former King of Holland. Italy thus became a second homeland to him. As a youth he considered himself an Italian patriot, planning an insane plot in Rome in 1830 and participating a year later in insurrections further north. Thereafter he turned his conspiratorial attentions to France, where, following a couple of farcical attempted coups, he became President of the Second Republic and four years later, in 1852, Emperor of the French. Although in 1848 France had for once stayed out of a conflict in Lombardy, the prospect of one day fighting on the soil of the first napoleonic triumphs remained a temptation difficult to discard.

Cavour was desperate for Napoleon's help, convinced that the emperor was the one sovereign in Europe prepared to assist the project he persistently referred to as 'the aggrandizement of Piedmont'. Since his fruitless adventure in the Crimea, the prime minister had become increasingly bellicose, talking repeatedly about expelling the Austrians from Italy and marching on Vienna. By the late 1850s, Napoleon was eager to promote the first part of this scheme, though he made various annoying demands of his putative ally. After Felice Orsini, a former Mazzinian, had tried to blow him up in Paris in early 1858, he insisted that Piedmont impose a censorship stricter than Cavour wanted, and as a result a small and harmless republican journal in Genoa was closed down. Earlier he had tried unsuccessfully to persuade the British to expel Mazzini from London although he, who had himself once been a refugee in England plotting conspiracies for the continent, might have felt some empathy with the Italian revolutionary.

Napoleon had a number of motives for bringing a French army

back to the plains of northern Italy. One of them may have been atavistic: warfare in the Po Valley between the great Catholic powers of Europe was a tradition going back so far that it seemed almost a normal form of international behaviour. A more important one was national and political. France's military prestige after Waterloo had not been sufficiently restored by its campaign in the Crimea, and it required a more solid victory on a more traditional battleground to regain pre-eminence in Europe. Such an outcome might bring a further bonus in the shape of territory, in particular Nice and Savoy, which Cavour was prepared to concede if he obtained Lombardy and Venetia. A third motive, also important, was the emperor's own need for prestige. Determined like his uncle to establish the Bonaparte dynasty among European royalty, he insisted that Victor Emanuel's young and high-minded daughter Clotilde should marry his middle-aged and dissolute cousin Prince Napoleon. Although not nearly as military or militarist as the first Napoleon, he also felt the need for a little personal *gloire* to increase his popularity at home. In this particular quest he succeeded, his victories against the Austrians in 1859 and the subsequent peace being celebrated with bonfires across his empire.

Yet there was another, more altruistic motive. Remembering his youth in Italy, he came to share some of the country's patriotic aspirations, even if he hoped that a future north Italian state would depend on France as an ally. Unusually for anyone, especially a sovereign, his attempted assassination made him feel more sympathetic to the cause of the aspiring assassin. He tried hard to save Orsini from the guillotine and, when this proved politically impossible – Orsini's bombs had missed their target but killed eight bystanders – he asked the Italian to appeal to him in a public letter to support the patriotic cause. Thereafter Napoleon was willing to fight for that cause so long as Cavour could make it appear that Austria was the aggressor.

In July 1858 the French emperor and the Piedmontese prime minister met secretly at Plombières, a spa town in Lorraine, where they broadly agreed on how a future Italy might be organized. After their war with Austria they envisaged that the peninsula would have three sizable states: Piedmont, expanded to include Parma, Modena, Lombardy-Venetia and the Romagna; Tuscany, enlarged by the addition of Umbria and the Papal Marches; and the Two Sicilies, where the

Bourbons might be removed and replaced by the emperor's cousin, Lucien Murat, a son of King Joachim. It was not an impossible plan though it was naive to expect the Marches, with few historic links to Tuscany, to submit to Florence on the other side of the Apennines. Apart from Austria, the chief loser in the scheme would be the papacy, which would be deprived of most of its territories, but the pope, as a compensatory gesture, might become president of an Italian confederation.

Yet none of this plan could be implemented if a pretext could not be found for starting a war. And how, wondered Cavour, could you provoke a conflict that your enemy didn't want while pretending it was you yourself who was reluctant to fight? Another difficulty was that public opinion in France and Piedmont was opposed to a war. There was little enthusiasm even among the patriots of Lombardy, where, after a repressive period in the early 1850s, Austrian rule had become more tolerant under the new viceroy, the Archduke Maximilian, later to be the ill-fated and short-reigned Emperor of Mexico. In England as well people were opposed to the idea of a conflict that was looking increasingly like a simple land-grab. When in January 1859 Victor Emanuel told the parliament in Turin about 'the cry of anguish' he was hearing from all over Italy – a phrase inserted at the request of Napoleon – the British were not impressed, suspecting rightly that the cries, if they existed, were extremely muffled. The leading figures of the Whig government that came to power in 1859 – Palmerston, Russell and Gladstone – were indeed supporters of Italian independence: Gladstone found it outrageous that the Austrians, 'glaringly inferior in refinement', were arbitrarily ruling 'a race much more advanced', while Palmerston, the prime minister, remarked that the Austrians had 'no business in Italy' and were 'a public nuisance there'.[7] Yet they did not think Vienna's occupation of Lombardy merited a European war, and they were concerned that Cavour seemed interested less in Italian freedom than in the expansion of Piedmont.

Alarmed by international opposition, Napoleon lost his nerve and suggested delaying the campaign for a year. Cavour was enraged, especially with the British, whom he accused of egotism and pettiness. When in March the Powers suggested a conference to discuss the situation, he rushed to Paris, harangued the French and threatened as revenge to ally Piedmont with England. He also declared himself ready to start a wider conflagration, to 'set Europe alight' to get his own way. One scheme was to encourage an uprising against the Austrians in Hungary, but the 20,000 rifles he sent the rebels by boat up the Danube arrived after the revolt was over.

International pressure persuaded Victor Emanuel and most of his cabinet to accept disarmament, but the prime minister held out until mid-April when France forced him to back down too. Although Cavour's dreams seemed to have dissolved, they were revived the following week when the Austrians lost their heads and delivered an ultimatum insisting that Piedmont reduce its army and disband its volunteers. On hearing of this blunder, Cavour was so euphoric that, unmusical though he was, he apparently flung open his study window and sang an aria from *Il trovatore*. In the eyes of a Europe astonished by the Austrian provocation, he had suddenly become the beleaguered statesman rather than the calculating aggressor. Furthermore, the much-desired war could now be fought against an enemy that had forfeited international sympathy and support.

The Habsburg government made a more honourable blunder by waiting three days for its ultimatum to expire and thus missing the chance to capture Turin before the French army arrived. The outcome of the campaign was decided by two battles in Lombardy in June, which ended in victories for France but in which its Italian allies played undistinguished parts. One of them, Magenta, was so sanguinary that it gave its name to the artists' colour magenta, but little Piedmontese blood helped inspire the name since the army did not arrive at the battlefield until nightfall, after the struggle was over. At the other, Solferino, the sight of wounded soldiers left to die was so horrifying to one Swiss witness that he went home and founded the International Red Cross.

At Solferino the Piedmontese did take part, fighting on the French flank near the village of San Martino. Yet this second contest was also a victory won by Napoleon's divisions; the Battle of San Martino was at best a draw between Victor Emanuel's army and a much smaller Habsburg force. For all their country's martial traditions, the Piedmontese commanders seemed to have no idea how to fight a battle. An artillery barrage and a concerted infantry assault might have compelled the Austrians to retreat. Yet much of the artillery was stationed too far away to be of use, and the infantry brigades, instead of combining in a massed attack, took it in turns to advance, charging with the bayonet and failing to break through.

The poor Piedmontese performance can be partly attributed to Victor Emanuel who, despite his lack of military experience, insisted on his constitutional right to be commander-in-chief. The king possessed courage and exposed himself to the enemy but he demonstrated no qualities relevant to generalship. Officers at the battle found him confused, indecisive and lacking any understanding of the geography of the battlefield. He galloped across the terrain, pursued by his staff, so that his field commanders could not tell where he was when they needed reinforcements. When one of them suggested he position himself on a height so that he could both see the battle and be seen by his troops, he seemed astonished by the idea.[8]

The Piedmontese could claim success, however, because in the evening the Austrians, after repulsing attacks all day, were obliged to fall back in line with their comrades whom the French had defeated; the villages the Italians had failed to capture in combat were thus occupied as the enemy withdrew, and a mighty victory was soon proclaimed. The battle acquired the status of a sort of Italian Austerlitz and was duly consecrated in textbooks and commemorated on site by a Risorgimento museum and a huge tower with a spiral staircase and frescoes of episodes from the 'wars of independence'. As in most memorials of the era, Victor Emanuel dominates both the frescoes and the sculptures: one painting depicts him being ushered into the Forum by a Roman legionary, as if he were about to join a pantheon with Caesar and Scipio Africanus. Close by is an ossuary containing on one wall of its nave the names of all Italian soldiers killed in 1859; at the east end their skulls are piled high on shelves above layers of human bones.

A fortnight after the battle, Napoleon suggested a truce and a meeting with his opposite number, the Habsburg Franz Josef. The two emperors met at Villafranca near Verona and, without consulting Victor Emanuel, agreed on the terms of a peace. Austria would retain Venetia; Piedmont would acquire Lombardy except for the fortified towns of Mantua and Peschiera; the Habsburg rulers of Tuscany and

Modena would return to the thrones from which they had recently been deposed; and an Italian confederation would be established which would include Austria in its role as a ruler of Italian territory.

After his two victories Napoleon might have carried on the war with the expectation of conquering Venetia. Yet he lacked his uncle's imperviousness to the sight of casualties and he was sickened by the carnage of Magenta and Solferino. He was also alarmed by signs that Prussia might enter the war on Austria's side if the conflict continued. A third factor in his decision was disillusionment with his Piedmontese allies. Led to believe that he would be fighting a war of liberation, he was disappointed to find that the Lombards seemed unanxious to be liberated. He was also disgruntled with the military performance of the Piedmontese. After Solferino he had planned to continue eastwards to the four Austrian fortresses known as the Quadrilateral, and he had allotted the task of capturing the north-western one, Peschiera, to his Italian allies. The Piedmontese should have been well equipped for the job because they had recently bought a siege train from Sweden, but unfortunately they had forgotten to bring it with them on campaign. After Napoleon learned of the oversight and was informed the artillery would not arrive for another three weeks, he decided to end the war.[9]

The fiasco over the siege train was not the only error for which Cavour, acting as minister for war as well as prime minister, was partly responsible. Perhaps his most egregious mistake was his failure to prevent his unseasoned and incompetent monarch from commanding the army. Other shortcomings were apparent in his handling of supplies and administration. The Piedmontese did not possess enough horses, and those they did have often went lame because there were not enough horseshoes. The army had neither reserves nor enough uniforms nor even proper maps of Lombardy; its soldiers were shod in boots that baked in the summer heat, making them feel they were wearing wooden clogs. At Plombières Cavour had offered Napoleon an army of 100,000 but in the event he could provide only half that number. The Piedmontese had also boasted that the cause would attract 200,000 volunteers, but only a tenth of that figure turned up – and there were not nearly enough weapons even for them. Those 20,000 rifles sent to the Hungarians would have been more useful at home.

Victor Emanuel accepted the armistice, but Cavour reacted so violently to its terms that observers believed he had become unhinged. He ranted at the king and tried to force him to carry on the war without the French. When Victor Emanuel rejected this lunatic idea, his prime minister resigned and retired to his estate at Leri, where he settled down to study Machiavelli. Regretting the impetuosity of his actions, he was soon plotting a return to power.

While planning the campaign against Austria, Cavour had simultaneously been preparing expansion into central Italy. His project was greatly advanced by a strange day in Florence, 27 April, when a peaceful demonstration of local patriots, supported by some soldiers, led within a few hours to a revolution and the fall of the Habsburg–Lorraine dynasty. Leopold II, the grand duke, had lost some of his popularity in 1849 when an Austrian army brought him back to power and quartered itself in Tuscany for several years at the state's expense. Yet the grand duchy's regime remained benign and tolerant enough to annoy the pope, who often rebuked Leopold for being too kind to Jews and Protestants. On the morning of the 27th few of the grand duke's subjects wanted him overthrown except for some radicals and republicans concentrated in Florence and Livorno. Even moderate patriots, headed by Baron Ricasoli and other liberal aristocrats, were happy to keep him if he was prepared to ally his duchy with Piedmont. At noon on that fateful day, Leopold accepted this condition. Alarmed by the size of the demonstration and the hoisting of the tricolour flag, he even agreed to join the war and appoint a government of liberal conservatives. As these concessions did not assuage the demonstrators, moderate leaders suggested that the grand duke might prevent revolution and save his dynasty by abdicating in favour of his son. We cannot know whether this tactic would have worked because Leopold refused to try it: instead of abdicating, he decided to leave the duchy altogether. After two dynasties and more than three centuries of grand dukes, Tuscans watched the departure of their last sovereign with much bewilderment and some sorrow.

In Tuscany the situation was thus ready to be exploited, but Cavour knew he needed evidence of popular support there and elsewhere in central Italy if his expansionist policy were to be acceptable to the rest of Europe. Lombardy had proved to be an embarrassment: Milan had

THE MAKING OF ITALY

not been engulfed by the patriotic fervour of 1848, and there had been no 'Five Days' of heroism and self-sacrifice on the barricades. The correspondent of the London *Times* saw no unrest in Lombardy and was unable to see signs of anti-Austrian sentiment even in parts of Piedmont: in Piedmontese country districts he even witnessed people welcoming the Austrian troops, helping them cross a river and reproaching them for not arriving earlier; they abhorred their own government, they explained, because it overloaded them with taxes to maintain an army they did not want and could not afford.[10]

Determined to conjure a better display of patriotism in the central duchies, Cavour ordered Giuseppe La Farina, the secretary of the National Society, to arrange 'spontaneous' demonstrations of support for the Italian cause. Although La Farina assured the prime minister that he could do this, the National Society proved incapable of organizing such affairs in the cities of the Po Valley. To the consternation of Cavour and the frustration of Napoleon, who felt he had been duped, patriotic enthusiasm in the summer of 1859 was neither strong nor widespread.

Austria's defeat at Magenta and the withdrawal of its garrisons from the Papal States had, however, created a revolutionary situation. The rulers of Parma and Modena fled their capitals, and in their duchies, as well as in Tuscany and the Romagna, provisional governments led by local patriots were established. These then organized assemblies of more patriots who rejected the terms of the Franco-Austrian agreement at Villafranca, formally deposed the ducal dynasties and demanded annexation by Piedmont. The crucial figures were Bettino Ricasoli in Florence and Luigi Carlo Farini in Modena, who acquired dictatorial powers in their cities and, at a time when Cavour was sulking on his estate, managed to undermine the armistice and maintain the momentum of the patriotic movement. Well-timed support for them soon came from the Whig government in London, which sanctimoniously rejoiced at 'the gratifying prospect of a people building up the edifice of their liberties, and consolidating the work of their independence, amid the sympathies and good wishes of Europe'.[11]

Cavour was still so much the dominant politician of Piedmont that in January 1860, despite the reluctance of the king, he was back in office. With his extraordinary talent for improvising and adapting to circumstances, he saw a chance to discard the provisions of both Plombières and Villafranca and by means of plebiscites of annexing central Italy to Piedmont. He disliked Ricasoli, who was haughty and principled and disrespectful of himself, but he realized that his co-operation was essential. With Tuscany, Piedmont would become the kingdom of northern Italy; without it, it would be just a bigger Piedmont.

Ricasoli was a Florentine patriot who had long supported the idea of Italian unification. Yet he wanted a genuine union – what he called 'fusion' – rather than mere annexation by Piedmont. Many Tuscans felt, as he did, that they were more Italian and more civilized than the Piedmontese, and they did not want to play a subordinate role in the new entity. Cavour tried to calm these anxieties by promising them autonomy, but Ricasoli remained hesitant about holding a referendum on annexation. A proud and high-minded man, his austerity tempered only by his pleasure in making Chianti wine, he had a fateful decision to make. The choice was between a 'finis Etruriae', the ending of a long tradition of independence, or preserving it and risking Tuscany's reduction to an unimportant statelet, perhaps a sort of Monaco surrounded by a new country that might become one of the great nations of Europe. Ricasoli agonized over the dilemma but he stuck to the national patriotic cause. Yet even after Tuscans had voted by a large majority to accept annexation, he was in a melancholy mood, wondering whether his fellow countrymen might one day curse the union he had brought about. Later he said he found the Piedmontese 'yoke' more antipathetic than the Austrian one because the new rulers could not understand how Tuscans wished 'to be Italian and to feel a new Italian spirit'.[12]

In the spring of 1860 patriotic fervour in northern and central Italy was undoubtedly stronger than it had been the previous summer. In the Tuscan plebiscite only 15,000 people preferred a separate kingdom to annexation by Piedmont, and in Farini's Emilia – a new region consisting of Modena, Parma and the Romagna – the minority was officially only 756, an impossibly low figure. Further plebiscites were held in Nice and Savoy, which had been promised to Napoleon first at Plombières and later in return for French support for the Italian annexations. Cavour had been forced to pretend that no promise had been made partly because Nice was Garibaldi's home town and partly because it would have been awkward to explain to Savoyard soldiers, whom he needed for the war, that they would be fighting for the privilege of exchanging their nationality. When the plan became public in March 1860, Garibaldi denounced it, pointing out that 'in 1388 Nice joined itself to Piedmont on condition that it should never be alienated to any foreign power'. The most famous of all Nizzards also allowed himself to become involved in a daft plot with an English adventurer called Laurence Oliphant. On the day of the plebiscite, the two men decided to sail to Nice with 200 volunteers, smash the ballot boxes in the city and burn the voting papers, after which, according to Oliphant's unverified and unreliable account, Garibaldi would have declared himself president of an independent Nice.[13] Fortunately for the great man's reputation, the plan was thwarted by a summons to Sicily and a journey to immortality. Oliphant went by himself to Nice, where he noticed that the polling station he visited was devoid of 'no' voting papers. In that city those voting for annexation by France outnumbered those against it by 100 to one, while the ratio in Savoy was more than 500 to one. As in Emilia, only pressure and manipulation could have obtained affirmative majorities of 99 per cent.

SICILY AND NAPLES, 1860

Garibaldi was diverted from the escapade in Nice by news of a revolt in Sicily and pressure from a number of patriotic colleagues who begged him to lead an expedition in its support. In early April a Mazzinian plot in Palermo, which was quickly suppressed, had touched off a wider rebellion in the interior: bands of hostile and impoverished peasants spread across the island, killing or ejecting policemen and tax collectors and eliminating all form of local government. Many educated Sicilians approved of the rebellion against the Bourbons but were nervous of the other aims of an essentially social uprising. A few of them wanted independence and a few others hoped for union with the rest of Italy; Francesco Crispi, a lawyer and a future Italian prime minister, opted for union partly because he considered his fellow islanders incapable of ruling themselves. Most Sicilians were autonomists, however, who would have been content with a revival of the 1812 constitution and the distant sovereignty of the Bourbons. Their dislike of Naples was more vivid than their desire to join Italy.

Garibaldi was delighted by the tidings from Sicily and enthusiastic about the idea of an expedition there. He was an idealistic man with a simplistic ideology. Italy must be free and united, and its enemies – principally the pope, the Bourbons and the Austrians – must be overthrown. Although originally a republican, he now realized that the national cause was only likely to succeed under the leadership of Victor Emanuel.

The Sicilian uprising seemed to be faltering in mid-April, when Bourbon forces regained control of the coastal regions. Garibaldi was disheartened by the news and vacillated over his impending expedition. He had criticized Mazzini for irresponsible adventures and he did not wish to emulate Carlo Pisacane, the socialist patriot whose followers had been annihilated after landing three years earlier on the Neapolitan coast. Another problem was munitions. Garibaldi's lieutenants had gone off to collect the money, arms and volunteers that were always available for any enterprise commanded by himself, but Azeglio, now the Governor of Milan, blocked a consignment of modern British rifles. 'We could declare war on Naples,' wrote the former prime minister, 'but not have a diplomatic representative there and send rifles to the Sicilians.'[14]

At the end of the month, after further dispiriting news from Sicily, Garibaldi called the expedition off, but two days later, apparently convinced by Crispi that the rebellion was still active, decided to go ahead after all. As soon as one of his lieutenants had seized two steamships in the harbour of Genoa, he dressed himself up in the outfit he had picked up in South America – red shirt, pale poncho and silk handkerchief – and set off with his 'Thousand' volunteers across the Tyrrhenian Sea, a voyage that propelled him and them into legend and into comparisons with the 'three hundred' soldiers of Leonidas, the Spartan king who had held the pass of Thermopylae against the Persian army in 480 BC. It was indeed an heroic enterprise but it was also, incontrovertibly, illegal. Apart from stealing the two ships, Garibaldi was making an unprovoked attack on a recognized state with which his country, Piedmont-Sardinia, was not at war. History may have forgiven him for the deed, but it was an act of piracy all the same.

The Neapolitan king, Francesco II, did not at first take the expedition seriously. To him it seemed another adventure in the manner of Pisacane and the Bandiera brothers, a raid by a rabble of revolutionaries who would easily be defeated, despite the support of local rebels, by his troops on the island. Yet Garibaldi was a successful and charismatic guerrilla leader who enjoyed other advantages as well. King Ferdinand had died the previous year at Caserta after a reign of twenty-nine years, and his son, nicknamed Franceschiello, was young, timid and inexperienced. The Kingdom of the Two Sicilies had few allies except Austria, which was no longer in a position to help, and it had broken off diplomatic relations with Britain and France following their governments' denunciations of Ferdinand's 'despotism'. The current Napoleon was unsympathetic to the Bourbons because he wanted their throne for his cousin Murat, and the British disliked them because Gladstone had convinced his colleagues that they presided over a uniquely awful regime. The hostility of France and Britain was fatal to the Bourbons because those nations had the means to decide whether ships might or might not reach their destinations in the Mediterranean. Had they wished to do so, their navies could have prevented Garibaldi from landing in Sicily in May and from crossing to Calabria in August.

While the expedition enjoyed the support of the small number of southern patriots, it also had backing, equivocal and confusing though this often was, from inside the Piedmontese establishment. Even those who opposed it did so halfheartedly. Cavour tried to dissuade the Thousand from embarking but he did not threaten force to deter them. Later he dispatched the Piedmontese navy to intercept the stolen ships, to prevent reinforcements from reaching Sicily and to delay Garibaldi's crossing of the Straits of Messina. But the navy's failure to achieve any of these objectives was not entirely the fault of the commander, the inept Count of Persano. Without some degree of official connivance, it is difficult to see how steamships could have been seized in Piedmont's principal port, how the expedition could have managed to reach its destinations, and how so many soldiers 'on leave' from the Piedmontese army could have enlisted with the volunteers.

Garibaldi was lucky with his landing at Marsala on Sicily's west coast on 11 May. The Bourbon garrison had just marched off to Trapani, and Neapolitan ships protecting the town had just sailed off to the south; later, when one of these vessels returned, it delayed firing at the red-shirted volunteers who were in the process of disembarking for fear of hitting two British ships in the harbour. The *garibaldini* had expected a welcome from islanders pining for liberation and were thus surprised to find a complete absence of enthusiasm for their arrival; also disconcerting was the invisibility of the revolt they had come to support. A few days later, however, the Thousand defeated a badly led Neapolitan force at Calatafimi and attracted a small number of Sicilians to their ranks. After the battle Garibaldi marched eastwards, capturing Palermo in June and Milazzo in July, landing on the Calabrian mainland in August and reaching Naples in September, four months after he had set forth from the Ligurian coast. In Palermo, where he established a government with himself as interim dictator and Crispi as secretary of state, he demonstrated his radical zeal by abolishing the grist tax and promising land reform for the peasants. Yet he could not go as far as he wished in this direction since he could not afford to alienate those landowners whose support was crucial for the achievement of political union with the north.

Although Garibaldi displayed courage and military skill in his campaign, the heroics were not quite on the scale that legend suggests. He did not defeat the 25,000 Neapolitan troops on the island with the thousand men he had arrived with at Marsala; over the summer, reinforcements from the north brought his own forces to more than 21,000. Nor was outrageous valour always required to overcome an enemy that, while well equipped, was poorly commanded and widely scattered. The young king was encumbered both with octogenarian ministers and with septuagenarian generals, one of whom had fought at Waterloo. These officers were not only old but also cowardly, incompetent and in some cases treacherous. At Calatafimi the Bourbon forces were positioned on a hilltop, inflicting casualties on the *garibaldini* attacking up the slope, when they were inexplicably ordered to retreat. One general foolishly suggested a truce which allowed Garibaldi to re-arm and take control of Palermo, another withdrew his troops unnecessarily from Catania to Messina, and officers from both the army and the navy deserted and took bribes. Some of these individuals were subsequently sent to the island of Ischia in the Bay of Naples, where the guilty ones were lightly demoted.

In Calabria Garibaldi found the opposition even feebler than in Sicily. Although the Neapolitan generals had 16,000 soldiers in the toe of Italy, they put up little resistance and sometimes submitted without firing a shot; one battalion surrendered to six wandering *garibaldini* who had got lost.[15] Reggio was handed over with hardly a fight, and so was Cosenza. In Naples the minister for war announced in the mornings that he was departing for Calabria to defeat Garibaldi but then changed his mind in the afternoons because he considered his presence in the capital was essential to prevent disorder.[16] Well did he and the other generals deserve a dismissive line in Richard Strauss's opera, *Der Rosenkavalier*: when the Marschallin thinks she is about to be surprised with her lover, she decides to confront her husband, the field marshal: '*Ich bin kein napolitanischer General: wo ich steh' steh' ich.*' ('I am not a Neapolitan general: where I stand I stand.')

On 7 September Garibaldi entered Naples by train, in advance of his army, where he was welcomed by Bourbon officials: the minister of police had already sycophantically told him that the city was waiting 'with the greatest impatience . . . to greet the redeemer of Italy and to place in his hands the power and destiny of the state'.[17] King Francesco had left the city the previous day, intending to carry on the war from Gaeta, the coastal fortress town near the border with the Papal States in the north. For all his limitations, he was a conscientious and honourable monarch who realized that a siege of Italy's largest and most densely populated city would cause terrible carnage. But he did not shirk or run away like the dukes of central Italy had done a year before. He left garrisons in the castles of Naples and marched out, leaving nearly all his money and his personal possessions in his capital. He expected to return.

In the north of the kingdom the Bourbon army was transformed. Loyal regiments from Naples and other provinces of the mainland fought valiantly and were victorious in several skirmishes against the redshirts near Capua. Yet once again the generalship was defective, too slow, too cautious, too lacking in imagination. An urgent and vigorous counter-attack might have defeated the smaller enemy force; but when the advance eventually came, Garibaldi halted it on the River Volturno, a dogged defensive action in which he lost more men than his opponents. Even then the Neapolitans might have remained undefeated if the contest had been limited to themselves and the volunteers.

As soon as Cavour realized that Garibaldi would conquer Sicily, he was eager to annex the island to Piedmont. He had always detested home-grown revolutionaries more than he disliked Bourbons and Austrians, and the last thing he wanted was to see Sicily and possibly Naples in the hands of democrats and other radicals. Once the redshirts had reached Palermo, he therefore sent his representative, La Farina, who arrived in early June with posters proclaiming 'We want annexation'. It was a strange appointment because La Farina was an insensitive individual and a well-known antagonist of both Garibaldi and Crispi. So much of his time in Sicily was spent intriguing and causing friction among members of the new government that after a month Garibaldi had him arrested and sent back north.

In Naples Cavour chose to employ a tactic similar to that which La Farina had failed with the previous year in the Po Valley: arranging a 'spontaneous' uprising in the city – and doing so before Garibaldi arrived. He duly sent Persano to the Bay of Naples with money in his pockets to bribe officials, and soldiers hidden on his ships ready to rush to the aid of the conspirators on land. In the city the Piedmontese ambassador duly gave the signal for revolt but, as so often with these Cavourian schemes, nothing happened. The Neapolitans were sensibly waiting to see which side was likely to win before committing themselves to the conflict.

Cavour's next project was more successful. Believing that Garibaldi would not stop at Naples but carry on to Rome, he decided to invade the Papal States, ostensibly to protect the pope from the redshirts, in reality to take the initiative from their leader, finish the war on an heroic note and ultimately acquire Naples. Garibaldi would be unable to offer resistance, he calculated, because although both his king and his prime minister considered him an enemy, he was publicly fighting for them with the slogan 'Italy and Victor Emanuel'. He was presumably unaware that the king was hoping for his defeat and even in September was urging Francesco to take the offensive, defeat Garibaldi and execute him. Cavour's tactics were more subtle and devious. In June he suggested an alliance with the Bourbons and as late as October was assuring Francesco that Piedmont's quarrel was not with him but with Garibaldi. But simultaneously he was plotting to undermine the Neapolitan regime and annex its territories. Although Cavour admitted he had little knowledge and no experience of Naples, he now managed to delude himself into thinking that its inhabitants were eager for annexation by Piedmont and could be absorbed by the expanding new kingdom without difficulty. A more perceptive calculation came from Azeglio, who knew the city and believed that only one Neapolitan in twenty wanted his country to be annexed.

Although Cavour professed protectiveness to the pope and amity to Francesco, he treated their subjects as if they were the eternal enemies of Piedmont. In September he dispatched an ultimatum to the papal government demanding the disbanding of its army and ordered his own troops to cross the border before an answer could be received; he also tried – and failed – to stage an uprising in Rome. The Piedmontese army, commanded by General Cialdini, then brushed aside a papal force before bombarding the port of Ancona into submission. At Ancona the army was joined by Victor Emanuel himself, along with Farini, the designated viceroy of Naples, and they moved south towards the Neapolitan border, still uncertain whether they were meant to be fighting the Bourbons or the redshirts. For Cialdini they were both enemies, as were the peasants whom he executed on the spot if they were found with firearms. It did not matter if they were trying to defend their property or support their legitimate sovereign; in the general's eyes they were simply 'rebels' and 'brigands'.

In Naples Garibaldi was more cooperative than his adversaries expected. After capturing the large Bourbon fleet there, he handed it over to Persano, thereby more than doubling the size of the Piedmontese navy and closing his option of using the ships to sail up the coast and attack Rome with his redshirts. Despite his undoubted authority, he did not attempt to thwart Piedmontese plans and he was willing to hand over his government to Victor Emanuel after the results of the planned plebiscites were known. He also submitted to the king's decision to take personal military command, a move that allowed Cialdini to turn his attention to Francesco's army and bombard the town of Capua. Garibaldi, who had never shelled a civilian population, was amazed and horrified, while Neapolitans must have been puzzled to observe how Victor Emanuel, who had ordered the bombardment, was proving to be so much more of a 'Bomba' than their old King Ferdinand.

While Cavour was reassuring both Pius and Francesco, he was pressing ahead with the annexation of most of the remaining Papal States (Umbria and the Marches) and the whole of the Kingdom of the Two Sicilies. He insisted that Garibaldi should hold plebiscites in Naples and Sicily as soon as possible and promised autonomy to both if voters chose annexation, though not everyone was convinced of his sincerity in this matter: Cattaneo's journal in Milan regarded the promise as 'a mere hoax to attract the public opinion of Naples and Sicily'.[18] Like Ricasoli in Tuscany, Crispi wanted to belong to a new entity, a new Italy, not to an old but greatly enlarged Piedmont. Yet Cavour insisted on 'annexation', though he was careful not to put the word on the ballot paper. Annexation plainly meant 'piedmontization', the imposition of northern laws, customs and institutions on distant regions with no experience of their workings. Such a process was already under way in Sicily, where Piedmontese laws were introduced in August, where the lira with the king's head appeared in the same month and where officials were forced to swear loyalty to Victor Emanuel and his constitution. In October the minister of justice in Turin persuaded his colleagues to agree to the abolition of the law codes in force in the southern lands and their replacement by the less enlightened legal system of Piedmont.

The plebiscites were held on 21 October and, as in the north, men went to the urns in an atmosphere of exhilaration, hope, pressure and intimidation. Undoubtedly a large majority voted for union with Piedmont and – also without doubt – the majority was not as big as the figures claimed: 99 per cent, with four-fifths of the Sicilian districts reporting no negative votes at all. The vote itself was hardly unbiased since the ballot paper offered the alternatives of simply 'yes' and 'no' to the supposition that 'the Sicilian people desire to form an integral

A jumble of Romes: the classical, the papal and the nationalist. The Capitoline Hill is on the left, the Victor Emanuel monument beyond, the Forum in front and the dome of San Martino and San Luca on the right

Cicero (*left*) and Virgil: great Romans and perhaps proto-Italians

Theodora, the formidable Byzantine empress, immortalized in mosaic in Ravenna

Dante reciting *The Divine Comedy* beside the dome built by Brunelleschi long after his death. Painted by Domenico di Michelino in the fifteenth century

Medieval Bologna

Apulian Romanesque: the Cathedral of Trani. For many crusaders embarking for the Holy Land, this was their last sight of western Europe

Pisan Romanesque: the Church of San Michele in Lucca, with the archangel on the top

Gothic Florence: the Palazzo Vecchio, headquarters of the republic, with the Chianti Hills behind

Renaissance Florence: Alberti's Church of Santa Maria Novella

Federigo da Montefeltro, builder and warrior, by Piero della Francesca

Isabella d'Este, daughter of Ferrara, ruler of Mantua, by Titian

The irascible Julius II, most martial of all popes, by Raphael

Cosimo de' Medici, first Grand Duke of Tuscany, by Agnolo Bronzino

The Doges' Palace by John Ruskin, self-proclaimed 'foster child' of Venice

The Miracle of the Relic of the True Cross on the Rialto, painted by Vittore Carpaccio in 1494, when the bridge was still wooden

Enlightened despots: the Habsburg emperor Joseph II (*right*) with his brother Peter Leopold, Grand Duke of Tuscany, by Pompeo Batoni

Napoleon Bonaparte at the bridge of Lodi (1796), one of his first Italian victories, by Louis Lejeune

Milan's La Scala in the mid-nineteenth century, by Angelo Inganni

'The Bear of Busseto': Giuseppe
Verdi mellowing in old age

Massimo d'Azeglio, artist turned statesman, by Francesco Hayez

Giuseppe Mazzini, the prophet in exile

Camillo Benso di Cavour, the arch-pragmatist of Risorgimento politics

Ferdinand of Savoy, Duke of Genoa, steadfast on his dying horse, by Alfonso Balzico

His brother, Victor Emanuel, first King of Italy, by P. Litta

Francesco II, last King of the Two Sicilies, with his wife Maria Sofia in exile

Pius IX, longest-serving of all popes and last sovereign of the Papal States

Crestfallen on Caprera: Giuseppe Garibaldi on his island home, by
Vincenzo Cabianca and Pietro Senno

The Piedmontese camp at Magenta (1859) by Giovanni Fattori, a
proclaimed victory although in fact the Italian troops arrived too late to
affect the outcome of the battle

Nineteenth-century Naples from the sea

Piazza Castello, the heart of Turin

Mussolini declaims in the early years of his dictatorship

The March on Rome (1922): fascists destroy photographs of Lenin and Karl Marx

In love with Olivetti: female emancipation begins its very long march

Fascist style: a nude Roman, a rearing horse and the Palace of Italian Civilization at EUR in Rome

The young leopard: Giuseppe Tomasi di Lampedusa (*right*) with his cousin, the poet Lucio Piccolo

Communist charisma: the Sardinian Enrico Berlinguer

Christian statesmanship: the Trentino Alcide De Gasperi

Populist and seducer: Silvio Berlusconi with friends

part of Italy one and indivisible under Victor Emanuel as their constitutional king'; people tempted to vote 'no' were not told what they
might get instead. It was difficult also to hold a free vote when Francesco was still holding out, when Cialdini was still bombarding Capua,
and when most voters were illiterate and had no idea who Victor
Emanuel was. In Naples the French writer Maxime Du Camp witnessed crowds of people shouting 'Long live Italy!' before asking him
to explain what Italy was and what it meant.[19]

The results of the plebiscites deceived Cavour into believing that
southerners wanted annexation and would not mind if he relinquished
complicated ideas of autonomy in favour of a programme of piedmontization. If he had only gone to Naples, he might have come to
understand the situation and avoid the mistakes that soon led to civil
war. But he refused to travel to the largest city in Italy because he had
already visited too many northern provinces with Victor Emanuel and
could no longer tolerate the royal company. So instead he sent the
Modenese Farini to take over from Garibaldi as governor of the
southern mainland. This appointment was even more disastrous than
that of the Sicilian La Farina to Palermo the year before. Both men
were tactless, self-important and personal enemies of Garibaldi. Farini
was also contemptuous of southerners, whom he described as a com-
pound of 'sloth and *maccheroni*'. Ten days after his arrival in October,
he concluded that the south was 'not Italy but Africa' and that 'the
bedouin' were 'the flower of civic virtue when compared' to Neapolitans. Writing from the 'hell-pit' of Naples a few weeks later, he
recognized that the plebiscite result had given an erroneous impression of the southern desire for annexation. People now appeared to
oppose unification in exactly the same ratio as they had voted for it in
October. 'In 7 million inhabitants of Naples there are not a hundred
who want a united Italy. Nor are there any liberals to speak of.' If the
Turin parliament did not impose its authority, he believed the annexation of Naples would become 'the gangrene of the rest of the state'.[20]

Garibaldi had offered to become viceroy instead of Farini, and he
would have been both a more suitable and a more popular choice. But
Cavour was intent on removing the man who had just handed him
such vast new territories to govern. Persistently churlish to Garibaldi,
he had even gone so far as to order his subordinates 'to hurl the

garibaldini into the sea' if they resisted Cialdini's advance. Other Piedmontese figures, jealous of the 'liberator's' success and fearful of his popularity, competed in the belittling of the one indisputably heroic figure among the leaders of the Risorgimento. Cialdini even told Garibaldi not to exaggerate his successes and claimed, absurdly, that the Piedmontese army had rescued him on the Volturno.

Garibaldi's behaviour during the handover of power was irreproachable. He asked for no reward and rejected the king's offers of money, estates, titles and a senior position in the regular army. In early November he handed over to Victor Emanuel and left for his home on Caprera, an island off Sardinia, with just a sack of seed-corn and a few packets of coffee.

The disparagement of Garibaldi and his redshirts continued after his departure. Within days the *garibaldini* – the men who had marched from Marsala to the Volturno and captured a kingdom – had been disbanded; although they had fought better than the Piedmontese in every war of the Risorgimento (and would do so again in 1866), very few of them were allowed to join the regular army. The humiliations of their leader were more petty and symbolic but still hurtful. At their meetings in Naples Farini had refused to shake hands or even speak to him. When Garibaldi sailed away to Caprera, British ships in the Bay of Naples fired their guns in salute, but Persano's fleet was ordered to stay quiet.

Garibaldi departed the scene as Cialdini was preparing to besiege Gaeta, where the King of Naples remained resolute. The northern general hoped to batter the town into submission from both land and sea, but unfortunately the French navy was patrolling the coast and preventing access to Persano's ships. The British tried to persuade it to leave, arguing that the Neapolitans had good reason to get rid of their 'tyrannical' dynasty, but Napoleon had a more nuanced view of the rights and wrongs of the conflict, and his ships remained off Gaeta for several months. In the meantime Cialdini persevered with the tactic of bombarding the enemy while keeping his own troops out of danger. Over the winter the defenders of Gaeta died in their hundreds from typhoid as well as artillery shells, and in February Francesco decided to negotiate a surrender. While the talks were taking place, Cialdini refused a ceasefire and even intensified the bombardment, killing numbers of civilians as well as soldiers, until the king departed. For this victory he was made Duke of Gaeta.

Francesco left with dignity, admitting he was a victim of his own inexperience as well as of the cunning and unscrupulous ambitions of Piedmont. His queen, the nineteen-year-old Maria Sofia, had behaved heroically during the siege. A member of the Bavarian ruling house and a sister of the Empress of Austria, she had stayed beside her husband, visiting the wounded, encouraging the soldiers and refusing to take safety precautions that were denied to others. She went to Rome with Francesco and lived in exile there and further north for another sixty-four years. Her husband died in 1894, and her sister, the Empress Elizabeth, was assassinated a few years later by an Italian anarchist. She herself died in penury, still wondering how the Piedmontese kings could have treated a legitimate fellow dynasty as they had, taking not only the riches of the kingdom but grabbing the family's private wealth as well. Marcel Proust wrote her a premature epitaph towards the end of his great novel, describing the aged former queen as a 'woman of great kindness' and much fortitude, a 'heroic woman who, a soldier-queen, had herself fired her musket from the ramparts of Gaeta, always ready to place herself chivalrously on the side of the weak'. After Proust's death – and just before her own – Maria Sofia listened to passages in the novel depicting her behaviour at a Parisian party and remarked that, although she could not remember 'this Monsieur Proust', he seemed to have known her very well because he had made her 'act as precisely as' she thought she would have done.[21]

Few Europeans mourned the fall of the Bourbons. Nor did later Neapolitans greatly regret the passing of a dynasty that had provided them with five kings over a century and a quarter – longer than the rule of either the Tudors or the Stuarts in England. Sentimental attachment was subdued perhaps by distant memories of earlier dynasties and by the presence of so many monuments of previous ages. The family had indeed produced no outstanding monarch but nor – despite what propaganda said – had it supplied a very bad one. In any case, was the general standard any lower than those of their cousins in Spain, the Savoia in Piedmont or the Hanoverians in Great Britain? The victors and their international supporters claimed that the Bourbon exit was an inevitable episode on the road to Italian unity, a necessary consequence of a war of liberation, the conflict having been simply a logical stage in the process of nation-building, a way of absorbing natural national territory – as Wessex had ingested Mercia or France had taken in Provence. Few people outside the Kingdom of the Two Sicilies saw it for what it ultimately was, a war of expansion conducted by one Italian state against another. The unusual feature of the contest was that it was a three-sided one, two sides playing the recognized parts of protagonist (the *garibaldini*) and antagonist (the Bourbons) while the third (the Piedmontese) took on a more subtle role, pretending to be a friend of the others but in reality being the enemy (and eventual conqueror) of both.

Moral and historical justifications for the conquest of Naples are perplexing. According to G. M. Trevelyan, the doyen of British eulogists of the Risorgimento, unification was necessary because of 'the utter failure of the Neapolitans to maintain their own freedom when left to themselves in 1848'.[22] Yet other people have failed in similar fashion without needing or deserving conquest. Another argument, still favoured by certain Neapolitan historians, is that the rapid collapse of the Kingdom of the Two Sicilies in 1860 proved that it was rotten and required elimination. Again, other regimes have collapsed before a sudden onslaught only to be resuscitated later by their allies. A distinguished historian of Naples, an elderly man whose great-grandparents were all Neapolitans, insists that his country could not have become a modern nation by itself after 1860, that it needed the partnership of Piedmont to give it the apparatus of a modern state.[23] His argument does not convince. Piedmont was undoubtedly a richer and more liberal state than the Two Sicilies in 1860, but for most of the eighteenth century Naples had possessed a more enlightened regime than Turin, and only a generation before union it had had more industry and more progressive codes of law. The belief that Naples, unlike other countries in western Europe, was incapable of evolving by itself is simply illogical, an example of that southern inferiority complex which was engendered by the triumphalism of the Risorgimento and reinforced by much subsequent talk, northern and condescending, about 'the southern question' and 'the problem of the *mezzogiorno*'.

VENICE (1866) AND ROME (1870)

On 17 March 1861 the Kingdom of Italy was formally proclaimed. Although it now included the territories of Parma, Modena, Tuscany, most of Lombardy, most of the Papal States and the Kingdom of the Two Sicilies, it was constitutionally still Piedmont with a new name but with the same monarch, the same capital and indeed the same constitution: the first legislature of the new state was labelled the eighth because it followed Piedmont's seven previous ones. The Piedmontese character of the kingdom was further emphasized by the king's retention of his old title, Victor Emanuel II, though of course Italy had never had a Victor Emanuel I.

The new parliament, consisting of an elected Chamber and a Senate nominated by the king, was populated overwhelmingly by men without parliamentary experience. In the Chamber, where fifty-seven seats were symbolically left vacant for future deputies from the unconquered regions of Venetia and Rome, few current members doubted that those seats would be occupied soon, and Cavour, who a few years earlier had dismissed the goal of unity as 'nonsense', was determined to fill them while he was still prime minister. It would be for the next generation, he suggested, to acquire further desirable territories such as Trieste and Istria, the Swiss Ticino and the South Tyrol.

Cavour himself was not destined to see any further accretion of territory. He had seldom paid much attention to his health, eating too much, working too hard and seldom taking exercise except walking along Turin's pavements between parliament, his house, his favourite cafés and the aristocratic Whist Club, which he had founded. Prone to gout, he suffered also from an undiagnosed fever that must have been malaria, probably picked up from the rice fields on his estate. The fever worsened during the spring of 1861, and, weakened by bleeding and poor medical care, he died in June, less than three months after the establishment of the Italy he had done so much to create. His death at the age of fifty was a catastrophe for the new state, which needed its inventor to make his invention work, just as a new Germany later needed his equivalent, Otto von Bismarck, who remained in power for twenty years after his country's unification under Prussian leadership. However unscrupulous in his dealings, Cavour had been an outstanding politician, intuitive and energetic, capable of exploiting even the most unpromising of circumstances. None of his colleagues approached him in stature except perhaps the Tuscan Ricasoli, whose effectiveness was limited by his rigidity and shortage of political skills. Cavour had been prime minister for almost a decade and was expected to continue in the role for many years to come. The governments of his four successors lasted on average for ten months, a duration typical of Italian politics – except in the 1880s – until Mussolini monopolized the premiership in 1922.

The conquest of Rome was not official government policy, but many people in Turin were hoping that the city would – like Naples – unofficially fall into their lap. In 1862 both the king and the prime minister, Urbano Rattazzi, were secretly encouraging Garibaldi to do the job for them. Although he had become a deputy in Turin, the conqueror of the Two Sicilies was uncomfortable in parliament, and he yearned for adulating crowds and exhilarating campaigns. He also yearned for Rome. In the summer of 1862, while he was speaking to an ecstatic audience in Palermo, someone in the crowd shouted 'Roma o morte!' ('Rome or Death!') The orator heard the cry and adopted it as his slogan for the rest of the decade. From Lombardy to Sicily, Italy is still studded with marble plaques affixed to buildings announcing that 'from this balcony Garibaldi harangued the populace and swore Rome or Death!'

Nobody prevented the idol of the people from assembling an army of volunteers in Sicily and then embarking them and sailing to Calabria, though the politicians in power were as equivocal about his current venture as they had been about his previous one in 1860. Perhaps they hoped the pope would run away when he saw Garibaldi coming; maybe they wished to repeat the trick of sending in a force to protect somewhere from Garibaldi and then taking it for themselves. Whatever they hoped or wished for, they lost their nerve. Fearing the anger of the Emperor Napoleon, who sought popularity with French Catholics by allying himself with the pope, they sent the Italian army to stop the volunteers at Aspromonte in Calabria. Although Garibaldi realized he had been misled and betrayed, he ordered his men not to fire on the troops advancing and shooting at them. A few volunteers were killed and their leader was wounded, badly in the ankle and less damagingly in the thigh. The others surrendered. After the affair Azeglio commented scathingly on the slogan 'Rome or Death!': of its alternatives, one had been renounced and the other had been chosen by fewer than 1 per cent of the *garibaldini*.

Most Italians did not want Turin as their capital. It was too French, too near the French border and too far from the centre of the peninsula; besides, it had little of the cultural character and historical resonance that had been the glory of Italy during the eras of the communes and the Renaissance. Rome was the choice of most patriots, but this was not an option, at least not for the time being. In 1864 Napoleon agreed to move his French garrison from Rome on condition that Italy established a new capital somewhere else and promised not to invade the remaining papal territory, the so-called 'Patrimony of St Peter' around Rome. An alternative thus had to be found. Milan, which has been tagged 'the citiest city in Italy', may have been the logical choice – and in retrospect the right one – but like Turin it was too northern and, moreover, it lacked resonance of a political kind; although it had succeeded Rome as capital of the western empire in the fourth century, it had been a viceregal court rather than the capital of an independent state for more than 300 years.

Naples was another possibility, one favoured by several cabinet ministers, but it would have been strange to turn a recently conquered and widely despised city into a capital. So the choice fell on Florence, a distinction it did not want and which Ricasoli described as 'a cup of poison'. Yet the Tuscan city satisfied all cultural and historical criteria, it was the country's financial capital (until overtaken by Milan in the 1880s), and it was favoured by the military because it could not be captured or bombarded from the sea. In May 1865 Florence duly became the capital of Italy, to the joy of Azeglio, who loved the city and hoped it would retain the position for all time. The Pitti Palace once again became a royal residence, while the older Medici palace near the cathedral housed the interior ministry, the Uffizi hosted the Senate, and the Palazzo della Signoria became the Chamber of Deputies. In Piedmont the news that Turin would lose its status led to a riot in the city and a massacre of its citizens by soldiers. The official report, which minimized the significance of the event, noted casualty figures of 52 dead and 130 wounded.

After Aspromonte and the agreement with Napoleon, the patriotic gaze moved from Rome to Venice, which was a less controversial target because its capture would not enrage the French emperor. It also seemed a more feminine one, 'the Queen of the Adriatic' being represented in the iconography of the time as a damsel in distress in need of rescue by a virile new Italy. A painting by Andrea Appiani (the Younger) in Milan's Museo del Risorgimento illustrates the sentiment in the early 1860s: entitled *Venice Who Hopes*, it portrays the city as a queen in white with her crown fallen on the ground and her lion impotent in the background. Another picture in the same museum, painted after the rescue of the distraught lady, depicts a female Italia welcoming two other women, Venice and Rome, into her home.

It was widely felt that, for the sake of its prestige, Italy needed to defeat Austria and complete its unification without the help of France. As Francesco Crispi, Garibaldi's former lieutenant in the south, insisted in parliament, Italian 'dignity' required an heroic victory against a foreign power, a 'baptism of blood' that would drive foreigners out of the peninsula for ever. In an argument repeated by Italian politicians for another eight decades, Crispi demanded such a victory so that 'the great nations of Europe should know that [Italy] too is a great nation, with sufficient strength to ensure that it can make itself respected in the world!'[24]

As it turned out, Italy did not need to fight alone because Prussia, eager to acquire hegemony in German-speaking Europe, was intent on fighting Austria and happy to help the Italians gain Venetia. The warmongers were given a fright in May 1866 when the Austrians, anxious not to campaign simultaneously on two fronts, offered to surrender Venetia in exchange for Italian neutrality in the war against Prussia. Italy was thus given the opportunity to achieve its territorial objective without the expense and suffering of a war. It refused to take it. Victor Emanuel claimed that honour forbade him to abandon the alliance with Prussia, but in truth he was mesmerized by the allure of military glory.

The unnecessary war could hardly have gone worse. At the Battle of Custoza near Verona in June the Italian army was beaten by a much smaller Austrian force and, instead of rallying, retreated twenty miles to the west. A few days later, the Prussians defeated a far larger

Austrian army at Sadowa in Bohemia, a decisive victory which effectively ended their war. The Italians could have stopped then too and would still have received Venetia, but they remained determined to have their 'baptism of blood'. This time the blood was maritime and it was shed off Lissa, an island in the Adriatic, where the Italian navy was defeated by a smaller and less well-equipped Austrian fleet. Even after this second reverse, Victor Emanuel was keen to try again and was only dissuaded from doing so by his chief of staff. The national mood of bellicose self-confidence became quickly transformed into one of embarrassment and despair, and it was scant solace to learn that Garibaldi and his followers had as usual fought better than the regular army and had won some skirmishes in the Trentino and the South Tyrol. A further blow occurred shortly afterwards when an uprising in Sicily demonstrated the islanders' true feelings about annexation. The insurrection captured Palermo and required 40,000 troops for its suppression.

Italy did in the end receive Venetia though it was ashamed of the manner of its acquisition. Austria refused to cede it to the country it had defeated and instead surrendered it to France, which then handed it over to the Italians. The Venetians, governed since 1797 by rulers they had not chosen, showed little enthusiasm for the latest lot: there was no popular rising in support of Italy or Victor Emanuel. Although the state organized the usual overwhelming vote in a plebiscite, the myths of the Risorgimento were never as popular or pervasive in the Venetian provinces as they were in other parts of Italy. The benefits of Italian unification remained a mystery to many people who for centuries had been finding it difficult to reconcile themselves to their ever-declining status. 'When Venice was a republic,' one of its patricians lamented in 1922, 'our word was law all down the Adriatic. Now that we are part of a greater kingdom, every petty little southern Slav can defy us with impunity!'[25]

Today you can still find traces of nostalgia for the Habsburgs in the regions of the Veneto and Friuli-Venezia Giulia. An official guidebook of Treviso criticizes the French historical role in Italy while praising the Austrians for their 'wise government' and their array of impressive public works.[26] In Udine, near the Slovenian border, people talk of the benefits of Habsburg rule as if they personally remembered them, and in Cormons, a pleasant town at the heart of the region's vineyards, a festival of music and gastronomy is held each August to celebrate the birthday of Emperor Franz Josef, the last Austrian ruler of Venice.

The demoralization induced by the defeats at Custoza and Lissa and by the events in Sicily did not dampen nationalist fervour for the next stage in the patriotic programme, the capture of Rome. An earlier generation of educated patriots had not been much inspired by the example of the capital of the classical world; events of the Middle Ages such as the victory at Legnano and the Sicilian Vespers had been more important in their creation of a national past than tales of Horatius and ancient Rome. Yet by the 1860s there was virtual unanimity among patriots, ranging from Mazzini to Victor Emanuel, regarding the importance and desirability of Rome. For ardent Garibaldi, the city was like a 'mistress' whom he 'worshipped, with all the fervour of a lover'. In a different mood he called papal Rome 'a cancer' which must be removed because Italy would not be Italy without Rome as its capital.[27] One of the few men who stood out against the clamour was the elderly Azeglio. He had warned that the annexation of Naples would create vast problems for Italy; he now predicted that the capture of Rome would create more, alienating the Church and Catholics everywhere at a time when the state needed their support. He himself was not an enthusiast for classical Rome, 'that immense monument of human arrogance', but he knew that others might be dazzled by its glory and realized that this would be dangerous for the young kingdom.[28] A new Italy needed a new capital, not an ancient one it might find difficult to live up to.

Rattazzi was again prime minister when in 1867 Garibaldi made another attempt to capture Rome; yet again he encouraged but did not endorse the enterprise. The volunteers invaded in October, coinciding with a failed uprising in Rome, and won a skirmish against papal troops. A few days later, under Catholic pressure at home, Napoleon came to the pope's aid by sending French forces back into Italy to stop Garibaldi. In early November at Mentana, north-east of Rome, the volunteers seemed on the verge of defeating the papal army when a couple of thousand French soldiers arrived and drove them off. A chastened Garibaldi retreated to the Italian border and surrendered to the authorities. As his decisions demonstrated, 'Rome or Death!' were not the only alternatives. There was a third option.

One notable feature of the campaign to capture Rome was the lack of popular support in the towns and countryside of the Roman state. Garibaldi was neither acclaimed by crowds nor assisted by peasants nor mobbed by aspiring volunteers. Even in Rome he had few supporters, and it must have been galling for him to learn afterwards that the French had been thanked for saving Rome from him. In 1870 there was a similar lack of enthusiasm for the national cause, even though the Italian government sent money to assist an uprising. Yet this time, as so often in the Risorgimento wars, the outcome was decided outside Italy. The French emperor withdrew his Roman garrison for his war against Prussia and ceased to be a factor in Italian politics after his defeat at the Battle of Sedan at the beginning of September. Later in that month, the Italian government took the opportunity of sending an army to Rome, where it breached the walls at the Porta Pia, overcame a symbolic defence and quickly captured the city. Garibaldi was not present at this occasion: quixotically he had gone to fight for the new republic in France.

The manner in which Italy had been unified was disheartening for many patriots: unity had been achieved without a 'baptism of blood' or a spectacular victory by anyone except Garibaldi in Sicily. In 1870, as in 1859 and 1866, Italy acquired territory as the result of a huge bloody battle fought between countries from beyond the Alps. Patriots liked to say that Italy would 'make itself', but Bismarck was closer to the truth when he observed that the nation was made by three battles beginning with S – Solferino, Sadowa and Sedan. Without these decisive contests it is difficult to see how Italy would have been united, at least while the patriotic idea enjoyed such exiguous popular support. There had been no eagerness for 'liberation' in Venice or Rome and not much in Lombardy. When Garibaldi was recruiting volunteers in Naples, the most populous city in the peninsula, only eighty men had responded to the call of Italy.

8

Legendary Italy

THE GENERATION OF GIANTS

In 1896 an American historian, A. Lawrence Lowell, described the makers of Italy in reverential prose.

> Victor Emanuel is the model constitutional king; Cavour, the idea of a cool, far-sighted statesman; Garibaldi, the perfect chieftain in irregular war, dashing but rash and hot-headed; Mazzini, the typical conspirator, ardent and fanatical; – all of them full of generosity and devotion.[1]

Other foreigners were even more laudatory. In 1907, on the centenary of Garibaldi's birth, George Meredith conjured a fair and bounteous Italia that owed her existence to the men

> Who blew the breath of life into her frame
> Cavour, Mazzini, Garibaldi: Three:
> Her Brain, her Soul, her Sword; and set her free
> From ruinous discords, with one lustrous aim . . .*

If he left out Victor Emanuel, another British poet rectified the matter: 'My King, King Victor, I am thine!' moaned Elizabeth Barrett Browning, placing the words improbably in the mouth of Garibaldi.†

British liberals were especially prone to adulation. The historian Trevelyan hailed the Italian prime minister as 'great Cavour . . . this marvellous man' and placed him in a category on his own, above Gladstone, Bismarck and Disraeli, when nominating him 'the most

---

*'The Centenary of Garibaldi' (1907).
†'Garibaldi' (1860).

wise and beneficent of all the European statesmen of the nineteenth century, if not of all time'; as a nation-maker he was on a pedestal beside William the Silent and George Washington.[2] Like many with his political views, Trevelyan regarded Italian unification as a triumph of progress and liberalism, a process comparable to the constitutional advances in England after the 'Glorious Revolution' of 1688.

Italian liberals preached a similar line and succeeded in persuading teachers and their students to accept it. One aim, as the historian Carlo Tivaroni tried to demonstrate, was to inculcate the idea that the main actors complemented each other.

> Thus the prudence of Cavour and Victor Emanuel helped, as did Mazzini's constancy and Garibaldi's audacity ... Without these four men, each with his own sphere of action, if only one had been missing, what would have become of Italy?[3]

As a way of implanting the message in the public consciousness, Italian governments embarked upon sprees of statue-making and street-christening in homage to the heroic four. In almost every Italian city you can find statues of Garibaldi and Victor Emanuel; in almost every smaller town you can follow an itinerary that with minimal variations takes you along a Via Cavour to a Piazza Garibaldi and thence through a Via Mazzini and a Corso Vittorio Emanuele before depositing you in a Piazza dell' Unità. Unlucky Mazzini usually comes last in the queue in the matter of nomenclature. In Turin his statue is in a side-street, in Lucca his name designates a car-park, and in Genoa, his home town, he is commemorated by a *galleria*, an elegant arcade of designer clothing shops. The last seems an especially unkind memorial to an impecunious, black-cladded ascetic whose only extravagance was cheap Swiss cigars.

Italy honoured other 'titans' (as they were labelled) apart from the famous four. Statues and routes also commemorate men such as Manin, Ricasoli, Azeglio and Crispi, though the last lost a few of his street names after the Second World War when people began to suspect him of having been a precursor of Mussolini. Patriots of the Romantic era had found it difficult to identify heroes since the Middle Ages, so it was natural to exalt contemporary titans and to recall, as the poet Giosuè Carducci recalled in 1886, 'those days of sun, liberty and glory of 1860', that sublime 'epoch of the infinitely great'. Before his death in 1876 the patriot Luigi Settembrini exhorted Italians to learn 'what posterity will say of us. It will say that this was a generation of giants because it carried out a task which had been impossible for many generations and many centuries.'[4] Settembrini did not stop to consider whether Italian giants, like most other giants, might sometimes be mythical.

THE WISEST STATESMAN

If Camillo Cavour had taken one on a gastronomic tour of Turin, it would have been an instructive and entertaining experience. Leaving his family's eighteenth-century palazzo in what is now Via Cavour, he might take one to Al Bicerin, a tiny café next to the Baroque church of the Consolata, which still serves by the glass its famous concoction of coffee, hot chocolate and cream. From there we might amble to Del Cambio, his favourite restaurant next to the parliament, and thence to Fiorio, the café which housed the Whist Club, an institution later moved to the Piazza San Carlo above his favourite confectioner, the Confetteria Stratta. One would be tempted to eat a lot in a city so liberal with *confetterie* and *gelaterie*, though it might be wise in restaurants to omit the *bollito misto*, a local speciality consisting of boiled meat in a stew that often contains donkey.

It would have been fun to sit at a café table and listen to this animated fellow with his blue eyes and spectacles, his tubby appearance and his curious wispy beard which he allowed to grow only under his chin. He was a clever and amusing man, affable in company, charming at most times and generous to the peasants on his estate. Yet he could be cynical and quarrelsome and was often odious to friends and to colleagues; in offensive moments, after listing their defects, he was apt to summarize them to their faces as 'useless nonentities'. He could also fly into such a rage, shouting and banging his fists on the table, that onlookers feared he had gone off his head. At a lunch with Azeglio and other colleagues in the early 1850s, he suddenly lost his temper, flung his plate and omelette on the floor and ran out of the room.

One victim of Cavour's rages and disdain was Victor Emanuel. The prime minister was often discourteous and condescending to his monarch and sometimes insulted him, as he did when presenting his resignation after Villafranca. On another occasion he lost his temper, kicked the palace furniture and broke one of the clocks. Even stranger was his behaviour when the king, whose queen had been dead for many years, decided to marry morganatically his favourite mistress, Rosina Vercellana. Cavour, who wanted him to marry a Russian princess, was so annoyed that he informed him that Rosina was an unfaithful mistress who enjoyed orgies. Victor Emanuel was tempted, understandably, to challenge his prime minister to a duel for telling such a story, which, apart from anything else, appears to have been untrue.[5]

The Piedmontese gaze traditionally swivels north, but Cavour's was directed even further north than most people's. His father's mother came from Savoy, a region he ceded to France in 1860, and his own mother was Swiss. He himself was born a French subject because in 1810 Piedmont belonged to the napoleonic empire, under which his family had prospered, his father being appointed chamberlain at the court of the governor-general, Prince Camillo Borghese. The chamberlain dignified his infant with Borghese's Christian name and with the more glamorous (though no more useful) prestige of having the governor's wife – Napoleon's sister Pauline – as his godmother.

The countries Cavour most admired were France and Britain, both of which he visited on numerous occasions. Their culture, however, was not a great draw because he himself had few cultural interests, although he took one of Walter Scott's novels on a visit to the Highlands to help him experience 'romantic emotions'. He was essentially a man of reason who would have been happy as a statesman of the Enlightenment; the Romantic era had little effect on his life until in middle age he became a convert to nationalism.

Cavour's journeys to England as a young man were industrious and practical. With energy and enthusiasm he inspected gasworks and railway stations, he toured the Arsenal at Woolwich, he visited shipyards in Newcastle and factories in the Midlands. While he found Parisian society more congenial than its London equivalent, he was impressed by English prosperity, by the sense of liberty and security there, by the workings of government; he thus became a liberal, convinced that political freedom was essential for the creation of wealth.

After looking at the careers of William Pitt and Robert Peel, he was also persuaded of the advantages of measured progress and an undoctrinaire approach. As an advocate for free trade, he applauded Peel's Repeal of the Corn Laws in 1846, though he himself would never have broken his party or sacrificed his career for a matter of principle. One journalist from southern Italy described him, not unfairly, as 'a cross between Sir Robert Peel and Machiavelli'.[6]

Cavour's knowledge of economics was a great advantage to Piedmont during his years as prime minister. So were his skills as a deputy, his energy and leadership and talent for debate; he did much to consolidate a parliamentary system in a country with few traditions of representative government. Yet in politics he could be both unjust and undemocratic: he sometimes managed to exclude opposition members from parliament and he refused, even after the victories of 1860, to allow Mazzini to return from exile. His chief defect, however, was the mendacity and unscrupulousness which he displayed in his parliamentary manoeuvres and his changes of policy. Azeglio, who in these respects was very much his successor's superior, thought that after long exposure to these traits people had simply learned to believe that what Cavour said was the opposite of the truth.

Turin has many wonderfully overblown monuments to Piedmont's kings, generals and politicians. The ugliest one is the huge and ridiculous statue of Cavour in the Piazza Carlo Emanuele, erected on the spot where the French revolutionaries had placed their guillotine. Known as 'the paperweight', it reveals nothing of its subject's character, no suggestion of the gregarious frequenter of cafés and gaming tables. Its bottom half is crowded with bronze reliefs and nude allegorical figures representing Cavour's great services to Italy. At the top stands the statesman in a toga, helping a curvaceous and semi-naked Italia to her feet while she clings to him and presents him with a laurel wreath.

This association with Italy was of course natural yet, while Cavour was a great Piedmontese, he was not a great Italian. Until near the end of his life he was simply incurious about what was happening in the peninsula beyond Piedmont. Although as a young man he had plenty of spare time, he had had no inclination even to see Tuscany; in his one visit to Venetia, in 1836, he contrived to find Venice and Verona uninteresting. He spent nearly a decade as prime minister of the King-dom of Sardinia* without going near the island of that name, although its impoverished inhabitants were subject to his rule and in great need of political and economic assistance. Cavour never travelled as far south as Siena, yet in the last year of his life he was legislating for vast areas hundreds of miles south of Tuscany. Had he only bothered to visit the former Bourbon kingdom, he would have noticed how differ-ent it was from Piedmont and might have devised a more appropriate system for its administration. He might also have realized that his free trade dogmas were unsuitable for an economy with a history of pro-tectionism. He might even have learned that Sicilians no longer spoke Arabic.

Cavour's reputation rests on a string of political and diplomatic successes in 1859 and 1860: the alliance with France, the defeat of Austria, the absorption of the centre, the annexation of the south and the establishment of the Kingdom of Italy. He was indeed a brilliant diplomat but he was also a lucky and sometimes irresponsible one. Bismarck in Prussia considered it immoral to start a general European war for the sake of German unity and expansion. Yet Cavour often talked of wide conflagrations, of 'setting Europe alight', stirring up the Balkans, bringing in the Russians, fomenting implausible civil wars in Germany and Switzerland. Nor was this just talk. In 1859 he sent thousands of rifles to Hungarian rebels fighting the Austrian Empire and a year later dispatched five shiploads of weapons for use by Romanian revolutionaries against the Ottoman Empire. When it was discovered that the ships' crates, which masqueraded as coffee containers, actually contained guns, there was a diplomatic uproar. Cavour tried to lie his way out of the scrape but did not fool Queen Victoria, who was appalled by the piratical actions of 'this really bad, unscrupulous Sardinian government'.[7] In the year of his death Cavour was still plotting a great European conflict that would result in an enlargement of Italy's borders.

Victoria's adjective 'unscrupulous' was one commonly applied to Cavour by foreign statesmen and diplomats as well as by political opponents at home. Yet few people were aware of the extent of his

*The legal title of the Kingdom of Piedmont-Sardinia.

deviousness and inconsistency. In 1855 Cavour had sent an army to the Crimea because he claimed it was essential to exclude the Russians from the Mediterranean, but two years later he allowed them to establish a naval base on Piedmontese territory near Nice. In the mid-1850s he was plotting to put Napoleon's cousin Lucien Murat on the throne of Naples and yet also suggesting an alliance between Piedmont and the Bourbons. More contorted still were his actions in February 1860, when he was simultaneously suggesting to the Prussians that they should jointly attack Austria and to Napoleon that together they should march against Prussia.

The wonder is that anyone in Europe put up with him. Part of the explanation is that the governments of Britain and France supported, for emotional as well as political reasons, the Italian national cause; however much they distrusted Cavour personally, they wanted to see a resurgent Italy. He himself undoubtedly achieved great successes, yet his behaviour set a tone for his country's diplomacy that was copied less successfully by his successors for almost a century. Through him and his example, Italy gained the reputation of being an unreliable and sometimes embarrassing ally.

THE NOBLEST ROMAN

Take down the Michelin guide to Italy and look at the maps of the towns. Start with the As (Alassio, Alessandria, Ancona, Aosta), go down to the Bs (Bari, Barletta, Belluno, Bergamo), and carry on to the Vs, the last letter to have proper towns in Italy (Venezia, Vercelli, Verona, Viterbo). All these places have something in common: they have at least one space – a via, a viale, a ponte, a corso or a piazza – named in honour of Giuseppe Garibaldi. Many also have statues of the great man, often astride a horse impassively directing his volunteers, or standing with a lion at his feet in case viewers need reminding of his leonine qualities of strength and courage.

In Genoa Garibaldi is represented not only by a huge equestrian bronze in front of the opera but also, in diverse and equally inappropriate ways, by a Via Garibaldi (a street of Renaissance palaces), a Piazza Garibaldi (a yard with a shop selling motorbikes), a Vico

Garibaldi (a gloomy cul-de-sac) and the Galleria Garibaldi, not an art gallery here nor a shopping arcade like the Galleria Mazzini but a tunnel for motorcars – useful in a city that tried to solve its traffic problems by erecting a motorway on stilts that separates the old town from the port. The next tunnel is dedicated to Nino Bixio, Garibaldi's most ruthless and violent lieutenant in 1860.

Garibaldi was an authentic hero, an idealist and a visionary but an achiever too, a valiant soldier and an incorruptible man. He also looked and sounded right for the part he had to play, wide-browed, fine-featured and possessed of a rich and melodious voice. According to Giuseppe Guerzoni, his friend and biographer, his 'superb head' made him look at different moments like Jesus, a lion and Jove on Olympus.[8] Others were struck by his resemblance to images of Christ, and people often referred to him as a 'saviour' and a 'redeemer'.

Garibaldi may have been the most commemorated secular figure in history; his only rival is Gandhi. Hailed in his lifetime for his exploits in South America as well as Europe, he was probably the most famous person on the planet. In England, which he visited in 1854 and 1864, he inspired the adoration of vast crowds, the love of several women, the business sense of the manufacturer of 'squashed flies biscuits' and the spirit of Nottingham Forest football team, which in his honour adopted his red shirts. The British of the period, whose education consisted mainly of Latin and Greek, saw him as a classical hero, *Punch* magazine saluting him with the words Shakespeare gave Mark Antony to describe Brutus – 'the noblest Roman of them all' – though whether Garibaldi would have relished comparison with Caesar's assassin is doubtful; although a revolutionary, he deplored assassination as a political weapon. One lord mayor of London claimed him as a modern embodiment of both the Spartan Leonidas and the Roman Cincinnatus, who was said to have rescued Rome in times of crisis and returned to his farm afterwards. Such classical comparisons were apt: like Leonidas, Garibaldi usually fought against superior forces and, like Cincinnatus, he often returned afterwards to his farm. Yet he was also likened to medieval paladins such as William Tell, William Wallace, Joan of Arc and Robin Hood, while Americans referred to him as Italy's George Washington (another of the cincinnati, a rare breed). Alas, he had a dreadful effect on poets. After Tennyson had planted a tree in his garden on the Isle of Wight, Britain's poet laureate was moved to write:

> Or watch the waving pine which here
> The warrior of Caprera set
> A name that earth will not forget
> Till earth has roll'd her latest year –*

Born in Nice in 1807, Garibaldi was a mariner by profession. From 1824 he worked as a merchant seaman on the Black Sea route before joining the Piedmontese-Sardinian navy in 1833. Almost simultaneously he became attached to Young Italy and soon deserted the navy to take part in Mazzini's planned uprising in Genoa in the following year. As happened quite often, this type of plot failed to get off the ground, and, although Garibaldi managed to escape, he was sentenced to death in absentia and forced to flee, first to Marseille and then to South America. He did not return to Italy for fourteen years.

In exile across the Atlantic, Garibaldi became a freemason and preached the message of Young Italy to Italian immigrant communities on the southern continent's eastern seaboard. To earn a living, he sailed up and down the coast, attempting to sell *maccheroni*, but he was not much good at this or any other commercial activity: while he was trying to herd 1,000 oxen to Montevideo, 400 of them drowned in the River Negro. Yet in South America he managed to discover his vocation: to fight 'for the ideal of freedom and independence'. As a result, he spent several years battling for the secessionists of Rio Grande do Sul who wanted independence from Brazil, followed by several more in the service of Uruguay in its wars against Argentina. He fought numerous skirmishes on land and at sea, winning a few more than he lost and suffering such vicissitudes as imprisonment, torture and capsized boats. José Garibaldi, *gaucho* and *guerrillero*, learned his new trade and became a leader of men. From the horse-

---

*This poem, 'To Ulysses', is not the feeblest verse about him written by an English poet. Swinburne, Meredith and Elizabeth Barrett Browning wrote even more gushing lines. A homier, happier image appears in *The Wind in the Willows*, Kenneth Grahame's classic Edwardian children's book. Along the walls of the Mole's burrow are 'brackets carrying plaster statuary – Garibaldi, and the infant Samuel, and Queen Victoria, and other heroes of modern Italy'.

men of the pampas he acquired his riding skills as well as his beige poncho and collarless red shirt, the uniform his followers in Italy loved and his opponents derided as vulgar and clownish.

Garibaldi's admirers have accepted their hero's own estimate of the struggles he waged in South America on behalf of oppressed peoples. Yet the politics of the continent are complicated, and it is not always easy to discern who were the oppressors and who the oppressed. The figure of the foreigner taking part in other peoples' civil wars is seldom an appealing one, and it may not have been obvious to everyone why a man determined to unite an independent Italy was so determined to disunite an independent Brazil. Garibaldi may have been the freedom fighter he claimed to be but equally accurate descriptions for this period, during which he preyed on his opponents' merchant shipping, would be bandit, corsair and buccaneer.

In 1839, while his ship was anchored off the Brazilian coast, Garibaldi saw a young woman through his telescope and was so captivated that he went ashore to find her. He instantly fell in love with the vivacious Anita, who reciprocated his passion strongly enough to abandon her husband, a local cobbler, and attach herself to Garibaldi, with whom in due course she had four children. In 1848 they sailed to Europe, in different ships and to different destinies, Giuseppe to celebrity and Anita to martyrdom.

On reaching Spain, Garibaldi heard about the spate of revolutions and rushed to fight for the Italian cause alongside the Piedmontese. Mazzini's revolutionary newspaper, established in Milan after the expulsion of Radetzky, saluted 'with brotherly love the brave, the long-awaited Garibaldi' and wished him 'new glory, for his glory is our glory, and is Italian glory'.[9] Although little glory was to be won in his campaign against the Austrians near Lake Maggiore, his enthusiasm for the cause and his belief in its righteousness remained absolute. In the following spring he fought heroically in Rome until, overwhelmed by foreign armies, Mazzini's republic collapsed. Garibaldi himself refused to capitulate and insisted on carrying on the fight in the hills of central Italy. His departure from the city illustrated his dramatic sense of occasion and his understanding of how to transform defeat into propaganda. While others yielded or slipped out of Rome with a British passport, he had his proto-Churchillian moment, sitting astride his horse in St Peter's Square, offering the republican army nothing but hunger, thirst, heat, cold, battles and forced marches – all without pay. Some 4,700 men accepted his unappetizing offer and marched with him that evening out of the Porta San Giovanni. Many later deserted and many others died (including Anita, who had insisted on accompanying him even though she was pregnant), but Garibaldi eluded his pursuers. On reaching Liguria, he was arrested by the Piedmontese army and released on condition that, after visiting his children in Nice, he left the country. After spending some time in North Africa wondering what to do, he crossed the Atlantic and reached Staten Island.

In exile Garibaldi resumed his trade as a merchant seaman. Acquiring a ship in Lima, he traded between China, Boston, the Philippines and South America; once he sailed from Peru to China with a cargo of guano only to find that the Cantonese did not want it. From afar he despaired at the plight of Italy, 'its servitude and the passivity of its sons', but he found some solace in 1854, when, on being allowed to return home, he bought his farm on Caprera, an island of granite boulders and an aromatic scrub of lentisk, cistus and stunted juniper. There he extended the house and created rooms with high ceilings; there he planted olive trees and cleared the land to make fields for his sheep and corn. When he was on the island, consoled by the solitude and the sweet-smelling breezes, he lived privately and frugally with his various children and (at different times) two of their mothers, one of them a nursemaid employed by his daughter Teresita, the other a peasant woman who became his third wife, Francesca Armosina. Before dawn he dictated letters and in the daylight he spent his time tending the farm. Although he served wine to his guests, he himself was a teetotaler, drinking only water at lunch and cold milk in the evening. Like Mazzini, he seemed to exist on coffee and cigars; his chief relaxation was to play the piano and sing arias from the operas of Vincenzo Bellini, the Catanian maestro of *bel canto*.

After this second return to Italy, Garibaldi broke with Mazzini, joined the National Society and in 1859 fought successfully with his volunteers against the Austrians in northern Lombardy. At the end of the war the Piedmontese government gave him command of its forces in the Romagna but removed him after he urged an invasion of the

Papal Marches. The years 1859–60 were the most dramatic of his long career; they were also the most tumultuous in his crowded and colourful private life. In the space of eight months he had a child with one woman (a peasant), proposed unsuccessfully to a second (a baroness), fell in love with a third (a countess), and married a fourth (the teenage daughter of a marquess), whom he discarded soon after their wedding on discovering that she was pregnant with someone else's child.

Angry and humiliated after the last episode, Garibaldi was luckily distracted by the call of Sicily, which he answered by sailing with his Thousand to vanquish the Bourbons. After conquering a kingdom, he returned to Caprera and resumed life as a farmer with his fields, his cowsheds, his henhouse and his horses. Published accounts of his fondness of animals made him still more popular with the British, but devout Catholics were not amused by the names of two of his donkeys, Pius IX and the Immaculate Conception.

Nothing else in Garibaldi's life could compare with the adventure in Sicily and Naples. Although tempted by an offer to fight for the Union in the American Civil War, he refused it when informed that he would not be made commander-in-chief or given the power to abolish slavery. Both his attempts to capture Rome were failures, and after the second in 1867 he returned in despair to Caprera and remained there for three years. His career as a soldier came to an end in 1871 after campaigning for the French Republic against Prussia, though for several years he dreamed of an expedition to 'liberate' the Trentino and the South Tyrol from the Austrians.

Garibaldi died in 1882, ten years after Mazzini. By the end of their lives both men had become disillusioned with the Italy to which they had dedicated their years. The revolutionary conspirator had 'hoped to evoke her soul' and admitted he had failed; the state that emerged in 1861 was 'only the phantom, the mockery of Italy'. The soldier's disenchantment was equally intense. Shortly before his death he wrote scornfully: 'It was a very different Italy which I spent my life dreaming of, not the impoverished and humiliated country which we now see ruled by the dregs of the nation.'[10]

A man of many talents, Garibaldi was also honest, modest and uninterested in money; in battle he was brave and inspiring; and in speech he was charming and articulate except when making a garbled attack on Cavour in parliament. In many of his views he was notably ahead of his time: he was a supporter of female emancipation, of racial equality and of the abolition of capital punishment. As with Mazzini, his patriotism was not a boastful, chauvinistic form of nationalism: both men would have liked to see the creation of a union of European states. Also unusual were his vegetarianism and his approval of cremation, which was illegal in Italy.

Garibaldi claimed he was an anti-militarist, that he was 'born to be an agriculturalist or a sailor' and that only 'tyrants and priests' had made him a soldier.[11] The explanation is somewhat disingenuous. Garibaldi may have been a humane warrior who took care to avoid civilian casualties, but he was not a pacifist manqué. His sword-arm became stiff with inactivity and soon itched to find people to liberate and oppressors to overthrow. He was an inspirational leader who enjoyed battles and was good at fighting them; he was also by far the best soldier that modern Italy has produced, winning his actions through decisiveness, boldness, improvisation and combative skill. Yet his tactical range was limited, and his habit of charging uphill against superior numbers did not always bring victory. Perhaps his military talents are fairly reflected in the calculations of one of his biographers, Jasper Ridley: of the fifty-three battles he fought in South America and Italy, he won thirty-four, lost fifteen and drew four.[12]

Garibaldi was regarded by many as politically naive, and sometimes he was. Yet he was more realistic than Mazzini and often more clear-sighted than Cavour. In Sicily and Naples in 1860 he governed calmly and wisely while simultaneously fighting a war against the Bourbons and dealing with the provocations of the Piedmontese government. His military feats, his courage and example, his ability to arouse pa-triotic enthusiasm – all were crucial to the success of Italian unification; without him, the Kingdom of the Two Sicilies might still be with us. Garibaldi was a man of the people who could inspire his fellow men to fight for a cause they might not otherwise have cared about. He was indeed the hero the Italian patriots had been searching for; he became the legend it was forbidden to doubt; and his aura prompted Mussolini to claim that he and his blackshirts were the descendants of Garibaldi and his redshirts. His most dramatic achievement – the con-quest of the south – certainly made modern Italy. Whether this was beneficial for either northerners or southerners is a subject for later consideration.

FATHER OF THE NATION

Cardinal Angelo Roncalli, the Patriarch of Venice, visited Turin in 1953 and was astonished by the abundance of enormous monuments he saw there. Officiating in a city whose republic had forbidden statues in public places, the future Pope John XXIII was perplexed. What were they doing, he asked a Torinese, all these warriors on horseback, waving their swords as if charging at the head of their troops?[13]

Most of the equestrian sword-wavers, cast in bronze and dominating their piazzas, are members of the House of Savoy. They include Emanuel Philibert, the sixteenth-century duke, who is thrusting his weapon back in its scabbard after a victory in alliance with Spain against France; Charles Albert who, despite his brief and disastrous military career, is depicted as a conqueror guarded by the figures of a gunner, a lancer, a grenadier and a *bersagliere*; and Ferdinand of Genoa, Victor Emanuel's brother, who is urging his men forward even though his horse has been mortally wounded and is already on its knees. The most majestic is of Victor Emanuel's second son, Amedeo, who, after a bizarre invitation to become King of Spain, duly took up his duties in Madrid and remained there for just over two years before abdicating in 1873. He sits high on a prancing horse in the Valentino park beside the River Po, the plinth beneath him ringed by dozens of horsemen representing the most illustrious members of the family since the founding of the line in the early Middle Ages. It is a tremendous tribute to a dynasty that over the centuries acquired the titles of Count of Savoy, Duke of Savoy, King of Sicily, King of Sardinia, King of Cyprus and Jerusalem, King of Italy, Emperor of Ethiopia and King of Albania.

Victor Emanuel is the only rival to Garibaldi in the number of statues in Italy. He too is frequently shown on a stallion, the helmeted image of a conqueror flourishing his sword, but he is often portrayed also as a standing figure, regal and uniformed, one hand holding his helmet, the other resting on his sword-hilt. This is how he poses in

Turin in the gigantic monument which you see looming above the trees as you walk along the Corso Vittorio Emanuele towards its intersection with the Corso Galileo Ferraris. The king himself, on top of a column, is nine metres tall; the whole structure reaches a height of thirty-nine metres.

The statues of the king, like his many portraits, were executed as acts of homage and propaganda. Yet they seldom attempted to disguise their subject's unhandsome appearance or to romanticize him or make him look intelligent. The monarch had a squat figure, a red face and unprepossessing features – a fat nose, a round face, bulbous eyes and an enormous moustache. So dissimilar was he to Charles Albert – who was tall, pale, thin-faced and aristocratic – that a biological connection between the two of them must be questionable. Rumours were whispered shortly after the boy's birth in 1820, before Charles Albert became king, that they were not father and son. A persistent one suggests that the royal infant perished in a palace fire and was substituted by a butcher's baby, a theory that was advanced to explain the coarse features and the unlikely story that a tiny child had escaped unscathed from a fire which had consumed his cradle and burned his nurse to death. Yet it would have been strange for the parents, who were extremely young, to have adopted an heir rather than wait to produce another one of their own. In fact they did have a son two years later, that Ferdinand on the dying horse, whose daughter Margherita married Victor Emanuel's heir, her supposed first cousin Umberto. So even if, for whatever reason, the king was illegitimate, the Savoia blood returned with his grandson, Victor Emanuel III.

In character and tastes the first King of Italy resembled few members of previous peninsular dynasties such as the Medici, the Farnese and the Habsburg-Lorraine. Indeed he seemed unItalian in a number of ways: apart from his inability to speak the national language properly, he was an uncouth figure who despised art and books. He had courage and a certain blustering charm but little else to recommend him as a sovereign. Much as he had desired to capture Rome, he did not like to visit the city or live there with his court: the people whose company he most enjoyed were his huntsmen, his mistresses and his Piedmontese generals, whom he liked to entertain whenever possible in one of his hunting lodges. Many of these places were inherited, along with castles and palaces, from the Savoia, and many more were acquired through conquest from the Bourbons and other deposed dynasties: by the end of his life he possessed so many properties that, beginning in January, he could have spent just a single day in each of them without returning to any until December. His extravagance was such that, although Italy was a much poorer country than Great Britain, the expenses of himself and his entourage were twice the size of Queen Victoria's.

The Piedmontese constitution of 1848 had reserved more powers for the king than was normal in constitutional monarchies. Victor Emanuel was determined to retain these and exercise his authority as head of government as well as head of state. He wanted to have governments that did what he told them and implemented the policies he put forward; despite his obvious boredom at cabinet meetings, he often insisted on presiding over these occasions. Naturally he seldom got his way with men such as Azeglio, Cavour and Ricasoli, but his constant interference in government exasperated all his prime ministers, drove several to resignation and encouraged others to avoid personal dealings with him.

The king's chief service to the Italian cause was performed in 1849, at the beginning of his reign, when he allowed Azeglio to persuade him to keep the constitution. Later he claimed the Austrians had put pressure on him to abolish it and that he had stood up to Radetzky and defied him. This was simply not true: there was no Austrian pressure. Victor Emanuel always disliked the constitution, its restraints and the system it produced, especially the members of parliament. There were only two ways to govern Italians, he informed the British ambassador, 'by bayonets and bribery'; the people did not understand parliamentary government and were anyway unfit for it. As potent as the legend of the eager constitutionalist is that of the patriot king. Victor Emanuel was in fact a monarch who liked to tell the Austrians how much he preferred them to the Lombards and who had even congratulated them for their repression of a Mazzinian insurrection in Milan in 1853. Fortunately, few patriots heard these opinions or his denunciations of Mazzini and Garibaldi whom – along with their followers – he described as 'vermin' that he would like to 'exterminate'.[14]

Like Cavour, the king was a Piedmontese nationalist but not an Italian one.

Victor Emanuel was very conscious of the military traditions of the Savoia, although the royal house had gained little recent glory and the family's most illustrious soldier, the great Prince Eugène – ally of Marlborough, vanquisher of France and saviour of Hungary from the Turks – had served as an Austrian field marshal. The latest member of the dynasty had had a military education but little personal experience and no aptitude for the job of commander. Yet he had extraordinary delusions about his abilities. Other crowned heads in Europe such as Napoleon III liked presiding over battles without wishing to direct operations; no British king had led his troops on the field since George II at Dettingen in 1743. Yet Victor Emanuel insisted on acting as commander-in-chief in 1859 and, despite his unskilful performance in that year, on resuming the post in 1866. Earlier he had offered to command the combined allied forces in the Crimea and ascribed his subsequent rejection to British fears that he might be too successful and put their generals in the shade. Self-deception on a similar scale was evident twenty years later when he offered to solve the 'Eastern Question', which he proposed to do by expelling the Ottoman sultan to central Asia and carving up his empire between the European powers.[15]

Foreign ambassadors were surprised and sometimes alarmed by the king's compulsive urge to go to war, by his endless talk about future battles in which he would lead his troops to victory. Once he told the Austrians, at a time when he wished for their support, that fighting wars was the only thing that gave him true pleasure. Like his generals and politicians, he wanted wars for the sake of Italy, but he desired them also for his personal delight. The boastfulness of his conversation was consistent and often astonishing. In 1862 he talked of fighting not only Austria but also France, his recent ally, and even Britain, his chief diplomatic supporter. Two years later, he told the incredulous British that Italy could defeat the Austrian–Hungarian Empire by itself and even take on the French Empire at the same time. Two years further on, he was fighting the Austrians in alliance with the Prussians and, a few years later, he was trying to fight the Prussians on the side of the French. This last folly was thwarted by the current prime minister, Giovanni Lanza, who may thereby have saved the dynasty and even the state. Both Bismarck and Napoleon had believed that another Italian defeat would lead to the break-up of the country.[16]

Like Cavour in the 1850s, Victor Emanuel became a meddler in the Balkans, stirring up trouble in Serbia and plotting to get his son Amedeo (the future King of Spain) on to the Greek throne. He enjoyed pursuing his own diplomacy, independent of the foreign ministry, and did so deviously through agents and secret missions. At the beginning of 1867 he was inciting Paris and Berlin to attack each other, each with Italian support, while suggesting to the Austrians that they should ally themselves with him against both the French and the Prussians. Later that year, the British foreign secretary, Lord Clarendon, talked to politicians in Italy and reported 'universal agreement' among them that the king was 'an imbecile', a 'dishonest man who tells lies to everyone' and, at the current rate, would 'end by losing his crown and ruining both Italy and his dynasty'.[17]

Victor Emanuel died of malaria in 1878 at the age of fifty-seven, at a time when he was again proposing to the Germans that they should ally themselves with Italy and take on both Austria and France. He died in the capital the month before Rome's other court, the Vatican, buried its leader, Pope Pius IX. Observers noted that far larger crowds turned out for the dead pontiff than for the defunct king, who was buried in Hadrian's Pantheon, far from the tombs of his ancestors in the basilica of Superga near Turin. The myths were created early and were soon emblazoned throughout Italy: Victor Emanuel, *il padre della patria*, father of the fatherland, a successor to Julius Caesar, the *pater patriae*; Victor Emanuel, *il re galantuomo*, the chivalrous gentleman-king; Victor Emanuel who was, according to one historian, 'the greatest Christian sovereign in all history'.[18] He was not in reality any of these things, not even *il padre della patria*. Italy was created during his reign but not by him.

SOME GENERALS AND AN ADMIRAL

Speaking to parliament in 1850, Massimo d'Azeglio observed that Piedmont was 'an ancient home of honour, an ancient warrior country'.[19] Although not much of a warrior himself, the prime minister understandably chose to emphasize his country's military ethos. Turin was not an imperial capital like Rome or an artistic capital like Florence or a capital of a maritime republic like Venice. It was the most military city in Italy, capital of a country in which the army had for centuries been identified very closely with the state.

The Piedmontese were eager to continue this association when they formed the new Kingdom of Italy. Distinctions between civil and military were quickly blurred by the presence of twenty-five generals and four admirals in the new parliament, some of them as elected deputies, others as senators nominated by the king. The chiefs of the army and navy could be parliamentarians and even cabinet ministers. There was thus little time for them to do their jobs properly and no chance of political neutrality. In June 1866 General Alfonso Lamarmora was not only prime minister and foreign minister but also chief-of-staff of an army on the verge of fighting a war.

The officer corps of the Italian army was dominated by Piedmontese veterans eager to implant their particular ethos in the new force, many of whose soldiers came from despised areas that had traditionally produced poor fighters. Unfortunately the Piedmontese themselves seemed recently to have lost their fighting skills, and their generals were fusty and unimaginative men who distrusted flair and initiative (especially when displayed by Garibaldi) and relied too much on conventional tactics and use of the bayonet. A typical example was General Alfonso Lamarmora, who had been prime minister after Cavour's resignation in 1859 and who was appointed again to the post in 1864. A commander with no sense of strategy, he was obsessed by drill and invariably hostile to innovation.

Lamarmora's statue in Turin, soaring in one of the city's finest squares, is an object so impressive that foreign visitors would be forgiven for believing that they were viewing a great conqueror, a sort of Piedmontese Hannibal. Like the Savoia, he rides a fine steed, and the plinth below him is decorated with lions' heads and inscriptions commemorating his career. The general made his name by his rough suppression of the revolt in Genoa in 1849, an action which hinted that the Piedmontese, recently defeated by Austria, might be venting their frustration on one of their own cities. Having established his reputation as a tough and reliable soldier, Lamarmora was rapidly promoted and selected to lead the expedition to the Crimea, where his brother Alessandro, founder of the plume-hatted *bersaglieri*, died of cholera. As chief-of-staff in 1859, serving loyally if awkwardly under Victor Emanuel, he won the small Battle of Palestro before his army arrived too late to fight at Magenta and later performed poorly at San Martino. Shortly afterwards the king, who longed for his premiers to be pliant generals rather than difficult politicians, appointed him prime minister. Lamarmora then spent the next seven years in politics, a sphere where his lack of skills and vision were all too evident. In June 1866 he resigned his political posts to concentrate on his duties as chief-of-staff and travelled to Lombardy eager for the much-trumpeted 'baptism of blood'. Almost everyone seemed confident of the outcome, partly because the Austrians were concentrating on Prussia and had only a small army in Venetia, a region they no longer wanted and had already offered to give up. Italy, by contrast, had been expanding its forces in recent years and could now outnumber its enemy by more than two to one for the contest which took place near Verona.

The second leading general in the campaign was Enrico Cialdini, a Modenese suspicious of Lamarmora and other Piedmontese generals, whom he regarded, in most cases rightly, as inferior commanders. He had served in Lombardy in 1859, but his earliest military experiences had been acquired in the fiercer circumstances of Spain's first Carlist War in the 1830s. The previous chapter has described the invasions of 1860 and the savagery with which he overcame any type of resistance in the Papal States and the Kingdom of the Two Sicilies: the declarations of martial law, the burning of villages, the summary executions of peasants caught with weapons, the pitiless bombardments of Ancona, Capua and Gaeta. He treated the inhabitants of states with which Piedmont was not at war as if he were wreaking vengeance on a barbarous people rather than hoping to persuade them of the merits of Italian unification. For his role in expelling the Bourbons in 1861, he was rewarded with a dukedom, as if to imply that as a commander he ranked alongside Marlborough or Masséna, Duke of Rivoli. Soon afterwards he returned to Naples as the king's lieutenant-general to deal with the civil war his actions had done so much to promote.

In the summer of 1866 the Italian army was divided: Lamarmora had the bulk of the army in Lombardy; Cialdini commanded a substantial force at Bologna; and Garibaldi led his volunteers in the Alpine foothills. This arrangement, a consequence of the jealousy and distrust among senior generals, made cooperation difficult. Lamarmora met Cialdini to discuss the campaign but failed to establish a joint plan. In the event he advanced without waiting for the others and marched his troops towards the fortresses of the Quadrilateral. Believing the Austrians to be east of the Adige, he crossed the River Mincio without making an effort to reconnoitre. He was thus astonished to discover, on the east bank of the Mincio, an Austrian force, which attacked his advance guard at Custoza and drove it back. Giuseppe Govone, the best of the Piedmontese commanders, counterattacked with his division and regained some ground but could not retain it without reinforcements. Desperately he appealed to the general to his rear, Enrico Della Rocca, to send his fresh divisions to the front, but his colleague refused to help. More of a courtier than a soldier, Della Rocca stuck to earlier orders from Lamarmora instead of following the elementary military rule of marching to the sound of gunfire.

Throughout the day Lamarmora himself panicked. His army was strung out over a considerable distance, and he galloped madly from one unit to another so that his subordinates were seldom able to find him; for some reason, inexplicable even to himself, he ended the fight about thirteen miles from the battlefield. A message was sent from the king to Cialdini ordering him to come to the rescue, but the general refused; he had in any case been positioned too far away to reach the battlefield in time to affect the result.

Both the senior generals mistook a reverse for a rout and chose to retreat. Yet Cialdini could have led his men towards the Po and threatened the Austrian flank, and Lamarmora could have regrouped on the Mincio and counter-attacked with the divisions that had not fired a shot during the battle; he had lost fewer than 1,000 men at Custoza, and his army was still far larger than the enemy's. His excessive and unnecessary retreat – the Austrians were not even pursuing him – added embarrassment to the humiliation of the defeat and deepened the demoralization of a nation that had been told victory was inevitable. The actions of Lamarmora, Della Rocca and perhaps Cialdini deserved examination before a court-martial. None of them faced one. Instead of being condemned as the incompetent general that he was, Lamarmora was posthumously rewarded with the magnificent statue in Piazza Bodoni.

Turin's military monuments were not all erected to commemorate individual kings and commanders. Some of them are collective memorials, representing units of the armed forces, principally the *bersaglieri* (who are always shown running) but also the cavalry, the *carabinieri* and the Alpine regiments. Only one monument, that dedicated to the men who went to the Crimea, contains a statue of a sailor.

Piedmont had no nautical traditions; indeed, until it was given Liguria by the Congress of Vienna, it possessed no coastline except around Nice. Its insignificant navy did little in the early wars of the Risorgimento and was never required to fight a proper battle. United Italy, however, had an extremely long coastline. Since it also had aspirations to join the Great Powers, it set about building an impressive fleet, though its only plausible enemy was Austria, which had little naval history or ambition of its own. By 1866 this new fleet included twelve new ironclads and was commanded by an admiral, four vice-admirals and eight rear-admirals. The Austrian navy was smaller, slower and less well equipped: it possessed only seven ironclads. The Italian force was thus superior in all material respects though generally inferior in most human ones, most markedly in the abilities of the admirals in command.

The Italian commander was Carlo Pellion, Count of Persano. Unlike Garibaldi, who was a seaman both by birth and by aptitude, the Piedmontese Persano had seafaring neither in his blood nor in his upbringing. He came from the inland rice-growing area of Vercelli and was apparently unable to swim. Some people believed he chose to be a sailor because there was so much less competition for posts in the navy than there was in the army. He himself owed his very rapid promotion not to his exploits but to his talent at flattery, intrigue and making himself popular at court. He managed to ingratiate himself with Cavour and became an unlikely friend of Azeglio, possibly because that amorous statesman was attracted to his English wife. A vain and quarrelsome individual with a taste for fighting duels,

Persano was both frivolous and irresponsible: he once asked Azeglio, who was prime minister at the time, to give him a false passport so that he could pursue a ballerina in Austrian-held Milan.[20] His friend refused to help.

Persano's seamanship could be embarrassing. In 1851 he ran his ship aground outside Genoa harbour when carrying Piedmont's contribution to the Great Exhibition in London. Two years later, even more embarrassingly, he ran aground again, this time while transporting the royal family to Sardinia for a hunting trip; apparently he was trying to take a short cut and hit some rocks that were not marked on his charts. Although he was arrested and reduced in rank for six months after this episode, the setback did not harm Persano's career. In 1860 Cavour entrusted him with the job of shadowing Garibaldi and stirring up trouble in Palermo and Naples, and in the autumn of that year Persano assisted Cialdini in the capture of Ancona by bombarding the papal port from the sea. Over the next two years he became a parliamentarian, the minister of the navy and the admiral who in 1866 found himself in charge of the fleet at Ancona under government orders to defeat the Austrians and rescue Italy's reputation after the fiasco of Custoza.

Persano was not, however, eager for combat and, although he had only brought his ships up from Taranto, claimed that they needed an overhaul. To repeated orders from Agostino Depretis, the current naval minister in Florence, he responded with a range of reasons for delay: the fleet was not ready, the crews were not trained, water had got into the cylinders and something was wrong with the coal; most important of all, the *Affondatore* (the *Sinker*), the best and newest ship, was still on its way from England, where it had been built. When Depretis told him to make himself master of the Adriatic, Persano replied that he had no proper charts of the one conceivable sea where his navy might fight. While the fleet was still being overhauled after its voyage from Taranto, the audacious Austrian admiral Wilhelm von Tegetthoff appeared with his navy off Ancona, fired a few salvoes and waited for the Italians to come out and engage him; when they remained in port without returning fire, he sailed away and claimed a moral victory.

An exasperated government eventually used the threat of dismissal to force Persano out and attack the island of Lissa off the Dalmatian coast. The navy was duly shelling the Austrian batteries on the island and preparing to land its troops when Tegetthoff reappeared and made a reckoning unavoidable. While Persano was organizing his line, the long-awaited *Affondatore* steamed up, its arrival persuading him to abandon his flagship, the *Re d'Italia*, and direct the battle from an armour-plated turret on the new vessel. Most of his captains were unaware, however, of the changeover and continued to look for signals from the *Re d'Italia* – until it was rammed and sunk by Tegetthoff's own flagship. The simultaneous loss of another ship, which caught fire and exploded, convinced Persano that the battle was lost, even though he still easily outnumbered the Austrians and could have carried on the fray. Like the generals at Custoza, he converted a setback into a disaster and, as with Lamarmora, ordered an unnecessary retreat, leading his ships back to Ancona, where expectant crowds were waiting to cheer captured Austrian vessels.[21]

Lissa ended the career of Persano, who was accused of cowardice but cashiered for the lesser sins of negligence and incapacity. The defeat had other repercussions, especially for the future of the Italian navy, which henceforth tried to avoid battles on the open seas; one consequence of this was the disaster of November 1940, when the British disabled half the fleet that lay anchored in the harbour of Taranto. Yet the most insidious effect of the 1866 war was its impact on the psyche of the Italian nation. The very names Lissa and Custoza became reproaches, incitements to redress and redemption. Instead of persuading Italians not to attempt to become a Great Power, they encouraged them to try even harder. As Austria seemed the obvious place to seek such redemption, Victor Emanuel suggested to Bismarck in 1878 that a joint attack on the Habsburgs would give each of them victory and new territory. When the chancellor replied that Germany was big enough already, Italy abandoned the idea, became an ally of Austria and embarked on colonial adventures in Africa. Yet the defeats of 1866 rankled and continued to do so well into the twentieth century. The obsession with amends was a fundamental motive in the decisions to take part in the world wars in 1915 and 1940.

THE RISORGIMENTO
WITHOUT HEROES

For many years after 1860, official Italy reiterated the claim that the nation had been made by a 'generation of giants', whose names honoured its streets, whose statues ornamented its squares and whose deeds filled its history books. Yet many people experienced doubts, feelings of unease and a sense of disappointment with the performance of the new state. If the Risorgimento had been such a splendid achievement, why was united Italy not more of a success? If the state was on the verge of becoming a Great Power, why could it not feed its own people? Why were so many Italians emigrating to the Americas?

Brain-washing by myth and propaganda may have been successful up to a point, but it failed to eradicate the suspicion that the wars of independence had not been as heroic as was officially claimed. Not many people had died, little glory had been won except by Garibaldi, and the outcome seemed to have been decided by foreign armies. The subsequent weakness of Italian nationalism made people wonder whether the patriotic movement had ever been very strong. Victor Emanuel had spoken of 'the cry of anguish' from all over Italy, Garibaldi had heard 'the groan of despair . . . from a million Italian throats', but few others had heard them, at any rate in great numbers. According to the Italian historian Alberto Mario Banti, patriots were inspired by an artistic canon of some forty works – novels, poems, essays, plays, heroic operas and paintings.[22] Doubtless these things did inspire literate young men in the cities, but most other Italians were not in a position to read the novels of Azeglio or study the paintings of Hayez. People may have had more opportunity to be inspired by music, although most opera houses were bourgeois enclaves for which the majority of Italians could not afford either a ticket or the appropriate clothes.

Italian historians are still prone to exaggerate the extent of patriotic valour. In a recent biography of Garibaldi the distinguished Neapolitan scholar Alberto Scirocco acclaimed 'the heroism with which young men from every corner of the Italian peninsula demonstrated faith in Italy's destiny'.[23] Yet several corners were virtually unrepresented: few of the young men came from the south or the islands or the countryside, as Garibaldi discovered when he marched around much of rural Italy without attracting volunteers. Scirocco's romantic youths were mainly northern, urban, middle-class and educated. The bravery of the Bandiera brothers and others like them is indisputable, but not many patriots were willing to sacrifice their lives: more Italians were killed in a day's fighting against the Ethiopians at Adowa in 1896 than in all the wars of the Risorgimento put together.

In times of revolution few revolutionaries think that events are moving too fast, but some Italian patriots did later wonder if the process of unification might not have been too swift. The seven kingdoms of Anglo-Saxon England had taken four centuries to become one, and a shared sense of English patriotism was forged towards the end of that time in response to the Danish invasions. Yet nearly all the territories of the seven Italian states were moulded into one between the summer of 1859 and the spring of 1861, while the remaining areas were absorbed over the following decade. This was obviously not long enough for a sense of nationhood to develop in a country with many regional traditions but few national ones. Nor did patriots have the assistance of an external danger, for only propagandists could claim that the Austrians were as grim or as aggressive as the Danes in their dragon-prowed longboats. Italian nationalism, such as it was, became real only after the nation had been made.

Three generations after unity, the communist intellectual Antonio Gramsci criticized the Risorgimento as a 'passive revolution' because its leaders had failed to ally themselves with the peasants; unlike the jacobins in France, they had thus failed to create a modern national state. Without sharing Gramsci's simplistic analysis of class behaviour, Piero Gobetti, a liberal and courageous opponent of fascism, came to a similar conclusion, arguing that the Risorgimento had failed because it had been the work of a minority with little popular participation. The arrival of fascism in the 1920s, he believed, was a consequence of the patriots' earlier failure to win the people's support or produce a creditable ruling class. The very title of Gobetti's book, *Risorgimento senza eroi* (*Risorgimento without Heroes*), published in 1926 after his death at the age of twenty-five, was considered a heresy requiring ponderous rebuttal. The problems after unification, declared a prominent historian, Adolfo Omodeo, were not a consequence of the Risorgimento but of 'the progressive loss of the sense of the Risorgimento'. The heroes must still be considered heroes because they had 'acted for the people', they had 'believed in the people and in the nation'. Cavour and his fellow giants had 'made themselves become the nation', just as the 7,000 ancient Israelites who had refused to bow to Baal had become 'the true Israel'. In a passage implying that the historian's job is not to write history but to preserve historical traditions, Omodeo argued that 'one must hold firmly to [the giants'] tradition and their spirit. One cannot abandon and destroy foundations laid with such difficulty.'[24]

Political nationalism may have subsided with the fall of Mussolini, but historiographical nationalism survived the Duce's exit. The appearance in the 1950s of a myth-breaker in the shape of Denis Mack Smith, a young Cambridge don, was thus highly unwelcome to the academic establishment. In two books, a study of Cavour and Garibaldi in 1860 and a history of modern Italy, Mack Smith fell upon the icons of unification, shattering the status of Cavour as 'the wisest statesman' of Europe and of Victor Emanuel as the great patriot king. Even more unpopular were his assertions that the revolts of the Risorgimento were 'largely social insurrections' tenuously connected to politics and patriotism, and that the wars themselves, far from being 'a simple story of deliverance from the Austrian oppressor', had been a succession of civil wars.[25] Although nationalist historians have preferred to ignore the fact, thousands of Lombards, Romans, Neapolitans and Venetians had fought against the patriots, and almost all the Italian blood spilt at the Battle of Magenta belonged to soldiers from Lombardy-Venetia fighting for the Austrians.

Italian critics praised Mack Smith for his mastery of sources, his discovery of new material and his attempt to explain what had been wrong with the Risorgimento and why it had led to colonial defeat and to fascism. Yet traditionalists were appalled by his iconoclasm, his lack of respect for the idols of the nation. Unable to confute him on matters of fact, the Englishman's detractors accused him of 'libellous language' and complained about his 'attitude', his use of irony, the 'arrogance' with which he had deprived the Risorgimento of its 'soul'. A century after unification, many historians still preferred romantic legends to revealed facts. The Risorgimento, proclaimed Professor Rodolico, the guardian of its 'soul', 'was spirit of sacrifice, it was suffering in the ways of exile and in the galleys, it was blood of Italian youth on the battlefields . . .' Above all, 'it was the passion of a people for its Italian identity'.[26]

9

Making Italians

PIEDMONT COMES TO NAPLES

Even today, when you arrive in Naples by train from the north, you feel you have crossed a frontier and reached another land. As you leave the station and find yourself in the Piazza Garibaldi, the feeling is intensified by the sight of so many foreigners, young men from Africa and Latin America selling bracelets, sunglasses and fake designer bags, young women from Senegal and Brazil selling themselves, standing in clusters around the market by the Porta Nolana, trying to look unobtrusive to the police but obvious enough for potential customers to realize what they are offering. Yet even without the immigrants, the place seems different. There are sensually distinctive qualities about the air and the light, the bay and its vegetation, the way the inhabitants talk and gesticulate, the way they exist.

The Piedmontese who came uninvited in 1860 felt they had arrived not in another country but in another continent. Accustomed to the straight gridded streets of Turin, they were disgusted by Spaccanapoli, the heart of old Naples, a warren of dark, intimidating alleys thronged with urchins and card-players and hostile *lazzaroni*. They were familiar with Baroque churches – they had them at home – but theirs were restrained, almost classical structures situated logically on sober streets; they were not like these weird creations, almost obscene in their extravagant curves and their lavish ornamentation. The architecture of Piedmont had little use for majolica tiles, so profusely and meretriciously flaunted in Naples on floors and benches and even up pillars. Nor had it been tempted by *guglie*, those colossal marble obelisks set in the middle of small squares, follies bursting with a promiscuous mass of cherubs, mermaids and coats of arms, with scrolls and fruit and scallop shells, with popes and saints and dedications to the Virgin. To northern eyes they were the summit of bad taste.

Naples has changed much in the last 150 years. The street-urchins have gone, and so have most of the monks; motor-cars have come, along with car-horns and lawless driving. Yet it is still a city with nuns and child accordionists, a place of plaster saints and nativity scenes, of pizza and the Camorra, of lines of washing strung across its alleys, of pavement stalls and tiny food shops that seem to have strayed from the souks in Tunis. The old palaces, built on such narrow streets that you can hardly see their façades, are still inhabited, though not by the families that built them. A representative example of an unrestored palazzo in Spaccanapoli today will have a courtyard of peeling plaster cluttered with motorbikes and small businesses: a hairdresser's, a travel agency and a jeweller's repair shop; on the first floor you will find a notary and a dancing school and, further up, below the residential flats at the top, an oculist and a bed and breakfast. Outside, the little streets still have life and bustle, yet they also emanate a sense of death and unchanging religious custom. Black-edged funeral notices are ubiquitous, announcing that Anna or Maria, the widow Mazzella or Fassari, has died, her 'dear existence extinguished' in the same serene manner in which she had lived her life. Little shrines dedicated to the Virgin are still illuminated in the angles of tiny lanes, Mary and Jesus bedecked with glittering crowns above vases of fading lilies and fake dahlias.

For the Piedmontese the nutritional prospect must have seemed as foreign as the rest of Naples: the profusion of tomatoes and their sauces, the anchovies fried in oil, the sea bass and the sea-urchins, the street vendors with their cauldrons of steaming pasta. It was all so different from the stews and sausages of their native land. Politically the conquest of the south may have seemed a victory of polenta over pasta, of the Bolognese *mortadella* over the Neapolitan *maccheroni*. But in culinary matters the southerners resisted with success. One Neapolitan chef achieved renown with a pizza of tomato and mozzarella, which he named after Queen Margherita, the most gracious and elegant member of the Savoia dynasty, who accepted the honour. Eventually the southern cuisine went on to the offensive and was victorious across Italy and further afield. Just as olive oil has defeated butter almost everywhere except in the Cisalpine redoubts, pasta has vanquished polenta, that yellow maize porridge with a vitamin deficiency that causes pellagra disease and is now used chiefly as an accompaniment to calves' liver.

In 1860 few northerners knew much about southern Italy and even fewer foresaw any difficulties they might have in governing their new acquisitions. They realized it had not recently been prosperous but thought this was a temporary problem, a consequence of Bourbon misrule, which they would soon be able to fix with parliaments, free trade and efficient administration. They had read about Magna Graecia and Campania Felix, they remembered what Virgil and more recently Goethe had written, and they believed the land was so fertile that southerners could afford to be lazy. They knew about the luxuries of ancient Sybaris, which was said to have invented the chamber pot as well as the 'Turkish' bath,[1] but they had not visited its site in Italy's instep and thus did not realize that the place could no longer support a sybaritic existence. They seemed quite unaware of drought and erosion and the other climatic and geographical disadvantages suffered by the south.

Ignorance was accompanied by the contempt of northerners from Italy and beyond. In the early nineteenth century one French traveller, Augustin Creuzé de Lesser, announced that 'Europe ends at Naples and ends there quite badly'; Sicily, Calabria and the rest belonged to Africa. Fifty years later, another Frenchman, Alfred Maury, described a journey south as if he were in a time-machine going backwards: in Turin and Milan you were in modern society, in Florence you were with the Medici, by the time you reached Rome you were in the Middle Ages, in Naples you had gone back to the pagan era, and further south you found customs that had 'all the naive simplicity of ancient times'.[2] Most observers found the southern landscape magnificent but its people squalid; it was 'a paradise inhabited by devils' and governed by them too. Southerners were spineless, idle, corrupt and so carnally sensuous that the Marquis de Sade – of all people – found them 'the most degraded species' in the world.[3] Yet they were also seen as savage, violent and irrational, perhaps taking after their earthquakes and volcanoes. Such prejudice was buttressed by historical example, pseudo-science and primitive anthropology. Racial differences, it was claimed, made southerners more likely to be corrupt than northerners, though it was accepted that not all southerners were the same. One theory, occasionally still uttered, held that western Sicilians have been *mafiosi* because they are descended from Arabs, whereas eastern islanders, especially the inhabitants of Syracuse, have been less violent and more civilized because their ancestors were Greeks.[4]

A politician who typified these attitudes was Cavour's first viceroy of Naples, Luigi Carlo Farini, the man who compared Neapolitans unfavourably with the bedouin. To the interior minister in Turin, he described the people as 'swine' living in 'a hell-pit' and their lawyers as 'tricksters ... law-twisters, casuists and professional liars with the conscience of pimps'; what a pity, he added, that Piedmont's civilization forbade floggings and 'cutting people's tongues out'. Farini began to have doubts about the wisdom of unification soon after he arrived in Naples at the end of 1860, but it was too late to go back. The 'entire Italian question', he believed, now revolved around Naples: 'to succeed there [was] to create Italy'.[5]

It soon became clear that few southerners were eager to help in the creation. Neapolitans from the poorer districts could sometimes be heard shouting 'Viva Garibaldi!' or even 'Viva Francesco!', for they much preferred the old Bourbons, who had spoken their dialect and possessed the common touch, to Victor Emanuel, a foreign king who did not conceal his disdain for his new subjects and referred to them as '*canaille*'. Giacinto De Sivo, a local historian, railed against the nationalists' misnomers: the destruction of his country should not be called a 'risorgimento'; the northern oppression should not be called 'liberty'; 'this servitude to Piedmont, the servant of powers beyond the Alps', should not be called 'independence'. 'Piedmont cries Italy,' he exclaimed, 'and makes war on Italians because she does not want to make Italy – she wants to eat Italy ...'[6] Other people held milder views yet still regretted the result of the plebiscite in which they had been voting less for Victor Emanuel than for Garibaldi, who was popular even though he was a northerner. They remembered that the Bourbon government had been often incompetent and sometimes irksome but they began to wonder if they really preferred to be ruled by an alien dynasty in distant Turin.

Since the summer of 1859 Azeglio had been warning it would be a disaster if the Piedmontese attempted to 'swallow down Naples'. Two years later, after the swallowing had been done and the swallowed were in revolt, he suggested that the Neapolitans should be asked 'once and for all whether they want us there or not'.[7] Cavour was by then dead but he had already decreed that the Neapolitans would not be asked. Bixio had told him that southerners were 'a bunch of orientals' who understood 'nothing but force', and he had agreed with Bixio. He was determined, he told the king, 'to impose unity on the most corrupt and weakest part of Italy', and to do so by force if necessary. Disorder would not be tolerated, nor would political opposition or even a free press. However much the Neapolitans disliked the prospect of unification, they were going to be unified anyway: it would be better to have a civil war than the 'irreparable catastrophe' of a break-up of the new nation.[8] It did not apparently occur to Cavour that, if southern Italy were denied liberty and social justice, its inhabitants might wonder what they were going to gain from unification.

Even northern populations resented the imposition of Piedmontese laws: the Tuscans, for example, had no desire to bring back the death penalty which they had first abolished in the eighteenth century. Yet the insensitivity of the Piedmontese in the south, and the arrogance of their assumption that they knew what was best for southerners, made their policies even more damaging in the former Kingdom of the Two Sicilies. Back in the twelfth century, at the Assizes of Ariano, King Roger of Sicily had wisely proclaimed that, as there were so many different peoples and cultures in his kingdom, they must be allowed as far as possible to retain their own laws and customs. Such wisdom was denied to Cavour, who would not permit the Neapolitans to keep a legal system they were rightly proud of. He certainly paid no attention to Giuseppe Ferrari, a federalist deputy from Lombardy, who informed him in parliament that the laws of the southern kingdom compared well with those of other civilized nations and were probably the best in all Italy.

The officials of the new government were too blinkered to notice certain basic and important features of Neapolitan history. They seemed unaware that the capital had no town hall, no parliament building and no medieval traditions of self-government. It was a royal city dependent on a court and a bureaucracy; such prosperity as it had would therefore decrease when its status declined from national capital to provincial city. Nor did they realize how disastrous a doctrinaire application of free trade would be to industries which depended on tariffs and state orders to protect them from northern and foreign competition. Equally crass was their failure to anticipate the effect of high taxes on people unaccustomed to paying them, especially those directed at the poor such as the grist tax. Increased taxation was required primarily to build a national army and navy, institutions the south did not want or care about. It was also needed to service Piedmont's large national debt, which was now shared with all the annexed territories. Naples, where the Bourbons had accumulated impressive gold reserves, was thus forced – on top of everything else – to help pay Piedmont's debts.

Another cause for resentment was the treatment of the Bourbon army after its defeats in 1860 and 1861. A number of senior officers, especially those who had deserted or fought badly against Garibaldi, were welcomed into the Piedmontese forces. Yet about 60,000 men were disbanded and left without jobs and pay, and 13,000 of Francesco's most loyal soldiers – those who had fought to the end at Capua, Gaeta and elsewhere – were kept as prisoners and incarcerated in Alpine fortresses. Conditions in the northern jails were so appalling that many of them died there of hunger, cold and disease.

In the south fighting continued for years after the arrival of Garibaldi. Within weeks of Francesco's departure – and just after the proclamation of united Italy – an anti-Piedmontese revolt broke out in Basilicata; within a few more weeks it had spread throughout the southern mainland, up to the Abruzzi and down to Apulia and Calabria. The rebels did not attempt to form an army but remained divided among several hundred armed bands; their tactics were guerrilla – consisting mainly of killings, kidnappings and ambushes – and their victims were the soldiers and officials of the new regime. The previous year Cialdini had dismissed resisters as 'brigands', and the label stuck: the enemies were not considered normal enemies but brigands and outlaws who could be treated as such. Historians followed suit, with the result that a civil war lasting five years became known as *il brigantaggio* or 'the brigandage'.

Some later historians, often marxists, regarded the revolt as a social insurrection and the rebels as freedom fighters defying a foreign aggressor. Like the earlier interpretation, this was simplistic because it ignored multiplicity of motive. Rebels may have shared the same target – the new regime – but they had diverse reasons for attacking it. Many were indeed brigands, the kind of men who had been around for many years and who had been encouraged to fight the French by both the Bourbons and the British half a century before. But there were many former soldiers as well, men loyal to the old monarchy who had been disbanded by the Piedmontese and who now joined the guerrillas in the hills. Other recruits included peasants fleeing conscription or refusing to pay the new taxes. As they moved around the interior, the rebels received support from the villages, from Bourbon loyalists and devout Catholics outraged by Piedmont's recent anti-clerical policies. Some of the bands obtained assistance abroad from Bourbon supporters and Francesco's exiled court in Rome.

The northern generals followed Cavour's instructions to use force and received statutory support for this from a new law which empowered them to employ repressive measures in 'those provinces declared by royal decree to be infested with brigands'. General Della Rocca, the future sluggard of the second Battle of Custoza, informed the prime minister that he had ordered his men 'not to waste time taking prisoners', and in his autobiography he boasted of the number of summary executions he had carried out; when told by the government to reduce the number and shoot only the *capi* (the chiefs), he and his commanders responded by calling all captured rebels *capi* and shooting the lot of them.[9] Other generals took a more Old Testament approach, urging their soldiers to show no mercy in 'purifying the countryside by fire and sword'. In August 1861 the inhabitants of Pontelandolfo, a large village north-east of Naples, were so overjoyed by the arrival of a band of brigands that they murdered the local tax collector and sang a *Te Deum* to King Francesco in the parish church. A small detachment of *bersaglieri*, which rashly went to see what was going on, was then wiped out by a force of armed peasants. Cialdini's response was predictable: Pontelandolfo and a neighbouring village were to be reduced to 'a heap of rubble', and their adult male inhabitants were to be shot. Some 400 people, a good number of them neither male nor adult, were killed on the day of the consequent slaughter.

By 1865 the Italian army had contained the revolt, though some fighting stuttered on for another five years. The number of rebel dead, those executed or killed in combat, is difficult to calculate, and assessments vary from under 6,000 to over 60,000. Whatever the true figure, unification had provoked a civil war of such atrocities and such dimensions that most of the Italian army was dispatched to the south to deal with it. It was so appalling a way to begin life as a 'united' kingdom that the government tried to suppress information about what was happening. Members of parliament hissed and shouted if a brave soul uttered the words 'civil war': no, no, they cried, it was a punishment of brigands. They were equally outraged when a Neapolitan parliamentarian compared the Piedmontese in Naples to the conquistadors in Mexico and Peru. Foreigners could also be hostile to those among them who doubted the sacred nature of Italian unity. One MP at Westminster risked unpopularity by dismissing the idea of brigandage and speaking of 'a civil war, a spontaneous popular movement against a foreign occupation'. In a debate in 1863 Benjamin Disraeli wondered why Parliament was allowed to consider the condition of Poland but not the situation in Naples. 'True,' he observed, 'in one country the insurgents are called brigands, and in the other patriots; but, with that exception, I have not learned from this discussion that there is any marked difference between them.'[10]

SICILY GOES DOWNHILL

As violence faded on the mainland, it flared up in Sicily, a large-scale revolt in 1866 following a smaller one three years earlier. Taking advantage of the withdrawal of the island's garrison (sent north in the summer of 1866 to fight the Austrians), armed bands emerged from the hills and occupied most of Palermo. The composition of the bands was similar to that of the Neapolitan 'brigands', a mixture that included criminals, peasants, deserters and other former soldiers. As usual the government failed to consider whether it might have been responsible for the revolt; instead of perceiving the outbreak as a social insurrection provoked by the policies of Turin, ministers blamed the Mafia* and sent in the army. Once again force was the policy adopted by the government and carried out by generals who believed that Sicilians were too barbarous to understand anything else. While the navy bombarded Palermo, the army went on the rampage, arresting and executing islanders.

The Sicilian desire for autonomy was not a new passion. It had reached insurrectionary point on many occasions over the previous six centuries and four times already in the previous fifty years; it remains an important political issue even though the island today enjoys an autonomous status. Cavour had taken note of this sentiment and promised he would satisfy it if Sicilians voted for annexation; after they had done so, he changed his mind and pressed ahead with 'piedmontization'. The islanders had also been promised a redistribution of land, but this too was revoked. Like the common lands, the former Church estates might have been utilized in some scheme of agrarian reform to benefit the poor; in the event they were sold cheaply to prototype *mafiosi* from the middle classes, and the peasants received nothing. Although Sicilians had been told they would benefit from annexation, the advantages must have been difficult for many of them to discern. As in Naples, the poor were often left unemployed by the consequences of free trade, they were conscripted by an army they regarded as an enemy, and they were forced to pay taxes that seemed specifically aimed at them: why else were heavy dues imposed on their beasts (donkeys and mules) and lighter ones levied on the landowners' cattle?

The imposition of liberalism upon Sicily seemed a good idea to Cavour and his colleagues: they were confident that everyone would

---

*The word was not commonly used in the 1860s and in any case it meant different things to different people. Individuals of the era often identified as *mafiosi* include agents of absentee landowners in the *latifondi*, gangsters running protection rackets in the lemon groves of Palermo, and newly rich men who had enclosed the common lands after 1860 and held on to them by force. Some people even then regarded the Mafia as different from other criminal organizations, as a secret society with its own rituals and arcane rules. Discussion of the Mafia and how to deal with it was for a century hindered by the refusal of many Sicilians to admit that it and its 'men of honour' even existed.

benefit from a combination of free trade, representative government and anti-clerical legislation, and they were thus puzzled by the reluctance of the population to embrace it. In 1875 two perceptive young Tuscans, Sidney Sonnino and Leopoldo Franchetti, went to Sicily and afterwards explained why: Italian institutions on the island, they reported, were 'based on a merely formal liberalism' and had simply 'given the oppressing class a legal means of continuing as they always' had done. The oppressing class may have been changing, as hard-headed businessmen replaced a dwindling aristocracy, but the oppressiveness remained: as a leading Sicilian historian, Rosario Romeo, later observed, the new ruling class had simply appropriated the worst characteristics of the old.[11]

In 1955 an impoverished Sicilian prince, Giuseppe di Lampedusa, decided at the age of fifty-eight to forsake his idle existence and become a writer. Over the following two and a half years, before he died of lung cancer, he wrote incessantly, his production including two short stories, a memoir of his childhood and his great novel known as *The Leopard* or *Der Leopard* in German but published in Italian as *Il Gattopardo* (denoting a serval or ocelot though the author intended the animal to be considered a leopard) and translated as *Le Guépard* (a cheetah) in French and *De Tijger Kat* (a margay or tiger cat) in Dutch. Set in the years of the Risorgimento, with aristocratic decadence as its theme, the novel depicts a Palermitan atmosphere charged with the optimism of liberalism. One character claims that unification will bring 'liberty, security, lighter taxes, ease, trade. Everything will be better ...' Yes, everything will be better, 'the only ones to lose will be the priests'. But Lampedusa knew that very little had got better and that few people had won except the opportunists, the men of 'tenacious greed and avarice' who had made fortunes from the state's seizure and subsequent sale of Church lands. Prince Fabrizio, the protagonist based on the author's great-grandfather, remains undeceived by unification and the advent of liberalism. He knows that nothing much will change. The Sicilian Risorgimento would be little more than a change of dynasty ('Torinese instead of Neapolitan dialect') and the substitution of one class by another. All the rest would be a veneer, a superficial application of liberalism on a rough and brutal society that was plainly unready for it. In his book Lampedusa was quite charitable towards the Piedmontese in Sicily, satirizing their naivety rather than their ignorance of the south or the arrogance of their behaviour. More critical was he of the opinions and activities of his fellow islanders, although he sympathized with their anxieties about the future, about their feeling that they were a conquered people and that they would not really belong to the new state. Prince Fabrizio, like his creator, understands that antagonism towards the Bourbons had not required so drastic a remedy, that it was crazy for Sicilians to think that heavy rule from Turin would suit them better than loose control from Naples.

Sicilians and other southerners suffered a number of disadvantages, among them the ancient miseries of drought and unproductive land together with dismal transport to their potential export markets in the distant north. After unification they also had to endure the government's ill-considered economic policies. The insistence on free trade at the time of independence had ruined heavy industry around Naples and silk and other textiles elsewhere in the south. So deluded had the government been that it thought it could inject the spirit of Manchester into southern manufacturers, men who had never been to Lancashire and had neither the capital nor the experience to adapt their industries. A generation later, the government itself repudiated the Manchester dogmas, and in 1888 the prime minister, Francesco Crispi, decided to pick a quarrel with the French by launching a tariff war so ruinous for Italy that its exports to France fell by two-thirds. Tariffs may have helped northern farmers and cereal growers in the south, who were not harvesting for export, but they were disastrous for the growers of fruit and vines. After the devastation of French vineyards by phylloxera in the years after 1875, southern Italian wine makers had invested in their businesses and had prospered with their exports. Yet they could not compete with the resurgent French vintners after the introduction of retaliatory tariffs in France. Nor were citrus growers able to export their produce when, in addition to transport costs, it was subject to import duties. The two regions most damaged by Crispi's tariff war were Apulia and Sicily, his own island.

In the 1870s a small number of remarkable parliamentarians began to visit the south, report on its condition and propose remedies that the government should adopt. Subsequently known as *meridionalisti*, the first generation of these altruists included Sonnino, Franchetti and Giustino Fortunato, a liberal, enlightened but deeply pessimistic land-owner from Basilicata. Their investigations were thorough and reliable, leading to devastating revelations of poverty, neglect, a dearth of public works and an almost complete absence of social, fiscal or economic justice. Perhaps they concentrated too much on the south's most benighted areas and thus missed certain nuances that might have tempered their stark vision of the 'two Italies'. Yet their findings were valid and their advice perceptive, and it was a tragedy for Italy that they failed to persuade governments to pursue policies that might have encouraged the south to feel it was part of the new nation.

In the Abruzzi Franchetti reported that agricultural workers were virtually slaves to the local landowners. In Sicily Sonnino concluded that the peasants were worse off than in any other part of Europe; they were even worse off than they had been before unification. Both men pointed out that liberalism was a meaningless notion in such coerced and impoverished societies; both also blamed landowners for showing such little interest in improving their land and building houses for their farmworkers. Estate owners, old and new, remained in control of enormous areas after 1860 and became even more powerful than they had been under the Bourbons. So weak was the new state in rural parts that they were effectively the government, the employers, the arbiters of justice, the selectors of members of parliament, and the providers of bridges and roads in places that suited themselves. Their position was secure because governments in Rome acquiesced in their dominance in return for their parliamentary votes. Projected reforms could thus be blocked or diluted whenever they wished.

Towards the end of the nineteenth century the wealth gap expanded in Sicily as it did in the rest of Italy and in much of Europe. In the west of the island the Florio family amassed a huge fortune from shipping, sulphur and wine; another bonanza was secured by an English family called Whitaker, whose profits from Marsala wine enabled them to build splendid villas and a palazzo in Palermo designed in Venetian Gothic. The capital's exotic, partly eastern character attracted the royal families of northern Europe, and a procession of princes, including Kaiser Wilhelm and King Edward VII, turned up on holiday in their yachts. The society of Palermo's Belle Epoque was no doubt frivolous, its members disporting themselves at balls and race meetings and fancy-dress parties, but it was majestic in its way, above all in scale, and glittering enough to attract the talents of Sarah Bernhardt and Giacomo Puccini. Yet its brilliance was brief, dulled by the squandering of fortunes and by the Messina earthquake of 1908, so that its style remained in the memory of its survivors as part of a transient golden age. Towards the end of his life the Duke of Verdura, who made his fortune as a jewellery designer in New York, recalled the garden parties of the epoch:

> ladies in light colours with boas, veils under enormous straw hats, gentlemen with their boaters under their arms and a few cavalry officers thrown in. Lace parasols against a background of palm trees and cypresses and long tables covered with white cloths spread with pyramids of strawberries and every sort of ice-cream.[12]

Yet throughout the epoch Palermo remained a city of slums as well as sumptuousness. The capital and its provinces were lawless lands, places of private violence where men did not wait for justice from the state; the murder rate in Sicily was fourteen times higher than it was in Lombardy. Much of the violence was committed by the enigmatic Mafia, but a lot of it had social causes. In the 1890s there were frequent peasant riots against both the actions and the inaction of the government: against the scarcity of land, higher rents, higher food prices (a result of Crispi's 'corn laws'), and against unfair taxes, especially the grist tax, a symbol of repression since the rule of the Spanish. Social unrest led to the creation of a movement called the *fasci*, left-wing peasant leagues that encouraged strikes, the seizure of land and sometimes the burning of tax-offices. Like the fascists of the following century, they took their name from the Latin word *fasces* (a bundle of rods surrounding an axe and symbolizing ancient Roman authority), but the two movements had little else in common.

Crispi, who became prime minister for the second time at the end of 1893, saw the *fasci* as promoters of revolution. In a move that would have appalled his mentor, this former *garibaldino* thus declared martial law, banned the *fasci*, arrested their leaders and deported many of them to penal islands. Angst and memories of his radical past may have persuaded Crispi subsequently to propose a land reform that would have emasculated the *latifondi*, but it was sabotaged by landowners and other conservatives in parliament. This reverse marked the ultimate defeat of the south: over the next two decades millions of people from Sicily and the southern mainland gave up on Italy and emigrated to the continents of America.

Those who remained continued to feel estranged from the new state. With the south's industry ruined, its agriculture in decline and its people so poor that many were forced to leave, what improvements were they able to see – apart from some new railways? Many southerners concluded that unification had been a mistake and, when confronted by nationalists who insisted it was their destiny, argued that at least it should have been done differently, that a federal system should have been established. Two of the greatest southern figures of the period pleaded early in the new century for such a system to be set up. Let the south grow, declared the Apulian historian Gaetano Salvemini, by letting it be autonomous of the central government. Leave us alone in the south, urged the Sicilian priest Luigi Sturzo, who became the inspiration for the future Christian Democratic Party.

> Leave us in the south to govern ourselves, plan our own financial policy, spend our own taxes, take responsibility for our own public works, and find our own remedies for our difficulties ... we are not schoolchildren, we have no need of the North's concerned protection.[13]

In 1899 Giustino Fortunato, one of the wisest of Italian politicians, declared that it was 'no accident that there are those who say – and I am quoting my father! – that the unification of Italy was a sin against history and geography'.[14] He himself sometimes felt the same and, loyal patriot though he was, he privately admitted that unification had ruined the south and prevented its economic revival in the 1860s; for him the nation frequently seemed to be on the verge of breaking up. In the same era a gentleman from Piedmont presented the French novelist René Bazin with an intriguing image: 'We are too long a country, *signore*. The head and the tail will never touch each other, but if they are made to do so, the head will bite the tail.'[15]

ROME AND PARLIAMENT

The new Italian capital was sometimes referred to as the Third Rome, distinguishing it from the Rome of the Caesars and the Rome of the popes. As the successor to such imposing forebears, politicians felt the need to refashion it with appropriate and equivalent splendour. Third Rome must have wide streets, imposing bridges and public buildings that were above all grandiose; it also required embankments to stop the Tiber from flooding.

Glorious as it still is, Rome lost a great deal during the transformation. Many convents and monasteries were pulled down, and old villas and gardens were flattened to make way for new development. The travel writer Augustus Hare complained in 1896 that old Rome had been 'spoilt', 'destroyed' and reduced by the Piedmontese 'occupation' to an 'inferior mediocrity'.[16] Some of the replacements are certainly monstrous, notably the huge Palace of Justice, a pompous and over-ornamented pile built on the banks of the river in 1893. As it was constructed without regard for the spring underneath it, subsidence in its foundations has brought it close to collapse. Another vast deformity is the Vittoriano, which commemorates the first king of united Italy and may be the largest monument to one person erected since the Great Pyramid of Giza. Often compared derisively to a wedding cake or a typewriter, it is the dominant symbol of the Third Rome. Its very position – blocking the view of Michelangelo's palaces on the Capitoline – suggests its designers wanted themselves to be considered superior to the builders of the first and second cities. Not only is the monument bombastic and badly sited, it is also built in a material – bright white Brescian marble – that contrasts flashily with Rome's local stone, the warm and lightly ochred travertine.

Apart from competing worthily with earlier Romes, Third Rome was intended to overshadow its rival and victim, Vatican Rome. One way of doing this was by building new streets near the papal enclave and naming them after pre-Christian Romans such as Scipio, Cicero, Pompey and the Gracchi. There is also a Piazza Cavour and a Piazza del Risorgimento, which adjoins the Vatican walls, though most martial episodes of unification (Solferino, Milazzo, Volturno etc.) are commemorated in streets further away, near the railway station.

Pope Pius IX reacted to Rome's capture in 1870 by excommunicating 'the sub-Alpine usurper' (Victor Emanuel) and refusing to recognize united Italy. Yet in spite of hostile relations, the new state understood the need for Catholic support and made some early concessions in the hope of attracting it. The Law of Papal Guarantees of 1871 granted the pontiff the status of a sovereign, with foreign ambassadors accredited to him, and gave him a generous income and free 'enjoyment' of the Vatican. This munificence was not excessive but, even so, it may have been unwise because it permitted the formation of 'a state within a state', one that could denounce the larger entity with impunity for the next sixty years.

The pope, who liked to describe himself as 'the prisoner of the Vatican', was not mollified by the law. Still resentful of the conquest, the closure of convents and the loss of his territories, he refused to have any dealings with the government and continued to insist that he was the rightful ruler of the Papal States. His response to Italian nationalism and to much of the modern world was to lead the Church into zones of obscurantism unvisited by most of his predecessors. In 1854 he had asserted that the doctrine of the Immaculate Conception – the belief that the Virgin Mary herself was conceived without sin – had been revealed by God. Ten years later, the Syllabus of Errors had condemned eighty modern 'errors' and declared it impossible for the pontiff to accept 'progress, liberalism and civilization as lately introduced'. More recently, in 1870, Pius had proclaimed the doctrine of Papal Infallibility, which asserted that the pope himself could make no errors when speaking, in his capacity as Bishop of Rome, on matters of faith and morals. Yet he and his four successors were curiously reluctant to exercise the power he had insisted upon. No pope claimed infallibility until 1950, when Pius XII declared that 'the ever Virgin Mary' had been 'assumed in body and soul to heavenly glory'.

In 1864 the longest-serving of all popes had told Italian Catholics it was 'not expedient' to vote in parliamentary elections, a position he reiterated after the fall of Rome and one which was strengthened by his successor, Leo XIII, who in 1881 forbade any members of his flock to stand for parliament or vote in national elections. Not until the following century did a pope publish an encyclical allowing Catholics to vote in order to preserve social stability – that is, to prevent the emerging Socialist Party from dominating the country's politics.

Many Catholics entitled to vote did so anyway, despite the papal pronouncements. All the same, the Vatican's refusal to recognize the Italian state was fatal to the cohesion and consolidation of the new nation. Catholicism was the one thing shared by nearly all Italians, and the papacy was the only institution in the country that could claim both longevity and continuity. Pius could have been a unifier yet decided alas to be a disruptor. His outrage and hostility encouraged many people to question the legitimacy of the new state and thus weakened the loyalty of millions of its citizens. An alliance of nationalism and Catholicism could have made a powerful force, as it did in Ireland, Spain and Poland. Instead, the animosity between them within Italy led to a divide in an already fractured country that lasted until Mussolini's Lateran Treaty of 1929. Devout Catholics were unable to play a commanding role in Italian politics until a christian democrat became prime minister after the Second World War.

The parliament of united Italy, chosen by an electorate of under half a million people,* had not begun auspiciously in Turin or improved much during its few years in Florence. Cavour's predominance in the 1850s may have obscured the innate instability of a system that gave too much power to a capricious monarch: the new kingdom had six prime ministers in its first three and a half years. In Rome the turnover of governments slowed down for a while before speeding up again and carrying on at a similar pace (except under Mussolini) until the beginning of the twenty-first century. As for the Chamber of Deputies, housed in the huge but unlovely Palazzo Montecitorio, this institution never succeeded in becoming a focus of national pride or a repository of the people's trust. Some of the blame for this situation should be assigned to Victor Emanuel, who despised parliament and told Lanza, one of his best prime ministers, that it had no business to discuss matters of high policy.

For fifteen years after 1861 Italy was governed by men who had

---

*419,846 from a population of 21.8 million in 1861 (i.e. without Lazio and Venetia); of these, 57 per cent (barely one-hundredth of the population) exercised their right to vote. A reform bill of 1882 increased the electorate to just over 2 million, and another in 1913 introduced universal male suffrage – five years before Britain. Italian women could not vote until after the Second World War, when they greatly assisted the christian democrats.

been Cavour's colleagues and supporters. These were liberal conservatives from the north, patriotic and high-minded on the whole, law-givers who sometimes liked to think they shared the virtues and values of Roman senators of old: a plaque in the baptistery of Pistoia cathedral commemorates one parliamentarian not only as a saint in his family life but also as an 'example of integrity', moderation, austerity and altruism. Known as *la Destra* (the Right), though they were not notably more right-wing than the so-called Left, they strove to turn unification into unity, a task that proved beyond them – as it was probably beyond anyone. A succession of able finance ministers managed to increase revenue and balance the budget, though at the cost of making Italy among the most highly taxed countries in the world. One of their most useful contributions to the state was their success in preventing Victor Emanuel and his generals from fighting more foreign wars after 1866. In 1870 the prime minister (Lanza) and the finance minister (Quintino Sella) stood firm when General Cialdini, a close ally of the king, demanded the resignation of the government because it would not declare war on Prussia. When Cialdini also demanded a stronger army to protect private property at home, Sella sensibly pointed out that a larger army would mean higher taxes and hence be an incitement to social disorder.

With all their limitations and their failures in the south, the Piedmontese leaders of *la Destra* were the nearest thing to a responsible ruling class that united Italy ever produced. They had hoped that Piedmont would become the Prussia of the peninsula, the kingdom around which the other states coalesced, yet it was always an unrealistic ambition. Their north-western state was too small, too weak and too remote – culturally and historically as well as geographically – to sustain such a role once Italy had been achieved.

The last government of *la Destra* fell in 1876 and was replaced by a ministry of the Left, headed by Agostino Depretis. The new prime minister was in certain ways very Piedmontese – sensible, cautious and incorrupt – but his political power came from the southern deputies, especially the lawyers among them, whose profession dominated the parliamentary benches. Apart from compulsory primary education, introduced by Depretis, differences between Left and Right were more discernible in moods and attitudes than in political ideology.

The liberal conservatives had stood for fiscal rectitude and a state that interfered as little as possible in the lives of its citizens. By contrast, many on the Left wanted a powerful state that could engender jobs and public works; it was also keener than the Right on foreign wars and colonial adventures. In consequence public debt grew to alarming heights during Depretis governments.

Under the dominance of the Left, politics became less principled and more corrupt, more a matter of deals and manipulation than of policies and programmes. Depretis encouraged this development with his reliance on '*trasformismo*', his method of retaining a parliamentary majority by constantly conjuring alliances between shifting and sometimes incompatible factions. At the heart of his coalition with southern deputies was a simple formula: he gave them control of their regions, and they gave him control of the nation. Depretis gained their votes but in exchange he lost the power to carry out reforms that the south so badly needed. His method, a bartering of votes for favours, prevented the emergence of a political class in the south and left power with what Sonnino called 'the oppressing class' – landowners and *mafiosi* – men who would deliver votes at elections on condition that at other times they were largely left alone.

Trasformismo discouraged the formation of political parties with distinctive programmes and led to paralysis in government. Lanza had hoped that Italy would adopt the British practice of two parties offering different policies and alternating in government. Leaving aside the fact that the Westminster customs had taken centuries to evolve, there was little chance of organizing an opposition in Rome when the government was able to seduce potential opponents with easy promises of favours. Depretis claimed to be governing in the interests of everyone and not of factions; in fact he was governing in the interests of those who gave him a majority in the Chamber. His power was secured by patronage, bribery and the fixing of elections, which he instructed the prefects in the provinces to implement. Francesco Crispi described in 1886 how parliamentary business was carried out during Depretis's third and longest term as prime minister.

> You should see the pandemonium at Montecitorio when the moment approaches for an important division. The agents of the government

run through the rooms and corridors to gather votes. Subsidies, decorations, canals, bridges, roads, everything is promised; and sometimes an act of justice, long denied, is the price of a parliamentary vote.[17]

The decline of parliamentary standards was not, of course, all the fault of Depretis. Deputies managed to damage the reputation of parliament by their involvement in bank scandals, their poor attendance record and their often rowdy behaviour, which sometimes led to the throwing of inkwells and to fights on the floor of the Chamber. Though duelling was illegal, one deputy was killed in 1898 while fighting his thirty-first duel. Such irresponsible behaviour was by no means confined to the backbenches. There were numerous challenges and duels involving ministers, including one such contest when the current premier (Marco Minghetti) fought with a former premier (Urbano Rattazzi). Depretis was witness to an extraordinary incident in his bedroom when, while he lay ill in bed, Giovanni Nicotera (the minister of the interior) tried to hit Giuseppe Zanardelli (a fellow minister and a future prime minister) with a chair and, having failed, apparently tried to push him out of the window. On a subsequent occasion Nicotera spat at a fellow deputy and forced his unwilling victim to fight a duel. Perhaps it was not surprising that Milan's *Corriere della Sera* should report that in this era the Chamber had not 'the slightest popular support' and was 'generally laughed at and despised'. Nor is it difficult to understand Sonnino's wider point, made in a speech to the Chamber in 1881.

> The vast majority of the population, more than ninety per cent . . . feels entirely cut off from our institutions. People see themselves subjected to the State and forced to serve it with their blood and their money, but they do not feel that they are a vital and organic part of it, and take no interest at all in its existence or its affairs.[18]

BEAUTIFUL LEGENDS

In 1865 the prime minister, General Lamarmora, claimed in parliament that Italy was 'far more united than older, more established nations'.[19] The statement was loudly applauded by deputies, who knew it was nonsense. Yet they believed it vital to pretend that it was true and to hope that repetition, together with various unifying measures, would persuade Italians to think it really was true. One urgent task for them was thus to cultivate the nation's founding myth, to promote and implant the idea that unity had been achieved by a united people determined to gain its liberty. The cultivators were well aware that the myth was indeed mythical but they were convinced of the need to nurture it. Giovanni Giolitti, the ablest prime minister since Cavour, understood the logic of protecting 'beautiful national legends': Italians needed to believe they shared a common glory and a common destiny.

Giolitti's point engenders sympathy. Nations need traditions, however distant and mythical, but a country cannot have genuine national traditions if it has only just become a nation. Even if the Lombard League had produced an iconic figure like William Tell or Joan of Arc, such a person would not have been inspiring to Sicilians and other peoples whose ancestors had fought against the League. Italy simply did not have the symbols or rituals that other European nationalities possessed through inheritance: no fleur-de-lis or 'Marseillaise', no Magna Carta or Union Jack; even the flag, the *tricolore*, was an adaption of the French revolutionary banner. Nor, even more crucially, was there that intimate connection between religion and monarchy that had been so useful in the establishment or strengthening of older nations, as in Spain with *los Reyes Católicos* or in England with Henry VIII. Italy may have been a Catholic nation, but the leader of the Catholic Church refused to recognize it.

Perhaps the most active promoter of the Risorgimento myth was Francesco Crispi, who had been one of Garibaldi's Thousand. In his later career the need for Italy to feel great and be thought great became the principal determinant of his policies. Governments and institutions, he told parliament, had 'a duty to immortalize themselves in marble and monuments'. So did monarchy. Although he had personally disliked and despised Victor Emanuel, Crispi believed that the cult of the founding monarch, whose funeral he had organized in the Pantheon in 1878, would be useful to the quest for national greatness. Fosterage of this cult also required the suppression of inconvenient evidence, and to this end officials were dispatched to the homes of the king's deceased correspondents to remove letters that might contain some of his unpatriotic and derogatory opinions of Italians. This problem was not, of course, unique to the royal correspondence. When Cavour's letters were published, descriptions of the 'cowardly' Tuscans and the 'disgraceful' and 'savage' Garibaldi were expunged; so too was the prime minister's desire to 'exterminate' the *garibaldini*.[20]

Garibaldi sometimes and Mazzini always had been regarded as enemies by the Turin government, but they had to be incorporated into the national myth because they had plainly been more romantic and self-sacrificing figures than Cavour and Victor Emanuel. Mazzini would have been astonished by his apotheosis and his posthumous appearance on monuments and city streets and in school textbooks (perhaps a more useful vehicle for childhood indoctrination than an endless array of statues). Educational primers were useful both for inventing glory – Magenta became a Piedmontese victory although the Piedmontese had not fought at it – and for identifying the nation's enemies: as we have seen, King Ferdinand was vilified as 'Bomba' for his bombardment of Messina in 1848, though Victor Emanuel naturally did not figure as the bombarder of Genoa, Ancona, Capua and Gaeta. Another scheme for the cultivation of patriotism was the creation of Risorgimento museums, which proliferated across the north but not surprisingly proved to be less popular in the south.

The most revealing exhibits in these museums are the prints and posters that encourage viewers to sense the harmony that had allegedly existed between the giants of the Risorgimento generation. Garibaldi and Mazzini may have parted company in the 1850s, but many years later they could be reunited in engravings with such titles as 'Thought and Action', their portraits framed by a wreath of oak and olive leaves floating above a sword and a pen. In one street poster they were joined together with Verdi under the title 'The Three Giuseppes – The Three Stars of Italy'. Above each bearded and incorruptible head is a scripted eulogy: Verdi's explains that he 'illuminated *la patria* with his melodies'.

Such articles in Risorgimento museums are invariably dwarfed by massive oil paintings depicting heroic scenes from the 'wars of liberation'. Favoured subjects include Garibaldi carrying the dying Anita through the marshes of Comacchio, Garibaldi on Caprera with the evening sun shining on his red shirt and mournful face, the Italian camp on the battlefield of Magenta (the depiction of wounded soldiers implying that they had taken part in the action) and the breach in the Roman walls in 1870, which was painted to suggest that the incident was a tremendous victory though the defeated side lost only nineteen men. The figure most commonly represented in the pictures is Victor Emanuel, almost always shown on a white horse leading his troops into battle; the scene is usually San Martino, with blue-coated Piedmontese soldiers advancing as if on parade and white-coated Austrians lying dead or dying or being captured in the foreground. The Palazzo Pubblico in Siena, which Lorenzetti and Simone Martini had once adorned, contains a large and garish room, the Sala Vittorio Emanuele, in which the king is acclaimed as 'liberator of Italy', 'bravest of leaders', 'best of princes', 'father of the nation' and 'restorer [sic] of national unity'. The enormous frescoes, three of which portray the monarch on a white or grey horse, are pure hagiography, gaudy and badly painted distortions of actual events. After looking at such displays, it is a relief to go somewhere else and look at the *macchiaioli* ('blotchers'), Tuscan impressionists, or artists of the next generation such as the Divisionists, who were more skilful, more human and more socially conscious, men such as Angelo Morbelli, compassionate chronicler of the old and the lonely, and Giuseppe Pellizza da Volpedo, the sympathetic painter of the working class in protest.

Wealthy middle-class Italians of the nineteenth century seldom established art collections as their counterparts did in Britain and Germany. Their most conspicuous expenditure on visual art was on funerary sculpture, on the creation of vast, ornate, often beautiful monuments to deceased members of their families. The erection of these was traditionally a private matter even for public figures – the Venetian Republic did not provide them for its doges – except in the case of remote heroes such as Dante, who was awarded a dismal cenotaph in Florence's Santa Croce in 1829. The state concerned itself with public statues of heroic and exemplary men, works that could be seen not in a chapel or a cemetery but in the middle of a square.

Many towns voluntarily commissioned statues of Victor Emanuel and his fellow giants. Others were encouraged and even chivvied by the government to follow suit. Yet a few remained relatively unmolested, including Cremona, home of the great violin makers, a delightful town which has retained this free-spirited tradition, which commemorates organists and choirmasters as well as generals and *garibaldini*, and which recently renamed its Piazza Cavour the Piazza Stradivari. It is a relief to walk into the town's Piazza Roma and find a statue not of the king but of its second-best composer, Amilcare Ponchielli; if you wander into the Piazza Lodi, you will then see a sculpture of the best, Claudio Monteverdi, the first of Italy's great musical dramatists.

Venice also stands out, permitted to retain its anti-public statue tradition with only a few exceptions such as a massive equestrian bronze of Victor Emanuel on the Riva and statues of its local Risorgimento heroes, Daniele Manin and Niccolò Tommaseo, in squares near San Marco. Lucca was less fortunate. That city too had a traditional aversion to statuary in public places: only the Madonna dello Stellario, a lovely Virgin with stars, dates from before the nineteenth century. The Restoration bestowed an ugly sculpture on the Piazza Napoleone of the Bourbon-Parma duchess, Maria Luisa, but at least she did something for her subjects, providing them with an aqueduct and a good water supply. The 'giants' did nothing at all for Lucca, yet here they are in the city: Garibaldi in marble, typically imposing outside the theatre, Victor Emanuel in bronze, typically bombastic near the main gate, Mazzini in stone, typically gaunt and forlorn, in a melancholy spot on the ramparts under the ilex trees. And all these are reinforced by the inevitable arteries, the Viale Cavour, the Corso Garibaldi, the Via Vittorio Emanuele and the Piazzetta del Risorgimento.

A cheaper and even more popular way of fostering the cult was the affixing of commemorative plaques in town centres all over Italy. These often contain a specific historical and political message, like the one in Cremona for a soldier who was killed in the capture of Rome during 'the final battle to lay low a priestly domination unwanted by Christ and condemned by reason and history'. The most ubiquitous are those recording where Garibaldi stayed and made a speech, inviting the local population to conquer Rome or to die in the endeavour, making the ultimate sacrifice for the redemption of Italy. Sometimes they are merely banal, recording that his brief stay in a house has glorified it for all time. A large marble tablet in Palermo's Piazza Bologna proclaims that from 'this illustrious building' Giuseppe Garibaldi 'rested his tired limbs for two hours'. Perhaps feeling that this was an inadequate inscription for all the effort entailed, its authors added a sentence relating how, 'with extraordinary valour', the 'genius-exterminator of all tyranny slept serenely' in the house in the middle of a battle.

Other means of buttressing the cult included the naming of ships and the celebration of anniversaries, though these sometimes commemorated pre-Risorgimento history as well: ships might be christened *Lepanto* or *Dandolo* as well as *Savoia* or *Italia*; the 600th anniversary of the Sicilian Vespers could be celebrated as well as the twenty-fifth anniversaries of the capture of Rome and the conquest of Palermo. The most common and least subtle exercise in Risorgimento propaganda was the renaming of streets. Communes had traditionally respected local traditions when choosing new labels, often, as in Pistoia, expunging a mellifluous-sounding name such as Via del Vento (Street of the Wind) in order to commemorate a long-dead, long-forgotten local worthy, in this case a Pistoiese who had once been a pupil of Bramante the architect. After 1861 such traditions were discarded in favour of a uniform policy of genuflecting to the giants. The name-changing epidemic swept all over Italy except Venice, partly protected by the strength of its dialect, though even there the street bordering the public gardens, aptly called the Strada dei Giardini, became the Strada (today Via) Garibaldi. Elsewhere there was a purge of local names, especially religious ones: a typical example is Arezzo, where Garibaldi replaced St Augustine and Mazzini took over from the Madonna of Loreto. In Padua three of the city's main squares were renamed in honour of Cavour, Victor Emanuel and 'the Unity of Italy'.

Patriotic citizens of Piedmontese and other northern towns may have welcomed the new names, but southerners often resented the changes even though they were authorized by their own municipalities. For centuries Neapolitans had been happy with their Via Toledo, their favourite street, and its alteration in 1870 to the Via Roma simply underlined their new subservience. Similarly insensitive was the substitution of the Foro Carlino (named after their best recent monarch, the Bourbon King Charles) by the Piazza Dante, named after a poet who had never visited Naples. Another example is the Piazza dei Martiri, with its monument to the 'glorious fallen', which commemorates men regarded as martyrs by northern patriots but who to most Neapolitans were rebels or even traitors who rose against their lawful sovereign.

A wanderer in Italian cities who sees all these statues and walks down all these streets may well ponder what effect they had on the people of the time. Crispi had insisted it was the duty of governments and institutions to immortalize themselves in monuments, but he did not explain why they had such a duty. Most citizens of the new state were doubtless less cynical than Pasquale Turiello, a writer who wondered why Italy was commemorating so many 'heroes' in marble when Italians had not won a battle by themselves since Legnano 700 years earlier.[21] Yet many of them were perplexed by the expense and effort involved. By the end of the nineteenth century their primary allegiances were more likely to be to the new socialism or the old Church than to the narrowly based liberal state that had disappointed so many of them. For those who had no vote, for those who planned to emigrate, for those who often had less to eat than their ancestors in the Middle Ages, the endless recycling of 'beautiful legends' was an irritation and an irrelevance.

THE QUEST FOR GLORY

The Italian peninsula had experienced much warfare in its history, but its peoples had created little in the way of martial traditions except in Piedmont and to a certain extent in Naples. Venice and Genoa had of course possessed their navies, as had Pisa and Amalfi for briefer periods. In the interior the city states had fought against each other throughout the Middle Ages and had expanded or disappeared in consequence. Yet this was not like fighting foreigners such as the French or the Germans, and the richer cities often preferred to delegate their campaigns to foreign mercenaries. At the beginning of the eighteenth century, the armies of most Italian states were pitiful: Tuscany, Modena and the Papal States were all incapable of fighting even a short war.

Yet it was an axiom of united Italy that the state must be martial. The ethos of Piedmont and the ambitions of its kings combined to give it a culture of warfare from the beginning. Victor Emanuel and his son Umberto, who became king in 1878, demanded huge armies and fought hard to prevent governments from cutting expenditure on the military. Umberto often said he would rather abdicate than accept a reduction in the size of the armed forces. Like his father, he got his way. By the early 1890s Italy had built itself an enormous navy although, as it was now an ally of Austria, it had no enemies. It had also created a great many admirals, virtually one for each ship, important-looking men splattered with medals acquired for reasons that few people understood, since after Lissa Italy did not fight naval battles. Military expenditure doubled under Umberto and was higher than spending on education, public works and all the rest of the ministries combined.

Other European countries spent more on their armed forces, but all were richer and some had empires to defend and enlarge. Italy's forces were excessive for a poor, unthreatened country without colonies until at the end of the century it acquired some outposts in the Red Sea. In the mid-1860s Italy had nearly 400,000 troops in its peninsula, more than Great Britain deployed in an empire spread across six continents of the globe.[22]

The state needed an army not for defensive purposes but for other reasons such as gaining prestige, quelling riots and putting down 'brigands'. Governments also saw it, quite reasonably, as a prop to the national project, an instrument that would help them weld the people into a cohesive nation. The army was thus considered a crucible into which young men would go as Sicilians or Ligurians and come out as Italians. One scheme to foster national understanding was to put men from different regions into the same regiment, an idea which seemed admirable in theory but in practice led to the formation of regional 'gangs' inside a unit whose members spoke in dialects that the others did not understand.

Although the Italians had no foes, except those they chose to make in the Red Sea, they had not stopped dreaming of a military triumph against someone. The defeats at Custoza and Lissa still rankled and, in the minds of many, still required a 'baptism of fire' to avenge them. Italian feelings of humiliation after those defeats were exacerbated in 1878 at the Congress of Berlin, called to settle borders after the most recent war between Russia and Turkey. The congress ended up allowing the British into Cyprus, the French into Tunisia (to which numbers of Italians had emigrated in recent years and which Italy also wanted) and the Austrians into Bosnia-Herzegovina. Italy received nothing. When its minister suggested that Austria might cede the Trentino, where Italian speakers were in a majority, the Russian delegate touched the rawest of Italian nerves by joking that Italy would need to lose another battle before acquiring further territory belonging to Austria.

The results of Berlin, followed by the French invasion of Tunisia three years later, enraged many Italians, who reacted by calling for the occupation of Albania and the building of an even larger army. The government responded with plans for colonization in east Africa and also by forming the Triple Alliance alongside Germany and Austria. This was a bizarre diplomatic move that gained Italy nothing except the chimerical prestige of being on officially equal terms with the other two Powers. The alliance forced the Italians to renounce their territorial ambitions in Trieste and the Trentino, it alienated France and Britain, who were meant to be their friends, and it encouraged nationalists to vent their frustration with Europe on the tribes of Eritrea.

Foreign policy at the end of the nineteenth century was dominated by the bulky figure of Francesco Crispi, who was prime minister from 1887 to 1891 and from 1893 to 1896. This former *garibaldino* was a man of energy, ability and massive self-importance; in the Chamber of Deputies he once compared himself to Mount Etna, the snowy summit of his formidable will dominating the fieriness of his spirit and the passions of his nature. The domestic policies of his ministries indicated that he retained vestiges of his revolutionary youth: he abolished the death penalty and carried out important reforms in public health, local government and administrative justice. Yet in foreign affairs he discarded his red-shirted, freedom-fighting background and stridently became a militarist, an expansionist and an imperialist. Once he had wanted Italians to be the 'Saxons of the Latin race', building parliamentary institutions like the English; now he renounced that aspiration, concluding that his countrymen were unsuited to representative government. Contemporary Italians, he believed, required discipline more than democracy; instead of remaining decadent and effete, they needed to be turned into soldiers and empire-builders. Crispi thought Italians had been injected with 'the morphine of cowardice' and he feared the nation would break up through lack of patriotism. In other countries, he noticed, people stopped talking and bowed their heads when their national flags were raised; in Italy the raising of the flag seemed to be a signal for everyone to start gabbling.[23]

Believing that an aggressive foreign policy was the best way of inculcating a sense of patriotism, Crispi was eager to quarrel – and if possible fight wars – with almost everyone (especially the French) except Britain and Germany. Yet not even these two nations were great admirers of Crispi or his projects. Lord Salisbury, the prime minister and foreign secretary, found him an 'embarrassing ally' and, in a comparison with his least favourite and most difficult colleague, he told Queen Victoria he was 'the Randolph Churchill of Italy'. Bismarck, to whom Crispi sent annual presents of Sicilian wine, was scarcely more sympathetic to the Italian's ambitions. He dismissed Italy as of 'no account' in international affairs and as 'the fifth wheel on the wagon' of the European powers; he also observed that its colonial failures in the 1880s showed that, although it had a very large appetite, it had very poor teeth. A quarter of a century before 1914, Crispi was eager for the Triple Alliance to fight a war against Russia and France. The German army, backed by the future and final Kaiser, was also keen, but Bismarck, entering the last year of his chancellorship, managed to defeat the scheme. 'What could Germany gain from a war now?' he asked. Within the country's current borders, there were 'more Poles than we need, and more Frenchmen than we could ever digest'.[24]

Italy could not realistically begin a war in Europe by itself. Yet it did not require foreign allies or the permission of others to fight colonial wars in Africa. Several other nations were busily engaged in 'the scramble': huge empires had already been acquired there by Britain, France and Portugal, and in the Congo the King of the Belgians was creating the largest colony on the continent. Colonial projects for Italy in other places had been mooted over the years. Victor Emanuel had been keen on either Sumatra or New Guinea, while his almost equally bellicose son wished to take Rhodes from the Turks and to establish a naval base in China. Expansion in the Balkans was another

Italian ambition though, until the First World War, Africa was to be the chief focus of the country's imperial hopes.

The French proposed Libya – then part of the Ottoman Empire – as a suitable colony, but the Italians were still so angry about Tunisia that they chose to go to the Red Sea instead. Colonies were expected to bring riches as well as prestige to their possessor, but neither of these options seemed likely to provide them. Assab, Italy's first colony on the Red Sea, looked especially unpromising. It was the terminus of caravans crossing the Danakil Desert and a place the Italians knew so little about that the colonel in charge of disembarkation admitted he had never seen a map of it. Three years later, another colony was founded further up the Eritrean coast at Massawa. As the troops landed there, Crispi (who was not then in government) insisted that they should have a single objective, to assert Italy's name in Africa and to show 'the barbarians' that Italians were strong and powerful. In the language employed earlier by Piedmontese officers in southern Italy, he added that, since the barbarians understood nothing but the power of guns, the artillery would soon be 'thundering'.[25] As it turned out, the guns did not always overawe the tribesmen. In 1887 an Italian force of 500 men ventured into the interior and was wiped out by Ethiopian troops at Dogali, a humiliating defeat transformed into an heroic sacrifice by nationalist painters who revelled in painting the courageous few being swamped by hordes of Africans. As a commemorative plaque still proclaims in the Apulian town of Locorotondo, the 'heroes' had died 'like Romans, devoted to the honour of the fatherland'.

On becoming prime minister soon after Dogali, Crispi sent a revenge force to the Red Sea to teach 'the barbarians' a lesson for their 'unjust aggression'. The expedition helped restore morale and led to the occupation of Asmara, which in turn led to the proclamation of Eritrea as well as Somaliland as Italian colonies. Crispi's exclusion from office between the beginning of 1891 and the end of 1893 brought colonial activity to a halt, but when he returned to power he was more pugnacious than ever. Even King Umberto, who was no slouch when war was on the agenda, was puzzled. 'Crispi wants to occupy everywhere,' he noted, 'even China and Japan.'[26] Yet in practice the prime minister restricted his ambitions to an expansionist drive into Ethiopia, where he intended to overthrow the Emperor Menelik and install Umberto on his throne. In February 1896, in a move that recalls the government's order to Admiral Persano thirty years before, Crispi told his reluctant commander in Eritrea to advance 'at whatever cost to save the honour of the army and the prestige of the monarchy'. Incompetently led, a large Italian force duly advanced and was annihilated by an Ethiopian army at Adowa. 6,000 men were killed, and many others were taken prisoner. No other European country ever suffered such a colonial calamity.

Fortunato thought Adowa a well-deserved defeat for a weak and impoverished country that was wasting its resources on trying to become a Great Power. Crispi's reaction to the disaster was to demand another expedition to punish the barbarians; even 'the little King of Belgium', he reminded the proud King of Italy, had done that. But Umberto realized that such a course would be unpopular and that it was time for Crispi, now in his late seventies, to retire. The new prime minister, Antonio Di Rudinì, was a Sicilian aristocrat who had succeeded Crispi after his first resignation in 1891. Now as then, Di Rudinì wanted to withdraw from Africa altogether but was persuaded that this would be too embarrassing and too heavy a blow to Italy's prestige. He thus reluctantly agreed to keep Eritrea and Somaliland but to recognize Ethiopia as an independent state.

Colonial adventures were not popular until 1911, when a reluctant prime minister felt obliged to go to war to capture Libya from the Turks. In Milan and other cities Crispi's aggression had provoked demonstrations in favour of Menelik, and many statesmen apart from Di Rudinì opposed colonial projects. One former prime minister, Rattazzi, believed the money squandered in Africa should have been used to develop Sicily, Sardinia and Calabria; one future head of government, Sonnino, who had visited Eritrea and was an expert on finance, mocked the idea that such places could be profitable to Italy. The notions that Eritrea might enrich its colonizer, that it could furnish it with a native army (as India did for Britain) or that it would become a magnet for Italians who wished to emigrate were laughable. Few people believed in them even if they subscribed to the ideas in public. How many of their countrymen could be expected to prefer to live in Eritrea than to begin a new life in the Americas? Even after Italy had acquired Libya before the First World War, only one Italian emigrant in a hundred chose to settle in the African colonies.

THE BEAR OF BUSSETO

The 1850s had been Giuseppe Verdi's great decade. With *Rigoletto* in 1851 he surpassed anything he had done before, a feat he repeated with its equally memorable successors, *Il trovatore* and *La traviata*. Although the next brace of operas, *I vespri siciliani* (*The Sicilian Vespers*) and *Simon Boccanegra*, were never so popular, he finished the decade on a high note with the glorious *Un ballo in maschera* (*The Masked Ball*). Verdi now was, and remained, Italy's favourite composer, overtaking Donizetti. In the ten years up to 1848 the playhouse at Ancona had staged twenty-five productions of Donizetti's operas and only four of Verdi's (fewer than for Bellini and Mercadante), yet over the following decade the number of Verdi's productions there rose to twenty-six, more than half of the total.[27]

However much they admired the recent operas for their music and drama, nationalists were unable to detect a whiff of jingoism in the librettos. Naturally, and often with reason, they complained about the behaviour of censors in the Italian states and in Lombardy-Venetia. In Austrian Venice, for instance, the authorities objected to the character of Rigoletto, a hunchbacked jester who has to drag his daughter's corpse across the stage in a sack, though in the end he was not prevented from being or doing either of these things at the première at La Fenice. Some of the censorship, however, was – in the mid-century circumstances – understandable. In the aftermath of 1848, following the defiance of the republics in Rome and Venice, the monarchies naturally did not wish audiences to watch lecherous kings, however fictitious, behaving badly in the theatre and even ravishing a subject. In consequence the monarch in Victor Hugo's *Le Roi s'amuse* became the Duke of Mantua (a title that no longer existed) in Verdi's operatic version of the play, *Rigoletto*.

Another thing monarchist censors disallowed was the killing of royalty on stage in case the sight encouraged members of the audience to emulate the assassins. Again, the anxiety was not wholly irrational.

Verdi's own sovereign, the Bourbon Duke of Parma, was stabbed to death by a saddle-maker in 1854, and Napoleon III was very nearly killed by the Italian Orsini four years later. In 1857 Verdi agreed to write an opera for the San Carlo in Naples and chose as his protagonist King Gustavus III, an amiable enlightened despot who had been assassinated at the Stockholm opera house in 1792. As a soldier had recently tried to kill the Neapolitan king, Ferdinand II, the Bourbon censors were understandably reluctant to stage a regicide at the royal opera house. In fact they demanded so many changes that the composer withdrew the work and put it on at Rome, where the papal censors also made demands. Gustavus eventually appeared in public as a governor of Boston in the seventeenth century, while his enemies, Count Horn and Count Ribbing, became Tom and Samuel.

Un ballo came out in 1859 at a time when patriots were eager to retrieve Verdi for the Italian cause. One consequence of their eagerness was the inception of the most enduring of all Verdian myths – the legend that audiences up and down the peninsula were forever shouting 'Viva Verdi!' during performances and using the composer's name as an acronym to indicate their loyalty to Italy: what they were really meaning was 'Long live Vittorio Emanuele Re d'Italia!' Recent scholarship limits the shouting to a few months at La Scala at the beginning of 1859, and some of it queries even that. One German scholar claims that the use of Verdi's name to mean Victor Emanuel is a propaganda trick invented many years after unification had been completed.[28]

Although Verdi was now writing operas which no one could claim were patriotic, he was still, of course, a patriot. In 1855 he became so angry with Eugène Scribe, the French dramatist who had written a libretto he disliked for *I vespri*, that he insisted on changing 'everything that attacks the honour of the Italians ... I am an Italian above all and ... I will never become an accomplice in injuring my country.'[29] Yet if his patriotism remained constant, his republicanism had diminished, as it had with Garibaldi, and he had concluded that the Savoia were now the best hope for Italy. In 1856 he accepted an honour from Victor Emanuel that made him a knight of the Order of St Maurice and St Lazarus.

At the outbreak of war in 1859 Verdi claimed it was only his health that prevented him from enlisting: he was 'unable to complete a three-mile march' or 'stand five minutes of sun' on his head. Yet he gave a generous donation to wounded soldiers and to families of those who died in battle. As in 1848, he was full of enthusiasm and was prepared to 'adore' Napoleon III for his role in the war. Yet he refused a request to write a national hymn after the victory at Solferino, which was just as well because news of the armistice that allowed Austria to keep Venice left him aghast and outraged by the French emperor's 'betrayal'.

After the overthrow of the ducal regime in his home city, Verdi was elected a deputy to the new assembly of Parma, which subsequently voted for annexation by Piedmont. He then went to Turin, where he formally presented Victor Emanuel with the results of the plebiscite, and visited Cavour, who was then briefly out of office. Much impressed by the politician, he afterwards wrote him an obsequious letter, hailing him as 'the great statesman, the first citizen, the man whom every Italian will call the father of his country'.[30] He even called him 'the Prometheus of our people', by which he presumably meant the titan who brought fire to mankind rather than the trickster of Zeus or the figure chained to a rock while an eagle gnawed his liver. Cavour replied that the letter had moved him 'very, very much'.

Verdi applauded Garibaldi's expedition to Sicily, while his wife Giuseppina Strepponi considered 'Giuseppe of Caprera' to be 'the purest and greatest hero since the world was created'. Although reluctant to stand for the new Italian parliament in Turin, the composer allowed himself to be persuaded by Cavour that his presence in the Chamber would 'contribute to the dignity of parliament in and beyond Italy' and that it was especially needed 'to convince our colourful colleagues in the south', who were so much more 'susceptible to the influence of [his] artistic genius . . .' than northerners. As a deputy, Verdi took an interest in such matters as agriculture and artistic copyright but he played little part in national and political debates. He was content to vote the same way as Cavour so as to be 'absolutely certain of not making a mistake'. When, soon after taking his seat, he told the prime minister he was thinking of resigning, Cavour said, 'No, let us go first to Rome.' 'Are we going there?' 'Yes', replied the statesman, but he would say nothing definite about the timing, though he assured him it would be 'soon'. Cavour's death a few weeks later left Verdi so distraught that he wept at the memorial service he had organized in Busseto. 'Poor Cavour! Poor us!'[31] He remained in parliament until 1865, when he did not seek re-election. He was later appointed a senator.

Official censors and morality-mongers had disapproved of Verdi's sympathetic treatment of 'fallen' women in three operas he wrote in the early 1850s, Lina in *Stiffelio*, Gilda in *Rigoletto* and Violetta in *La traviata*. His neighbours near Parma were even more appalled when the composer came to live in Busseto in 1849 with Giuseppina Strepponi, his mistress for years before she became his wife in 1859. A woman as 'fallen' as any of the characters in his works, Giuseppina possessed charm and talent and had combined a career as one of Italy's leading sopranos with a succession of lovers as well as babies, who had been adopted or left at foundling hospitals. She had produced at least three children by at least two fathers, continuing to sing throughout her pregnancies and giving birth to one baby six hours after a performance.

Giuseppina was happy to live as the mistress of Verdi in Paris or Naples or whatever city he happened to be working in, but she loathed being in Busseto, where the townsfolk refused to speak to her. Verdi came to hate the place too, and after a while they moved out to Sant' Agata, the farm he had bought in 1848, where he was soon extending the acreage and transforming the farmhouse into an attractive and unpretentious villa. He admitted the countryside was not pretty – it was even ugly – but it was his, where he had been born and where he could now afford to buy. He felt comfortable in the flat Emilian landscape with its fogs, its ditches, its poplar trees and its large fields of corn. It was to him what Caprera was to Garibaldi. He appreciated the solitude, which gave him peace to think, and he liked working in his own fields and living in a place where he did not have to tip his hat to counts and marquesses. At Sant' Agata he was close to the earth, could call himself 'a peasant from Roncole', could even pretend that all he wanted to do for the rest of his life was to plant beans and cabbages and trade livestock in the market at Cremona. Giuseppina, who was sometimes bored there, grumbled at her husband's mania for getting up at dawn to inspect his trees and crops, to watch the digging of an artesian well or to supervise construction work on the farm buildings. Eventually he agreed to break the monotony of the Po Valley year by making a summer visit to the Tuscan spa of Montecatini and by wintering in Genoa, renting an apartment of the Palazzo Doria Pamphilj, which must have been an idyllic place before its grounds were expropriated to build roads, a railway line and a motorway on stilts.

As he grew older, Verdi frequently felt depressed. Pessimistic by nature, he became increasingly gloomy about the future of Italy and even of life itself. When people complained that *Il trovatore* had too many deaths, his revealing reply was that 'death is all there is in life. What else is there?'[32] At home he was often gruff and grumbly, especially with his wife and servants, and he admitted that Giuseppina was right to call him a bear. Yet while he could be a difficult man to do business with, his conductors and singers adored him, and even the prima donnas did not flounce out. He was innately, if undemonstratively, a kind and generous person. Near his home he constructed a hospital and in Milan he built the Casa de Riposo, a retirement home for impoverished musicians. Throughout his life he gave money to victims of earthquakes and other disasters, and in his will he left large sums to hospitals and schools as well as to individuals, including an annual payment to the fifty poorest people in Roncole.

Verdi's pace of composition slowed down after 1859. In twenty years he had written twenty-one operas but over the next four decades he produced only five, each of them a masterpiece. He returned to La Scala in 1862 with *La forza del destino*, went to the Paris Opéra in 1867 for his immense *Don Carlos*, and in 1871 sent to Cairo his opera *Aida*, a work often supposed to have been performed at the opening of either the Suez Canal or the Cairo Opera House, though both events had in fact taken place two years earlier. There was then an operatic gap of sixteen years until *Otello*, though the abstinence did produce the incomparable Requiem, composed in honour of Manzoni, the only man apart from Cavour whom Verdi revered. Although the composer claimed to have retired, Arrigo Boito, his last and ablest librettist, was able to cajole him into writing the great final works, *Otello* and *Falstaff*, the old man producing the latter in 1893, his eightieth year. Boito was so skilful in condensing Shakespeare and conflating several minor characters that he made the opera a far finer and funnier work than the original, *The Merry Wives of Windsor*. People sometimes complain that there are no tunes in *Falstaff*, but actually there are a great many, only they do not last long enough to become arias.

The acclamation and adulation that greeted the two operas made Verdi mellow and more relaxed and much less like a bear. Yet if he was happier with himself and kinder to his wife, he was still anxious about what he called his 'troubled *patria*', which seemed to him to have been going downhill ever since the death of Cavour. The politicians were now so bad that they just made '*coglionerie*' (balls-ups) after *coglionerie*. The composer had been so distraught by Austria's victories in 1866 and by Italy's consequent humiliation – receiving Venetia as a gift from Napoleon III – that he even tried to cancel *Don Carlos* for Paris because he felt it would be embarrassing to be an Italian in France at that moment. Although he recognized that the capture of Rome four years later was 'a great event', it left him 'cold' because he could not imagine how a *modus vivendi* could be arranged between 'Parliament and the College of Cardinals, a free press and the Inquisition, the Civil Code and the Syllabus of Errors'. Verdi's concern about a possible break-up of Italy may have been reflected in a revision of *Simon Boccanegra* in 1881, in which the Genoese protagonist confronts demands for war against the Venetians with the argument that the two great maritime republics share a common *patria* and must not behave like Cain to Abel.[33]

The rise to power of Crispi, his near contemporary, briefly persuaded Verdi that Italy had found its saviour. He saluted the prime minister who, so he thought, controlled the 'destinies of our beloved country' with such wisdom and energy, and he even sent him a photograph dedicated to 'the great patriot'.[34] Verdi's strong social conscience welcomed Crispi's social reforms, but the rest of him was soon disenchanted, particularly with the military and colonial adventurism. How, he wondered, could the government waste so much money in Africa when there was so much poverty in Italy to contend with? Verdi was especially appalled by the advance against the Ethiopians, whom he regarded as 'in many ways ... more civilized than we'. For him Adowa was a salutary defeat for a country 'playing the tyrant in Africa'.

After Verdi's death in January 1901, the novelist and senator Antonio Fogazzaro acclaimed the composer as 'our great unifier', the man who 'deserved, more than anyone, to be the symbol of the heroic era of our Risorgimento, because of the mystic fusion of his music [and] the longed-for, prayed-for, unity of the nation'.[35] Verdi had for years been hailed as '*il maestro della rivoluzione italiana*', the artistic herald of the Risorgimento; posthumously he became a hero of school textbooks, the man whose name was taught to generations of children as the symbol of Italian aspirations: 'Long live Verdi! Long live Victor Emanuel King of Italy!'

Scholarly revisionism has done little to dent the mythology surrounding Verdi's life and political role. In the BBC's fine television series on Italian opera, broadcast in 2010, the excellent Antonio Pappano, music director of Covent Garden, was still extolling the maestro for his patriotism and the symbolism of *Nabucco*. Without doubt Giuseppe Verdi was a great man, a great composer and a great philanthropist, but he was not Italy's 'great unifier'. He was not even a great nationalist.

10

Nationalist Italy

LITTLE ITALY

Nations are often accused of being divided into two, of being split into hostile, opposite and even irreconcilable parts. A character in Disraeli's novel *Sybil* famously declared that England consisted of two nations, the rich and the poor, whose peoples were so ignorant of each other that they might have been 'dwellers in different zones, or inhabitants of different planets'.[1] The Spanish dictator, General Francisco Franco, also divided his country into two: one half was 'true Spain', valiant, Catholic and hierarchical; the other was 'anti-Spain', composed of liberals, marxists and freemasons, people so infected by the ideas of the Enlightenment and revolutionary France that, even if born on Spanish soil from Spanish parents, they could not be regarded as true Spaniards.

As befits a country of such diversity, the idea of 'two Italies' has several variants. The polarity between secular Italy and religious Italy goes back a long time, and that between town and country is even older. Yet the standard division is of course that between the north and the south. Sometimes this is mentioned simply to illustrate different degrees of wealth and economic development. More usually it comes with nuances and insinuations about race and lifestyle and habits of thought. Putting most of the clichés into a single sentence, many northern Italians today would subscribe to the view that the real division is one between a civilized, hard-working, law-abiding, European north and a backward, Arabized, idle and violent Mediterranean south. A century ago, a young nationalist intellectual, Giuseppe Prezzolini, claimed there was 'an Italy of deeds and an Italy of words, one of action, the other of chatter and drowsiness, one Italy in the office, the other in the parlour'.[2] As the editor of *La Voce*, a review that defined itself as 'militantly idealist', Prezzolini became a creator of another Italian divide, between those who supported and those who detested Giovanni Giolitti, the statesman who was prime minister four times between 1892 and 1914 and again for a year from the summer of 1920. Prezzolini disliked the dominant politician of the day so much that a special issue of his publication was called simply '*Abbasso Giolitti!*', 'Down with Giolitti!'

La Voce's target was a clever and pragmatic liberal from Piedmont, an empiricist, an administrator, a believer in measured progress. Giolitti was not a great visionary but he was a great reconciler, which is what Italy needed at the start of the twentieth century. The previous decade had ended with a series of dreadful events – martial law in Sicily, colonial defeat in Africa, and bread riots causing at least eighty deaths in Milan – that culminated in the assassination of King Umberto by an anarchist at Monza in the summer of 1900. The atmosphere of the epoch reinforced Giolitti's belief that the country needed social peace more than political reform just as it needed economic growth more than colonial adventures. Although he had stressed the importance of 'beautiful legends', he had done so for political reasons, not because he had much time for heroes or ideals or for attempting the task of turning Italy into a Great Power. Prosperity, he believed, would do more for national unity than expeditions to Eritrea. In the years before the Great War, when Giolitti was the most powerful politician even when he was out of office, national income increased by more than 50 per cent. Agricultural wages rose, the industrialization of the north-west took off and, owing to a determined government campaign against malaria, mortality rates were reduced.

Giolitti believed that the wealth gap in Italy was wider than in other countries and blamed the rich for provoking class conflict by making the poor pay high taxes on salt and cereals while they themselves were unwilling to levy a tax on wealth. Like his ally and predecessor as premier, Giuseppe Zanardelli, he insisted on remaining neutral during strikes, a stance that earned him the enmity of conservatives. When one aristocratic landowner from Mantua complained that, in consequence of a strike, he – 'a senator of the realm' – had been forced to drive his own plough, Giolitti's response was to suggest he did this more often because he would then understand what a tiring job it was and perhaps pay his labourers better.[3] Instead of dealing with strikes by sending in the army, as earlier premiers had done, he let them succeed or fail of their own accord. As a determined social reformer, he also reduced food taxes and introduced legislation on working conditions in factories.

Giolitti was a unifier who understood that national unity could not be achieved simply by repeating old formulas combining ideas of patriotism, conquest and self-sacrifice. It required the inclusion of groups that had not existed in 1861 such as political Catholics, who from 1904 began to participate in elections and whom he helped to incorporate into the body politic. More controversially, he reached out to the radical Left, to a collection of socialists, radicals and republicans, who at the polls in 1900 had succeeded in electing nearly 100 deputies to the Chamber. To the fury of the Right, Giolitti was prepared to go far to accommodate the socialists, not only by introducing social reforms but also by inviting them to join his governments. Moderates in the Socialist Party were tempted to cooperate but they invariably came up against the intransigence of dogmatic colleagues who refused to consider anything other than revolution; their inflexibility later did much to assist the rise to power of Benito Mussolini. In 1900, after the assassination of King Umberto, most socialist (and republican) deputies failed to attend the funeral or send condolences to the royal family or even turn up for the new king's coronation oath in parliament. In 1912 the party expelled its most talented reformist leaders principally because they had gone to the Quirinale Palace to express sympathy with Umberto's successor, Victor Emanuel III, after he had survived an attempt on his life. The socialists preferred to threaten revolution and preserve their ideological purity rather than collaborate with Giolitti and take some responsibility for running the state. Their history for thirty years from 1892 is one of schism and expulsion, a period that saw the departure from the party of syndicalists, anarchists, reformists and communists.

Despite the refusal of the socialists to play a constructive part in national life, the period of Giolitti's ascendancy was a hopeful one, a time of civic progress, of relative prosperity and, with the enlargement of the franchise, of greater political participation. In fact it provided the best opportunity Italy ever had of becoming a successful, liberal nation-state. Yet few contemporaries were able to recognize this. The liberal philosopher Benedetto Croce later hailed it as an epoch of affluence and liberal ideas, but at the time he was a haughty critic. So was Piero Gobetti, another liberal, and so too was Gaetano Salvemini, a radical who condemned Giolitti as a dictator and as minister of the *mala vita* (criminal life) because, like most of his predecessors, he acquired his parliamentary majorities with the use of corruption and sometimes force, especially in constituencies in the south. Although Salvemini, like Croce, later admitted that his criticism had been excessive, it was by then too late. The calumnies that assailed Giolitti from the Left as well as the Right did much to damage the credibility of the liberal regime and weaken it to the extent that it could later be overthrown without difficulty by Mussolini.

The prime minister's most vocal and virulent opponents were on the Right, men who loathed Giolitti because he had abandoned the project of making Italy great in favour of making it prosperous. They derided his idea of Italy as '*Italietta*' ('little Italy'), a place of bourgeois values, of citizens aspiring to leisurely lives with domestic servants and seaside villas at Viareggio or Posillipo. Giolitti's most eloquent critics were the nationalists, a group of bellicose intellectuals who transformed themselves into a political party in 1910 and won seats in parliament three years later. Disappointed by the results of the Risorgimento and the national humiliations that had followed, they shared the frustrations of Carducci, the poet who had lamented that 'the epoch of the infinitely great' had been succeeded by 'the farce of the infinitely small, the busy little farce of ponderous clowns'.[4] Petulantly, they scoffed at democracy and liberalism – and even at the notion of individual liberty – because these had failed to make Italy a real state or Italians a real people. What the country required was strength and discipline sufficient for conquest and expansion and economic development. Still talking about the need to avenge Lissa, a battle fought before most of them had been born, they preached violence, glorified war and demanded an empire that included Libya,

Corsica, Dalmatia and dominance in the eastern Mediterranean. Among the benefits of warfare listed by Giovanni Papini, an essayist and friend of Prezzolini, was the fact that corpses made better and cheaper fertilizers than chemicals. 'What beautiful cabbages', he reflected, could be grown in a field where hundreds of soldiers had been killed.

> We love war, and we will savour it like gourmets as long as it lasts. War is horrifying, and precisely because it is horrifying and tremendous and terrible and destructive, we must love it with all our male hearts.[5]

Closely linked to the nationalists were the Futurists, a group of painters and intellectuals who exalted speed and worshipped technology. For their founder, the poet Filippo Tommaso Marinetti, 'a roaring automobile that seems to ride on a hail of bullets' was more beautiful than a great Hellenistic sculpture in the Louvre, the *Winged Victory of Samothrace*. This hysterical character revelled in his iconoclasm, his desire to shock and his rejection of the world's artistic heritage. He aspired to introduce punching into 'the artistic struggle' and encouraged people 'to spit every day on the Altar of Art'. Library shelves should be burned, canals should be diverted to flood museums, and both Venice and Florence should be flattened for the sake of human progress. Yet the Futurists' targets went beyond the artistic. In their notorious manifesto, published on the front page of *Le Figaro* in 1909, Marinetti announced, 'We will glorify war – the world's only hygiene . . . and scorn for women.' Since women had been scorned for decades and in parts of the country enjoyed fewer rights than before unification, there was little the Futurists could do to make things worse. Their movement's cult of violence, however, which was extolled in similar terms by nationalists and by that saturnine poet and sometime politician Gabriele D'Annunzio, helped create a political-cultural atmosphere that encouraged people to think of war as something necessary, inevitable and indeed hygienic. Even after the Great War, when the hygiene had taken over 600,000 Italian lives, Marinetti was calling for the abolition of pasta on the grounds that it encouraged pacifism. Luckily, any credibility he may have possessed when launching this campaign was punctured when he himself was photographed munching his way through a bowl of spaghetti.[6]

In 1911 the Futurists joined the nationalists and other adventurists in demanding the conquest of Cyrenaica and Tripolitania, the Otto-man provinces of Libya. For years, as they reminded their fellow Italians, they had 'glorified love of danger and violence, patriotism and war', which they defined afresh as 'the only hygiene of the world and the only educative morality'. Many on the Left opposed the proj-ect, including a young socialist journalist, Benito Mussolini, whose violent anti-imperialism landed him in jail. So did some of the country's finest and most independent minds, such as Einaudi and Salvemeni, who realized the expense would be huge and guessed that rewards from this 'enormous sandpit' would be meagre. Giolitti him-self was neither eager for a war nor deluded about the economic benefits of colonialism. Other liberals shared his views yet reckoned that Italy should try to do something manly somewhere. The British were in Egypt and the French were in Tunis, almost in sight of the Italian islands of Lampedusa and Pantelleria; Italy thus ought to acquire some space in north Africa, even if only to prevent the French from occupying it. The country required a modicum of military prestige, as even so great a liberal as Fortunato admitted. After 'a mil-lennium and a half of shameful history', he thought Italy needed to 'secure a virile victory' over somebody so as 'to be able to face the future with confidence'. Unlike the Greeks, who had gained indepen-dence in 1830 by defeating the Turks, the Italians had never won anything by themselves. 'For the first time in my life,' he told his friend Salvemini, 'I have a vision of the sanctity of war.'[7]

Nationalists and Futurists knew that Italy was a signatory of the Hague Conventions and a guarantor of the territorial integrity of the Ottoman Empire, yet this knowledge made an invasion of Libya seem all the more exciting. They were proud that aggression would entail the breaking of treaties, the defiance of Europe and a revival of 'the traditions of Cesare Borgia and Machiavelli'. While itching for a real battle, they were, however, convinced that conquest would be easy because the Turkish garrisons in north Africa would surrender, and the Arab population would not fight. Little notion of *une mission civilisatrice* entered their heads. They would go to Libya to enrich and aggrandize Italy; they would find minerals, they would find water, they would make the desert bloom. A leader and theorist of national-ism, Enrico Corradini, visited a Libyan oasis and went into ecstasies about the wild trees laden with olives and vines so heavy with fruit that bunches of grapes were lying on the ground. 'Instead of a desert,' he announced, 'we are in the Promised Land.'[8]

The clamour for war became so loud that Giolitti decided with some reluctance to invade in the autumn of 1911. The Italian navy bombarded Tripoli, the army defeated the Ottoman garrisons there, and after a few weeks Italy announced the annexation of Libya, even though its forces occupied only 1 per cent of that enormous territory. As Turkey needed troops for its war against the Balkan League, it signed a treaty in 1912 that recognized Italy as the de facto ruler of both Libya and the Dodecanese islands, which had also been captured. The Italians believed the war was over and congratulated themselves on a great victory.

The treaty, however, applied only to Italy and the Ottoman Empire. With considerable naivety, the Italians had assumed that Libya's Arabs would be pleased to see them and grateful to be rescued from their Turkish oppressors. They were thus astonished and furious when early on in the war an Arab force attacked them and won a small victory. Claiming that the Arabs had proved themselves to be 'treacherous rebels', Italian commanders sanctioned reprisals so murderous that even Kaiser Wilhelm objected. This policy was in any case a failure. The revolt intensified, and, after three more years of fighting, Italy retained only a few towns along the coast. Although the Italians struck some 140 different campaign medals to commemorate their Libyan triumphs, the real victors of the war were their opponents, the bedouin of the Senussi Islamic order.[9]

The prime minister was under no illusions about the performance of the army, but he could not let the public know the truth. He thus invented victories and falsified figures to protect Italians from learning that their generals were so inept they could not win battles unless they outnumbered their enemies by a ratio of ten to one. Neither could Giolitti let people know that the war had been expensive, cruel and ultimately unsuccessful. Returning soldiers might wonder why so many people had been killed to acquire a few palm trees and a desert, but the government succeeded in convincing a jubilant populace that resurgent Italy had performed feats worthy of the Roman Empire. The war thus became popular and led to a sprouting of establishments

with African names, a Bar Tripoli in a town's piazza or a Caffè Ben-
ghasi on its Via Cavour. Monuments were erected and street-names
were changed to reflect the recent glory, especially in the north, where
most of Italy's armchair imperialists lived: the city of Turin named
streets and piazzas after almost every place that had been occupied by
Italian forces in Libya, Eritrea and Somaliland. The pretence of victory may have been Giolitti's greatest disservice to his country, because
the lie encouraged too many Italians to rejoice and feel warlike. Thus
they soon became tempted to participate in the great conflict that was
about to engulf Europe.

BELLICOSE ITALY

The third monarch of united Italy was Victor Emanuel III, who became
king after his father's assassination in 1900. Short in stature, modest
in character and retiring in disposition, he was not at all like his predecessors. Although he too had suffered a mainly military education,
he liked reading books, and his interest in warfare was historical
rather than physical. Neither as pompous as his father nor as bombastic as his grandfather, his sense and moderation in the early years of
his reign did much to raise the prestige of the monarchy. Yet he was
also a marrowless man, whose characteristics of fatalism and irresolu-
tion led him to make a series of decisions between 1915 and 1946
that were disastrous for his country and fatal to his dynasty. In 1915
and 1940 he joined world wars that were unpopular with most of his
subjects; in 1922 he refused his own government's request to declare
martial law and prevent Mussolini from coming to power; and in the
1940s his failure to acknowledge his unpopularity by abdicating in
favour of his son (until it was too late) encouraged Italians to vote for
a republic.

In 1914 Italy was still a member of the Triple Alliance with Austria
and Germany, which seemed no more logical then than it had at its
conception in 1882. It certainly made no sense to Victor Emanuel, an
anglophile who disliked the Germans, especially their Kaiser, who
treated him with arrogance and condescension. Nor was it in the
interests of Italy to be aligned against Britain, a country which, apart

from supplying it with coal, had always supported it, had never tried to conquer it, and whose navy would be extremely threatening to its coastline in the event of hostilities. At no stage in its 150-year-old history has Italy needed to fight a war, and it should have been easy to avoid one that pitted its old supporters, France and Britain, against its more recent allies. Yet the country never liked to stay on the sidelines, at least not for very long, and the belligerent Powers in 1914 suspected that, despite the neutrality proclaimed in August, it would join the side most likely to win and demand a high price for doing so.

Italy's dilemma about whose side to join in a European conflict was not a new one. Indeed it had existed for so long that military planners had never known whether to build fortifications on the north-eastern Alps against Austria or in the north-western mountains facing France. At the outbreak of the Great War the dilemma hinged on the question of how much territory the rival sets of allies could offer. War against France was often a temptation because the French were irritatingly successful neighbours who had grabbed Tunisia, even though it was closer to Italy. Yet apart from a slice of north Africa, Italy could not aspire to gain very much from France except possibly Nice and perhaps Corsica, an island with associations with Genoa and the (originally Florentine) Bonapartes, but not likely to be much more of an asset than Sardinia.

More tempting was the idea of fighting the traditional enemy Austria, even though it had been a formal ally for thirty-three years, because victory would gain Italy the *terre irredente*, the 'unredeemed lands' still in Habsburg hands such as the Italian-speaking city of Trento and the partly Italian city of Trieste. Known as 'irredentists', the Italian aspirant redeemers promoted this scheme of conflict as a fourth 'war of independence', as what the philosopher Giovanni Gentile considered a struggle to complete the Risorgimento, to obtain the desired lands and to achieve for the nation a sense of regeneration. They did not pretend that they would be fighting to liberate an oppressed people because even their foreign minister had recently praised the Austrians for their excellent administration of Trento and Trieste. Instead they would be fighting so that they could consider themselves – and be considered by others – as a martial nation.

In the spring of 1915, encouraged by Germany, the Austrian

government offered Italy territorial concessions to induce it to remain neutral. Vienna was willing to give up Trento and most of the surrounding province, to grant autonomy to Trieste, to withdraw in Friuli as far as the east bank of the Isonzo River, and to approve an Italian occupation of Valona on the Albanian coast of the Adriatic. For Giolitti as for most politicians, this seemed a generous offer that should be accepted. Yet the government, led by Antonio Salandra (the prime minister) and Sidney Sonnino (the foreign minister), dismissed it as 'dubious and absolutely inadequate'. This pair of politicians had decided that Italy must join the war and obtain for itself territory far in excess of the 'unredeemed lands'. Realizing that they were in a minority, they worked in secret – 'we two alone', as Salandra told his partner – preventing anyone except in due course the king from knowing what was going on and keeping parliament in recess for six crucial months in case it demanded the right to debate matters of war and peace. The behaviour of Sonnino was perplexing to those who remembered him as a social reformer, a prudent economist, a sceptic of colonialism and a scoffer at the idea that Italy had any serious claim to either Trento or Trieste. Although in August 1914 he wanted Italy to join Austria's side straightaway, he then completely changed his mind. Together with Salandra, he also abandoned the essential Mazzinian tenet that people should own and govern their own territories for a policy that would gain Italy expanses of Habsburg territory where Italians were in a minority, often a very small one.

Salandra and Sonnino haggled hard in their secret negotiations with the Triple Entente – Britain, France and Russia. As the prime minister admitted in an unfortunate phrase, Italy's 'sacred egoism' was the determinant of his country's foreign policy; no moral considerations were apparently involved. At the secret Treaty of London, which Victor Emanuel authorized in April 1915, the Italians were promised, along with Trieste and the Trentino, Gorizia, Istria, the South Tyrol, part of Dalmatia, a bit of Albania and most of the islands of the eastern Adriatic. If all went well in the war, the nation would acquire a million people who were not Italians but Croats and Slovenes and German-speaking Austrians. In return for these promises, Italy was obliged to declare war on both Germany and Austria, though in the event it delayed its declaration against Berlin for another sixteen months, persisting until September 1916 in exporting goods to its allies' chief enemy.

Very few people were aware of the treaty's terms until they were published by Russia's Bolshevik government at the end of 1917. Many Italians were then appalled to learn that they had been fighting not only for the unredeemed lands but also for territory that was not by any standards Italian. Their country's support had been put up for auction, and their young men had been dying not, as in the Risorgimento, for the *patria* but for what war memorials were soon calling 'greater Italy', a grander, larger and more powerful Italy that included Slav territories as well as the German-speaking South Tyrol. Salvemini lamented that Italy had thus entered the war with 'the knife of Shylock rather than the liberating banner of Mazzini'.[10]

A majority of parliamentarians opposed the idea of their country going to war, and over 300 of them left their visiting cards in Giolitti's hotel in Rome as a sign of support for the old statesman's attempt to stop Italy from joining the hostilities. Opponents of the war included the socialists, most active Catholics in parliament and the pope, Benedict XV, who refused to sanction it as a just cause. The principal interventionists were the nationalists, men such as Papini who had trumpeted the need for blood to oil the wheels of the future and for 'cadavers to pave the way of all triumphal processions'.[11] Nationalists and Futurists were united in believing that a bloodbath would 'purify', that it would regenerate the nation, that it might even be a spiritual experience that would wipe out the stain of Lissa and Custoza. Giolitti's opposition gave them new opportunities to ridicule the former premier and to brand him and other 'neutralists' as defeatists and even traitors: D'Annunzio excelled himself by inviting cheering crowds to kill such people. Although the interventionists were easily outnumbered by opponents of the war, they were well organized and knew how to influence public opinion. During what they called 'the radiant days of May' 1915, they brought huge crowds on to the streets and into the piazzas, arousing them to a state of delirium and inciting them to shout day after day for war. While this support was doubtless pleasing for the government, it did not influence the decision that had already been taken by the three men who counted, the prime minister, the foreign minister and the king. Victor Emanuel admitted later to the British ambassador that Italy had gone to war despite the fact that large majorities of its population and its parliament had been opposed.

The leaders of the combatant powers were criticized later for not foreseeing the length of the conflict or the scale of the carnage. Yet they had the excuse that, as their countries had not fought in Europe for several generations, it was difficult to predict the effect that machine guns, trenches and barbed wire might have on the tactics of a battle. Salandra and Sonnino had no such excuses. Although the prime minister claimed that an Italian invasion of Austria would quickly finish the war, he had had ample time since August 1914 to notice that invasions were no longer the speedy affairs they had once been. A glance at the stalemate on the Western Front should have been enough to convince him that the tactical advantage lay with the defending force, while a study of the battles that had already been fought, from the Marne to the Masurian Lakes, should have shown him that the war he demanded would cost hundreds of thousands of casualties. Lack of foresight was accompanied by such incompetence as a war leader that Salandra was forced to resign in 1916. In later years he advised the king to appoint Mussolini as prime minister and, despite subsequent qualms about fascism, he became a senator of the kingdom.

The chief theatre of war for the Italians was the valley of the Isonzo in Friuli, where they expected to defeat Austria (which was simultaneously fighting the Russians in the north and the Serbs in the south) before crossing the Carso Plateau and capturing Trieste. It turned out to be the most contested zone in the whole war. While their allies on the Western Front fought three battles of Ypres, the Italians engaged the Austrians in no fewer than twelve battles of the Isonzo, a statistic that by itself testifies to the limited imagination of the Italian commander, General Luigi Cadorna. The first eleven ended in stalemates, the front line advancing or sometimes retreating a few kilometres, but the last in 1917 (usually known as Caporetto) was a thumping victory for the Austrians and their German allies.

All countries, especially Britain, had unimaginative commanders who ordered their infantrymen to advance in straight lines, elbow to elbow, against well-defended positions, but Cadorna was in a league of his own. He failed to concentrate his forces, he attacked on too wide a front, he sent his men over open ground against barbed wire and machine guns, and he repeated these mistakes. His forces invariably outnumbered the Austrians, who were busy on their other two fronts, by a ratio of five to two, and he almost always suffered higher casualties than his opponents. These would have been even higher if Austrian soldiers had not sometimes felt pity for their enemies and risked court martial by encouraging them to retreat before they were gunned down.[12]

Cadorna was an obtuse and deluded general who liked to compare himself with Napoleon: when things were going really badly on the Isonzo, he consoled himself with the thought that not even the great Corsican could have fought better on the banks of that accursed river. His reaction to setbacks for which he was responsible was to sack or transfer his officers, singling out those who had shown spirit and originality: during the two and a half years of his command he removed more than 200 generals and over 600 colonels and battalion commanders. Another habit of his was to blame the poor fighting qualities of his soldiers, who were punished for their failings more savagely than their counterparts in the armies of Germany, France, Austria and Britain. Cadorna insisted that even mildly mutinous behaviour should be countered with summary executions. He also revived the ancient Roman custom of decimation, executing by lot a proportion of a censured unit's soldiers, a practice guaranteed to kill innocent men. Before offensives military police with machine guns were stationed behind the trenches, ready to shoot at soldiers who appeared to dawdle as they were going over the top.

In the summer of 1917 Rudyard Kipling travelled to the Italian front and convinced himself that he was viewing a 'new Italy' in possession of an army comparable to the old Roman 'exercitus': even the generals – 'wide-browed, bull-necked devils' or 'lean narrow hook-nosed Romans' – resembled sculptures of classical times.[13] A few weeks later, the illusion dissolved as the exercitus crumpled before the German–Austrian offensive at Caporetto and was forced to retreat all the way way back to the River Piave, not far north of Venice. 40,000 soldiers were killed or wounded, 300,000 were taken prisoner, and 350,000 deserted, disappearing into the hills and attempting to find their way home. The army lost vast quantities of weapons including

3,000 machine guns and 300,000 rifles. And the nation lost 14,000 square kilometres that contained a million of its citizens. There is little evidence that the return of the Austrians to Friuli, fifty years after their departure, was greatly regretted by the region's inhabitants.

Cadorna had held on to his post for so long because he had secured the king's support, and this allowed him to browbeat the prime minister and the cabinet. The disaster of Caporetto failed to dent his complacency, and he even managed to convince himself that public opinion would not tolerate his dismissal as the army's commander. When the British and French insisted on his resignation, he blamed 'the notorious ingratitude of the House of Savoy'.[14] His replacement was General Armando Diaz, who held the line on the Piave and sensibly refused to launch costly offensives. In October 1918 the new commander eventually ordered an advance and won the Battle of Vittorio Veneto, a victory hailed as one of the greatest of all time, one that by itself caused the destruction of the Austrian–Hungarian Empire. In fact it was achieved with the support of French and British units at a time when the Germans were already beaten, the empire was already dissolving, and the Viennese government was seeking an armistice.

The First World War cost Italy a million casualties – one-third wounded, two-thirds dead – from a population of 35 million people. At the front its soldiers had suffered at least as badly as those of any other nation. Except perhaps for the Turks, they were the worst fed, worst led, worst clad and worst equipped in the conflict; they were expected to cut through Austrian barbed wire with implements resembling garden secateurs. Such deprivations may help explain why so many men deserted and why over half a million were taken prisoner. One German officer, the future General Rommel, recalled how at Caporetto Italian soldiers were so delighted to surrender that hundreds of them threw away their rifles and rushed at him, shouting 'Evviva Germania!'[15] Yet the prisoners had a miserable time in captivity. Since their own government feared that the thought of eating well in a prison camp would be an incentive to surrender, it refused to send food parcels to its captured soldiers in Germany and Austria. This policy, which no other country adopted, resulted in the deaths of 100,000 men from hunger and diseases brought on by starvation.[16]

It has often been claimed in Italy that the Great War made the country feel more patriotic, but there is little proof of this except among people who were patriots already. Conscripts naturally saw parts of their country beyond their provinces, and they were thus able to meet other Italians, even if their dialects made it difficult to communicate with them. Yet the evidence does not suggest that they cared very much for the cause, especially the soldiers who came from the south and were sent to northern mountains to die for places they had never heard of. Soldiers seldom exhibited signs of patriotic sentiment and sometimes they even spat at the national flag. Nor did they display much hostility to the enemy; it seemed that Italians no longer even pretended to hate the Austrians. Southern men employed ingenious methods to avoid conscription, including putting tobacco leaves under their arms, which gave them an artificial fever that appeared to be malaria. An American anthropologist found a Sicilian villager who made himself ill by eating cigars, while two of his neighbours even blinded themselves so as to be unfit for military service.[17]

Vittorio Emanuele Orlando, the prime minister in 1918, told parliament that Italy's victory had been one of the greatest in recorded history, a fantasy that encouraged him and his supporters to make extravagant claims at the peace conference in Paris that opened in January 1919. In addition to gaining what he called Italy's 'God-given' borders in the Alps, Orlando demanded Fiume, a Croatian port with an Italian middle class that had formerly been administered by Hungary. Although the city had not been included in the provisions of the Treaty of London, and though it was superfluous now that Trieste was in Italian hands, Orlando insisted on acquiring a place which, he mysteriously asserted, was 'more Italian than Rome'.[18] Sonnino, who was still foreign minister, was even more demanding than Orlando. In Paris the Italian delegation claimed it was 'a matter of no significance' that the South Tyrol (as Austria called it; for Italians it was the Alto Adige) contained over 200,000 German speakers, because they were there only as a 'result of violent intrusion and foreign invasions' in the past.[19] Italy needed the Alpine watershed, insisted Sonnino, for its security and independence; it required a strategic 'natural' frontier rather than a purely ethnic one. He did not explain why Italy needed a strategic frontier when, in all recent wars between Italy and Austria, the aggressors had been the Italians.

If its western allies had remained limited to Britain and France, Italy would have stood a reasonable chance of gaining most of its demands; the Treaty of London had after all promised it a good deal of extra territory. In 1917, however, the United States had entered the war under a high-minded president with strong views about the right of peoples to self-determination: the ninth of Woodrow Wilson's famous Fourteen Points stated that the 'readjustment of the frontiers of Italy should be effected along clearly recognizable lines of nationality'. This was plainly an appalling principle for Sonnino, who was intent on acquiring a large chunk of Dalmatia even though its population of 610,000 was almost entirely Slav and included only 18,000 Italian-speakers. One Italian diplomat supported his view by arguing that self-determination may have been 'applicable to many regions but not to the shores of the Adriatic'.[20] Arguments of this sort bewildered the American president, who could not understand how the nation of Garibaldi and Mazzini could aspire to rule subject peoples.

The Italian government's response to Wilson was to send troops to the eastern Adriatic and impose Italian rule, a policy so provocative that it led to the resignation of the two most left-wing members of the cabinet in Rome. When he could not get his own way in Paris, Orlando tried another tactic. He walked out of the conference and waited in Rome for the allies to offer concessions and implore him to come back. As the delegates of the other three principals shared the view that Italy had contributed little to the conference except in discussions about its own borders, they were content to let him stay there until he decided, somewhat sheepishly, to return. Wilson had already agreed to let the Italians have the South Tyrol, a decision he later regretted, but he refused to concede Dalmatia, which was ear-marked for the new Yugoslavia.

Spurred on by the rhetoric of D'Annunzio and the nationalists, Orlando and Sonnino had raised such expectations that Italians were bound to feel disappointment at a settlement that was inevitably a compromise. Since Italy did not receive everything it wanted, its people were encouraged to believe that it had done badly out of the war, that it had been betrayed by its allies (who according to propaganda had been saved from defeat by the Italian army), and that the settlement was, in D'Annunzio's searing phrase, a 'mutilated peace'.

Yet in fact Italy did quite well from the Treaty of Rapallo (1920) which, while denying it Dalmatia and Fiume, granted it the Trentino and the South Tyrol, Trieste and the Carso, plus Gorizia, Zara and several islands in the eastern Adriatic. Another gain for Italy was the defeat and dismemberment of its traditional enemy, the Austrian–Hungarian Empire, whose chief component was now confined to the Austrian heartland. Some Italians resented their exclusion from the allocation of the German colonies in Africa, from running a mandate in the Middle East, and from receiving no colonial additions except for a few border changes in Libya and east Africa. And they had a point, even if Italy had proved itself an inept colonial power so far. France and Britain liked to boast of their administrative skills as colonizers, but French policy in Lebanon led to predictable conflict and eventually to a ferocious civil war, while British policy in Palestine introduced a bloody antagonism that was showing few signs of abating nearly a century later.

Trento had been linked with Trieste to create Italy's chief slogan of the war, a fact reflected by changes in street names all over the country. The Neapolitans had to sacrifice St Ferdinand so that his square could become Piazza Trento e Trieste, just as the Sardinians of Cagliari awoke one day to find a Viale Trieste meeting a Viale Trento in the long Piazza Trento. The city of Trento itself had once been the capital of powerful prince-bishops and, as the natural meeting-place between the Italian and Germanic peoples, had been chosen as the site of the great council that in the sixteenth century proclaimed the dogmas of the Counter-Reformation. With 90 per cent of its population speaking Italian, the Trentino was a legitimate national objective, as the Austrians had recognized by offering most of it to Italy before the fighting started. Its northern neighbour, the South Tyrol (now the Italian province of Bolzano), was a correspondingly unjustifiable aim because 90 per cent of its people were German-speakers. Italy's insistence on possessing it has led to disputes and occasional violence since the Second World War. Tyroleans from both sides of the Alpine border – men wearing *Lederhosen* and fancy braces and dripping with folksy *Gemütlichkeit* – still gather at the city of Innsbruck to demand *ein Tirol*. Even today, when one visits the town of Bressanone, north of Bolzano, one feels one is not in Italy but in Italian-occupied Austria.

The 'Fourth War of the Risorgimento' provided its quota of martyred heroes. The most prominent Trentino was Cesare Battisti, a passionate irredentist who enlisted in the Italian army in 1915, was captured by the Austrians soon afterwards and was executed in the moat of Trento's Castello di Buonconsiglio. Parts of that majestic castle now form a shrine to Battisti. You can see the room where he was sentenced and the spot where he was hanged, and you can tell from the photographs of his last minutes that he died well: having made no attempt to avoid death by renouncing his beliefs, his gaze is fierce, fearless, stern and unrepentant. A square in the old town is named after him, but his chief memorial is a vast mausoleum erected on a hill across the river. Consisting of fourteen bridged pillars in a circle, its lettering proclaims that Cesare Battisti prepared Trento for its new destiny and its union with the *patria*.

Yet the story of Battisti's last year is more complicated than a simple and moving tale of martyrdom. A leader of the Trentino Socialist Party, Battisti had been a deputy in the parliament in Vienna and also, for a brief time, of the Diet of Innsbruck. However noble his behaviour and understandable his motives, he was by any legal standard a traitor to Austria who had joined the army of a foreign power that had reneged on its alliance and attacked the state of which he was a citizen. Similarly treacherous had been the earlier actions of Battisti's most conspicuous counterpart in Trieste, the nationalist Guglielmo Oberdan, who deserted from the Austrian army and fled to Italy before returning in 1882 with the intention of killing the Habsburg emperor, Franz Josef. As Italy had just become a formal ally of Austria, the attempted murder of his legal sovereign might thus be seen as an act of double treachery. Yet memorials to this aspirant assassin can be found not only in Trieste but all over Italy. Even the small Sardinian island of La Maddalena contains a Via Oberdan; even sensible Bologna has a plaque on its town hall saluting the martyr's stand against 'tyrants abroad and cowards within'.

Trieste had been a fishing village until the Habsburgs transformed it into a free port at the beginning of the eighteenth century. Thereafter it grew to be a vast commercial emporium and a vital deep-sea port for the Habsburg Empire. It became one of those great multi-ethnic cities on the shores of the Mediterranean, as Venice had once been and Istanbul and Alexandria still were, a tolerant, open-minded place where its foreign businessmen – Greeks, Germans, Armenians, Egyptians – lived prosperously among an indigenous population of Italians, Slovenes and Jews of diverse origins. Its multicultural complexity is well illustrated in the person of its most famous writer, who called himself Italo Svevo (Italo the Swabian), whose real name was Schmitz, whose father's family was Jewish-Hungarian and his mother's Jewish Triestino, who went to school in Germany, who wrote badly in Italian and who felt comfortable only when speaking and writing in the dialect of his native city. Svevo was a businessman and an unsuccessful novelist when in 1907 he employed an Irish tutor to improve his English. The Irishman, also obscure at the time, was James Joyce, who became an enthusiast for Svevo's work, promoted its author as 'the Italian Proust' and gained for his friend a late but enduring fame by persuading a French firm to translate and publish *The Confessions of Zeno*, written when Svevo was in his sixties. Recognition in Italy soon followed.

Italians were in a majority in Trieste itself but were outnumbered by Slovenes in the suburbs and the surrounding countryside. Although they included a smattering of nationalists, mainly students, very few of them volunteered to fight for Italy in 1915. The inhabitants understood a basic truth about their city: economically, Italy did not need Trieste – just as Trieste did not need Italy – but Austria and Trieste needed each other. The port is today linked to Italy only by a strip of land to the north-west; its real hinterland is Croatia and Slovenia, and its natural trading relationships are with central Europe, which is why the Austrians had encouraged its development. No rational person really believed that Trieste would prosper from unification with Italy. Even Sonnino, in the days when he cared more about economics than expansionism, admitted that the city would be ruined if it became part of the Italian kingdom.

Trieste is still a nineteenth-century city, one that was prevented from becoming a twentieth-century metropolis because the Paris peace conference abolished its role, severing it from its hinterland and handing it to Italy. Its new masters did little to retard its now inevitable decline. While it became Italian so late that it was spared an epidemic of statues, its streets were renamed – one even commemorates the ineffable Cadorna – and it received a Museo del Risorgimento which, perhaps because Trieste took no part in the real Risorgimento, is seldom visited and is only open two mornings a week. After unification with Italy, the city's trade languished – and failed to recover – and its population declined. Today the steamers have gone, the docks are idle, the quays are used mainly by pleasure vessels. Trieste's contact with the non-Italian world has also withered. Until the advent of budget airlines, you could not fly from it direct to any foreign city except Munich and even in 2008 you could not travel by rail to Ljubljana (the nearest city) unless you were prepared to arrive at a quarter to two in the morning.

Trieste is an evocative place for sentimentalists, for connoisseurs of decadence, and for a travel writer who depicts ambience as well as Jan Morris, who has written of 'the sweet tristesse that is onomatopoeic to the place'.[21] You can sip hot chocolate at a café in the great square (the Piazza Unità d'Italia), you can follow in the footsteps of Svevo and Joyce, you can listen to a town band playing the 'Radetzky March', and you can sense the enchantment of Miramar, the seaside castle built by the Archduke Maximilian before he went to Mexico and was shot as its emperor. Yet you will feel, even if you are not a nostalgist like Morris (and myself), that it is a place without a purpose and you may wonder why it had to be ruined for so tawdry a cause as Italian expansionism. Today, when nationalism in Italy barely exists, the exercise strikes one as peculiarly pointless. According to an opinion poll taken at the end of the twentieth century, a large majority of Italians did not even realize that Trieste was in Italy.[22]

RUPTURED ITALY

In 1915 a middle-aged Italian left France, where he had gone to escape his creditors, and at the age of fifty-two enlisted in his country's armed forces. In the course of the war he served in the army, the navy and the air force, and his extraordinary exploits, which cost him an eye and other injuries, included both a torpedo-boat raid and a flight over Vienna, which he 'bombed' with pamphlets written by himself. The name of this improbably exotic hero was Gabriele D'Annunzio, a sorcerer with words, a novelist of the erotic life and a poet of twilight and sensuality too talented to deserve Croce's dismissive label, a 'dilettante of sensations'. He was both a cruel and a charismatic man, part nietzschean and part narcissist, an occasional politician and a perennial philanderer. He inaugurated the trend of the shiny scalp that was copied by Mussolini and later by Yul Brynner and later still by millions of youthful-hearted men throughout the western world.

Like the nationalists and Futurists, D'Annunzio despised those who preferred the assurance of comfort to the risks of adventure. Like them, he desired colonies and national grandeur, he wanted Italians to recover their masculine vitality and thus he exhorted his compatriots to do what he himself often did – 'to dare the undareable'. He insisted the Mediterranean should become *'mare nostrum'*, a phrase that reverberated in fascist heads with an effect similar to his words 'mutilated peace' which persuaded many people to share his views on the injustice of the peace treaties and the perfidy of allies who liked to belittle Italy. His post-war aims were the same as the government's – the Treaty of London plus Fiume – but the politicians eventually and reluctantly accepted the settlement. D'Annunzio did not. In September 1919 he decided to dare the undareable and capture Fiume for Italy.

Before the war Fiume had served the eastern parts of the Austrian–Hungarian Empire in the way that Trieste had provided for the northern portions. Like Trieste, it was an important city for its Italian businessmen but not important, economically, for Italy: its commercial focus was fixed firmly on the Balkans. Even more than in Trieste, its divisions of class and ethnicity coincided: an Italian bourgeoisie dominated a Croatian working class to such an extent that none of the town's schools taught in Croatian. After the war and the collapse of the Habsburg Empire, the Croatian majority moved to take over the city in line with the principles of Wilson's Fourteen Points. Alarmed by this development, Italians in Fiume clamoured for unification with the 'fatherland', a cause that dismayed the government in Rome, which knew that international opinion was against it and that France was already positioning itself as the protector of the nascent Yugoslavia.

In Italy Fiume became a rallying-cry for nationalists and adventurers who volunteered alongside disbanded veterans known as *'arditi'* to fight for its 'liberation'. In a classic case of history repeating itself as farce, the volunteers shouted 'Fiume or Death!' while the inhabitants of the city responded with 'Italy or Death!' At a crucial moment D'Annunzio arrived to lead the volunteers into the city and from a palace balcony proclaimed the annexation of Fiume to Italy. Officers of the Italian army stationed around the city were ordered to prevent his entry, but they behaved like Marshal Ney in March 1815, and the poseur in D'Annunzio delighted in playing the part of Napoleon, even baring his chest and telling them to shoot him. He duly became director of a vulgar and hedonistic Ruritania known as the 'Regency of Carnaro'.

The Italian government under Francesco Nitti had no idea how to deal with the 'operatic dictatorship' of D'Annunzio, which lasted over a year and was not overthrown until Giolitti returned as premier and sent troops into Fiume at the end of 1920. Although D'Annunzio quickly surrendered, he could claim a victory of sorts because Fiume became a free port and, four years later, was annexed anyway by Mussolini; as with Trieste, its incorporation into Italy deprived it of its hinterland and ruined it economically. Although nationalists claimed the Fiume episode was a triumph, Salvemini regarded D'Annunzio's adventure as 'a source of dishonour and ridicule for Italy'.[23]

One observer who found it neither dishonourable nor ridiculous was Benito Mussolini, who supported D'Annunzio in the pages of the newspaper he then edited, *Il Popolo d'Italia*. He noted how the *comandante* (as the dictator liked to call himself) manipulated crowds with speeches from a balcony, how he elicited the desired responses (as Garibaldi had once done) and how he stirred audiences up with crescendoes culminating in a mysterious and meaningless cry, '*Eia, Eia, Eia, Alalà!*' The journalist in Milan could also appreciate the importance of uniforms and parades, of the resonance of the word *duce*, of the usefulness of such gestures of masculinity as the arm outstretched in a 'Roman' salute. It would be simplistic to call D'Annunzio Mussolini's John the Baptist (as many people later did), but he was a precursor, at least in style. Soon after Mussolini became prime minister, D'Annunzio tactlessly told him that fascism had taken all its ideas from *dannunzianesimo* and invented nothing by itself.

Mussolini was thirty-six at the time of Fiume and had for long been displaying that volatility and inconsistency that were essential features of his character. As a socialist revolutionary he had described the Libyan war as a crime against humanity, had helped to organize protests and a strike against it and had gone to prison for five months as a result. His subsequent zeal in expelling reformists from the Socialist Party led to his appointment as editor of the party's newspaper, *Avanti!*, a post that gave him a useful platform to attack the interventionists and argue for neutrality at all costs in the Great War. In October 1914, however, he changed his mind completely and decided that the war would be a good thing after all, especially if it ended in a bloodbath which resulted in revolution. He therefore left *Avanti!* and set up a rival newspaper, *Il Popolo d'Italia*, which received subsidies from countries eager for Italy to join them in the fighting. The lavish new life that Mussolini was soon relishing in Milan was largely funded by the British secret service.

The editor of *Il Popolo* welcomed Wilson's Fourteen Points but, on realizing their implications for Italy's ambitions, changed his mind and denounced them. The former enemy of nationalism and imperialism now became a proponent of Italy's 'imperial destiny', demanding territories and 'booty' in the Balkans and the Middle East. In March 1919 he founded a movement called the *fasci di combattimento*, composed of a few hundred Futurists, nationalists, war veterans and former revolutionaries united by not much more than post-war disgruntlement. Although this group evolved into the Fascist Party two years later, it had few characteristics – beyond a propensity to violence – that would later be regarded as fascist. Its jumble of policies and lack of identity must have been evident to voters, who gave it less than 2 per cent of the vote in Milan in the elections at the end of 1919. Yet even before then these early fascists had revealed their preference for force over the ballot-box. A group of them, consisting mainly of *arditi*, had smashed up the office and printing-works of *Avanti!* in the spring. The leader of the *fasci*, a former socialist and editor of the paper, had by then identified their chief enemy as the Socialist Party.

There were good reasons for many people, even socialists, to feel exasperated with the performance of Italian socialism. At the elections that humiliated the *fasci*, the socialists had won more than 150 seats, making them the largest party in the Chamber, ahead of the Popular

Party (the new Catholic party), which had 100 deputies, and Giolitti's liberals, who were reduced to 92. In a functioning democracy the socialists would have entered the government, either in coalition or as a minority with outside support, as social democrats had already done in Sweden and the Labour Party did soon afterwards in Britain. In Italy they refused. When Victor Emanuel opened the new parliament, the socialist deputies walked out, singing 'The Red Flag' and shouting 'Long live the socialist republic!'

In retrospect the 'socialist threat' to Italy seems to have been exaggerated but it appeared real enough at the time. 'Red Week' in the summer of 1914, when Emilia-Romagna seemed on the brink of revolution, had been a warning. The summer of 1920, when hundreds of thousands of people went on strike and occupied factories and shipyards, seemed still more like a pre-revolutionary situation. Giolitti, who was nearly eighty, refused to intervene and managed to defeat the socialists – and the possibility of revolution – with a policy of nonviolence. He also invited moderate socialists to join his last cabinet and help him create that social peace which had been the chief object of his political life. Again they declined. The largest party in Italy refused to act responsibly and continued to frighten conservatives by talking about republicanism and revolution. Even when it became clear that its intransigence was driving Italians towards Mussolini, it concerned itself more with issues of ideological purity than with the fate of the country. Under Lenin's orders from Moscow, the extremists tried to expel the moderates at the party conference in Livorno at the beginning of 1921; when the vote went against them, they marched off to form the Italian Communist Party. Later in the year the socialists again refused to collaborate in government and in the summer of 1922 committed the folly of calling a general strike. Three years of remorseless irresponsibility had by then convinced millions of people that liberal Italy was destitute, ungovernable and ripe for bolshevism. Only too late did some socialists realize that they had allowed the *fasci* to transform themselves from a motley group of malcontents into a force capable of becoming a government. Similar behaviour by the German Left led to a similar result in its country ten years later.

Giolitti's refusal to use force to break the strikes and end the occupations may have scuppered the chance of a socialist revolution, but it alarmed northern landowners and industrialists, who concluded that in future they would have to protect their interests themselves. At hand were growing numbers of tough and violent fascists only too eager to assist them. Not content with a defensive role, squads of black-shirted thugs soon went on to the attack, beating up and killing socialists and burning their offices, their cooperatives and their local clubs, the *case del popolo*. Giolitti tried to tame the fascists by offering them an alliance in the election he called in 1921. Their candidates, he believed, would be like 'fireworks': they would 'make a lot of noise but . . . leave nothing behind except smoke'.[24] He was disastrously mistaken. His offer gave the fascists a measure of respectability and the means to win thirty-five seats, and in return they gave him nothing at all, not even support after the election, following which Giolitti was forced to resign. Nor did his gesture lessen their violence. Scenting that the socialists were already beaten, the party's *squadristi* went on the rampage in 1922, marching through the Po Valley, occupying town halls, expelling socialist councils, killing hundreds of 'reds' and again setting fire to their buildings. Surprised by their success, and by the fact that the police and the army did little to impede them, the fascists turned north to occupy Trento and Bolzano. They had succeeded in creating an extraordinary situation, transforming themselves into a counter-state that was tolerated by the real state.

Even with Giolitti's help in the elections, the Fascist Party held only 7 per cent of the seats in parliament, less than a third as many as those gained by either the Socialist Party or the Catholic *popolari*. Yet in the late summer of 1922, while the socialists were calling a general strike, the fascists were baying to take over the state, by constitutional means if possible, by coup or insurrection if not. In October they decided to force their way into government by staging a 'march on Rome', and on the evening of the 27th their squads occupied government offices and telephone exchanges in key areas. They could easily have been stopped by the army and the police, but the prime minister Facta, a liberal lightweight, dithered until after midnight. Eventually he and the cabinet advised the king to declare a state of emergency and impose martial law. At two o'clock in the morning Victor Emanuel agreed, and the army quickly recaptured the occupied buildings and blocked the roads and railways into Rome. Later in the morning, however, the king changed his mind and refused to sign the decree of martial law that his prime minister had prepared. After Facta resigned in consequence, Victor Emanuel offered his job to Salandra, the former premier, who asked Mussolini to join him in government. When the fascist leader declined to serve under him, Salandra successfully urged the king to resist the claims of Giolitti – the one politician who might still have been able to save Italy from fascism – and invite Mussolini to become prime minister.

It was a remarkable case of collective liberal suicide. Political Italy had suddenly and unnecessarily saddled itself with a prime minister who was the leader of a small political party which had gained power as a result of an armed insurrection. As Donald Sassoon has suggested, this could not have happened had the 'establishment' not decided it wanted Mussolini to 'cleanse the country of the red menace and then turn himself into a figurehead. The old establishment would rule in the shadows, as it always had done.'[25] In the event the king became the figurehead, and the establishment – or much of it – was excluded from power.

Many liberals acquiesced in Mussolini's takeover and continued to do so for some years. They believed that their state had been too weak and the political system – which had not become a party system – too unstable. Sixty-one years of liberal government had produced eighty-six ministers of education, eighty-eight ministers of justice and ninety-four ministers of the navy; one minister of agriculture had taken office on Christmas Eve and left it on Boxing Day.[26] How could administration function in such a manner? Certainly the liberals underestimated Mussolini, as did Catholics and socialists; like the king, they did not believe that the fascist leader intended to make himself a dictator. Even intellectuals of the stature of Gobetti and Salvemini could not see much difference between him and Giolitti; even Croce was ecstatic about the prospect of having Mussolini as prime minister.

The world's first and most quintessential fascist dictator thus achieved power by constitutional means – as did his future ally Adolf Hitler a decade later. Mussolini did not need a revolution like Lenin, or an army revolt like Franco, or the usual coups and murders that have cleared the way for other tyrants. Yet, just as he wanted people to think him more brutal than he really was, so he liked to claim that he had seized power by marching on Rome rather than receiving it at the hands of the king. There was in fact no march on the capital. A few thousand fascists, bedraggled and ill-equipped, gathered in the rain outside the city gates on 28 October, but, if the king had signed the decree of martial law, the armed forces could have dispersed them without difficulty. Mussolini himself did not pretend to march. He travelled by sleeping-car from Milan to Rome, a journey he compared to Julius Caesar crossing the Rubicon.

Mussolini gave notice of his intentions when, after becoming prime minister on 29 October, he addressed the deputies, telling them he could have converted their 'deaf and grey' Chamber into a barracks for his 'legions', that he could have abolished parliament and formed a government consisting solely of fascists, and that he had not done those things only because he had 'not wanted to, at least not for the moment'. The new premier often made it plain how much he despised democracy, how he regarded it as a foreign import unsuitable for Italians, but his liberal opponents seldom took him seriously. They seemed satisfied that at least he had acted legally, swearing allegiance to the king and the constitution and appointing a cabinet with a majority of non-fascists, including four liberals and the Great War's triumphant general, Armando Diaz. They did not notice signs of incipient megalomania when Mussolini made himself foreign minister and interior minister as well as prime minister – a trend that accelerated crazily so that by 1929 he held eight of the thirteen posts in the cabinet. Nor did enough of them worry that his squads were beating up and sometimes killing political opponents, notably and notoriously his most courageous critic, the socialist deputy Giacomo Matteotti, who was murdered in June 1924. A supine parliament passed laws that muzzled the press, guaranteed a fascist majority in the Chamber and established the apparatus of an authoritarian state. It paid a predictable penalty: all political parties were soon abolished except for one, the Partito Nazionale Fascista.

Giolitti was the first of the liberals to realize their mistake, but by then it was too late to rectify it. In January 1925 he voted to censure Mussolini in the Chamber but received the support of only thirty-six deputies. Many more would have voted with him had the socialists not chosen to 'secede' from parliament, one of several gestures they made that played into the hands of Mussolini. Giolitti observed that Italy had got the government it deserved; he might have said more aptly that the socialists had the government their behaviour had merited. In 1928 the old statesman, the greatest figure of Italian liberalism, died at the age of eighty-five. Mussolini did not attend his funeral. Nor did the king, whom he had served well.

II

Fascist Italy

ITALIA ROMANA

The early fascists liked to think of themselves as revolutionaries, and until lately many of them had been socialists, syndicalists, republicans, anti-clericals and even libertarians. Mussolini claimed he too was still a revolutionary and he often talked about 'the fascist revolution'. Yet it was difficult for them to take revolutionary positions when their main enemies were the socialists, their main supporters were the petty bourgeoisie, and their main backers were the landlords and capitalists who had paid them to defend their property.

Mussolini's way of dealing with this problem was to insist that fascism was both modern and traditional, conservative and revolutionary, a movement that drew from the past yet looked to the future. He thought of himself as an iconoclast like Marinetti and longed to destroy the image of Italians as innkeepers and mandolin players. Like the Futurists, he was an enthusiast for speed and technology, and he enjoyed the backing of their leader, who thought fascism a logical extension of Futurism and invented a new movement, *aeropittura futurista* (Futurist painting from the air), which he baptized as 'the daughter of fascist aviation and Italian Futurism'.[1] Yet Mussolini could not endorse Futurist yearnings to flood Italy's museums and burn down its libraries because he needed to reassure Catholics and conservatives. He also needed to promote the past – specifically the classical past – to remind Italians of what they were capable of achieving. With modern history, however, he had to be selective: thus he identified Garibaldi and Crispi as antecedents who had tried to make Italy great but simultaneously he derided most other politicians.

Fascism was happy to be regarded as the final stage of the Risorgimento so long as people realized it was also a revolutionary rupture with the liberal past and its futile spokesmen.

It is difficult to find intellectual coherence in Italian fascism, perhaps because its own leader contradicted himself so frequently. Corporatism, government not by individuals but by bodies representing different economic groups, is sometimes claimed as the great fascist idea, one so brilliant that it was copied by, among others, Spain's General Franco and Portugal's António de Oliveira Salazar. Mussolini announced that the fascist state was corporative or it was 'nothing' and claimed that corporations were the 'fascist institution par excellence'. Yet the corporate system was not organized properly until 1936, when it proved to be expensive, cumbersome and useless to the economy. The idea that industrial strife would cease because capital and labour would each be represented in government by like-minded fascists was at best naive. Fascism claimed it ran a 'direct' democracy rather than a representative one, but there was little democratic content to either the regime or its corporations. Corporatism was in effect a cloak for dictatorial control of the economy.

Mussolini liked to identify things he regarded as fascist. Boxing, for example, was 'an exquisitely fascist means of self-expression'.[2] Virility was fascist, speed and sporting prowess were fascist, fecund women with swarms of children were fascist, and above all war was fascist – it was to men what maternity was to women. He was less good at clarifying fascist ideas. He liked to conflate Italy and fascism, regarding them together as forming an organic whole, which enabled one party secretary, Roberto Farinacci, to assert that 'the anti-fascist' could not be an Italian. Beyond that was the vague idea that fascism was a sort of faith and the nation a spiritual entity. As Farinacci again put it, fascism was 'not a party but a religion'; it was 'the future of the country'.[3] Such nebulous thoughts make one sometimes wonder whether fascism was anything beyond ways of speaking, acting, fighting and controlling. Giovanni Gentile, who was supposed to be its philosopher, described it as mainly a 'style' of government, while D'Annunzio, as we know, regarded it from the beginning as simply *dannunzianesimo*. Even Mussolini occasionally wondered whether fascism was a strategy rather than a doctrine, a technique for acquiring and then retaining power. In such moods he thought of fascism almost as an extension of himself, *mussolinismo*, a personal thing that would die with him.

In the 1930s the regime's style became more ostentatious. There were more parades, more uniforms, more censorship, more hectoring, more speeches from the leader, more shouting, gesturing and grimacing from a balcony to vast crowds, which greeted Mussolini's every reference to *patria* and *gloria* with roars and chants of '*Du-ce! Du-ce! Du-ce!*'. Some of this change of style can be attributed to military successes in Africa and also to the influence of Adolf Hitler, which will be discussed later, but part of it was the responsibility of another party secretary, Achille Starace. Nobody made the fascist regime look more pompous and silly than Starace, who banned hand-shaking because he deemed it effete and unhygienic and made visitors to the dictator's office run in and out of the room at the double. When asked why he had appointed a 'cretin' as party secretary, Mussolini admitted that Starace was indeed 'a cretin, but an obedient one'.[4] The Duce was the type of leader perennially worried that he might be outshone by intelligent subordinates. When Italo Balbo, one of the ablest and most successful fascist ministers, became too popular with the Italian public, he was removed from the air ministry and sent off to govern Libya.

One of Mussolini's chief projects was to change the character of the Italian people. In an interview with an American newspaper he claimed that fascism was 'the greatest experiment in our history in making Italians'.[5] Previous attempts may have failed, but if fascism could create a new nation, surely it could create a new native? Mussolini wanted to fashion a fascist way of living, one that abhorred comfort and sloth and embraced courage, discipline and respect for authority. A favourite verb of his was *plasmare* (to mould or shape), which illustrated his ambition to be the new Italians' designer, though he later substituted this for the stronger *forgiare*, which implied he saw himself as their blacksmith.[6] When explaining to the fascists' Grand Council why he wanted to restore the death penalty, which had been abolished in 1889, he said he wanted 'to make Italians more virile, to habituate them to the sight of blood and to the idea of death'.[7]

Certain parts of the project were carried out sensibly and to some extent successfully. The regime's Opera Nazionale Dopolavoro created 'after-work' clubs which gave opportunities of sport, theatre and other recreations to people who had seldom experienced such pleasures. By the late 1930s nearly 4 million Italian adults were members of the clubs, while 7 million of their children belonged to the fascist youth organization, the Balilla, named after the boy from Genoa who had touched off the riot against the Austrians in 1746. This gave children the chance to become little fascists at the age of six, when they became *figli della lupa* (children of the she-wolf), and to advance through other stages to become *avanguardisti* (advance-guards) and finally adult party members. At summer camps in the mountains or by the seaside, they were told that they were descendants of the Romans and that Musssolini was the spiritual progeny of Caesar. Yet in spite of the brain-washing, these predominantly working-class children from northern cities were able to enjoy holidays their parents had never dreamed of.

The fascist regime wanted Italians to become more aware of their history or at any rate of the historical periods it approved of. Little was done to remind people of their Baroque past, which was considered a decadent and effeminate age, but the Middle Ages, with their phallic towers and their Gothic town halls, were extolled. Much effort and money was thus spent on restoring the town of San Gimignano to its medieval glory; modern windows were replaced, crenellations were added, and a Baroque church was deprived of its nave because it blocked the view of the Porta San Giovanni. The 'medieval' embellishments still look remarkably authentic. Linking the town's two squares is a vaulted loggia that seems to belong to the fourteenth century; in fact it was built in 1936.[8] San Gimignano's architecture looks more medieval today than it did in 1902 when E. M. Forster visited the setting of his first novel, *Where Angels Fear to Tread*.

Garibaldi was predictably the figure from the recent past whom the fascists exalted above all others. In appropriating him as a proto-fascist, the regime was assisted by one of the great man's grandsons, Ezio, who argued that the 'march on Rome' and the seizure of power had been very Garibaldian events; fascism, he claimed, was the continuation and fulfilment of his grandfather's dream. In 1932, fifty years after Garibaldi's death, the body of Anita, the hero's first wife, was brought to Rome and reburied with much ceremony on the Janiculum Hill. Mussolini, who understood the propaganda value of the 'Lion of Caprera', dominated the celebrations. He even interfered with the design of the commemorative statue, insisting that the heroine on her galloping steed should cradle a baby as well as a gun – maternity and warfare in unison. Yet in the speech he gave at the unveiling of the statue he virtually ignored Anita and concentrated on establishing connections between his regime and the *garibaldini*. The blackshirts, he declared, the men who had fought and died to make the fascist revolution, were the political heirs of the redshirts and their gallant leader. If Garibaldi could now come to life and open his eyes, he would recognize the descendants of his men in the veterans of Vittorio Veneto and in the blackshirts of the fascist regime.[9]

Although many fascists saw themselves as the heirs of Garibaldi, so inconveniently did many anti-fascists. While fighting on Franco's side in the Spanish Civil War, Mussolini's corps of so-called volunteers was defeated at the Battle of Guadalajara (1937) by an enemy force that included the Garibaldi Battalion of Italians fighting in the International Brigades. In 1945, as he was trying to escape to Switzerland, Mussolini was discovered and captured by the 52nd Garibaldi Brigade of anti-fascist partisans. And in the elections of 1948 the Italian Communist Party used Garibaldi's face as its emblem. The old hero would have been bemused and possibly amused, but he would surely have preferred the partisans to the blackshirts, just as he would have fought with Spain's republicans rather than Franco's nationalists.

No recent allusions, however, appealed to fascism as much as the example of ancient Rome. Mussolini, who claimed the word Rome was 'like a boom of thunder' in his soul, saw himself as the descendant of Julius Caesar and Augustus, triumphant, omniscient and imperial; perhaps he anticipated that he too would have a month named after him. He loved the idea of *romanità* ('Romanness') and wanted Italians to inhale it so deeply that they would become more disciplined, more feared, more courageous and less Italian. The official emblem of the regime was the *fascio littorio*, the bundle of rods enclosing an axe that Roman lictors used to hold; another emblem was the she-wolf, who had suckled Romulus and Remus, who gave her name to child fascists and whose image from the Capitoline Museum was used at celebrations of *romanità*. If any commune in the country was still without a Via Roma, it was ordered to create one forthwith and to ensure that it was a principal thoroughfare and not a secondary street. In Sicily new settlements were christened Dux and Mussolinia, and old towns were given more resonantly Roman names, Girgenti making way for Agrigento and Castrogiovanni reverting to the ancient Enna; one impoverished hamlet on the island suddenly became the village of Roma. Much of this 'Romanizing' was self-evidently trivial and obsessive: Mussolini changed the date of Labour Day from 1 May to 21 April, the mythical date of Rome's foundation in 753 BC, and he altered a regional boundary so that Monte Fumaiolo, source of the River Tiber, would be in the Romagna instead of Tuscany. Not all of this programme was strictly Roman, even if it pretended to be. Shortly before Hitler's official visit in 1938, Mussolini ordered his army to adopt the goose-step style of marching, but he called it the *passo romano* so that he could deny he was imitating the nazis.

Yet there had to be a serious side to a policy that set out to retrieve, instil and export classical Roman values. One important achievement of the fascist era was the excavation and restoration of ancient buildings. The Ara Pacis, the 'altar of peace', erected in Rome to celebrate the age of Augustus, was unburied and reassembled on the banks of the Tiber; the neighbouring mausoleum of the first emperor was also restored, its vast structure liberated from the debris of centuries and a history that included spells as a vineyard, a bullring and a concert hall. Both projects were timed, along with the 'Augustan Exhibition of Romanness', to coincide with the 2,000th anniversary of the emperor's birth. To emphasize the connection between the Rome of the Caesars and the Rome of Mussolini, the monuments were framed on three sides by a piazza of fascist buildings designed by the Jewish architect Vittorio Morpurgo. As with the Garibaldi celebrations, Mussolini placed himself at the centre of the enterprise and was photographed wielding a pickaxe outside the mausoleum as he commenced the demolition of the surrounding buildings. The Duce liked to remind people that he was a destroyer as well as a builder. He once planned to knock down all of Rome that had been constructed during 'the centuries of decadence' after Augustus, but in the end he contented himself with razing the quarter (including its churches) between the Colosseum and the Piazza Venezia to make way for an imperial thoroughfare (now the Via dei Fori Imperiali) along which his 'legions' could parade.

Fascism's architectural style was intended, like the regime itself, to be a hybrid between the classical and the modern. Some of it simply took the form of pastiche (for instance, the sports stadium in Rome once known as the Foro Mussolini) or even pillage (the Duce copied Augustus by stealing an obelisk from Africa). Yet most of it was serious, as one can still see in the outskirts of Rome at EUR (Esposizione Universale di Roma), an unfinished attempt to create an 'ideal city' for an exhibition that was planned for 1942; its Palace of Italian Civilization, a cube of six storeys containing fifty-four arches on each side, is the first beautiful building that travellers arriving at Fiumicino see on their way into the city. Guidebooks routinely dismiss the architecture of the era as 'bombastic' and 'typically fascist', but many buildings do not merit such dismissals. The architect Marcello Piacentini designed the lumpy and inappropriate Piazza della Vittoria in Brescia, but in neighbouring Bergamo he built in an elegant, restrained and unheroic style. In Como the young Giuseppe Terragni constructed several fine buildings, including the Casa del Fascio, one of the most beautiful examples of modernist architecture in Italy. Fascist buildings are often disparaged not because they are bad buildings but because they happen to have been built by fascists.

Italy under Mussolini is sometimes regarded as a cultural desert, its artists reduced to conformity and even servility by a police state and an oppressive censorship. This was not the case. Artists worked with a freedom unthinkable in nazi Germany or soviet Russia, and many of them were convinced fascists. Such was Pietro Mascagni, the composer of *La cavalleria rusticana*, and both Puccini and Toscanini were sympathizers, though the former soon died and the latter changed his mind after Mussolini came to power: later he refused to conduct the fascist anthem ('*Giovinezza*'), was beaten up in consequence and took himself into exile. No composer had an opera banned apart from Gian Francesco Malipiero, one of whose works aroused the whimsical fury of the Duce. Yet it was an exception. There were enough cultured and broad-minded fascists, including the arts minister Giuseppe Bottai, to deter those burners of books and destroyers of canvases who flourished in other dictatorships. Mussolini himself found museums rather boring and sometimes wished they contained fewer paintings and more captured flags. Yet unlike Hitler or Stalin, he did not interfere with artists or force them to produce paintings of valiant soldiers and heroic proletarians. He also had a more sophisticated attitude to art than the Führer, appreciating both modernist painting and rationalist architecture. He wanted art to be – like everything else – a blend of the modern and the traditional, but he did not try to impose a 'state art' until near the end, under the influence of Hitler and on the eve of the Second World War, Farinacci sponsored the Cremona Prize awarded to painters who created 'fascist art'. Even in 1939, however, Bottai established the rival Bergamo Prize, which gave awards to artists irrespective of their style or political views.[10]

The regime was active in its support for theatre and cinema. After Luigi Pirandello had made his name as a playwright in Paris, Mussolini saw his potential as an adornment of the state and helped him set up a theatre company in Rome. The potentialities of cinema were even greater. What splendid propaganda messages could be made through a film about the Roman general Scipio Africanus, or through Alessandro Blasetti's *1860*, which ended with a mutual saluting scene between ancient redshirts and youthful blackshirts. The regime subsidized and promoted cinema and built Cinecittà in Rome, the largest film studios in Europe. Yet few overtly propaganda works were in fact produced, and many were not more nationalistic than those made in more democratic nations. British film-makers liked to show the valour of the British on the North-West Frontier, and American film-makers managed to depict 'Red Indians' as hordes of aggressive savages unreasonably objecting to the presence of a few white-skinned pioneers.

Mussolini was not cast by nature for the role of censor. While it was absurd to claim, as he did in 1928, that the press enjoyed more freedom in Italy than in any country in the world, he initially kept the same censorship laws set in place by his liberal predecessors. The situation worsened from 1934, when publishers were forced to send in their books for vetting, and in 1940 it deteriorated further. Yet Croce was allowed to publish his anti-fascist writings throughout the dictatorship, and Cesare Pavese could have a book published in 1936 even though he had been a political prisoner the year before. Wisely, the government thought it preferable to influence writers with perks and subsidies than to ban their books. Several members of the left-wing intelligentsia after the Second World War had been avid supplicants for fascist funds, a fact they later tried very hard to conceal. Mario Alicata, a future stalinist, received money for his journal from the Ministry of Popular Culture. Alberto Moravia, the novelist and a future MEP on the Communist Party list, was so eager for state money and assistance that he sent grovelling letters to Count Ciano (Mussolini's son-in-law), whom he hailed as a role model for Italian youth, and to the Duce himself, to whom he shamelessly lauded the achievements of the regime and its 'exemplary and extraordinary' leader. It was difficult for Moravia to be critical of a state while he was begging it to give him $500 in order to travel to the East and write about China.[11]

Fascist Italy was a braggart state, a bully state and a police state, but for all its rhetoric it was not – within its own boundaries – a very bloodthirsty state. It kept files on more than 100,000 subversives, but very few went to prison. In 1931 Italy's 1,200 university professors were forced to swear an oath of loyalty to fascism as well as to the king, but the action did not greatly inconvenience the academics: only a dozen refused to swear and consequently lost their positions. The usual way of punishing political dissidents was *confino*, internal exile, a method that liberal governments had employed against malcontents in Naples and Sicily in the nineteenth century. During the fascist dictatorship a few thousand dissidents were exiled, usually to remote villages and islands in the south, where they were prevented from travelling and forced to report to the police each day. Many years later, Silvio Berlusconi scoffed at the punishment and said *confino* was like being sent to a holiday camp. It was of course nothing of the sort, but neither was it Dachau or the Gulag.

More crass and vindictive was the regime's policy towards the country's ethnic minorities on the frontiers. Slovene was banned although half the people in and around Trieste were Slovenes. Italian was the obligatory language in the Alto Adige, where 90 per cent of the population spoke German as a first language. No suggestion of autonomy was permitted in the province. The teaching of German was forbidden even in private, newspapers in German were suppressed (except one produced by the government), and Italian immigration was actively encouraged. As a way of emphasizing the status of the ex-Austrians as a conquered people, Mussolini erected an enormous victory monument, its giant pillars sculpted in the form of the Roman *fasces*, in Bolzano, their provincial capital. Some of the inhabitants, who continued – and continue – to consider themselves Tyrolean, later hoped that nazi Germany would come to their rescue. But Hitler had no intention of rescuing these quarter of a million members of the *Volk*. He had 9 million Germans from Austria and Czechoslovakia whom he planned to gather to his reich, and he needed Italian friendship for his schemes. After the Anschluss in March 1938 he guaranteed Italy's frontier with Austria near the Brenner Pass and forced Tyroleans to choose between emigrating to Germany or staying in the Alto Adige and renouncing their cultural and linguistic rights.

A minority that was not oppressed during the first sixteen years of fascism was Italy's Jewish community. Consisting of only 48,000 people, it was considered neither a 'problem' nor a threat by even the most extreme nationalists. One Italian diplomat recalled in a memoir published in 1938 that Jews were not regarded as aliens but as 'patriotic and useful members of the community' who were 'not conspicuous enough to figure as scapegoats in times of depression'.[12] Jews were welcomed into the Fascist Party, some took part in the 'March on Rome', and a few became ministers; Italo Balbo acknowledged that the three 'best friends' of his life had been Jewish.[13] Within the Jewish community there was little discontent or anxiety, and only a handful of its members chose to become zionists and go off to colonize Palestine. Giorgio Bassani, the Jewish novelist whose books include *The Garden of the Finzi-Continis*, wrote mainly about the Jews of Ferrara, his home town (and Balbo's), and admitted he could not remember anyone in the community who had not been a fascist.[14]

Mussolini himself was not innately anti-Semitic, though later he pretended to be in order to refute accusations that in 1938 he was simply imitating Hitler's policies. His favourite mistress in the 1920s was Jewish, and he chose a Jewish architect to do the work on the Ara Pacis and its surroundings. Although he hoped to 'give Italians a feeling of race so that they [wouldn't] create half-castes',[15] and though he encouraged them to treat Arabs and Africans and later Slavs as inferior peoples, he did not share the racial doctrines of the nazis and he was understandably uncomfortable with theories that exalted fair-haired, blue-eyed northerners above all other races. Yet in 1938, plainly influenced by Germany, he declared racialism to be an essential fascist dogma and said that the purity of the Italian race could only be preserved by the expulsion of the Jews. As Governor of Libya, Balbo protected the colony's Jewish inhabitants but in 1942, after his early death, Mussolini persecuted them with new edicts; fortunately General Montgomery and his Eighth Army soon arrived and made the new policy redundant. In the autumn of the following year 183 members of Ferrara's Jewish community were deported to nazi concentration camps. Only one returned.

Visitors to Italy after the Second World War received the impression that most of its people had been anti-fascists. It was simply not true. The dictatorship could not have lasted for twenty years if Mussolini had been despised and fascism had been detested. In recent years there has been much debate about how popular Mussolini really was, how much *consenso* – a word somewhere between acceptance and approval – he enjoyed among the Italian people. For a decade after his victory in the last real elections in 1924, *consenso* seems to have been fairly general. The diplomat Daniele Varè expressed the view of many when he claimed that fascism 'embodied an ideal of Order, Discipline, Authority, wedded to the Italian temperament'.[16] This was what most people wanted, especially the middle classes and above all the members of the petty bourgeoisie. Mussolini himself had charisma – to men and to women – and also a certain charm, difficult though this may now be to discern. It is revealing to look at a newsreel of him making a speech in the late 1930s in Padua's Prato della Valle, one of the largest squares in Europe. The piazza contains nearly the entire population of the city, tens of thousands of people cheering every sentence and throwing their hats in the air or twirling them deliriously at the end of their sticks. The event was, of course, orchestrated, but the enthusiasm was genuine. Those who failed to attend such spectacles were not arrested and put in prison.

Mussolini survived so long partly because he incarnated certain strands of *italianità*; he embodied the hopes, fears and grievances of a generation that believed Italy had been cheated of its due, both by its liberal politicians and by the attitudes of its wartime allies, who had forced it to accept the 'mutilated peace'. Until 1934, before he began to squander Italy's wealth on invasions of Africa and Europe, he faced little opposition to his rule from his countrymen. Probably he made Italy feel more united than ever before – or indeed since. As the historian Alberto Mario Banti has suggested, the middle years of Mussolini's dictatorship were 'the apex of the process of nationalizing the masses', the moment when 'Italy's national identity was at its strongest and most widespread'.[17]

Anti-fascist views seldom reached the ears of the Italian populace, and organized opposition rarely consisted of much more than a few clandestine cells of the Communist Party. The regime's few outspoken critics were mainly dead (Gobetti and Giolitti), imprisoned (Gramsci), in exile (Salvemini and the *popolari* leader, Don Sturzo) or murdered (Matteotti and Giovanni Amendola as well as later victims such as the Rosselli brothers, whose anti-fascist group Justice and Liberty tried to create a united opposition of politically disparate elements). Few Catholics followed Sturzo into opposition because Mussolini made intelligent concessions to the Church. He allowed Catholic Action (an organization of 2 million people in 1930) to continue to operate, and in 1929 he gave the Vatican the status of a sovereign and independent state. Also, in one of his many about-turns, he abandoned his early anti-clericalism and his enthusiasm for contraception. However much Catholics might dislike other aspects of fascism, many of them shared the regime's view that women's priorities should be maternity, domesticity and religious observance.

Fascism's appeal was blunted, however, by its failure to provide prosperity. Italians might be deceived into thinking they were well governed but they could not be deceived into thinking they were well off. They could see in American films that other people were much richer than they were, and they could observe this discrepancy in person when emigrants returned for spells in the homeland with plenty of dollars to spend. Mussolini himself was not an acquisitive person and he wanted Italians to care more about their country than about their wealth. His economic policies duly reflected this priority: it was for reasons of prestige rather than financial advantage that in 1926–7 he kept the lira overvalued against sterling. A more damaging result of his craving for prestige was his insistence that Italy became self-sufficient in wheat. The so-called Battle for Grain did indeed achieve this objective, but the consequent monoculture led to soil exhaustion, a decrease in animal farming and a decline in exports of more profitable crops, especially fruit; for a while, Italy even became an importer of olive oil. Italy also suffered from a lack of coal and other raw materials, which meant it could never hope to compete as an industrial power with Britain and Germany. Yet it could have become wealthier if its rulers had shown any zeal in looking for oil in Libya. Foreign oil companies offered to help in exploring the sands, but Mussolini rejected their approaches, once again for reasons of prestige. Proud of the technological inventiveness of his countrymen, he thought it would be humiliating to accept foreign assistance.

Fascism was a phenomenon of the north. It was made in the Po Valley, and its leaders were northerners; Gentile was almost the only Sicilian who became an important figure in the regime. In the south, where the petty bourgeoisie – its natural recruiting-ground – scarcely existed, fascism was imposed and then accepted without enthusiasm. The Duce did not like the south, and he especially disliked Sicilians, who did not care very much for him. Many of the island's noblemen viewed the regime with aristocratic disdain; on seeing Mussolini for the first time, the Prince of Butera observed, 'Too many spats! Too many spats!'[18] The fascist government did virtually nothing to develop the southern economy, though it created some employment by erecting prestigious buildings such as headquarters for the party and barracks for the *carabinieri*. Little was done to exploit Sicily's gas, and nothing was done to reform the *latifondi* until the Second World War, when it was too late.

On a visit to a Sicilian town in 1924, Mussolini was upstaged by a local *mafioso*, who hogged the publicity and made him feel inferior. The episode goaded the Duce to fight and try to destroy the Sicilian clans, and before long the annoying *mafioso* found himself in prison.

Fascists could not in any case have been expected to tolerate what they considered a state within a state. A year later, Mussolini appointed a Lombard policeman, Cesare Mori, as prefect of Palermo with wide-ranging powers for a campaign against the network of criminal gangs collectively known as the Mafia.

Mori was a man with a sense of mission. He believed that the 'great soul of Sicily' could be recovered only by extinguishing the Mafia. The task of extinction was complicated, however, by the fascists' failure to agree on who in fact belonged to the Mafia. Radicals among them identified it with the old ruling class, but conservative fascists found it among bourgeois arrivistes. Others seemed simply to equate *mafiosi* with their political opponents. Mori himself, who believed the Mafia was a 'parasitic' middle class, admitted that its members could not be empirically unmasked. 'The figure of the *mafioso*,' he declared, was 'recognized above all through intuition: he is divined, sensed.' In the event, Mori sometimes used his intuition to ensure the downfall of fascist rivals, revealing to Mussolini their alleged links with the Mafia. His campaign against the *mafiosi* consisted of sweeping police operations, thousands of arrests and massive trials. Many *mafiosi* were caught, many others escaped, and many innocent people suffered. Although the crime rate dropped, the fascists did not manage to destroy the Mafia, partly because they insisted on seeing it as a secret and sinister organization, when in fact it was more than that; it was also a way of living that could not be extinguished by mere repression.[19]

The Duce's insistence that the Mafia had been destroyed meant that the subject could not be mentioned by the press and, as a result, many murders and robberies went unreported. This was a typical Mussolinian situation. A decree of 1925 stated that the Duce had 'meditated with passion and knowledge' on 'the Southern Question' and had thereby cut 'the gordian knot of its solution'.[20] In consequence the issue was no longer an issue and could not be a subject for public discussion. When Luigi Barzini was sent by the *Corriere della Sera* to report on Sardinia in 1933, he was ordered not to mention poverty, malaria or banditry because officially these no longer existed. Soon after his arrival, a captain of the *carabinieri* invited him to watch a shoot-out with some bandits.[21]

Visitors from the north could see very well that 'the Southern

Question' had not been solved, and they were, like the *meridionalisti* before them, appalled by the poverty and the sight of people living in one-room hovels together with their animals. They met young men volunteering to fight in Africa and Spain not as enthusiasts for those wars but as people who knew they had no future in their villages. Many observers were struck by the sheer joylessness of rural life in the south, where nobody sang, not even at harvest-time. One witness was an anti-fascist intellectual from Turin, Carlo Levi, who in 1935 was sent to *confino* in a village in the hills of Basilicata, which was then known by its Roman name, Lucania. A doctor by training and a painter by profession, Levi managed to empathize with the poor of the rural south in a way that few northerners have been able to do. A decade later, he distilled his experiences in *Christ Stopped at Eboli*, a hauntingly evocative work, part memoir, part study and part fiction.

Levi's title came from a saying of the villagers of Aliano (a place he called Gagliano in the book), who felt they were outcasts treated by other people as if they were not Christians or civilized people or even normal human beings. They inhabited a world 'hedged in by custom and sorrow, cut off from History and the State', a 'land without comfort or solace, where the peasant lived out his motionless civilization on barren ground in remote poverty, and in the presence of death'.[22] The most vigorous villagers had emigrated to Argentina. Those who remained tramped for hours to distant fields, they suffered from malaria and other diseases, and they were still further oppressed by the regulations of the regime. The government had decided that crops should be protected by a national tax on goats, but in Aliano, where there were no crops for goats to eat, they survived on thorn and scrub. All the same, the Alianesi were as subject to the tax as anyone else and, since they could not afford to pay it, they were forced to slaughter their goats and thus deprive themselves of milk and cheese.

The case of Aliano illustrates a widespread phenomenon in the south, one that long predated fascism. It is the concept of people from *fuori*, people from outside, from 'over there', people from the state, officials who are automatically distrusted and from whom no good can be expected. Peasants felt no attachment to the state, whoever controlled it, because they had never been made to feel that they belonged to it. No peasants in Aliano were members of the Fascist Party because fascism meant power, and they had no power. For them the state was a distant and alien entity that taxed them, conscripted them and made them kill their goats. They had absolutely no reason to feel affection for those 'guys in Rome'. In the peasants' houses, which he frequented as a doctor, Levi never saw prints of the king or Mussolini or even Garibaldi; alone on the walls were images of President Roosevelt and the Madonna of Viggiano, who in their different ways represented hope. When Aliano's mayor tried to enthuse the peasants with talk of empire and the conquest of Ethiopia, they remained silent and uninterested. Nearly all their families had lost sons in the Great War for a cause they had not understood, and they did not wish to support the even less comprehensible project of an empire in Africa. As they told Levi, if the 'guys in Rome' had enough money for a war, why did they not spend it on providing Aliano with a reservoir or repairing its bridge or even planting some saplings?

Aliano no longer feels lost in time or 'cut off from History'. Much of the landscape is still desolate, the jagged slopes of its eroded hills stretching away towards the mountains of Calabria. But between the hills there are new fields and young olive groves as well as scraggy clumps of incongruous eucalyptus. Money from the government, remittances from emigrants and pilgrimages from the writer's admirers have erased the sense of poverty that so troubled Carlo Levi. There is now no misery or malaria in the village, but neither is there much sign of wealth creation. Aliano today is a silent place, populated mainly by the old, by women in black who chatter from windows to their neighbours across alleyways, by old men in berets hobbling about or sitting together on benches under the ilex trees. Most of the people they knew as children went to Buenos Aires or further south to Bahía Blanca; there are far more Alianesi living in Argentina than in the old village in Basilicata. Most of the young have also left, and the village football team has been reduced to playing five-a-side soccer. The dismal demographic statistics listed in the parish newsletter tell a story that is only too typical of the south. There are more deaths than births, more women than men, more emigrants than incomers, and, among those who remain, unemployment is high.[23]

ITALIA IMPERIALE

Mussolini's first appearance on an international stage was at Lausanne at a conference summoned in late 1922 to settle Turkey's borders after the fall of the Ottoman Empire. His fellow delegates were not impressed by Italy's new prime minister. The British foreign secretary, Lord Curzon, found him 'a very stagey sort of person' who was always trying to create an effect, sometimes with a band playing '*Giovinezza*' in attendance. On the opening day of the conference Mussolini contributed nothing to the discussions and spent his time strutting around with his blackshirts and making eleven statements to the press. Although he left Lausanne the following day, still without any achievement, Italian newspapers managed to describe his performance as their country's first diplomatic success since 1860.[24]

Mussolini's directives to his delegation soon convinced Curzon that, apart from being 'stagey', the fascist leader was a 'thoroughly unscrupulous and dangerous demagogue, plausible in manner, but without scruple in truth or conduct'. From Rome he threatened almost daily ruptures of the alliance with the Great War victors and warned he would withdraw from the conference unless he was promised a slice of the Middle East, a stance that suggested to Curzon 'a combination of the sturdy beggar and the ferocious bandit'. Soon he went beyond threats and adopted a policy that the South African prime minister, Jan Smuts, described as 'running about biting everybody'.[25] When four Italians working for an international boundary commission were mysteriously killed on Greek soil, Mussolini delivered an impossible ultimatum to Athens and then bombarded and occupied the island of Corfu, killing a number of civilians. Although the Italians were eventually persuaded to evacuate, they did so only after the Greek government was made to pay a large indemnity for a crime it knew nothing about and which was probably committed by Albanians. The Duce was determined, like the Venetians of old, to control the Adriatic and demonstrate the fact.

Mussolini was converted to imperialism in his thirties at a time when the idea of empire was losing ground in other parts of the world. The Atlantic empires of Spain and Portugal had long gone, and Britain and France were faced with increasing opposition in some of their colonies. The British may have been building a new imperial capital in Delhi, but by now much of the subcontinent's administration was being conducted – except at the very top – by Indians. Yet when Mussolini embraced an idea, he invariably hugged it to excess. He talked about reviving the Roman Empire and incorporating within it Malta, the Balkans, parts of France, parts of the Middle East and most of north Africa. Although he had signed the Treaty of Locarno in 1925, which was intended to guarantee peace in western Europe, he later raved about defeating France and Britain by himself, of marching 'to the ocean' and acquiring an outlet on the Atlantic. Like Crispi, he wanted colonies for reasons of prestige rather than for their wealth – such as it was – or their potential as a place to settle land-hungry Italians.

Fascist Italy inherited certain colonial positions which it quickly resolved to strengthen. Somaliland thus had to be properly subdued and ruled more vigorously than before. The situation was more complicated in Libya because the liberal regime, aware that by the end of the Great War it controlled only a few areas along the coast, had made an agreement with the Senussi leader which gave the Arab tribes autonomy and economic assistance in exchange for accepting Italy's sovereignty. This created a very unfascist state of affairs, and the policy was soon abandoned in favour of subjugating the tribes, first in Tripolitania and later in Cyrenaica. In 1930 two senior generals, Pietro Badoglio and Rodolfo Graziani, herded the entire population of Cyrenaica into detention camps where conditions were so bad that thousands of people perished along with nearly all their goats and camels. The following year the 'rebel' leader in Cyrenaica, the septuagenarian Omar al-Mukhtar, was captured and executed in front of his followers. Half a century on, when a film called the *The Lion of the Desert* was made about this heroic figure, it was banned in Italy on the grounds that it was 'damaging to the honour of the Italian army'.[26]

Mussolini believed that a nation could only remain healthy if it fought a war in every generation. The Italian army had been fighting for years in Libya, but its activities there did not count as a war: it was carrying out the 'pacification' of a territory that already belonged to Italy. The real thing would be to conquer and annex a foreign country. Mussolini was old enough to remember the defeat at Adowa and he had long-nurtured ideas of avenging it by conquering Ethiopia and overthrowing its emperor, Haile Selassie. It was unfortunate that the country was Christian, independent and a member of the League of Nations, but the Duce was not deterred by such things. He had generally disliked and affected to despise the League, a body formed in 1920 from which his new admirer, Adolf Hitler, had already withdrawn; he also had some support from the French foreign minister, Pierre Laval, who had allegedly offered him 'a free hand' in Ethiopia.

Mussolini had assembled a huge force of 400,000 men, consisting of regular troops and fascist militiamen, and in October 1935 he ordered them to invade Ethiopia from Eritrea and Somaliland. Although he knew the invasion was initially unpopular at home, he believed that a rapid victory and the consequent prestige of imperial ownership would change public opinion. After a triumphant entry into Addis Ababa, fascism would be unstoppable; it would next turn against Egypt, throw the British out and liberate Italy from the 'servitude of the Suez Canal'. Seven months after the campaign's inception, Badoglio's troops entered the Ethiopian capital, an event which earned their commander the title of Duke of Addis Ababa. Victory justified the prediction of the Duce, who informed ecstatic crowds at home that, after a gap of fifteen centuries, empire had returned to the seven hills of Rome. Gentile seemed to embody the national mood when he claimed that Mussolini had not only founded an empire but 'done something more. He ha[d] created a new Italy.'[27] One ludicrous aspect of the enterprise was the military boastfulness that followed. The victory may have been Italy's first ever without allied support but it was hardly, as its propagandists claimed, one of the most brilliant campaigns in world history: you did not have to be brilliant in the 1930s to defeat an enemy that possessed neither artillery nor an air force.

Victory was achieved with the help of poison gas and bombing raids on civilian targets. One of Mussolini's sons wrote a book about his experiences as an air force pilot in Ethiopia, describing fighting as 'the most beautiful and complete of all sports' and recalling how 'diverting' it was to watch groups of tribesmen 'burst out like a rose after [he] had landed a bomb in the middle of them'. [28] The sport did not cease after the proclamation of victory. As in Libya in the decade before fascism, most of Ethiopia remained unoccupied by Italian troops, and native resistance continued after the fall of the capital. Mussolini reacted by ordering a systematic policy of terror, burning hundreds of villages, executing prisoners without trial and shooting all adult males in places where resistance was discovered. When weapons were found in the great monastery of Debra Libanos, at least 400 monks and deacons were murdered; the Coptic Archbishop Petros, who had come from Egypt to be head of the Ethiopian Church, was also executed. When in February 1937 two Eritreans threw grenades at the viceroy, Marshal Graziani, killing seven people and wounding others (including the viceroy), the local fascist boss gave his men three days to go on the rampage, 'to destroy and kill and do what you want to the Ethiopians'. At least 3,000 Africans – and probably many more – were slaughtered in consequence. The victims had nothing to do with the bomb throwers; they did not even belong to the same part of the fascist empire.[29]

Italian soldiers used to enjoy the reputation of being *brava gente*, good fellows, 'the good soldier Gino' who remained good even in uniform. Italians claimed they were not like the nazis. Nor were their generals, whose decency is supposed to have been certified later by the fact that none of them faced a trial like the leading nazis at Nuremberg. Yet in recent decades an Italian historian, Angelo del Boca, has gone through the colonial records and painstakingly compiled, in volume after volume, evidence that the generals committed horrific atrocities in Africa and later the Balkans and that 'the good soldier Gino' is a myth: the *brava gente* were as adept at massacring as anyone else. The Italian army reacted by trying to have Del Boca prosecuted for 'vilifying the Italian soldier'.[30]

In July 1936, two months after the capture of Addis Ababa, Mussolini decided to fight another war, this time in support of Franco's insurrection against the republican government in Spain. He dispatched a squadron of bombers, which he soon added to, and a small army of blackshirts, which he increased with regular soldiers so that ultimately Italy sent 73,000 Voluntary Troops to the Iberian peninsula. Fascists and their apologists claimed they were sent to counter the 'Bolshevik threat', but at that moment no such threat existed.[31] The Spanish Communist Party had sixteen deputies in a Cortes of 473, it was not part of the government, and communism was not even mentioned in the manifesto that Franco issued to justify his rebellion. Communism only became a force in Spain because the government, opposed by Italy and Germany and ignored by Britain and France, had to appeal to the Soviet Union for arms.

Mussolini decided to intervene in Spain because he believed intervention would add to the glory of Italy and its Duce. This time he was wrong. Fighting Spanish republicans backed by Russian tanks was very different from fighting African tribesmen, and it was demoralizing to be facing fellow Italians in the International Brigades who kept the volunteers awake at night with loudspeakers urging them to show solidarity with the workers by deserting to the Spanish government's side. At the Battle of Guadalajara in March 1937, Mussolini's troops were blocked by republican units that included the Italians of the Garibaldi Battalion, and they were forced to retreat, losing a lot of men, arms and prestige in the process. Although it was a clear defeat for the fascists, the Duce managed to proclaim it a victory.[32]

Historians have long been divided between those who believe that Mussolini intended all along to build an empire and an alliance with Germany and those who see the Duce as more of a predatory opportunist than a dedicated expansionist and aggressor. The sheer erraticism of the man, his frequent doubts and changes of mind, make one wonder whether he could really have been as single-minded as the 'intentionists' believe. He had the eye of a chancer, looking for easy pickings such as Corfu and later Albania, which he invaded a week after the end of the Spanish Civil War. He admired the German Reich much more than the French Republic yet, when in 1934 Austrian nazis murdered his ally Chancellor Dollfuss in Vienna, he signed a treaty with France and talked about war against Germany. Mussolini was a show-off who thought in slogans which he seldom wholly believed in – he did not, for example, really think it better to live one day as a lion than 100 years as a sheep. And he was always talking about fighting wars even when he had no intention of waging one. His neutrality in 1939, his dithering in 1940, his failure to produce a half-decent army and his refusal to join the war until France was beaten – none of this suggests the character of a conqueror.

Yet it is easy to build up a case on the other side, and certainly there is space for a compromise. Even before the rise of the nazis, Mussolini had hoped for an alliance with a revived Germany and a joint war against France and Yugoslavia; he also believed that 'the axis of European history passes through Berlin'.[33] In 1932 he ordered Italian newspapers to support the nazis in elections that brought them to power, and in the same year he sacked his foreign minister for allegedly being too fond of the French and the British. Although Mussolini held ambivalent views about Hitler and liked to belittle him, he supported most of the Führer's actions in the years before the Second World War. He accepted the German army's occupation of the Rhineland, like Hitler he fought for Franco, and he eventually acquiesced in Germany's annexation of Austria in 1938 and its occupation of Czechoslovakia the following year. Renzo De Felice, the author of a seven-volume biography of the Duce, used to argue that fascism was very different from nazism, that Mussolini desired to be a mediator in Europe, and it was only Britain's championing of economic sanctions against Italy after its invasion of Ethiopia that drove Mussolini into the German camp. Yet this sounds too much like the plea of the apologist. Had he wished, Mussolini could have preserved peace and contained Hitler by aligning himself with Britain and France. He chose instead to join Germany, securing the support of a powerful ally to protect his position in Europe while he pursued his dream of empire in Africa.[34]

On a state visit to Germany in 1937 Mussolini was hugely impressed by the sight of armament factories and army parades staged in his honour. Soon afterwards he took Italy out of the League of Nations, made anti-Semitism a fascist policy and signed an anti-communist pact with Germany and Japan. In March 1938 he was perplexed (and privately furious) that Hitler grabbed Austria without warning him, and later in the year he made his sole appearance as a mediator, going to the Munich conference to persuade the Führer to opt for the peaceful cession of the Sudetenland rather than a military invasion of Czechoslovakia. Yet Mussolini felt uncomfortable in the role of peacemaker, as he soon demonstrated when he told the fascist Grand Council that Italy must acquire Nice, Corsica, Albania and Tunisia.

At Munich the Duce was deeply unimpressed by the British prime minister (Neville Chamberlain) and the French premier (Édouard Daladier), whose feeble performances in the face of Hitler's pugnacity reinforced his view that Britain and France were decadent and geriatric states that could easily be defeated by the young and virile nations of Germany and Italy. Much influenced by a meeting of the Oxford Union in 1933, when idealistic undergraduates had voted against fighting 'for king and country', Mussolini had decided that the British were effete and unhealthy (and too fond of umbrellas), that their empire was in terminal decline, and that their country should be destroyed like Carthage. He also convinced himself that Italy could capture Egypt without difficulty because the British were unable to fight in the heat; perhaps he was unaware that they had won a few summer battles over the years in India. Such views were strengthened by reports from his ambassador to London, Dino Grandi, who watched British soldiers on parade and dismissed them as 'marionettes of wood' who would be too cowardly to defend their country.[35]

In March 1939 Germany enacted another aggression without warning Italy, this time overturning Mussolini's 'success' at Munich by seizing Prague and setting up a German 'protectorate' in Bohemia and Moravia. Although the Duce felt humiliated by this episode, he decided to stand by 'the Axis' and to demonstrate parity with Germany by conquering something for himself. After briefly considering Croatia as a target, he opted for Albania, a strange decision considering that the little country was already largely under Italian control. In May Germany and Italy formalized the Axis with the 'Pact of Steel', a name that, while professing equivalence between the two signatories, drew attention to the disparity in industrial might: Germany produced ten times as much steel as Italy. Once again the Germans were dishonest with their ally. They told Mussolini that no European war would take place for over three years, which would give him time to strengthen his armed forces and to hold his big exhibition, the EUR in Rome. They also pretended they had no intention of attacking Poland, although Hitler had already selected September 1939 as the month for his invasion and on the day after the pact's signature he informed his generals of his plans. When Mussolini finally learned that the Germans were about to strike, he panicked and sent Ciano, his foreign minister, to entreat them to desist. Although keen to fight and make territorial gains – what he called 'our share of the plunder' – he was beginning to have doubts about Italy's armed forces and how they might perform in battle.

Among his other posts, the Duce was minister for the army, the navy and the air force, and he talked so much about the invincibility of each service that Italians were led to believe they were as good as any in Europe. He boasted that he could raise an army of 8 million men – a figure he later raised to 12 million – yet he was unable to produce rifles for more than a sixth of that number; he vaunted Italy's technological skills, though some of his best artillery had been captured from the Austrians in the Great War; and he claimed to possess enormous tanks, though the Italian model was little more than an armoured car, and its vision was so limited that it had to be guided by infantry walking ahead, often with fatal results for the guides. No wonder Farinacci told Mussolini he was the commander of 'a toy army' or that, after inspecting it, the German war minister in 1937 had concluded that his country would stand a better chance in the coming war if Italy was on the other side.[36]

A great deal of money was spent on speedy new battleships, but these were ineffective in action, and their guns apparently failed to hit a single enemy ship at any time during the war; far more dangerous were the courageous Italian frogmen and the manned 'slow speed torpedoes' (known as *maiali* – pigs) entering the harbours of Gibraltar and Alexandria and inflicting considerable damage on British ships. More sensible than building battleships would have been the construction of aircraft carriers, which would have been useful for attacking Malta, a strategic goal that Mussolini ignored until it was too late; they might also have protected the rest of the fleet from devastating raids by the RAF. The greatest deficiencies, however, were in the air force, which the Duce had taken charge of in 1933, when he sensed that Balbo was doing too well in the job – a replacement that proved disastrous for Italy. Mussolini claimed to have over 8,500 aeroplanes, so many that they could 'blot out the sun' and so effective they could reach London or destroy Britain's Mediterranean fleet in a single day. Yet in fact he had fewer than a tenth of that number, and he failed during the war to build a great many more. At the height of the conflict Italy was manufacturing as many aeroplanes a year as the United States was producing in a week. One of the most revealing statistics about the inefficiency of fascism is that Italy managed to produce more aeroplanes in the First World War than it did in the Second.[37]

While Mussolini vacillated during the August of 1939, news of the Ribbentrop–Molotov pact made some fascist leaders question the wisdom of an alliance with Germany; communism was after all meant to be their chief enemy. At a meeting of the Grand Council earlier in the year, Balbo had criticized the policy of 'licking Hitler's boots' and later he suggested that Italy should fight on the side of Britain and France. This suggestion had no appeal to Mussolini. Although in September he declared Italy's neutrality or 'non-belligerence', his sympathies had been long with the nazis, and he wanted to fight with them when he was ready. Meanwhile he played for time by demanding from the Germans more millions of tons of oil, steel and coal than they could possibly supply and transport. All the same, he knew that a position of neutrality was rather ridiculous for a man who had been threatening wars for seventeen years and who was still telling Italians that warfare was 'the normal condition of peoples and the logical aim of any dictatorship'.[38] At the beginning of 1940 he warned his government that Italy could not remain permanently neutral and ordered the armed forces to be prepared for war against anyone, even Germany. Soon afterwards he issued bizarre instructions to the navy, which in the coming war was to go on the offensive everywhere, to the air force, which was to remain passive, and to the army, which was to stay on the defensive in all places except east Africa, where it would attack the British colonies. Even more bizarrely, he continued to erect costly fortifications along the Alpine frontier with Austria, a policy he did not abandon during the war and which understandably annoyed the Germans, who had already demonstrated in the case of the Maginot Line that such defensive schemes were outmoded and useless.

The nazis' rapid conquests of Denmark and Norway in April 1940 convinced some waverers that Germany would win the war. Yet Mussolini continued to hesitate until France was close to collapse in June. Believing that Italy would somehow gain prestige as well as territory by defeating an already defeated enemy, he then announced a 'lightning war' against France and Britain to a crowd in Rome which, as leading fascists admitted, showed little enthusiasm for the enterprise. Many Italians were undoubtedly embarrassed about joining a war after Paris had fallen and the British army had scuttled back across the Channel. Yet a large majority did not want to fight anyway: even Victor Emanuel later claimed he was against the war although, as in May 1915 and October 1922, he did not try very hard to make the right decision.

On 17 June the French asked Germany for an armistice, and three days later Mussolini ordered an attack on them. An Italian army was dispatched to the Alps, where it suffered many casualties and failed to defeat a far smaller French force that suffered hardly any. Once France was out of the war, the Duce made territorial demands in Europe, Africa and the Middle East, but the Germans told him to curb his appetite until Britain had also been defeated. In the meantime they suggested he used his huge army in Libya to attack the British in Egypt and capture the Suez Canal. Yet Mussolini was now more interested in conquest close to home and, instead of attacking an enemy power in Africa, he wanted to invade a neutral country in Europe, Greece. In October 1940 a large Italian army duly assembled in Albania and invaded Greece, where it was stopped by numerically inferior opponents and forced to retreat. By then the Duce had at last ordered an attack on Egypt, but the results were even more disastrous. Graziani's army of over 250,000 men was defeated in a series of engagements by 36,000 British troops, and 135,000 prisoners were taken. The Italians fared no better at sea: after defeats by the British at Taranto in November 1940 and at Cape Matapan the following spring, the navy remained in harbour and played little further part in the war.

Hitler had made an offer of German tanks for Italy's Egyptian campaign, which Mussolini had rejected because he wanted his troops to win glory on their own. As a result, the Führer had to send an army under Field Marshal Rommel to defeat the British in north Africa and regain the initiative. The Italians also had to be rescued in Greece, which the Germans quickly overran in an operation that delayed their invasion of Russia and thus contributed to their later defeats on the Eastern Front. This series of military failures reduced Italy to a very subordinate role in the Axis. It had already lost Addis Ababa and Italian Somaliland, and the main task of its armies was now to garrison the Balkans while the Germans and later the Japanese did most of the fighting. The behaviour of their forces in south-eastern Europe rivalled the savagery of their allies and buried the myth of 'the good soldier Gino'. After provoking guerrilla warfare from partisan groups in Yugoslavia, Italian troops carried out extensive reprisals against civilians.

In the province of Ljubljana alone, a thousand hostages were shot, 8,000 other Slovenes were killed, and 35,000 people were deported to concentration camps.[39]

In July 1943 Anglo-American forces invaded Sicily, landed a few weeks later on the Italian mainland and spent the next twenty months slogging their way north through the Apennines against a German defence brilliantly conducted without air support. Soon after the landings in Sicily, the Grand Council in the presence of Mussolini approved a motion to return military command to Victor Emanuel, a move that led to the dismissal of the Duce and his eventual imprisonment at a skiing resort in the Apennines. He was replaced as prime minister by the vain and elderly Marshal Badoglio, a disastrous choice.* Together with the king, this former chief of staff dithered for six weeks, remaining in the Axis, until the imminence of the Allied landings at Salerno forced them to accept Anglo-American terms for an armistice. They continued to dither even after that, failing to do anything to prevent German reinforcements from rushing south to occupy the peninsula as far down as Naples. Although they had promised to help the Anglo-American forces, the two changed their minds and even cancelled an Allied attack on Rome, which Badoglio himself had requested, on the very day it was planned to take place. Fearful for their personal safety, premier and sovereign fled across the peninsula to Pescara and, accompanied by hundreds of courtiers and generals, took ship to Brindisi, far from the threat of the Germans. It was a very thorough abdication of responsibility. Badoglio did not even inform his fellow ministers he was leaving and gave no orders to his troops except to tell them not to attack the Germans. Left on their

---

*Like those earlier chiefs of staff, Lamarmora and Cadorna, Badoglio enjoyed a career of constant promotion despite evidence of consistent incapacity. After the disaster of Caporetto he had been appointed deputy chief of staff although he was widely regarded as having been more responsible for the defeat than anyone except Cadorna: after a commission of inquiry wrote its report on the battle, thirteen pages on his contribution had to be deleted from the published version for him to retain some credibility in his new post. As Governor of Tripolitania and Cyrenaica, he had even outdone Graziani in the butchery of his repression and, although he had captured Addis Ababa, his 'triumph' had been no more difficult or heroic than General Kitchener's massacre of Sudanese at Omdurman in 1898. He was chief of staff during the invasion of Greece but resigned half way through the campaign.

own in increasingly chaotic circumstances, Italian forces offered little resistance to the Germans in Italy or the Balkans, and nearly a million of them were quickly captured; on the island of Cephalonia, where Italians did resist, 6,000 soldiers and prisoners of war were murdered by the nazis. In mid-October, from the safety of Apulia, Victor Emanuel declared war on Germany, a move that gained Italy the status of 'co-belligerent', eased the country's post-war relations with the victors and enabled hundreds of men to avoid trials for war crimes.

The collapse of the state made it easier for the Germans to rescue Mussolini from his mountain prison and install him as their puppet ruler of the Republic of Salò, a new fascist state based on Lake Garda in the nazi-held north. Many young men volunteered to fight for this new entity, which intellectuals such as Gentile, Papini and Marinetti were also prepared to support. Mussolini himself returned to the beliefs of his youth, insisting once more that fascism was a revolutionary ideology and that industry should be nationalized. Yet he was too demoralized and too powerless to do much except whine about the defects of his countrymen. The chief significance of Salò was that it encouraged the growth of the Resistance, the Italian partisans, and within a short time led to a civil war in the north marked by terrible atrocities, most of them committed by the republic's 'black brigades'.

Even in his impotence Mussolini deluded himself with the thought that he was a great man, comparable to Napoleon, and that he had been brought down by the character of the Italians. Even Michelangelo, he had earlier pointed out, had 'needed marble to make his statues. If he had had nothing else except clay, he would simply have been a potter.' At Salò Mussolini grumbled that he had tried to turn a sheep into a lion and had failed; the beast was still 'a bleating sheep'.[40] Yet he himself did not die like the lion he had pretended to be: in April 1945 he ran away to the north, disguised as a German, with wads of cash in his pockets. Captured by communist partisans on the western shore of Lake Como, his final moment may have been slightly more impressive. According to one report, he opened the collar of his coat and told his executioner to aim for the heart.

The flight of Badoglio and Victor Emanuel marks one of the lowest points in the history of united Italy. The nation dissolved: all real power was now in the hands of the Germans, the British and the Americans. Italy might be built anew, but it could never be the same Italy.

Both Italians and foreigners have liked to think of fascism as an aberration, as an unlucky and almost accidental episode in the history of a constitutional country. Sforza regarded 'the vain show of the fascist years' as 'only a brief interlude of unreality',[41] while Croce described the dictatorship as a 'parenthesis' in his nation's story, implying that it was not closely connected with what happened before or after. The genuine connection, so it was claimed, was between the regimes that preceded and succeeded Mussolini. The young liberal Piero Gobetti may have got closer to the truth when he observed in the 1920s that fascism was part of Italy's 'autobiography', a logical consequence of unification's failure to be a moral revolution supported by the mass of the people. That fascism was 'the child of the Risorgimento' was also Gentile's verdict, a view much derided in the years to come but supported intrinsically at the time by the fact that so many liberal fathers had fascist sons without having family ruptures.

Fascists liked to present themselves as a continuation of the Risorgimento but at the same time as a breach with its liberal heirs. The exercise was never very convincing because, apart from the abolition of parliamentary elections, the fascist 'revolution' changed little of substance, certainly in comparison with the French Revolution of 1789 or the Spanish Revolution of 1931. It retained the monarchy, protected private property, exalted the family and established good relations with the Church. Abroad its policies were aggressive and avaricious but not so very different from those of some preceding governments. Both Crispi and the earlier Victor Emanuel had wanted war in Europe and colonies outside, and they and many others had spoken in tones almost as bellicose as those of Mussolini.

The real break in Italy's twentieth-century history came not in 1922 but at the end of the Second World War. The essence of Risorgimento thinking, which had been liberal, nationalist and anti-clerical, evaporated after 1945 and was replaced by the anti-nationalist ideologies of communism and christian democracy. At the same time Italy abandoned its pretensions to become a Great Power and concentrated, with far more success, on achieving prosperity for its citizens.

12

Cold War Italy

CHRISTIAN DEMOCRATS

In Verona's Piazza Brà, beside the great Roman amphitheatre, a small patch of ground contains four commemorative images of united Italy. Two of them are by now familiar and obligatory: a statue of Victor Emanuel II on a horse waving his sword, and a marble tablet on a house recording the window from which Garibaldi had sworn 'Rome or Death!' The third, a rarer species, is a bronze sculpture of a woman representing Italy, surrounded by a marble memorial listing the names of young Veronesi who were sent to kill or be killed in Africa: 'To her sons who died heroically in Libya'. Close to the equestrian monarch is another unusual statue, that of a young fighter of the Resistance, handsome and fearless, a rifle slung over his shoulder and an inscription with the words, 'To those who died for Liberty'. This fourth memorial is the significant one for modern Italy because it represents atonement for fascism, it symbolizes the rebirth of the nation in 1943, it tries to assure those who observe it that the country was in essence anti-fascist. Yet like the other three, it is representing something that is at least partly a myth.

After the armistice in 1943 Italians joined the Resistance for a variety of motives. Some were anti-fascists who wanted to defeat fascism, some were patriots who wanted to expel invaders, and more were communists who aimed for both of these things and a political revolution as well. Many, however, simply drifted into it because they were on the run from German and fascist forces. Although they were unskilled in open combat, the partisans proved to be effective in guerrilla warfare: they blew up bridges and killed fascist officials, they helped liberate the cities of the north from the German occupation, they punctured the credibility of Salò and they signalled the redemption of Italy. For some twenty months they fought courageously, and about 40,000 of them were killed. Yet there were never very many of them, perhaps 9,000 at the end of 1943, some 80,000 at the end of 1944, and about 100,000 by March 1945, when victory was certain.[1] Comparable numbers had volunteered to fight for the Republic of Salò even though most of them must have known that defeat was inevitable. The Resistance was thus not the nation in arms: it was about one-third of 1 per cent of it in arms, roughly the same proportion that had volunteered to fight the Austrians in 1848. Nor were its achievements of the magnitude claimed on its memorials, which sometimes leave the impression that the partisans 'vanquished the nazi-fascist tyranny' by themselves. At the entrance of the town hall of Bologna photographs are still displayed of partisans liberating the city without giving a hint that Allied forces had helped them to do so.

Official Italy has liked to claim that, even if the Resistance was not numerically large, it was supported by the bulk of the population. This again is not true. For reasons of self-preservation many Italians preferred to remain neutral in the fratricidal war between the partisans and their fellow countrymen who fought for Salò. Many feared the partisans because they stole food and money, shot suspected collaborators and left villages vulnerable to reprisals from German and fascist forces.[2] More than 10,000 civilians were executed in revenge for attacks on nazis and fascists. In March 1944 communist partisans detonated a bomb in Rome's Via Rasella and killed thirty-two policemen who had been recruited by the nazis in the province of Bolzano (which Germany had seized after the armistice) and a couple of civilians as well. Hitler was so enraged by the event that he demanded an instant reprisal, and a decision was made to kill ten Italians for each dead policeman, which meant at first 320 executions, then 330 when one of the wounded died, and finally 335 after a counting error. They were murdered in the Ardeatine Caves outside Rome in retaliation for a terrorist attack that had no impact on the course of the war but caused 370 deaths as well as misery for the dead men's families. Some Italians took the view that the communist perpetrators should have given themselves up for execution and thus spared the lives of at least a few innocent people.

It used to be joked in Italy and outside that on 25 July 1943 – the day Mussolini was arrested by the king – the Italian people had gone to bed as fascists and woken up as anti-fascists. While this was of course an over-simplification, there was some truth in the jibe. After the Second World War Italians consistently underestimated the numbers of them who had been fascists just as they exaggerated the strength and importance of those who had been anti-fascists. For them the Resistance became a sacred experience which could not be profaned because it represented reparation for fascism and credibility for the future. It was the true successor to the Risorgimento. In the words of Carla Capponi, a partisan and a future communist member of parliament, 'In the Resistance each of us found our mother country. We felt [our] country was the country of the Risorgimento; of democracy and liberty.'[3] The moral sense of the Resistance was succinctly expressed in a poem by Piero Calamandrei, which was later reproduced in an inscription on the town hall of Cuneo: 'This pact of free men who joined voluntarily out of dignity, not out of hatred, determined to redeem the shame and terror of the world'.

In September 1943 the Italian government had been forced to accept an armistice that was in effect a surrender. Yet the king's later declaration of war on Germany, and the 'co-belligerency' thus acquired, convinced many Italians that they were Hitler's victims rather than his allies and that they were in fact 'co-victors' in 1945. This feeling was brazenly reflected in Italy's attitude to Austria after the war. There were plenty of foreigners, including nearly 200 British MPs, who believed that the Alto Adige, the former South Tyrol, should be given to the newly independent state of Austria. Italy was adamant that it should not, retorting that the scheme was iniquitous because Austria had fought with the nazis from beginning to end and had not even produced a resistance movement. The Italian position thus implied that there was a wide moral gap between a nation that had been invaded and annexed – and thus forced to fight for the Reich – and one that had voluntarily joined Hitler even if, as a result of military defeat, it had only stayed the course for three and a quarter years.

Nearly two years of war on Italian soil had left the country a battered and unhappy place, much of it in ruins after the Allied bombing campaigns. Food shortages were everywhere, and so was the black market, flourishing in the trade of items such as salt and tobacco. The hunger and poverty in Naples shocked outsiders who went there. Little girls gathered cigarette butts and sold them on trays in the street; over 40,000 women worked as prostitutes; even ladies of elegance went to the San Carlo in coats made from stolen army blankets. Much of the population survived on bowls of *maccheroni* which were distributed both by nuns and by volunteers of the Salvation Army.

Retribution may not have been so extensive in Italy as it was in France because the fascist regime had not excited as much revulsion among Italians as the Vichy collaboration with Germany had among the French. All the same, some 12–15,000 fascists were pursued and killed at the time of liberation, and thousands more perished over the next couple of years. Bombs were thrown by extremists on the Left and the Right, and communists murdered the editor of the Milanese newspaper that had revealed the name of the partisan who shot Mussolini.* Some fascist leaders, such as Starace, Farinacci and Gentile, were captured and shot, but other senior figures of the regime, including Badoglio and Grandi, died peacefully as prosperous octogenarians. Graziani, who had been defence minister for Salò, was tried and imprisoned but released after a few months, after which he became honorary president of the Movimento Sociale Italiano (MSI), the neofascist party sometimes known by its members as *Mussolini sempre immortale*.

There could be no real purge of the administration without destroying it altogether: the civil service would have had no civil servants because all of them had been obliged to join the Fascist Party, and the universities would have had no professors because all these had sworn an oath of allegiance to the regime. In 1946 the government thus issued a general amnesty for former fascists and at the same time permitted the MSI to operate, a move convenient for the other parties,

---

*Not that the Communist Party was ashamed of the execution or of the executioner, Walter Audisio, who became one of its parliamentary deputies. In 1947 its leader, Palmiro Togliatti, said that the Duce's execution had been 'one of the greatest, perhaps the greatest contribution that the movement of national liberation made to the nation'.[4]

which could now demonstrate their anti-fascism by scorning it. So lenient a policy left former fascist officials in control of local administration as well as the civil service: as late as 1960 all the police chiefs, all their deputies and all but two of the provincial prefects had been functionaries under Mussolini.[5] The easiest form of *epurazione* (purging) was the time-honoured one of changing street-names, erasing those associated with the regime and replacing them with victims of fascism, so that almost all towns soon acquired a Via or a Piazza Matteotti and many had a Via Amendola as well. New boulevards often received more sonorous names. In Modena the Viale Martiri della Libertà comes from the Viale delle Rimembranze and passes into the Viale dei Caduti in Guerra.

One indisputable Italian loser in the world war was the monarchy. In June 1944, as the Allied armies liberated Rome, Victor Emanuel surrendered his powers to his son Umberto, appointing him lieutenant-general of the kingdom. Had he abdicated and moved abroad, he might have given the crown some time to recover the popularity which his own behaviour had lost. Yet he insisted on remaining king and living near Naples, refusing to abdicate until a month before a referendum on the monarchy's future was held in June 1946. Umberto thus had little chance to show himself as the decent, responsible, if rather limited prince that he was. In the ballot he received 10,700,000 votes, mainly in Naples and the south, where people seemed to be voting more for the monarchical idea than for the northern dynasty that had evicted their own kings. Yet 12,700,000 other citizens chose to vote for the abolition of the monarchy and the establishment of a republic. Although urged by some to stand firm and resist, Umberto decided his throne was not worth the bloodshed such a stance would have entailed; he therefore accepted the verdict and went into exile in Lisbon, a victim of the many mistakes made by his father. No male heirs of the Savoia were permitted to return to Italy until 2002, when they were allowed to do so on condition they renounced their claims to the throne. Soon after they came back, the family's reputation hit a new low when Umberto's violent and disreputable son, another Victor Emanuel, was arrested and charged with corruption and the recruitment of prostitutes for clients of a casino on Lake Lugano.

Until the summer of 1944 Marshal Badoglio had deluded himself into thinking he had a future as the prime minister of an anti-fascist Italy. But his past obviously made him objectionable to the new National Liberation Committee, the umbrella organization of the Resistance, which consisted of anti-fascist groups ranging in ideology from liberalism to communism. He was duly replaced by Ivanoe Bonomi, a mild and elderly figure of the moderate Left, an appointment that demonstrated a certain agreeable symmetry and an affirmation of democratic revival: the second last prime minister before Mussolini now became the second one after him. Bonomi lasted until the end of the war, when he was succeeded by Ferruccio Parri, a long-standing anti-fascist and a partisan leader from the Party of Action, the second largest group in the Resistance. Yet the new premier's talents in guerrilla warfare were not matched by skills in politics, and after a few months he was supplanted by a christian democrat from the Trentino, Alcide De Gasperi, one of the great figures of Italian political history. From December 1945 De Gasperi led a coalition government that included the communist leader Palmiro Togliatti as minister of justice.

Elections for a constituent assembly were held on the day of the referendum on the monarchy for the explicit purpose of producing a new constitution. The principal victors were the Democrazia Cristiana (the christian democratic descendants of the pre-fascist Popular Party), which obtained 207 deputies of a total of 556, and the socialist and communist parties, which both gained more than 100 seats. In an augury for the future of republican Italy, the chief losers were the secular parties of the Centre and the Centre-Left. The Party of Action was decimated even though it had been prominent in the Resistance and some of its leaders had been opponents of Mussolini since the 1920s. So were the liberals, the heirs of the Risorgimento now being represented by just forty-one deputies. In 1949 liberalism received a consolation prize when the great economist, Luigi Einaudi, was elected first president of the republic, but it was already clear that it had no future as an independent force. As Luigi Barzini had warned Umberto shortly before the referendum, Italy was no longer in the hands of the people who had brought the Savoia to Rome. It was 'in the hands of those who had nothing to do with the Risorgimento', of the women who had not been allowed to vote, of the Catholics who had been told not to vote and of the poor who had been too poor to be enfranchised before 1913.[6]

The Constituent Assembly did its duty, its various parties being cooperative, deliberating with speed and producing a constitution that, if sometimes anodyne and uninspiring, was clearly democratic and anti-fascist. The rights and duties of citizens were defined, as were their civil and political liberties, and mention was made of the state's obligation to address social and economic inequalities. As of old, the legislature would consist of two chambers, with the lower house again predominant, but the senate would now be almost entirely elected. Although both De Gasperi and Einaudi wanted a 'first-past-the-post' voting system, the assembly opted – as a precaution against any party gaining too much power – for proportional representation in multi-member constituencies. The head of state would be a president, who would enjoy less power than Victor Emanuel but more than a British monarch, and the head of government would be as usual the prime minister, the 'president of the council of ministers' (the cabinet). A glance at the roles of the various branches of government, including the judiciary, reveals why and how they have been able to restrain the activities of each other. The constitution may have been a charter for liberty but it also seemed a guarantor of weak government. The founding fathers of the Italian republic were apparently so anxious to prevent anyone from governing with too much power again that they created a constitution that made it difficult to govern at all. Endemic political instability was a result.

At the end of 1946 Pope Pius XII was urging De Gasperi to remove 'godless' communists and socialists from his government, but the prime minister resisted the pressure and waited until the following May before deciding to break up the coalition. At the spring elections of 1948 the christian democrats won an emphatic victory, gaining nearly half the vote and over half the seats, while the godless parties between them obtained less than a third of the votes cast. The cause of the Left was not helped by either a recent communist takeover in Prague or a split in the socialists, which prompted Giuseppe Saragat, a future president of the country, to lead the moderates into a new social democratic party. The christian democrats also possessed certain advantages of their own, even if few of their members could boast of having fought in the Resistance.* The party itself was a coalition ranging from the Right to the Centre-Left, but all factions were committed to representative government, and their belief in political liberty was symbolized by the word 'LIBERTAS' emblazoned on the party's icon, a crusader shield. As the descendant of the Popular Party, which had won 100 seats in the 1919 elections, the christian democrats were assured of a mass following, and their conservative views on the family and the Church greatly appealed to newly enfranchised women voters.

One factor important to their success was the backing of the United States, which was eager to retain military bases in a democratic Italy as part of its strategy to contain the influence of the Soviet Union in Europe; as a result, large amounts of Marshall Aid were offered to Italy, and millions of dollars were paid annually to the anti-communist parties, principally to the christian democrats. Even more significant was the support of the pope and the Catholic Church. Although the Vatican had cooperated with the fascists, it had not much liked them, and it was delighted to have a christian democrat as prime minister for the first time. Papal encouragement was especially valuable in an era when most Italians were still practising Catholics. It gave the party not only the backing of hundreds of bishops and thousands of priests but the auxiliary assistance of the Catholic press and publishing houses, of the religious bodies that ran schools, hospitals and charities, and of a trade union, an association of small farmers and the nearly 3 million members of Catholic Action.

Alcide De Gasperi was an unusual politician, a Trentino whose political career had begun in 1911 when he had been elected a deputy for the parliament in Vienna. After his province had been transferred to Italy, he became a deputy for the Popular Party in the parliament in Rome, but his hostility to fascism led to his arrest and a period of imprisonment that lasted until the pope, Pius XI, secured his release; in 1929 the pontiff made him a librarian in the Vatican, where he

---

*One province in which Catholics were prominent in the Resistance was Lucca, which lacked the anti-clerical traditions of the rest of Tuscany. Fifty-seven Lucchese priests were executed by the nazis.[7]

remained until 1943. Towards the end of the Second World War De Gasperi re-entered politics, joining the Resistance and reorganizing the *popolari*, who had been banned by Mussolini, as the Democrazia Cristiana (DC). A man of wisdom, honesty and sound judgement, this austere northerner eschewed party matters to concentrate on broader concerns, chiefly the need to return Italy to a state of international respectability, to bring it into the western fold, and to give it a novel role, no longer as a colonial power or a destabilizer of Europe but as a responsible participant in international affairs. Foreign policy would now be relatively straightforward, based on attachment to western Europe and, at least for a time, guidance by the United States. In 1949 Italy joined NATO and three years later the European Defence Community.

Carlo Sforza, a former and future foreign minister, declared in a book published in New York during the war that 'the integrity of our national life and the future of our country hang on the coming of that free and federated Europe of which Mazzini was the first prophet'.[8] In his view nationalism was out of date and ready to be jettisoned in favour of international cooperation. Einaudi and De Gasperi agreed, and the three of them helped steer Italy along an unfamiliar road. As a borderer from territory that had changed hands many times in its history, De Gasperi hoped and believed that European integration would prevent future wars as well as help solve some of Italy's stoniest economic problems. In 1952, together with France, Germany and the Benelux countries, he took his nation into the European Coal and Steel Community which five years later became the European Economic Community. After nearly a century of costly endeavour trying to match the power of France and Germany, Italy was now on peaceful and equal terms with them as a founder member of the future European Union. The Treaty of Rome, signed in 1957, led to a huge surge in exports over the following decade and gave under-employed southerners the chance to earn a living in the factories of northern Europe.

At the end of the war the great division in Italy had been one between fascists and anti-fascists, yet within a couple of years it had become one between communists and anti-communists. De Gasperi's break with the Left, inevitable though it was, polarized the country.

For Italians the Cold War between the West and the Soviet bloc thus became an internal reality as well as a global rivalry. In Germany communism and christian democracy were governing in two separate states, but in Italy they were competing in the same arena. As the ideology of each contestant was essentially international and even universal, Italian nationalism soon became, as Sforza had hoped, outmoded and limited chiefly to supporters of the neo-fascist MSI. For a century Italian rulers had tried to bully their subjects into becoming nationalists, most recently by dragging them into a war in which they had ended up fighting on both sides. Now most of the people were fed up with nationalism and all its trimmings; for years after the war designers did not even dare put the national flag on postage stamps. Not much of the Risorgimento – and even less of its rhetoric – was left after 1946. Liberal anti-clericalism had gone the same way as nationalism, the Piedmontese monarchy had also disappeared, and the parties descended from Cavour (the liberals) and Mazzini (the republicans) were pitifully reduced. The country's chief political rivals were now parties formed after the First World War.

After breaking with the Left, De Gasperi governed for another six years in a coalition of christian democrats and the small parties of the Centre. He knew it would be fatal to take his party to the Right or to allow it to be too closely identified with the Church; thus he rejected heavy-handed pressure from the Vatican to form an alliance with the neo-fascists in Rome's local elections in 1952. The following year, at the age of seventy-two, he resigned after a parliamentary vote and, a year further on, he died from a heart attack. Italy is not full of statues of De Gasperi or of streets named after him, but there is a memorable sculpture in his native Trento of the statesman declaiming between two vast triangles of bronze that remind one of Lorenzetti's frescoes of the well-governed and badly governed cities in the town hall of Siena. The evil panel portrays the recent past with a dive bomber and a vampire bat flying above a scene of devastation, of destroyed buildings and a collapsed church tower, a wasteland peopled only by a dead soldier and a dying woman with her baby. The good panel indicates the present and the future, a land of happiness and prosperity, of churches, factories, ships and aeroplanes; in the foreground a mother is shown suckling her baby and being embraced by her son, while a man sits on a tractor, surrounded by his cattle and a horse that nuzzles his shoulder. Italy's post-war revival was not quite like this, but the economic side of it was indisputably impressive.

De Gasperi was succeeded by lesser men, who continued to rule in coalitions and to try to limit the Vatican's interference in politics. Their governments were seldom very energetic. According to Piero Ottone, a distinguished journalist, ministers rolled up at their offices in the late morning, made a few telephone calls, signed a couple of documents and then 'dedicated their time to party matters, which for them were the most important. Spanish hours prevailed for the rest of the day, including the siesta.'9 Yet increased energy levels would not by themselves have remedied the inherent instability of government. In the forty years after De Gasperi, twenty-seven prime ministers were sworn in, all but two of them christian democrats. There was an innate weakness in the system, as there was in the French Fourth Republic, but Italy had no figure like de Gaulle either willing or able to challenge it. One problem was the weakness of the executive. Another was the electoral system itself. Proportional representation and the party list meant that candidates did not need to be liked or even known to be successful in their multi-member constituencies. They needed to be popular only with party leaders in Rome and party secretaries in the regions for them to gain a place high enough on the list to secure election. Ostensible loyalty to his party was thus essential for a deputy's chances of re-election, but it was not necessary to demonstrate it at critical moments in parliament because the secret ballot allowed him to vote against party policy without anyone finding out; the budget bill was defeated seventeen times in 1988 because dissidents in the government coalition furtively voted against it.

For nearly half a century after 1945, the christian democrats were always in power and never in any real danger of being overthrown by a disunited Left. Without a single spell in opposition, they resembled a regime in which all the important decisions on policy and government are made through deals inside the party. The DC was divided into factions, known as *correnti*, usually grouped around such canny operators as the dynamic Tuscan Amintore Fanfani, and the artful Roman Giulio Andreotti, who was prime minister seven times, a cabinet minister for twenty-one years and a deputy continuously from

1946 to 1991, when he was appointed a life senator. Governments used to fall about once a year but never as a result of a vote of no confidence moved by the opposition in parliament. They fell because either a faction within the DC or a small party in the coalition (such as the liberals) withdrew its support, an action that persuaded the prime minister to resign without a parliamentary vote. This was followed by frantic negotiations among the same people and the same factions until they agreed on the next prime minister, who often turned out to be the old one leading a largely unchanged team of ministers. Such a system ensured that the chief skill a politician needed was not the statesmanship of De Gasperi but the subtlety of manoeuvre as exemplified by Andreotti.

As the century progressed, the christian democrats lost many of their natural supporters: there were far fewer small farmers and practising Catholics in 1980 than there had been in 1948. There were also fewer women who divided their day between their church and their kitchen and were prepared to follow the instructions of their priests. Yet the christian democrats remained the largest party because people were frightened of the alternative, the Communist Party, which by the mid-1970s was gaining three and a half times as many votes as the socialists. Politics were thus effectively paralysed. Italians turned out at elections in impressive numbers but they knew they were not voting for a change of government; at best they hoped their party might increase its vote by a couple of percentage points. In the early years of the republic attempts had been made to end the paralysis by building a 'Third Force' of the secular Centre, a project supported by the weekly *Il Mondo* and by many of the country's leading intellectuals. Yet loyalties to the Catholic and communist parties had been cemented so early that in the elections of 1953 the parties of a potential Third Force – the liberals, the republicans and the social democrats – between them received less than 10 per cent of the vote. *Il Mondo* closed down in 1966, its final issue leaving an unhappy last message: 'What reigns in Italy above all else is the deep-rooted and penetrating presence of a soft and priestly secret government that conquers friends and foes alike and tends to enervate all initiative and all resistance.'[10]

COMMUNISTS

Communism attracted more adherents in Italy than in any other country in the West. By the end of 1944, just a year after it had emerged into the open, the Partito Comunista Italiano (PCI) had half a million members, many of them living in the then German-occupied areas of the north. Thousands of young fascists mutated quickly into young communists, relishing their opposition to a defeated regime while appreciating the familiarities of discipline and authoritarianism offered by this alternative 'system of truth'. In her novel *La storia* Elsa Morante captured this spirit in the character Nino, who becomes in turn a fascist, a partisan and a black marketeer although, whatever he is pretending to be, his behaviour is always an imitation of Mussolini.

Partisans and other party militants hoped the end of the war would leave them in a position to seize power and carry out a revolution – as their comrades in Yugoslavia were doing just across the border. They were thus dismayed by the cautiousness of their leadership. Palmiro Togliatti, a stalinist and former functionary of the Comintern, was a realist who guessed that the British and Americans would not allow a country to go communist just after they had taken the trouble to liberate it. Italy was not like eastern Europe; it was more like Greece, where communist guerrillas were in the process of being defeated by royalist forces that had British and later American help. Togliatti was convinced that, in order to survive, communist parties in western Europe had to adopt the Popular Front strategy of alliances with the democratic Left that the Comintern had promoted in the mid-1930s. What he called 'the Italian road to socialism' would be one that led first to national unity and only later, when the time was right, to socialism. In his new identity as conciliator he accepted the monarchy until its demise and also the place of the Church in national life. He got very little in return except for a short spell as a minister before De Gasperi expelled him and his party from the government in 1947.

The Italian road to socialism might be leading to an unhappy destination – that of permanent opposition – but at the time it proved attractive to millions of voters who flocked to communist festivals and enjoyed the amenities of the *case del popolo*, the 'people's clubs'. The Communist Party was especially strong in areas of the former Papal States, in which misgovernment had fostered a strong tradition of anti-clericalism. By 1976 it had nearly half a million members in a single region, Emilia-Romagna, and in two of the most prosperous provinces in the country, Bologna and Modena, nearly half the votes in local elections regularly went to the communists. Although excluded from national power in Rome, the party dominated the 'Red Belt' (Tuscany, Umbria and Emilia-Romagna), controlling both municipalities and regional governments. The towers of San Gimignano overlooked one of the few towns in the world that voluntarily gave nearly two-thirds of its votes to a communist party. Visitors to Bologna were impressed by the communists' administration of the city, by the hospitals and public transport, and by the absence of that drabness and bureaucracy associated with Eastern Europe. In Emilia and Tuscany it was easy to get the impression that Italian communists were different from other communists, that they were harmless social democrats who enjoyed their pasta and salami and ran their cities with admirable efficiency.

Yet they were not social democrats: if they had been, they could have joined the socialist or social democratic parties. The PCI revered Stalin and remained unctuously attached to the Soviet Union for many years. On the death of the Russian dictator in 1953, its newspaper hailed 'the man who [had] done most for the liberation of the human race'. Party intellectuals, who must have known the truth, were especially servile in their praise for the achievements of the Soviet Union: one of them, Mario Alicata, a former fascist, went to Russia and described it in 1952 as 'the first country in the history of the world in which all men are finally free'.[11] In 1956 the Italian communists supported the Russian invasion of Hungary and refused to break publicly with the Soviet Union even when later they criticized its policies in Czechoslovakia, Poland and Afghanistan. The leaders felt the need to balance criticism with 'fraternal' messages of support for the principles of the Bolshevik Revolution; they also seem to have feared that a real break would have led to a schism within their own party and the creation of a rump of hardliners financially backed by the Kremlin.

The communist leader from 1972 until his death in 1984 was

Enrico Berlinguer, a Sardinian of clear integrity and intelligence. Like Togliatti, he put national unity before other priorities and believed that it could be achieved in Italy only through a partnership, or at least a compromise, between Catholics and communists. He himself embodied this approach not only in his ideas but also in his life, for his family was of noble origin, his wife was religious, and his children were brought up as Catholics. Under his leadership the party's electoral popularity increased, and many people believed it might displace the christian democrats as the largest force in parliament after the elections of 1976. Like Santiago Carrillo in Spain, Berlinguer epitomized the idea of 'Eurocommunism', a somewhat nebulous term suggesting a more modern and moderate form of the ideology, one that was more democratic, more independent of the Soviet Union and more inclined to cooperate with non-marxist parties. Yet he was nervous of coming to power in a left-wing coalition because he feared it would provoke a civil war or a right-wing coup or even some kind of intervention from the United States. Perhaps he was too cautious. In any case, as soon as Chile's left-wing government was overthrown in 1973 in a coup that ended the life as well as the regime of Salvador Allende, he offered the christian democrats what he called 'an historic compromise'. At the beginning he envisaged that the communists would cooperate with the government and help deal with the post-1973 economic crisis but later, he hoped, they would receive tangible benefits in the shape of social reforms and ministerial posts. In his quest for conservative approval, Berlinguer even declared that Italy should remain in NATO and announced that his party opposed any extension of public ownership, a statement that put Italian communists to the right of French socialists and the British Labour Party.

The communists' attempt to join the government failed chiefly because few christian democrats were interested in the idea of an historic compromise. Aldo Moro, prime minister from 1974 to 1976, was one of the few but he was a procrastinator who kept begging the communists to be patient while he 'educated' his own party's right wing. His successor, Giulio Andreotti, was another delayer, keen to have Berlinguer and his colleagues support the unpopular measures of his unpopular government while giving them nothing in return. Moro, however, remained their best hope, and he was close to making them formal partners in the parliamentary majority when, in the spring of 1978, he was kidnapped and later murdered by the revolutionary Red Brigades, whose aim was to sabotage the chances of the historic compromise, an ambition they duly achieved.

Terrorism was a tactic used by groups on the extreme Right as well as the extreme Left, and some 500 people were killed by it in the two decades after 1969. Fascists committed the more spectacular atrocities, such as the bomb in Bologna's train station in 1980 that killed eighty-five people, while left-wing terrorists carried out a selective campaign of assassination and kidnappings of industrialists, politicians, lawyers and journalists. Curiously, both sets of terrorists had a similar objective: they hoped that, by creating tension and destabilizing the state, they could provoke a military takeover and the installation of a regime that the Right would love and protect and the Left would loathe and overthrow. Both were trying to take the country back to the conditions of 1920–22, yet neither of them enjoyed popular support. 'Front Line', 'Workers' Power', the Red Brigades and similar groups claimed to be taking 'proletarian action', but their members were middle-class students and intellectuals playing fatally at being Che Guevara. Over the years they were defeated by a patient and intelligent police campaign led by a general of the *carabinieri*, Carlo Alberto Dalla Chiesa.

Left-wing terrorists were contemptuous of the Communist Party, which had long renounced its revolutionary pretensions. Even in 1968 party leaders had criticized the student revolt, and by 1974 they seemed to have abandoned socialism altogether: Berlinguer was offering his supporters nothing more than the prospect of 'implementing measures and guidelines that are in some respects of a socialist type'.[12] After the elections of 1979, when the communists lost an eighth of their 1976 vote, even Berlinguer realized that his pursuit of the historic compromise, however laudable as a sentiment, had been a mistake and a failure. In elections to the European parliament in 1984 the communists received, for the first and only time, slightly more votes than the christian democrats. Yet commentators recognized that this was not a sign of resurgence. It was more in the nature of a sympathy vote, a consequence of the death six days before the poll of the most respected man in Italian politics, Enrico Berlinguer.

The 1980s were the decade of the *pentapartito*, government by a coalition of five parties – the christian democrats, the social democrats, the socialists, the republicans and the liberals. For the four middle years of the decade, the DC relinquished the premiership and allowed it to go to the leader of the Socialist Party, Bettino Craxi, a man who had little in common with earlier Italian socialists. He was a leader, he understood power, he preferred government to opposition and he liked and admired wealth; he made friends with both Ronald Reagan and Silvio Berlusconi, the Milanese businessman, who asked him to become the godfather of his son. Many of Craxi's subordinates also discarded their socialism and became notorious for their taste for fast cars, smart nightclubs and luxurious holidays. Their party soon became regarded as the most corrupt in Italy.

In the meantime the communists grew increasingly irrelevant. They supported Mikhail Gorbachev's policies in the Soviet Union and hoped that some kind of reformed and democratic communism would survive. Yet their support was being eroded at home both by the decline of the traditional working class and by the visible fragility of their ideological *raison d'être*. The fall of the Berlin Wall in November 1989 signalled the end of the Communist Party in Italy, but its half-century of influence had not been wholly negative and unproductive. Although it had been excluded from power in Rome, the party had run local governments and, from Togliatti to Berlinguer, it had played a stabilizing role in the life of the nation. Its influence was especially clear in Italian culture, which it dominated for decades after 1944. Italy naturally had a conservative culture as well, a largely anti-communist press and many non-marxist publishers; Feltrinelli, itself a left-wing publishing house, achieved success through the publication of two very unrevolutionary novels, Pasternak's *Dr Zhivago* and Lampedusa's *The Leopard*. Yet cultural glamour belonged to the communists: they had the support of the celebrities, of most of the artists and writers and directors who were famous and revered both in Italy and abroad.

In 1947 Pier Paolo Pasolini declared that only communism could provide 'a new culture' for Italy, a view with which thousands of people in the arts, especially those in literature and the cinema, agreed. It

became axiomatic that a serious director had to be 'engaged' in political issues, that he had to have *impegno* (commitment), that his films
had to take political sides and make ideological statements. Marxism
and the Resistance had fused to create a left-wing *Zeitgeist*, and many
artists found life simpler if they joined the Communist Party or at
least became fellow travellers.

'Neo-realism' was an obligatory first phase for post-war directors
who wished to be taken seriously, and some fine films resulted from it,
such as *Ladri di biciclette* (*Bicycle Thieves*) by Vittorio De Sica or
La terra trema by Luchino Visconti, who was the champion of neo-
realism until decadence became a more appealing theme. The products
of this genre are usually gritty, worthy and well made, shot on the
street often with non-professional actors. Yet they are also humour-
less, comfortless and unglamorous, and they were not very popular
with Italians. Working-class people understandably found it more
diverting to watch John Wayne fighting 'Red Indians' or Charlie
Chaplin outwitting huge bullies than to see themselves represented as
exploited fishermen in Sicily or Romans so poor that they could not
afford a bicycle. Yet neo-realism continued, alongside brighter genres,
for decades. In 1978 Ermanno Olmi directed one of the longest and
bleakest of all films about the misery of peasant life, *L'albero degli
zoccoli* (*The Tree of Wooden Clogs*). It begins with scenes of warm-
hearted rustic life in Lombardy in the nineteenth century: the peasants
are trying to make the best of a hard existence, singing as they tear the
husks off the corn-cobs and sitting together in the evenings, the men
telling stories and the women knitting and saying prayers. But the central story recounts the tribulations of a hard-working peasant, who is
persuaded by the local priest to send his clever son to school; as the
little boy's shoes are broken – and he has a long way to walk – the
father cuts down a small tree to make him some clogs, the landowner
notices the stump, and as a result the entire family is evicted. Olmi's
political message could not be clearer: rural Italy was divided between
pure and good-hearted peasants and brutal and rapacious landlords.*

---

*One director who ignored neo-realism was the great Federico Fellini, who took audi-
ences into his private worlds of fantasy and surrealism. Instead of following the trend
of filming on location, he preferred to recreate the Via Veneto or the streets of Rimini,

One era of Italian cinema is often said to have ended with Mussolini, and another, largely unrelated, to have succeeded it in 1944. Naturally it did not happen in quite this way: like other Italians, film directors changed their spots, and the creators of fascist films mutated into makers of committed, left-wing, neo-realist cinema. One of them, Carmine Gallone, was briefly ostracized for his work under the dictatorship but redeemed himself with a film about the opera *Tosca* set in nazi-occupied Rome.[13] Others escaped ostracism. Roberto Rossellini had been a friend of Mussolini's children and the director of three war films known as his 'fascist trilogy'. Yet in 1945 he reinvented himself as an anti-fascist by making the famous Resistance film, *Roma città aperta* (*Rome, Open City*). This is a work that realistically and evocatively conveys the atmosphere at the end of the German occupation, but it is also a work of distortion and propaganda. The only bad people in Rossellini's film are oafish German soldiers under the command of an effetely sadistic officer. The Italians are nearly all good, high-minded folk who make sacrifices in expiation for the fascist aberration. The new Italy rising from the ashes is represented by a stoic priest, an indomitable partisan and a compassionate working-class woman, who are respectively executed, tortured to death and shot by the nazis. Neither of the two men blink or shake or show the slightest sign of nervousness, even when they know they are about to be tortured or shot. Their deaths symbolize the rebirth of the nation, their Christian resignation heralding a resurrection of its people.

Another, much later, work that combined neo-realism with political propaganda was *Novecento* (*1900*), a film made for international audiences in 1976 by Bernardo Bertolucci, a young but already famous director whose previous film had been *Last Tango in Paris*. The beauty of both the photography and the music – a typically haunting score by Ennio Morricone – is undoubted, but the work is dominated by the politics of the director, one of the Communist Party's celebrities, a man who made no secret of his belief in 'the victory

---

his home town, in the studios of Cinecittà. Fellini was untypical in other ways, being uninterested in politics and claiming he had never kicked a football in his life. His films were more appreciated at foreign film festivals than by cinema-goers in Italy.

of the masses'.[14] In his film the entire history of the inter-war years is reduced to a Manichaean struggle between a small number of ugly fascist bullies and a multitude of handsome, down-trodden and noble-hearted peasants.

It opens with a scene in the Emilian countryside on Liberation Day 1945. The peasants are up in arms – the men grabbing rifles, the women wielding pitchforks – and are hunting down the local fascist leader, a brute played by Donald Sutherland, suitably sinister in a bald wig and suitably named Attila. Eventually they capture him, together with his sadistic wife, and are on the point of killing him when the scene stops and the film goes back to the beginning of the century. We have to wait five hours, until the end of Part Two, before we observe his end.

We are now in 1901, on the day of Verdi's death, and the film is appropriately shot near the banks of the River Po, close to the composer's home, with many of the extras gathered from Roncole and Busseto. The early scenes are almost uplifting. Peasants with austerely noble faces toil in the fields and sometimes take time off to dance under the poplar trees; the sense of camaraderie is ubiquitous and even shared by the old landowner, an eccentric aristocrat played by Burt Lancaster, who feels a sense of obligation to his employees. Yet soon the action advances a few years, and it becomes clear that matters have deteriorated. Burt is dead, his inheritance grabbed fraudulently by an appalling younger son, and the peasants, now enrolled in the Socialist Party, are on strike with red flags flying, while an ancient accordionist, dressed symbolically in a Russian smock, strolls along a railway platform playing the '*Internationale*'.

Things get even worse after the next skip, which takes us to the end of the First World War. A peasant woman's bastard son, who was born in an early scene, has now grown up to become Gérard Depardieu, acting very poorly as a demobbed soldier transformed into an heroic socialist with the assistance of his girlfriend, a young marxist teacher. An agricultural crisis is upon us, and the evictions of peasants have begun, cartloads of families with their pitiful possessions traversing the countryside along paths beside the river. When some peasants refuse to be evicted, Depardieu and the schoolteacher organize defiance by persuading the women to lie down in front of a cavalry charge aborted only at the last moment by a relatively humane officer. All this is happening, somewhat surreally, in full view of the ghastly landowner and his equally repellent friends who, clad in fur coats, are shooting duck from boats on adjacent canals. Disgusted by the withdrawal of the mounted troops, one of the duck-shooters fires both barrels of his shotgun at the peasants. He and his fellow sportsmen then retire to a church in which, having realized that the liberal government is not going to suppress the socialists, they give money to Attila to establish a branch of Mussolini's *fasci di combattimento*. There are only two dissenters, one of them played by Robert De Niro (the landowner's son), who has spent part of the duck shoot masturbating his insatiable cousin Regina (Attila's future wife) with the butt of his shotgun. His role is to spend the rest of the film as the weak, cowardly, non-fascist aristocrat who allows himself to be manipulated by the fascists.

Soon a drunken band of Mussolini's thugs appear, brandishing clubs and lurching about in a lorry. After they have burned down a *casa del popolo*, killing some pensioners, Depardieu drags the charred corpses around in a cart; a vast crowd of mourners in red scarves unexpectedly gathers – perhaps they are not real – and a band plays the '*Internationale*'. The camera shifts back to the fascists, some of them lounging in a bar while others are at a tailor's, watching Donald Sutherland trying on a black shirt and urging his followers to buy one too. Snarling demonically, he is suddenly inspired to demonstrate his virility by head-butting a cat, screaming as he kills it that this is the way to treat communists.* In Part Two of the film his Attila becomes even more revolting. The director evidently thinks that a fascist cannot be simply a fascist: he must also be a sadist, a paedophile, a pervert and a murderer. In a moment of pederastic delirium, Attila kills a young boy and blames the murder first on Depardieu, who is duly beaten up by his fascists, and then on a wandering simpleton, who is carted off to prison as a result. Next, Attila murders a widow and impales her on her railings and soon, after angry workers have pelted him with horse manure, he carries out a general massacre of peasants

---

*By this moment of the film, the Socialist Party must have split, which allows Depardieu to join the communists.

in the estate farmyard. Eventually (and far too late), blue skies arrive along with liberation, and Sutherland is captured and shot in a grave-yard.

Italian literature after the war evolved in similar fashion to cinema. Neo-realism and *impegno* were the first essentials, and radical commitment remained almost compulsory, but writers in due course drifted away from realism towards innovation and avant-garde 'experimentalism'. By the late 1950s intellectuals were agonizing over the future of the novel, trying to work out new roles for writers and new 'paths' for their writing. Literary journals sent questionnaires to authors and printed their answers to questions about the place of 'social realism' in contemporary fiction. Pasolini even invented rules for writing poems which could make poetry 'radically innovative but regulated by an awareness of political and social realities'.[15]

In Spain a number of intellectuals who in the 1930s had supported the Falange, a blue-shirted fascist party, recanted and became democratic critics of Franco even during the most repressive years of the dictatorship. One young poet, Dionisio Ridruejo, rose to be chief of nationalist propaganda before repudiating fascism completely; in atonement for his youthful years in the Falange, he founded an illegal social democratic party and spent the rest of his life criticizing Franco and frequently going to jail. Few of Italy's fascist writers became social democrats. Indeed, many of them travelled from the far Right to the far Left without feeling the need to stop anywhere, even temporarily, on the way. The novelist Curzio Malaparte was in turn a nationalist, a fascist, a communist and an enthusiast for maoist China. Other fascist writers who anchored themselves on the Left included the Sicilian Vitaliano Brancati, a one-time eulogist of Mussolini, and the Tuscan Vasco Pratolini, who distanced himself from his black-shirted youth by adopting *realismo socialista* to write about the Florentine working class.

In his novel of the Resistance, *Uomini e no* (*Men and not Men*), Elio Vittorini even extended the idea of good versus bad to the corpses of the combatants – dignified partisan against fascist 'dog' or 'carrion'. Yet this communist intellectual had been a fascist who had toadied to the leadership, approved of its censorship and praised the invasion of Ethiopia. He only turned against Mussolini after the dictator had backed Franco and his supporters, whom Vittorini regarded as too Catholic and reactionary – and insufficiently fascist – to deserve support. Later he bolstered his anti-fascist credentials (which hardly existed until the regime's fall) by joining the communists and putting himself in charge of what he called the 'modern renovation of literature'.[16] Vittorini epitomized that near uniformity of intellectual standpoint that made it so hard for anti-communist writers to achieve success. Committed left-wingers were regularly preferred and promoted above more deserving liberals and conservatives. The writer Salvatore Quasimodo, who was a communist, acquired a status so exalted in Italy that in 1959 the Nobel Prize Committee was persuaded to choose him ahead of Eugenio Montale, a much finer poet, who had to wait until 1975 for the Committee to recognize his merits.

One writer who suffered discrimination was Giorgio Bassani, who had been persecuted at the end of fascism because he was a Jew and was now belittled by the Left because he was not a marxist. His nostalgic semi-autobiographical novels set in Ferrara had no place in Vittorini's 'renovation'. Nor did Lampedusa's *The Leopard*, a novel that Bassani discovered and arranged for publication after its author's death. Vittorini had already done his best to bury the work by rejecting it for publication, once as an adviser for Mondadori and again as a director of Einaudi. But he could not stop Feltrinelli from publishing it on Bassani's advice in 1958. Nor could he or his left-wing allies prevent large numbers of Italians from enjoying this beautiful novel, one that Luigi Barzini suggested 'made all us Italians understand our life and history to the depths'[17] – a work, moreover, that made no concessions to socialist realism or avant-garde experimentalism. Yet Vittorini made an effort, and his fatuous complaint that *The Leopard* was 'right-wing' was repeated by other writers and by the heavy guns of the communist press, which blasted the book's 'ideological deficiency'. The campaign of denigration was blunted, however, by the French writer Louis Aragon, one of the leading marxist intellectuals in Europe, who mocked Alberto Moravia's grumble that Lampedusa's work was 'right-wing' and a success for the Right. Even more disconcerting was Aragon's assertion that *The Leopard* was 'one of the great novels of this century, one of the great novels of all time', and most crushingly, 'perhaps . . . the only Italian novel'.[18] Italian readers sided with Aragon. In an opinion poll carried out by a literary weekly in 1985, *The Leopard* was chosen as 'the most loved' novel of the twentieth century; it was also voted, together with Svevo's *Confessions of Zeno*, as one of the two 'most important'.[19]

AFFLUENT ITALY

Italians had been the richest people in Europe from the early Middle Ages to the end of the sixteenth century. They had subsequently dropped behind the French, the Dutch and the English, and in the years after unification, Italy was the poorest nation in western Europe outside the Iberian peninsula. Italians after the Second World War were still impoverished, as the neo-realist films remind us, and their country was much the least prosperous of the six founder members of the European Coal and Steel Community in 1952.

Yet the 1950s and 1960s turned out to be the most successful decades in the economic history of united Italy. Between 1951 and 1969 the economy increased by an average of nearly 6 per cent a year, and the rate of export expansion was even higher. Considering that Italy had been a predominantly agricultural country at the beginning of the 1950s, the industrial statistics are astonishing. By 1967 Olivetti was producing nearly a million typewriters a year, FIAT had become the largest car manufacturer in Europe, and the nation was annually making over 3 million refrigerators, more than any country in the world except for the United States and Japan. Within the space of a single generation, Italy had become a consumer society. Its people could afford not only fridges but also cars, televisions, washing-machines and good clothes. They spoke with some justice of an 'economic miracle'.

In 1948 the young Piero Ottone was sent to London as the correspondent of an Italian newspaper. At Calais he parked his car in the wrong queue for Dover, whereupon a gendarme came up, lectured him on his mistake and, on observing the number plate, sighed contemptuously, '*Ah, les Italiens . . .*' An outraged Ottone was tempted to make an official complaint. Born in 1924, he had been educated to believe that Italy was a great country, that Mussolini was a great ruler, and that Britain, France and the United States were 'old, grey and decadent' powers, worthy of an Italian's disdain. Admittedly Italy had just lost a war, but that could happen to anyone, and to be patronized by a French policeman was intolerable.[20] Ottone, who later became editor of the *Corriere della Sera*, soon understood why his country's reputation was so low, and he was naturally delighted when, by its own efforts, it began to rise. The prestige of Italy eventually grew not as Crispi and Victor Emanuel and Mussolini had intended – by becoming a mighty power – but because the country was an innovator in such peaceful and productive fields as film, fashion and industrial design. The Ferrari factory outside Modena was one of many enterprises that made Italy seem chic and stylish, just as the manufacture of Vespa scooters in the Arno Valley made it feel 'cool' – especially when Gregory Peck and Audrey Hepburn rode one in the film *Roman Holiday*. The fashion business, based first in Florence and later in Milan, was another success for Italian style. The country may have been infected by London and the 'Swinging Sixties', by the Beatles and by Carnaby Street, but the infection was temporary. Carnaby Street is now folklore, but Gucci and Armani are great international brands.

Italy's rise owed much to Marshall Aid and much also to the dynamism and skills of its people. The government too played its part. Although Italy was a full member of NATO, it allotted barely 1 per cent of its GDP to defence and, without wars to fight or colonies to conquer, it could now invest money in infrastructure, especially motorways, which were built quickly and well. Only eight years were needed to complete the whole Autostrada del Sole, running 755 kilometres from Milan to Naples, a project that included the construction of thirty-eight tunnels, 113 bridges and five chapels. Motorways in the north are today often congested, partly because Italians have more cars than other Europeans, and partly because governments invested a lot of money in roads and very little in railways. The first thing you notice about travelling by train in Italy is that everything is very old: network, tracks, coaches, locomotives, goods wagons and, except in certain large cities, stations. Those of us who like to meander about the country by rail soon become aware that the so-called *accelerato* is the slowest train in Italy. Even the rest are slow compared to their equivalents in other parts of western Europe, and in some cases they are getting slower. The Inter-City service from Milan to Turin now takes ten minutes longer than it did in 1987. If you get up early to go from one end of Sicily to the other, from Ragusa in the south-east to Trapani in the north-west, you will spend nine and a half hours in trains, waiting-rooms and a connecting bus to travel 440 kilometres.[21]

Italy suffered along with other western countries from the economic crisis of the 1970s, but it recovered more quickly than most. It owed this success to the rise of the 'Third Italy', thus termed to differentiate it from the industrialized north-west and the agricultural south. Located in the central regions and the Veneto, 'Third Italy's' chief characteristic was the small family business, which often stayed small as well as successful but sometimes became huge and international, as in the case of the Benetton family near Treviso, which, sensing a market for colourful knitted clothes, started off with one second-hand knitting machine and came to acquire over 6,000 stores in 120 countries. In the provinces of Third Italy Italians rediscovered those talents and that entrepreneurial flair with which they had led the European economy in the Middle Ages. Concentrating on quality and style, they came to be ranked among the world's finest manufacturers of ceramics, glass, shoes, clothes and furniture. At a time when such skills were vanishing in Britain, it was not surprising that by 1986 the Italian economy was larger than the British. Italians were jubilant about this *sorpasso* (overtaking), which made their economy the fifth largest in the world, and some predicted they would soon overtake France and become the fourth biggest. Italy at the end of the 1980s was a success story.

One of the casualties of the 'economic miracle' was the natural environment. The post-war constitution had specified the protection of Italy's landscape as a government duty, but the stipulation has been very largely ignored. The city centres of the north and the centre have generally been well preserved, but their suburbs are invariably ugly, sprawly and chaotic. To the outsider it often seems as if there had been a tacit agreement between citizens and the state whereby, in return for keeping their medieval centres intact, Italians were allowed to build whatever they liked in whatever style they chose outside them: fruitful plains, scenic woods, Alpine valleys – few of them have been safe from the industrialist or the building speculator. Even where there were regulations about spaces and population density, these were widely disregarded, especially in the south. Some regions looked after their landscapes better than others. Tuscany was the best, while Sicily was among the worst; anyone who had known Palermo's plain, the Conca d'Oro, in 1950 would not have recognized it in 1970 because its citrus groves had been concreted over to enrich both the Mafia and the city council, whose personnel overlapped. During the boom years Italy's coastline suffered as tragically and irreversibly as Spain's Mediterranean shores and the Balearic Islands. In an effort to appear modern and industrial, Italy built far more oil refineries than it needed and sited them, along with petrochemical works and other factories, in unsuitable places such as the eastern seaboard of Sicily or the Venetian lagoon. Almost any sandy patch on the peninsula was regarded as suitable for development, and those few areas of shoreline beauty that survive – such as the Amalfi coast and the Ligurian Cinque Terre – have done so because they are rocky, difficult to reach and unembellished by convenient beaches.

Another consequence of the miracle – one shared by all industrializing states – was a massive exodus from the land. Although its productivity increased, agricultural acreage shrank, and new machinery meant that farmers no longer needed to employ so much labour. In 1950 nearly half the population worked the land: a half-century later, only one Italian in fifteen earned a living from agriculture. Millions of young men, mainly from the south, began leaving in the 1950s, boarding the trains from Palermo and Apulia or catching the ferries from Sardinia, country boys saying farewell to their families and carrying their possessions in parcels or in cardboard boxes tied with string, eventually arriving outside a factory in Turin or somewhere else in the unwelcoming north and having to adjust to an unfamiliar life in a shanty town or a concrete block on the outskirts of a frightening city. Their departure left countless villages populated mainly by women and the old; most farmers and labourers you saw in the early 1970s were born before the First World War.

The southerners who remained became richer, though, as in the village where Carlo Levi had lived, less as a result of their own efforts than because they received government handouts and remittances from those who had emigrated. Italy's economic miracle did not reduce the gap between the north and the south, and in 1997 income per capita was still more than twice as high in Emilia-Romagna as it was in Campania, Calabria, Basilicata and Sicily. Yet without government intervention the gap would presumably have been even wider. In their early days the christian democrats implemented some measure of land reform, which enabled about 120,000 peasant families to settle on land expropriated from the *latifondi*. More importantly, De Gasperi created the Cassa per il Mezzogiorno (Development Fund for the South), which in its first years accomplished valuable work on the infrastructure, building roads, aqueducts and irrigation systems. In the 1960s, however, it began to invest in industry – with less happy results. Vast sums were spent on building huge factories in places where skilled labour and suitable communications were absent. Before long it became obvious that the christian democrats were using the Cassa for purposes that previous democratic governments from Depretis onwards would have appreciated: they were bribing the south, providing jobs and projects for their clients and receiving votes and political power in return.

At Gioia Tauro in Calabria a beautiful and fertile landscape of olive trees and orange groves was flattened to make way for a huge industrial complex to be dominated by a steel works that had to be abandoned before an ounce of steel was produced. The chief effect of this choice, apart from the environmental desecration, was vicious warfare among local gangs vying for building contracts which resulted in the murder of hundreds of people. Other schemes in the south – in Sicily, Apulia and Sardinia – also collapsed because they were selected for political rather than economic reasons: some failed to produce anything at all, and others were closed down soon after construction. Such projects were known as 'cathedrals in the desert', but at least real cathedrals functioned and were visited. The Cassa ceased to operate in 1984, a victim of its investment policies but also of its failure to prevent local criminals from stealing so much of its money. One of the worst examples of southern corruption took place after the 1980 earthquake near Naples, in which 2,400 people were killed: funds allocated by the government to rebuild the area were simply diverted to enrich a new breed of businessman linked to the criminal gangs of the Camorra.

Unhealthy though it was to gain votes through bribery, it was still more poisonous to acquire them by protecting criminals. In the years after the war the christian democrats had increasingly come to rely on Sicily and the Veneto as their strongholds of electoral support. Yet while the people of the north-east voted democratically, in accordance with their interests and traditions, many Sicilians voted according to the wishes of the Mafia bosses. The christian democrats needed the *mafiosi* to obtain these votes, and the *mafiosi* needed the politicians to protect them from prosecution. Although this relationship was resented and denounced by party members in other areas of Italy, it endured and became ever more shameful and in the end dangerous. Leading Sicilian christian democrats had to play a dual role, national politician and sometimes government minister in Rome, and protector of the Mafia in Sicily. They may not themselves have been 'men of honour' (*mafiosi*), but they were 'friends' who, as E. M. Forster put it in another context, preferred to betray their country than to betray their friends.

The most controversial figure at the heart of the DC–Mafia connection was Giulio Andreotti, a man who was scrupulous about religion but not about politics and who was regularly described as wily, 'machiavellian' and even 'Jesuitical'. Andreotti came from Lazio, where his power base was small, and he needed and acquired Sicily to have himself installed with such frequency in the cabinet, seven times as prime minister of coalition governments in the twenty years after 1972. Although he evidently had connections with the Mafia – and could be perceived as its ultimate protector – he operated on the island through two infamous lieutenants, Salvo Lima and Vito Ciancimino. However particular in his personal habits, Andreotti was not fastidious in his choice of subordinates. Both men served as mayors of Palermo and city councillors for public works, jobs that enabled them to carry out the 'sack' of the Sicilian capital by issuing thousands of building permits to Mafia frontmen and enriching themselves in the process. Ciancimino was a notorious figure whose power was so farreaching that he personally decided which singers should be employed by the Palermo opera house; yet eventually he overplayed his hand, was arrested in 1984 and later convicted of corruption and collusion with the Mafia. Lima was luckier for a time, and he even became a minister under Andreotti in Rome. He personified the dual role of the Sicilian christian democrat, a man regarded simultaneously as the Mafia's ambassador to Rome and Andreotti's viceroy in Palermo.

Until the 1970s many people in Sicily continued to deny the existence of the Mafia. One cardinal-archbishop claimed it was an invention of the Communist Party, while his successor shrugged it off with the astonishing observation that it killed fewer people than abortions. Yet soon the revelations of *pentiti*, penitent *mafiosi* who gave evidence against former colleagues, proved that it was – or at any rate had now become – a highly structured and organized entity. Gone were the old-style provincial bosses who, inviolate in their strongholds, had dispensed favours, arranged killings and managed protection rackets from a café in their home piazza. Their replacements were less visible and more violent, men who moved into the cities and made millions in the building industry and even more millions in the narcotics trade; in the 1970s Palermo became the global capital of the heroin market. The most ruthless of these new men belonged to the Corleone clan, which gained a spurious glamour in foreign imaginations because it shared the surname of the characters in Mario Puzo's novel *The Godfather*, which in the films based upon the story were played by Robert De Niro, Marlon Brando and Al Pacino. Yet it is hard to think of many people less resembling Robert De Niro than Totò 'Shorty' Riina, the squat psychopath and principal boss of the 1980s, or his henchman Giovanni Brusca, who admitted to murdering 'many more than one hundred but less than two hundred people'.[22]

At the beginning of the 1980s the *corleonesi* exterminated their rivals and in the same period declared war on the nation. Until then, the Mafia had been careful not to target members of the Italian 'establishment'. Now, under Riina, it reversed direction and chose to challenge the state by assassinating policemen, politicians, journalists and magistrates. Their victims – known collectively as 'the eminent corpses' – included the president of the Sicilian regional government, the chief prosecutor in Palermo, the communist leader in Sicily and the christian democratic leader in Palermo, a man whose father had protected the Mafia as a minister in Rome but who himself was bravely trying to detach the DC from the criminals. Despite the outrage of many islanders, there was woefully little response from the christian democrats who, while doubtless disapproving of the murders, did not dare to break with the Mafia. It was not until 1982 and the most audacious killing of all – that of the police general Dalla Chiesa, vanquisher of the Red Brigades and newly appointed prefect of Palermo – that the ruling coalition made any serious response. One consequence of the murder was a law criminalizing 'associazione mafiosa', a phrase difficult to define and an offence even more difficult to prove, but it enabled the courts to convict Ciancimino and several other politicians later on. In 2003 a court in Palermo accepted that even Andreotti was guilty of Mafia associations but judged that these had taken place too long ago for that octogenarian politician to be imprisoned now.

Another consequence of Dalla Chiesa's killing was the establishment of a pool of deft and dedicated magistrates in Palermo who, armed with the evidence of numerous *pentiti*, were able to round up hundreds of suspected *mafiosi*. At the end of 1987, after a 'maxi-trial' in Palermo that had lasted nearly two years, some 350 suspects were convicted and sent to prison. The guilty men were not too concerned about this because they knew that under Italian law they still had two chances of getting off, both in the appeal court and in the Supreme Court, the Court of Cassation. At the appeal stage they had the good fortune to come up against a judge notorious for acquitting *mafiosi* on technicalities and who himself was later charged with *associazione mafiosa*. Many of them were duly released and remained confident of equally benign treatment when their cases came up for review in the Supreme Court. They thought that Salvo Lima would fix the trial, that the presiding judge would be on their side, that ultimately Andreotti would protect them from having to serve their sentences. They were wrong and, when many of the original verdicts were upheld, they responded predictably with vengeance. One of their first victims was Lima, their 'friend' for over thirty years, who was murdered both as a reprisal for his failure to protect them and as a warning to Andreotti and the christian democrats that they too were in danger. Next, they targeted the magistrates who had caught them, Giovanni Falcone and Paolo Borsellino, men who had grown up with *mafiosi* in the Kalsa district of Palermo and who knew how greatly they were risking their lives when they took up the challenge. Italians were convulsed by the murders in 1992 of these heroic figures – and their wives and their police escorts – and some declared themselves ashamed of being Italian. Reactions were so strong that the state was goaded into taking sustained action; even the Polish pope, John Paul II, who had been reticent for too long, condemned the Mafia while on a pastoral visit to Sicily in 1993. Over the next three years thousands of *mafiosi* were arrested, including the ineffable Riina, and the murder rate dropped dramatically. For the only time in the history of the Italian republic, it seemed that the Mafia might be defeated.

The Mafia in Sicily had gained the reputation of being a uniquely brutal, secret and effective organization of criminals. In fact there were others in southern Italy with rival qualifications. Calabria had the 'Ndrangheta, which was equally ruthless, and Apulia had the Sacra Corona Unita (United Sacred Crown), against which magistrates in Bari fought with some degree of success. The most powerful of all was the Neapolitan Camorra which, like the Mafia, had close connections with the christian democrats. One of its 'friends' was Antonio Gava, who was known as the 'viceroy of Naples' and who in the 1980s was appointed to several ministerial posts in Rome, including minister of the interior, the man supposed to be in charge of fighting organized crime; he subsequently spent thirteen years trying – ultimately with success – to clear himself of the charge of *associazione mafiosa*. At the time the Camorra rivalled the Mafia in the scale of its violence, the two between them murdering on average over 500 people a year, but it later overtook its Sicilian equivalent in size, wealth, killings and corruption. In the thirteen years after 1991 seventy-one municipalities in Campania were dissolved because they were being run by gangs of the Camorra. In the twenty-six years up to 2005, 'the system' – as its members liked to call it – murdered 3,600 people.[23]

The Italian state had helped make its citizens prosperous but it had failed to provide them with security or to protect the lives of its officials. Politics, prosperity and corruption seemed to mix very easily – and not only near the tentacles of the Mafia and the Camorra. In the late 1970s corruption brought about the resignation of a president of the republic (Giovanni Leone) and the imprisonment of a former minister for defence (Mario Tanassi), and in the following decade the disease became endemic in the parties of the governing coalition. As magistrates soon discovered, building and other business contracts were being awarded only to those companies prepared to pay bribes to the politicians who were awarding them.

In February 1992 a prominent Milanese socialist was caught redhanded receiving a bribe from a company that did the cleaning at a geriatric hospital administered by himself. Taken into custody, he stayed silent for a while until, finding himself reviled by his party leaders, he was persuaded to answer questions put by local magistrates. It soon became clear that this was not an isolated case but a piece of a vast, rambling and seemingly infinite jigsaw puzzle of corruption. The chief prosecutor of Milan decided to investigate the alleged crimes and put together an effective team of magistrates,* men whose detective work and interrogation skills persuaded many of the guilty to confess. Their investigations, known as the 'mani pulite' ('Clean Hands') campaign, found hundreds of people from the government coalition guilty of receiving bribes and putting the money into their parties' coffers and, in many cases, their own pockets.

The scandal engulfed and destroyed the political system of the previous half-century. Over the sixteen years of Craxi's reign as their leader, the socialists had already acquired a reputation as Italy's most dishonest party, and the magistrates' investigations now confirmed it. Craxi himself brazenly denied the many charges of corruption against himself but, on realizing a conviction was inevitable, he fled to his villa in Tunisia, never to return. He was declared a fugitive of justice and sentenced to twenty-seven years in prison; meanwhile his deputy went to jail, and his party disappeared. Other parties, also guilty of corruption, disbanded or simply disintegrated. The christian democrats dissolved their party in 1994, although many of them refused to accept that their political lives were over. Whatever future they might still have made together was sabotaged, however, by internal divisions, and their members were soon dispersing in different directions, some to the neo-fascists, some to new formations and others to a

---

*In Italy magistrates are divided between the prosecuting and adjudicating components of the judiciary. A magistrate can therefore be a detective as well as a judge.

Centre-Left coalition known as 'the Olive Tree'; one independent group tried for years to make itself a pivotal force at the centre of politics but never quite succeeded in doing so.

As well as rejecting their discredited politicians, Italians also condemned the process that had produced them. Fed up with proportional representation, a system that had immobilized politics and kept the same party in power, they voted in a referendum in 1993 for something more like Westminster. As the appropriate legislation proceeded through parliament, the Governor of the Bank of Italy, Carlo Azeglio Ciampi, was appointed prime minister to take care of the economy. By the time he resigned, a few months later, Italy had a new system: the Chamber of Deputies would have just one-quarter of its members elected by proportional representation and the rest by a 'first-past-the-post' system in single-member constituencies.

13
Modern Italy

CENTRIFUGAL ITALY

United Italy had begun its life designed as a centralized state by Camillo Benso di Cavour, and it had become more centripetal during the dictatorship of Benito Mussolini. Yet after the Second World War many of the constitution-makers wondered whether Cattaneo might have been right and Cavour wrong on the issue of federation; they also wondered whether fascism might have been more difficult to establish in 1922 had the administration been less centralized. Aware that a certain degree of federalism could be justified by Italy's historical traditions, they therefore divided Italy into regions, five of which were to be considered 'special' and granted a substantial measure of autonomy. Sicily, Sardinia, Val d'Aosta and Trentino-Alto Adige all became autonomous regions in 1948, with Friuli-Venezia Giulia following in 1963 after various problems with Yugoslavia had been resolved.

The government's reasons for giving these places their own executives and legislatures were practical and pragmatic. Autonomy was an attempt – a largely successful one – to neutralize separatist demands, which were especially strong in Sicily, and to defuse tensions in those northern regions where large numbers of people did not regard themselves as Italians and spoke French, German and Slovene as their first languages. After 1948, however, enthusiasm for regional plans waned, partly because the christian democrats were reluctant to see a great belt of central Italy run by communist councils in Florence, Perugia and Bologna. The 'ordinary' regions came into existence only in 1970, when they elected their first assemblies, and they then proved something of a disappointment. While most Italians were happy to be dealing with councillors who were aware of local issues, they were sometimes frustrated with both the poor quality of their new administrators and the limits set on their autonomy, which was much more restricted in the ordinary regions than in the islands and the linguistically divided areas of the north. The establishment of the regions also sometimes led to violence. In the Abruzzi there were riots in L'Aquila and Pescara, which both wanted to be the capital, while in Calabria protests left several people dead and more than 300 wounded when the population of Reggio discovered that Catanzaro had been chosen as the region's administrative capital.

Demands for more autonomy increased in the 1990s, and at the turn of the century additional powers in such areas as tourism, transport and welfare were transferred to the regions. When in 2008 the finance minister proposed to devolve tax-raising powers and thus give the regions what was called 'fiscal federalism', it seemed that Italy was at last on the road to becoming what it should have been all along, a state that recognized the importance of regionalism and diversity. Yet sceptics sometimes wondered whether the creation of the regions had done anything more than add another tier of government and bureaucracy. Italy is now divided into twenty regions and subdivided into more than one hundred provinces and more than 8,000 *comuni* or municipalities. This situation leads to much duplication in local government and to some bewilderment for the population: until recently the citizens of Udine were under a left-leaning separatist mayor, a right-wing provincial president and a centre-left president of the region.

The obvious solution would have been to abolish the provinces, which became increasingly irrelevant after 1970, especially in those regions that had only two: Umbria, Molise, Basilicata and the Trentino-Alto Adige (the Val d'Aosta has none at all). Yet anyone who suggested such a thing was assailed with shouts of 'Hands off the provinces!', branded a heretic and told that the provincial system was part of the nation's heritage as the departments were in France. In consequence the provinces survived without any real purpose: local government remains mainly in the hands of the *comune*, and wider issues are dealt with by the regions, yet Italians still have to pay large salaries to the provincial presidents, the deputy provincial presidents, the presidents of the provincial assemblies and a total of 4,000 provincial councillors.

Regionalism has led to considerable extravagance and self-importance on the part of these devolved governments and their leaders. In 2004 the entertainment expenses of the president of Campania were twelve times higher than those of the president of Germany. Across the Straits of Messina one Sicilian president spent much of his reign trying to expand his powers, requesting a cabinet place in Rome whenever his island was discussed and attempting to conduct a personal foreign policy with Colonel Gaddafi and other north African neighbours. Regional officials are especially keen on inventing international roles for their regions, whether establishing little 'embassies' for themselves in Brussels or promoting their regional products in expensive and unsuccessful ventures such as Casa Sicilia, branches of which were set up in such unpromising places as Sofia and Beijing. Lombardy alone has twenty-five 'consulates' dispersed among twenty-one countries, including Cuba and Uruguay.[1]

In recent years much of the passion for devolved government has come from the north, particularly in those areas of Lombardy and the Veneto where people had traditionally voted for the christian democrats but became disillusioned both by the party's corruption and by its heavily southern bias. Inspired by the example of the communes that had defeated Barbarossa at Legnano 800 years earlier, the Lombard League was formed in the 1980s by a small group of northerners determined to fight for their rights against the exactions and inefficiencies of the central government. Joined in 1991 by the Venetian League and a few other groups, it was renamed the Northern League and instantly became an electoral force.

Folklore and nostalgia were a part of the League's appeal from the beginning. Rallies were held at Pontida, where the communes had sworn an oath against Barbarossa in 1167; efforts were made to revive dialects and recover the north's 'linguistic heritage'; followers were encouraged to put on fancy dress, carrying toy swords and wearing helmets with horns on them when attending medieval ceremonies and re-enactments. Although protection of the environment was not one of the League's priorities, green was chosen as the party colour, and a Miss Green Shirt beauty contest duly came into being. As for the anthem, the choice went to '*Va pensiero*' from *Nabucco*, an odd choice considering that northerners, whatever grievances they had, could not easily empathize with the slaves in Babylon; the only connection with Verdi (who was not even a Lombard) seems to have been that the composer also wrote an opera about Legnano.

Yet the League's real appeal is not sentimental but economic. Its message attracts those with a visceral resentment, people you hear grumbling in bars how they pay high taxes and receive few benefits, how they make the money which the government in Rome then steals or squanders on bureaucracy, mismanagement and allowing corrupt and idle southerners to live beyond their means. Without the north, they very reasonably point out, Sicily and Calabria would be unable annually to spend 50 per cent more than they earn. One town which exemplifies the hard-nosed side of the League is Treviso in the Veneto, a place so unsentimental about its past that it erects modern structures in its centre and, even when it is moved to 'restore' a building, guts it almost completely and starts again. In Treviso you do not find souvenir shops or knights in armour but citizens living for the future rather than in the past, people determined to keep their revenues and spend them on projects in their own region.

The League's founder and leader was Umberto Bossi, a wayward, mercurial and charismatic figure with a talent for demagoguery and political acrobatics; he also had a touch of megalomania, was intolerant of dissent and was derided by a leading member of his own party as the Lombard 'Braveheart'.[2] He delighted in being provocative and he appealed to the rankest instincts of his followers when he mocked homosexuals and referred to southerners as Africans or *mafiosi*. Apart from their commitment to federalism, he and his party were unencumbered by ideology and even on the federal question they were happy to adapt to the times and their electoral prospects. In the early 1990s they campaigned for an Italy of cantons, as in Switzerland, and were astonished by the degree of support they received. Their blunt and primeval message – 'the north for the northerners' – had such appeal that between 1987 and 1992 their vote was multiplied by a factor of seventeen. They elected fifty-five deputies in elections in the latter year, won Milan and fifteen other cities of the north and indicated that they would henceforth play a pivotal role in the making and unmaking of governments. In 1994 they did even better, fighting the election in alliance with Silvio Berlusconi and doubling their representation in parliament. The League was suddenly in national government.

Success stimulated ambition. Federalism was not enough, declared Bossi in 1995, he now wanted secession and independence for the north, a region he called 'Padania' that stretched southwards from the Alps to the River Po. The following year he led a multitude to the banks of the river and held a ceremony at which he declared the independence of Padania. 'Padanians,' he cried, 'no longer feel Italian', a sentiment often repeated in later years, even on T-shirts for children carrying such slogans as 'Padania is not Italy', 'Born to kill Italy', or simply 'Bossi's boys'. Other gimmicks included a 'shadow parliament' in Mantua, a Padanian Liberation Committee and a foray by militants into Venice, where they occupied the campanile in San Marco and flew the flag of the Venetian Republic from its top.

How much secessionism was a tactic and how much a principle is still debatable. In the event, influenced by political developments in Britain, Bossi soon changed his mind and declared that the League's aim was now 'devolution, Scottish style', pronounced in a thick Lombard accent. Although the League had withdrawn its support from Berlusconi within a few months of the 1994 elections they had jointly won, thereby causing the downfall of his government, it joined forces with him again in 2001 and also agreed to respect Italy's national sovereignty. While this concession did not hinder League supporters from chanting 'Devolution or Death' or Bossi himself from again threatening secession, the party was with Berlusconi once more in the Right's victory in 2008, when it persuaded its allies to support the cause of 'fiscal federalism'.

The League owed its success to its populism and emotional appeal but also to economic arguments that attracted people who were not personally inclined to vote for it. Such a man was Riccardo Illy who, apart from intermittently running his family's coffee company, became successively (with support from the Centre-Left) mayor of Trieste, a deputy in Rome and the president of the autonomous region of Friuli-Venezia Giulia. Illy did not wish to disunite Italy but he did want it to become a truly federal state. Rome could remain the national capital, and the government there would retain control of defence, foreign affairs, security and public order; it would also preserve some authority over health. All other matters, he believed, should be handled by properly autonomous regions.

From the perspective of Rome, it seemed fair and natural for the richer areas to subsidize the poorer ones. A businessman in the north might also see the justice of this principle, but his chief concern was to keep his business going in conditions that allowed him to compete successfully with rival firms in neighbouring parts of Europe. His competitors in Austria, for example, were in 2004 paying substantially lower corporation tax than he was. In Slovenia, which was enjoying 7 per cent growth and receiving structural funds from the EU, an industrialist was paying labour costs a third lower than those burdening his Italian equivalent. The situation was so unbalanced, observed Illy, that a sensible businessman in Italian Gorizia should simply relocate his business across the road to Nova Gorica in Slovenia. Difficult though this situation was for Friuli-Venezia Giulia, it was even worse in non-autonomous regions such as Lombardy, the Veneto and Emilia-Romagna, which annually lost between a fifth and a sixth of their incomes through their subsidization of other parts of the country. Warning Italians that they were in danger of losing the north, Illy argued that the people making the economic decisions there must be northerners, people familiar with their regions' needs and complexities.[3] By 2009 most Italians agreed with him that fiscal federalism was a good thing, but not many were seeking to answer the question, 'Who is going to pay for the schools and hospitals of Calabria?'

The least attractive side of the League was its xenophobia, its dislike of foreigners and its habit of playing on the electorate's fears of illegal immigration from Africa and the Balkans. In the general elections of 2008 one of its posters portrayed a 'Red Indian' chief, whose noble image and feathered head-dress were accompanied by the words, 'They were unable to stop immigrants, and now they live in reservations!' Certain senior figures in the party sometimes sounded like neo-nazis ranting about ethnic purity. At a festival of the 'Padanian people' in Venice in 2008, a long-serving mayor of Treviso known as the 'sheriff' fulminated against Muslims and gypsies, raged at the building of mosques in Italy and denounced the idea of 'black or brown people teaching our children'. In the same year a Trevisan councillor urged the council to 'use the same system as the [nazi] SS' when dealing with illegal immigrants, 'punishing ten of them for every slight against one of our citizens'.[4] Occasionally the League made a gesture of conciliation such as supporting the election of a black mayor (the son of an American soldier and an Italian woman) or choosing a coloured girl to be Miss Green Shirt and to sing 'Va pensiero' at party festivals. Yet for all that, it remained a party suffused with racism, one which owed much of its appeal to its skill in persuading people that Italy was being swamped by foreigners.

The League and its supporters had similar feelings towards Italians of the south. It was an old gag that Italy stopped at the Garigliano – the river that once marked the boundary between Naples and the Papal States – but the ancient mockery was rejuvenated with new insulting epithets such as 'Calafrica' and 'Saudi Calabria'[5] or with the banner at Milan's San Siro stadium that greeted Neapolitan football fans with the words, 'Welcome to Europe'. Especially provocative was the jibe that 'Garibaldi did not unite Italy: he divided Africa', because it mocked the central tenet of the Risorgimento that Italy was a nation. In its declaration of Padanian independence in 1996, the League took this further by alleging that united Italy's history had been one of 'colonial oppression, economic exploitation and moral violence'. The state had 'deviously compelled the Peoples of Padania to endure the systematic exploitation of the economic resources created by their hard work, and see them squandered in the thousand streams of support for the Mafia clienteles of the south'.[6]

One of the Italians most appalled by such heresies was President Ciampi, the former partisan, Governor of the Bank of Italy and interim prime minister in 1993. During his presidency from 1999 to 2006 he constantly urged his countrymen to remember the Risorgimento and even implored directors to make more films of that courageous and 'wonderful adventure'.[7] It was a strange plea, in itself an admission that unification had not built a nation, and in any case it was too late. Italians cared increasingly little about those 'beautiful legends' Giolitti had been so eager to preserve, and they seldom visited the places designed to enshrine them. I have been to a dozen Risorgimento museums and find myself invariably alone with the ticket-seller and an attendant unless I am in Rome, where the museum is at the top of the Vittoriano and attracts tourists who have been taking photographs on the terrace. Few Italian children today have any idea what events are commemorated by all those streets in their cities called 4 Novembre, 25 Aprile or 20 Settembre. In 2008 the municipality of Rome even ridiculed the last date – the day the capital was 'liberated' in 1870 – by turning the anniversary ceremony upside down. Instead of remembering the forty-nine *bersaglieri* and other infantrymen killed at the Porta Pia, the event commemorated only the nineteen soldiers of the papal army who had died in the defence of the city. It seemed a gesture as derisive of the Risorgimento as the jibe about Garibaldi dividing Africa: by implication the true martyrs had been those fighting to defend the temporal power of the papacy.

BERLUSCONI

As Italy's traditional parties disintegrated in 1994, a very remarkable thing happened. A Milanese businessman without political experience set up a new political party, won a general election and became the country's prime minister. Although his government was brought down only a few months later by his ally, the Northern League, Silvio Berlusconi bounced back to win another election in 2001 and yet another in 2008. In May 2010 he became the third-longest prime minister in Italian democratic history, ahead of De Gasperi and not far behind Giolitti and Depretis.

Berlusconi's success in 1994 was extraordinary. After just a few months of preparation, he announced in January that he was 'getting on to the pitch' as the boss of a new party he christened with a football chant of a name, Forza Italia ('Come on, Italy'). Two months later, he employed the most simplistic of messages to persuade Italians to vote for him as their leader. He was a successful man and he was going to make them also successful. He had become the richest man in Italy, he had rescued AC Milan and turned it into the finest football team in Europe; he was a clever operator, he got things done, he was the man to transform the country. In case voters might need some kind of programme, he promised tax cuts, a free market and victory over the 'communists', who were now masquerading as the Partito della Sinistra (PDS), the Party of the Left.

As the 'first-past-the-post' – or 'winner-takes-all' – electoral system tends to lead to contests between two power blocs, Berlusconi knew he had to unite the Centre-Right in order to defeat the Centre-Left and win the election. His most promising potential partners were the Northern League and the Alleanza Nazionale (National Alliance), but these unfortunately disliked each other so much that they would not join the same coalition. Whereas the League was sometimes federalist and sometimes secessionist but always anti-southern, the Alliance favoured centralized government and received the bulk of its support from the south. It was in fact the old neo-fascist party (the MSI) with a new name and a new leader, the presentable and articulate Gianfranco Fini, who had been national secretary of its youth front. Although he was still in this period describing Mussolini as a great statesman, Fini did not look or sound like a fascist and, as he grew older, he became positively anti-fascist. He came to regard fascism as an 'absolute evil', an opinion that drove the Duce's granddaughter, Alessandra Mussolini, out of the party, and in 2008 he threatened to expel any fascists from his (until recently) neo-fascist organization.[8] By then he had become one of the most coherent liberal voices in the country.

Since Berlusconi could not form a single coalition, he decided to construct a couple of them in different parts of the peninsula. In the north he joined forces with Bossi and the League in the 'Liberty Axis', and in the south and the centre his Forza Italia united with Fini and the Alliance in the 'Axis of Good Government'. The success of this manoeuvre was astonishing, for at the election the coalitions won 366 seats in the Chamber against 213 for their opponents on the Left, and Berlusconi became prime minister. Yet he had little time to enjoy the office because Milanese magistrates began investigating him for corruption before the year was out and the Northern League deserted him.* A government of technocrats then took over until new elections

*See p. 384.

were held in 1996, when the parties of Bossi, Fini and Berlusconi did even better than in 1994, the three of them plus a small christian democrat group winning over 52 per cent of the vote. Yet as Forza Italia and the League were competing with each other in the northern constituencies, they both lost out, which allowed their opponents, the Olive Tree coalition, to take power despite winning only 44 per cent of the ballot.

The Olive Tree was the first government of the Left that Italy had ever had and relied in parliament on the former communists of the PDS, the largest party in the coalition. Berlusconi and his colleagues strenuously insisted that the Party of the Left was still communist, an accusation its leaders did little to refute when they retained the hammer and sickle as its symbol, albeit now placed under an oak tree. Yet although the cabinet contained nine ministers from the PDS, it did nothing very radical. It was headed by Romano Prodi, who had run the state's Institute for Industrial Reconstruction (IRI), and most of its ablest members were men of the Centre or Centre-Right, including two former employees of the Bank of Italy who had briefly been prime minister (Ciampi and Lamberto Dini) as well as the very popular Antonio Di Pietro, the most prominent of the Milanese magistrates in the Clean Hands campaign. The main achievement of Prodi's ministry was to reduce inflation and the deficit to a level that enabled Italy to enter the European Monetary Union. With higher taxes, cuts in spending and a special 'Euro-tax', the government met the criteria and adopted the euro as its currency. By then, however, Prodi had been brought down by a faction inside his coalition and had gone unwillingly to Brussels as president of the European Commission. He was succeeded by Massimo D'Alema, the leader of the PDS, who made the mistake, which the Left was to repeat, of underestimating Berlusconi. His chief error was his failure to legislate on media monopolies and 'conflicts of interest', which in consequence allowed Berlusconi to control almost all commercial television and, if ever he returned to power, the state channels as well. The leaders of the Left seemed unable to understand charisma – they had little of it themselves – and they did not foresee how charisma plus television control would be a powerful electoral combination.

The Olive Tree was in disarray by the time it fought the elections of

2001. It had lost Rifondazione Comunista, the communist hardliners who had refused to join the PDS (now called the DS, Democratici della Sinistra), and it lost potential voters to a new party called 'Italy of Values' set up by Di Pietro to oppose Berlusconi and corruption. Its leader this time was the mayor of Rome, Francesco Rutelli, a former member of both the Radical and the Green parties, who was now the leader of the Margherita (Daisy Party), a name which understandably gave the Olive Tree a rather fey and wimpish image. Although Rutelli himself was an attractive and plausible candidate, he was no match for Berlusconi, who managed to resurrect his 1994 coalitions with both the National Alliance and the Northern League. Bossi and Berlusconi liked to insult each other – the Lombard Braveheart doing so in public, 'Berluskaiser' (as Bossi called him) choosing to do so in private – but they were aware that they could only win the election if they fought side by side in the north.

At the head of a coalition he now called 'The House of Liberties', Berlusconi promised to lower taxes and the crime rate, to increase pensions and to create at least a million jobs. The programme sounded appetizing but it was not accompanied by explanations of how he was going to achieve these goals or how he was planning to pay for them. It certainly did not fool the *Economist*, the influential London weekly that would normally have supported a politician of the Right who believed in free enterprise. After a front-page headline proclaiming that Berlusconi was 'unfit to govern Italy', the magazine observed that he was under judicial investigation for corruption on several counts, that the conflict of interests arising from his media empire should make him ineligible for office, and that 'it would be unthinkable in any self-respecting democracy' to elect such a man.[9] Berlusconi's acolytes dismissed the *Economist*'s survey as a communist plot, though the application of the adjective to such a dogmatically free trade publication was as laughable as it was to the author of the devastating judgement, Xan Smiley, who was the journal's European editor and a liberal conservative.

The *Economist*'s views were widely publicized in Italy but evidently had little effect on the electorate. Berlusconi duly used his commanding ownership of commercial television to project his image into Italian homes, and he employed his wealth to print and distribute an illustrated book displaying his qualities to 18 million families. (Some years later he claimed to be the greatest prime minister Italy had ever had.) Yet most Italians refused to become indignant. They did not seem to care about the conflict of interests, just as they were apparently unperturbed by the criminal charges against him of corruption, tax evasion and the bribing of judges. In the elections Berlusconi had no difficulty in trouncing the Left, his coalition winning 367 seats in the Chamber against the Olive Tree's 248.

After occupying the premiership for a full term of five years, it was predicted that Berlusconi would be badly defeated in the elections of 2006. Of all the pledges he had made in the previous campaign, he had managed to fulfil only one, an increase in pensions. He had failed to create the jobs he had promised, he had failed to reduce the crime rate and he had failed to lower taxes, though he had made it easier for the rich to evade them. Above all, his assertion that the Italian economy needed an entrepreneur like him to get it moving had been made to look ridiculous. Over the course of his second premiership Italians became poorer, and their economy grew at an average annual rate of just one-third of 1 per cent, slower than in any other country in the European Union. Nor were there identifiable political achievements to set against this dismal economic record. In fact the prime minister had demonstrated his contempt for parliament by ignoring it, preferring to rule by decree, even though he had a large majority, rather than suffer the tedium of having to debate bills in the Chamber. Under his rule the chief political forum became the one he felt most at home in, the TV studio. When he made the decision to withdraw Italian troops from Iraq, where he had sent them to support the American invasion of 2003, he chose to announce the move not in parliament but in an interview on television.

The Right lost heavily in the regional elections of 2005, and opinion polls suggested it would suffer a similar defeat in the national elections a year later. Yet as the contest approached, Berlusconi's alliance began creeping up in the polls, and in the end the result was surprisingly close, Romano Prodi's Union coalition, successor to the Olive Tree, gaining power with only 24,000 more votes than its opponents. Berlusconi came so near partly because of his command of television, partly because he changed the voting rules – reviving proportional representation which the electorate had rejected in 1993 – but mainly because the Left fought an incredibly inept campaign. Leaders of the Union behaved as if victory was inevitable because the electorate had seen through Berlusconi and identified him as a charlatan; they assumed voters would recognize that Prodi was the better man but were unable to see that, serious and intelligent though he was, he came across on television as a boring professor of industrial policy (which he also was). Yet the Left had been equally feeble and passive during its years in opposition. In exasperation the novelist Umberto Eco asked how a country could be healthy if 'comedians and artists [were] the only people to inspire argument and debate, obviously without being able to suggest solutions?' One of the comedians was Roberto Benigni, who at the San Remo Festival in 2002 both shocked and delighted Italians with his plea, 'Please Berlusconi, please do something that, when we go to bed at night, will make us proud to be Italians.' One of the artists was Nanni Moretti, the left-wing film director, who turned his anger on his own side, mocking its failure as an opposition and predicting that, with leaders like the current bunch, it would not win again for another three generations.[10]

Prodi's second spell as prime minister ended in the same manner as his first – by a rebellion within his coalition. Fresh elections were held in the spring of 2008 at which the Left's leader was another mayor of Rome, Walter Veltroni, a decent candidate but one who, like Prodi, lacked charisma and who, unlike Berlusconi, made the mistake of lecturing the electorate. The outcome was a third emphatic victory for Berlusconi, a result which showed, as the elections in 1948 had first done, that Italy has a natural conservative majority encompassing some 55 to 60 per cent of the electorate. As Beppe Severgnini, an Italian journalist once based in London, said to me at the time, 'Italians are conservatives pretending to be progressives, whereas you British pretend you are traditionalists though in fact you are quite radical.' The Left could draw an election, as it did in 2006, if the Right had been governing very badly, but it was unable to win one without a charismatic leader. Unfortunately for its supporters, the only charismatic leaders in recent Italian history have been the right-wing populists, Umberto Bossi and Silvio Berlusconi.

Berlusconi's talents and personality went on display at an early age.

The child of a modest, middle-class family in Milan, he earned money as a boy by helping schoolfellows with their homework, and as a student by singing and playing the guitar on cruise ships. Ever after, he retained the manners of a crooner: sleek and smarmy, smiley and jokey, a self-assured entertainer who wanted everyone to love him as much as he loved himself. In his early thirties Berlusconi became a property tycoon, constructing a huge suburb near Milan that, according to *mafiosi* allegations over the years, was funded by the Mafia, which later used these dealings to blackmail him. Yet his natural habitat was the media rather than real estate, and he made the bulk of his fortune in television.

Berlusconi had a hold over the Italian people as no other politician had had since Mussolini. Of course the allure of the fascist leader had been very different, for women as well as for men. He had not been one for serenades and lingering siestas: he liked to take women roughly and briskly, on the floor or up against a wall. Berlusconi by contrast was a seducer and a caresser, an archetypal giver of chocolates and pearl necklaces. A smiler rather than a scowler, he appeased his narcissism with a face-lift and a hair transplant and by surrounding himself with gaggles of young women, to some of whom he gave political careers and occasionally a post in his government. He liked making remarks that were crass, sexist and insensitive, as they were when he advised an unemployed woman to marry someone like himself, but most women forgave him. He was an Italian male.

Berlusconi's message to men was equally simple: I am like you, and you can be like me if you try; you too can be famous, rich and seductive even if (like me) you are small and not very handsome. With all his vulgarity, Berlusconi was able to talk to voters in a way that nobody on the Left could begin to emulate. Instead of telling them what they should think or do, he would wink and grin at them: we are all sinners, he was saying, but life is good, and we should do our best to make it better. He appealed to many men because they thought that, unlike intellectuals such as Prodi or Veltroni, all his pleasures were their pleasures, especially those connected with football, sex and making money. And they voted for him, not only because they recognized that he was clever and *furbo* (a greatly respected quality meaning 'cunning') but also because he was the archetype of many. They did not seem to mind if he made gaffes, told lies, betrayed his wife or faced criminal charges. They even seemed to enjoy his tactic of deflecting criticism by labelling it communist: it was quite a clever joke to call the *Economist* the 'Ecommunist'. When he was rebuked for something he had said, he sometimes denied he had said it and then, when proof was given, would laugh it off, claim it had been a joke and remark that the 'communists' had no sense of humour. Other responses to criticism were to state that the 'communists' were jealous of his wealth and that they had no taste in women: right-wing ladies, he declared, were much more attractive than left-wing ones.

Berlusconi had little interest in philosophy or ideas. He was the supreme master of *l'arte di arrangiarsi*, of getting by, of making deals, of governing by intuition and opportunism. He did not pretend to be chaste, devout or obedient, but he genuflected to the Church and won its support with expedient and well-timed stances on bioethics and other moral issues. Few prime ministers of any epoch have been so ignorant of – and indeed uninterested in – the history of their country. In an interview in 2003 with the British weekly the *Spectator*, he made the astonishing claims that Mussolini had not 'murdered anyone', that his dictatorship had been 'benign' and that he had punished his opponents not by jailing them but by sending them 'on holiday' to islands in the Mediterranean.[11] Later he became a little more cautious or perhaps just rather bored with the subject of Mussolini. When members of his coalition were rancorously arguing in 2008 whether fascism was sometimes excusable or always deplorable, Berlusconi declared that the matter was simply irrelevant. He was a busy man with a lot of projects to attend to, and his duty was not to worry about the past but to concentrate on the future.[12]

Berlusconi had never thought of politics as his vocation and, when in his late fifties he went 'on to the pitch' of the political stadium, he had no statesmanly vision of the Italy he wanted to fashion. As his friends admitted, he became a politician by accident and calculation, choosing the profession in 1994 as a means of protecting his business empire and of evading charges of corruption. A few years later, one of his closest associates even confessed that, had Berlusconi not gone into politics and formed Forza Italia, they would by then be in prison or hanging under a bridge – a reference to the corpse of the corrupt banker Roberto Calvi, which had been found under London's Black-friars Bridge in July 1982.[13]

Radiotelevisione Italiana (RAI), the public service broadcaster, used to have a monopoly of national transmissions, which meant that Berlusconi's company Mediaset, the owner of the three main commercial channels, was restricted to local broadcasting. When in 1984 magistrates discovered that Mediaset was breaking the rules and broadcasting nationally, they ordered that its channels be partially suppressed. An indignant Berlusconi reacted by appealing to his friend Bettino Craxi, who was prime minister at the time, and succeeded in having the rules changed. Subsequent legislation allowed Mediaset to broadcast nationally and gave him a virtual monopoly of commercial TV. This in turn gave him the chance to create another monopoly for one of his companies, the advertising agency Publitalia, which came to handle and control the hundreds of daily advertisements on his television channels. Berlusconi was thus in the happy position of being able to pay himself to advertise his own products on his own TV stations. Later, as a politician, he hatched another wheeze, making the news himself and getting his employees to report it as prominently and favourably as possible.* In 1993, however, Mediaset's profits were threatened by the stance of the PDS which, if it formed part of the next government, was expected to push for limits to the control of the media by individuals and companies. This perceived danger was one of the factors that impelled the magnate into politics.

As prime minister Berlusconi had ultimate control of his own channels plus the three state ones which, in order to compete with Mediaset, lowered their standards to such an extent that for a generation Italian television has been regarded as the most inane in Europe – an endless succession of game-shows, talk-shows, phone-ins, advertisements and news bulletins aimed at audiences with an attention span of about seven seconds. Yet more invidious than the abysmal quality has been the fact that a single individual, a politician in a democracy, could have the power to command almost the entire output of the most important sector of his nation's media. Berlusconi

---

*Another tactic, as Umberto Eco noted, was to 'use his own formidable mass media apparatus to accuse the mass media of persecuting him'.[14]

regarded the notion of an independent broadcasting corporation as simply ludicrous. After becoming prime minister in 1994, he declared it would be 'anomalous' for a country to have a state television that did not support the government elected by the people;[15] a month later, he removed the RAI's directors and replaced them with nominees of his own. On a visit to Bulgaria in 2002 he even went so far as to denounce three journalists who had either mocked him or allowed someone else to mock him on TV: the trio were duly sacked and effectively banned from working in television. Berlusconi's threatening behaviour towards journalists, and the curbs placed by his governments, persuaded an American Freedom of the Press report in 2009 to downgrade its rating of Italy's press from 'free' to 'partly free' and to list the country seventy-third in the world's press freedom rankings, below Ghana, Chile, Mali and Namibia.[16] The Sienese writer Antonio Tabucchi was so appalled by the situation that he chose to live in Portugal, where he found life was now more agreeable and civilized than in Italy.[17]

There can be little doubt that Berlusconi's control of television perverted the electoral process in Italy. The country's many serious and responsible newspapers refuse to make concessions to popular taste and as a result have small circulations and little influence on public opinion. Television is the real opinion-former, and two-thirds of Italians admit that they make up their minds whom to vote for entirely from what they see on TV.[18] This might not matter if the broadcasting companies were neutral in their views and balanced in their coverage; when, however, they are controlled by one of the two prime ministerial candidates, balance and neutrality are obviously impossible. In the month before the election campaign started in 2006, television viewers saw sixteen times as much of Berlusconi as they did of his rival, Romano Prodi. Even during the campaign itself, when the competitors were supposed to receive equal time on the screen, the right-wing coalition obtained 60 per cent of the coverage on RAI and a great deal more than that on Berlusconi's own channels.[19] Perhaps the Right's chief advantage was the sycophantic treatment its leader secured from interviewers, who were often his own employees and had been told what to ask him beforehand. This allowed Berlusconi to spend hours in front of the camera, chatting and joking in a relaxed mood in the knowledge that he would be untroubled by probing questions.

In 1990 the Court of Appeal in Venice had convicted Berlusconi of the charge of giving false testimony in a libel case two years before. In the subsequent decade he was charged with numerous other crimes, including embezzlement, tax evasion, false accounting, illegal funding and the bribing both of judges and of tax inspectors of the Guardia Finanza, who consequently 'forgot' to check the accounts of some of his companies. Two incidents in 1994, the year he went into politics, illuminate the nature of Berlusconi's regard for the law. As his first minister of justice he chose a close associate, Cesare Previti, a lawyer of such dubious repute that President Scalfaro refused to accept him. While Previti was allowed to become minister of defence instead, Scalfaro's judgement was later vindicated when this shady character was found guilty of corruption and, after a lengthy appeal, sentenced by the Supreme Court to six years in jail. Berlusconi seemed to have suffered another embarrassment when his brother Paolo admitted he had indeed bribed the tax police to overlook the accounts of his sibling's companies. Yet the prime minister was unabashed by the confession. Although he did not deny that the wrongdoing had taken place, he claimed that the bribe was as insignificant as a litre of water in the Mediterranean.

Berlusconi employed a dual strategy in his counter-attack on the law, attempting to circumvent it and to discredit its representatives. Circumvention was a complicated business requiring a subtle use of delaying tactics and a clever changing of the rules. One court in Milan had to acquit the prime minister of false accounting after his government had decriminalized the offence. Several cases against him were protracted for so long that, in accordance with the Statute of Limitations, they had to be closed. But the most effective ploy of all was a law of 2003 that gave the prime minister and other holders of the highest offices legal immunity for the duration of their tenure. It has been estimated that by 2010 Berlusconi had passed as many as eighteen laws 'to meet his own personal needs'.[20]

Denigration of judges and prosecutors was a more straightforward business. Berlusconi simply ordered his political supporters and his employees in the media to wage a vicious and often hysterical

campaign against Di Pietro and his colleagues, denouncing and accus-
ing them of corruption and abuse of power. The accusations were so
insistent that investigations had to be set up, which wasted a lot of the
magistrates' time and which regularly found the charges to be
unfounded. Berlusconi's contribution to this campaign was entirely
typical, starting with the incredible assertion that, as he had been
elected by the people, he could not be judged by individuals who had
merely been appointed to their positions. More predictably he claimed
that the prosecuting magistrates were politically motivated and
accused them of using the 'old communist practice' of putting their
opponents in jail. He also became vituperative, declaring that the
magistrates were insane, mad politically and 'mad anyway. To do that
job you need to be mentally disturbed, you need psychic distur-
bances'.[21] The prime minister was speaking of people who did more
than anyone else to keep Italy a civilized place in the 1990s, men who
had exposed political corruption and had struggled – sometimes at
the cost of their lives – to defeat the Mafia.

When Berlusconi first came to power, the *mafiosi* were in a cowed
and dejected state. Hundreds of them were in jail, put there by a combination of evidence from *pentiti*, a courageous Piedmontese prosecutor
in Palermo and the public outrage at the murders of Falcone and
Borsellino in 1992, which had impelled the government to take action.
Under new leadership the Mafia ended its suicidal policy of assassinating senior officials and politicians of the state. Yet it was no less
criminal in its business activities and it even managed to increase its
economic control of Sicily through extortion and protection rackets.
As it became more invisible, it also became more invasive. According
to a report by the Censis research institute in 2009, it received protection money from 80 per cent of the shops in Catania and Palermo
and, together with its counterparts in the Mezzogiorno, enjoyed an
annual turnover of 130 billion euros and adversely affected the lives
of 13 million Italians.[22]

It is no coincidence that the Mafia's resurgence coincided with the
political ascendancy of Silvio Berlusconi. Even in 1994 Sicilians who
had traditionally voted christian democrat had few doubts about
transferring their allegiance to the new leader of the Right, who by
2001 had acquired even greater support on the island than Andreotti

had enjoyed: his coalition captured all sixty-one of the directly elected seats in the Chamber and the Senate. Evidence about Berlusconi's links to the Mafia, which allegedly went back to the 1970s, was often given but never proved in a court of law. He himself was clever enough neither to criticize the Mafia nor to suggest he was indifferent to it, though one of his ministers reflected his government's relaxed attitude to the matter when he observed that, as the Mafia had always existed and always would exist, Italy would have to 'learn to live' with it.[23] Like Andreotti, Berlusconi himself learned to live with it by employing Sicilian lieutenants as 'go-betweens'. His equivalent of Salvo Lima was Marcello Dell'Utri, widely credited as the man who had persuaded him to save his neck by going into politics. This devious and unsavoury person, who had been head of Berlusconi's advertising company Publitalia, was convicted and sentenced for tax fraud and false accounting in 1999, was found guilty of association with the Mafia and sentenced to nine years' imprisonment in 2004 and was given a third prison sentence for attempted extortion in 2007. These setbacks did not, however, dissuade Berlusconi from nurturing Dell'Utri's parallel career as a politician, giving his friend's followers seats in parliament and enabling their leader to go from deputy in 1996, to member of the European parliament in 1999, to senator in 2001 and to be re-elected to the latter post in 2006 and 2008. The appeal system in Italy goes on for such a long time that by 2010 Dell'Utri had still not served any of his sentences.

RESILIENT ITALY

Italy entered the third millennium in a mood of some despondency. The euphoria of a few years before, when the economy was flying and politics were being cleansed, had evaporated as a cascade of statistics suggested that the nation was in incurable decline. Especially worrying was the decrease in the birth rate which, despite the Vatican's stance on birth control, had fallen to 1.18 children per woman (or 118 children for every 200 adults), the lowest in the world, perhaps the lowest in all history, one that suggested the Italian people would die out within four or five generations; in the month of January 2005

Italians seemed to give an indication of their priorities when they produced fewer than 46,000 babies and bought more than 212,000 new cars.[24] The accumulation of gloomy data led to a decline in self-esteem and to a widespread crisis of identity. Why, people asked, did Italy not function? Why was it apparently ungovernable? Was it in fact a real nation or was it just a nineteenth-century invention? Except in a purely formal sense, could it really be said to exist?

The economic *sorpasso* was by now a memory. The British economy had caught up with Italy's and then surged ahead; France remained out of reach; even more depressing was the discovery, a little later on, that Spain's GDP per capita had surpassed Italy's. Further gloom was caused by the industrial rise of China which, at a fraction of the cost, was able to manufacture goods the Italians had become experts in making such as spectacles, shoes, glass and clothing; in June 2010 Venetian police seized 11 million objects for sale in their city as Murano glass which were in fact fakes made in China.[25] Yet the pessimism was not only induced by comparisons with what was happening abroad. That economic dynamism which had characterized the 1960s had been replaced – at any rate in public schemes – by lethargy, corruption and indecision. Any large project in Sicily, the construction of Palermo's ring-road for example, was now likely to need a quarter of a century to complete. It had taken just eight years in the late 1950s and early 1960s to build the 755 kilometres of motorway from Milan to Naples, but thirty-four years were required to open (in 2008) just the first stretch of an autostrada planned to run the mere 140 kilometres from Syracuse to Gela.[26]

The most conspicuous economic activity over the last generation has been the construction of illegal housing, which has made Italy the biggest producer and consumer of cement in Europe, producing twice as much of the substance as France and four times as much as Britain. Speculators built hundreds of thousands of houses without permission wherever they could buy land, preferably in fields or along the coast, confident that bribery would win them retrospective permission or that they would be beneficiaries of the amnesties which the government periodically and incomprehensibly offered. Three-quarters of the illegal construction took place in the south and, although Sardinia was able to preserve most of its coasts, those of Sicily, Calabria and much of Apulia were irredeemably ruined. Cement was poured over much of the north as well, particularly the shores of Lake Garda, the coastline of Liguria and the valley of the Po. The old Lombard landscape of brick barns and bell-towers, of poplar trees and great fields of maize, virtually disappeared as land equivalent to twenty football pitches was daily consumed by asphalt and cement. Italians still talk about their *bel paese* without seeming to realize that much of it is no longer *bello*; for many of them, a picnic in a field is a picnic in the country even if the neighbouring field contains a factory. Most of the Po Valley is now neither town nor country but *periferìa*, an endless and unplanned sprawl (a noun that has entered the Italian vocabulary) of factories, fields, car-parks, pylons and largely treeless suburbs. Destruction of the landscape under the christian democrats was bad enough, but it accelerated after they had gone. Between 1990 and 2005 rural Italy lost 2 million hectares, an area the size of the entire region of Lazio. Nearly a half of Liguria's farmland disappeared under concrete in that period.[27]

The Clean Hands campaign may have limited the scope of political corruption, but it did little to stem avarice and fraud in other spheres. In 2004 Transparency International's corruption index rated Italy more corrupt than any other country in Europe except Greece and more than many states in the developing world, including Jordan, Oman, Costa Rica and Barbados.[28] In one spectacular incident a senior official of the ministry of health was found to have embezzled enough money to hold fourteen Swiss bank accounts, large quantities of gold and diamonds, $120 million hidden in cushions in his homes and an art collection that included works by Modigliani and De Chirico.

The most lethal forms of corruption were inevitably those linked to organized crime in the south. There is an obvious connection between two statistics for Casal di Principe, a nondescript town a few miles north of Naples which in the 1990s had both the highest murder rate in Europe and one of the highest volumes of Mercedes car sales in the world. In his brilliant and courageous exposé of the Camorra, published in 2006, the journalist Roberto Saviano observed that what he called 'Gomorrah' or 'Italy's other Mafia' had turned his region of Campania into the homicidal record-holder of Europe, the most violent place in Italy, the drugs capital of the continent, the toxic waste dump of the West and a world centre of illegal arms trafficking.[29]

While most Italians might remain unaffected by crime and corruption, few were able to circumvent the obstacles set up by a slow, cumbersome and extremely inefficient bureaucracy. Even a minister for the civil service once admitted that Italians wasted between fifteen and twenty days a year simply trying to cope with the problems it caused. The tax system was so complicated and confusing that citizens often found it difficult to calculate even roughly how much they might have to pay. Nor was it easy to navigate the nation's legal system because, according to different reckonings, Italy had between five and twelve times as many laws as France or Germany.[30] The law was perhaps the most frustrating of all aspects of Italian life. In the late 1990s it was estimated that there were 2 million criminal cases and 3 million civil cases pending, and the figure had apparently risen to a total of 9 million early in the next century. It is not surprising, then, that most civil cases are abandoned, four out of five crimes have gone unpunished and, even when a guilty verdict has been returned, the convicted in non-violent cases could spend an average of eight years at liberty before being in danger of going to prison.[31]

Politicians remained the principal focus of their electorate's disdain. In 2009 the veteran journalist Piero Ottone argued that Spain's economy had overtaken Italy's because the ruling class in Madrid was greatly superior to the one in Rome; Italy's inferiority could be traced among other things to its leaders' lack of 'moral sense'.[32] Spain's constitutional progress after Franco's death in 1975 had indeed been remarkable. Within a few years the country possessed a stable two-party system and had peacefully elected a socialist government in spite of threats from the army and a terrorist campaign in the Basque provinces. Nearly a century and a half after unification – and more than sixty years after Mussolini's death – Italian politics had still been unable to settle into any kind of rhythm or consistency. To many of their compatriots, politicians seem an innately frivolous breed. As Beppe Severgnini observes, they prefer 'brilliant declarations to unostentatious planning. They like first nights but not rehearsals and want to be onstage rather than behind the scenes.'[33] When they have to retire backstage, they spend their time playing number games, plotting new combinations, making and unmaking coalitions. And journalists abet these activities, endlessly interviewing politicians, discussing possible alliances, wondering how factions will react and speculating on who might desert one grouping and team up with another. Italy has had more political parties than any other country, so many of them including the word *democratico* in their name that it is not always easy to distinguish them clearly.* Perhaps that explains the recent proliferation of 'nature' names, not only the Ulivo and Margherita whom we know, but also the Girasole (Sunflower), a small left-wing group founded in 2001, and the Arcobaleno (Rainbow), an unsuccessful alliance of Greens and hardline communists in 2008.

Many Italians resent the wealth and lifestyle of their parliamentarians. In the 1950s few deputies had a telephone or a private office or even a secretary at the Chamber of Deputies in the Palazzo Montecitorio; many were too poor to rent a Roman flat with a bathroom, and some came to the capital only for Thursdays, the day when bills were voted on. Yet at the beginning of the twenty-first century Italians were the richest parliamentarians in the world, earning over twice as much as their counterparts in France and three times that of deputies in the Swedish Riksdag. They were driven around in chauffeured cars and often lived in suites in Rome's smartest hotels; perks included free haircuts, free cellphones, subsidized meals and life pensions even after spending only a few years in parliament. Extravagance permeated every level of official life, from the foreign junkets of regional councillors to the splendours of living for the president of the republic. It cost four times as much to keep the Italian president in the Quirinale as it did to maintain the Queen of England in Buckingham Palace.[34]

Another cause for dissatisfaction was the performance of Italian members of the European parliament. Italy has long been vocally enthusiastic about the European Union and a supporter of closer integration among its members. A federal Europe was naturally an attractive idea to what had become the least nationalistic state on the continent, and such a goal had after all been the dream of Mazzini

---

*The Communist Party, for instance, metamorphosed successively into the Partito Democratico della Sinistra (PDS), the Democratici della Sinistra (DS) and the Partito Democratico (PD).

and Garibaldi. Instead of moaning about the 'tyranny of Brussels', Italians have long believed that the EU, with its regional funds and insistence on free trade, would help modernize the economy: a survey made in the spring of 2004 found that nearly two-thirds of Italians 'trusted' the Community, compared to barely one-quarter of the British.[35] Yet this enthusiasm was not reflected in the behaviour of the government, which regarded Brussels as a sort of exile for its politicians and supplied commissioners who, with a few notable exceptions, were second-rate performers, both unskilled and unprepared in international negotiation. Italy has seldom had a European policy and as a result it has not enjoyed the degree of influence possessed by France or Germany, fellow co-founders, or even by notoriously eurosceptical Britain. During Berlusconi's second government its attitude changed for the worse, from negligent to obstreperous: Italy even threatened to sabotage much of the EU's programme if Helsinki was selected instead of Parma as the headquarters of the European Food Safety Agency. The country also acquired the worst record among member states for compliance with EU laws.

Like their colleagues in Rome, Italian deputies in the Strasbourg parliament are paid far more than other Europeans. Yet they play little part in the deliberations of the assembly, many of them seldom taking part in debates or even opening their mouths in public. Despite their high salaries, most of them regard Strasbourg as a place of banishment, as a hotel in which to live comfortably while they plot to acquire more attractive jobs at home. This practice, which is followed by few deputies from other countries, is remarkably successful. Nearly half of Italy's MEPs elected in 2004 resigned before the end of their term to take up more tempting posts such as a job in the Rome government or the presidency of their own region. Since while serving at Strasbourg they were allowed to retain their domestic jobs as mayors or provincial presidents, they consequently had poor attendance records and rarely bothered to turn up on days when no votes were scheduled. One MEP for the National Alliance was absent for two-thirds of the sessions because she found it more congenial to stay at home and concentrate on two of her other jobs, mayor of Lecce and party boss in Apulia.[36]

In recent years it has been rare to hear impartial Italians make appreciative remarks about their leaders unless they are talking about certain unusual individuals such as Di Pietro (a politician by accident), Fini (an extremist turned moderate), Prodi (who twice defeated Berlusconi), Emma Bonino (a veteran civil rights campaigner) or Nichi Vendola (the gay communist president of conservative Apulia). An international survey in the spring of 2008 discovered that only 16 per cent of Italians have faith in their politicians, the lowest proportion, along with the Poles and Bulgarians, in Europe.[37] The low calibre of the country's politicians has prompted some people to wonder whether Italians are congenitally incapable of producing great leaders. Two of the best, it was pointed out, had been more or less foreigners, De Gasperi, once a member of the Austrian parliament, and Cavour, who was francophone, anglophile and half-Swiss.[38] One writer lamented the fact that Italy even produced inferior villains, less remarkable xenophobes and dictators than other countries. Franco had been better – and more successful – than Mussolini; the Austrian Jörg Haider and the French Jean-Marie Le Pen were more cultured chauvinists than Umberto Bossi; and Nicolas Sarkozy's romance with Carla Bruni had seemed more glamorous than Berlusconi's escapades with prostitutes and aspiring actresses. When asked abroad how things were going in his country, Piero Ottone found himself replying that three institutions still functioned there: the navy, the Bank of Italy and the ministry of foreign affairs.[39] Perhaps he might have added the *carabinieri*.

Italy's unease at the start of the millennium was exacerbated by intellectuals who demonstrated their anxieties by writing books with titles as stark as *The Death of the Fatherland, If We Cease to Be a Nation* and *Is Italy a Civilized Country?*, sometimes containing an equally pessimistic subtitle such as *Why Italy Cannot Succeed in Becoming a Modern Country*. Many were fixated by the 'problem' of the national character, and one newspaper editor ascribed the country's shortcomings to the nature of its people, who were wily, deceitful and amoral, who possessed no 'spirit of service' and who were too attached to their mothers.[40] The sense of national identity, such as it had been, seemed to have disappeared, and increasing numbers of Italians were now questioning the legitimacy of the state. The Northern League, which became the third party in Italy in 2008, had long denounced the Risorgimento and claimed that unification had been a mistake. Now the Resistance, the second sacred experience of modern Italian history, was being discredited by politicians of the Right. A mayor of Rome publicly denied that fascism was evil, a minister of defence praised the brutal soldiery of Salò, and a speaker of the Senate pronounced the Resistance to be a myth that ought to be abandoned. Berlusconi made his own opinions clear in 2002 by refusing to lay a wreath to the partisans and going on holiday to his villa in Sardinia instead.

By the start of the millennium it was hard to discern a sense of pride in being Italian, unless the country's football team was playing well, except for that pride understandably engendered by the high quality of exports exhibiting 'Italian style' and 'made in Italy'. Although Italy was still a unitary state, it was evidently not a united one. Even the name Padania, an entirely imaginary idea, attracted more loyalty and enthusiasm than the name Italy. According to the journalist Massimo Nicolazzi, Italy had been 'a state without a language but has now become a language (almost) without a state':[41] *la patria* had not evolved into *la nazione*. In his book *Italiani senza Italia* (*Italians without Italy*), Aldo Schiavone suggested that what Italians had always really wanted was to be 'a people without a nation but with a distant identity'.[42] Dante would have agreed.

As the 150th anniversary of the Italian state approached in 2011, commentators found it hard to see how it could be celebrated with any genuine enthusiasm. The first fifty years had been commemorated with nationalist gusto in 1911, the centenary had been held at a time of economic optimism in 1961, but the 150th birthday was being organized by a government whose second-largest component condemned unification and daily disparaged the southern half of the country. As the journalist Ilvo Diamanti observed in the summer of 2009, the antics of the Northern League – and the reactions to them around the peninsula – meant that Italians had never felt less united or part of the same nation.[43]

Italian grumbles are directed chiefly at the state, which is widely regarded with disdain and dislike and as an obstacle to be negotiated in the pursuit of happiness. Yet the state is weak and cannot prevent its citizens from enjoying their lives beyond its reach. Italians may be tired of the foreigners who tell them that, though they are incapable of running their own country, they know how to live, they possess 'the secret of life', yet there is more than a superficial truth in this view. Britons I have known living in Italy, as well as Italians I have known living in Britain, have generally agreed that people are happier near the Mediterranean than near the North Sea. I have a Modenese friend who chooses to live in Edinburgh, and a Lucchese acquaintance who prefers to live in the London borough of Ealing, but they do not deny that pleasure and happiness are more accessible in Italy; like a group of Neapolitan friends, who chose to open a restaurant in Scotland, they found themselves unable to deal with the corruption and bureaucracy at home: 'too many problems', they say with a sad smile. Italy has a visible vibrancy and a degree of economic activity that makes it hard to believe some of the statistical indications of malaise. In any case, one cannot measure the 'quality of life' by simply comparing GDP per capita between countries and regions. Using other criteria, such as health care and the environment, an international survey in 2009 found that, while Lombardy is the richest region in Italy, its population has a lower quality of living than seven poorer regions, including Tuscany, the Marches and Friuli-Venezia Giulia.[44]

Italian society revolves around the family to an extent unimaginable in what are still bizarrely called the Anglo-Saxon countries. Whether the family is, as Luigi Barzini claimed, 'the only fundamental institution in the country', it is certainly, as the historian Paul Ginsborg has written, 'very important, both as metaphor and as reality'.[45] Northerners may snigger at the ubiquitous molly-coddling, at the way Italian parents pamper their children, keeping them up late, stuffing them with ice-cream, spending twice as much money on their clothes as other nations do. Yet they may also notice that such genuine and enthusiastic affection rarely leads to the 'Anglo-Saxon' problems of hooliganism, alcoholism and teenage pregnancies. Fellini's comedy of 1953, I Vitelloni, mocked Italian men who remain tied to their mothers, which is another subject for northern ribaldry. British newspapers relish reporting about 'mammoni', 'mamma's boys' who are still living at home in their thirties – not looking for work though perhaps vaguely doing a degree – especially when law courts take their side and order divorced fathers to maintain adult sons living idly with their mothers.[46] Yet whatever else this custom is, it is a sign of social cohesion.

A more serious criticism of the Italian family was made in 1958 by the American political scientist Edward Banfield, who employed the phrase 'amoral familism' to describe the 'inability of villagers [in Basilicata] to act together for their common good, or indeed for any good transcending the immediate material interests of the family'.[47] Rather than use their skills and energy for the good of the state or the community, they were applying them exclusively for the benefit of their relations. Banfield's research was done long ago in the south, and there was clearly some validity to this argument, which is illustrated today in a hideous, concave distortion in the southern criminal organizations. But its thesis could not be accepted, especially today, in northern or central Italy. Family strength has anyway been both a result as well as a cause of the traditional weakness of Italian government. As the BBC's Matt Frei once observed, the family is 'Italy's secret shock absorber in times of social upheaval'.[48] It provides what the state fails to provide, a point often made to justify the Italians' propensity to evade taxes.

The benefits of belonging to an Italian family far outweigh the drawbacks. In his book *La Bella Figura* Beppe Severgnini enumerated them, starting with the family as a bank, lending its children money without interest for buying cars, homes and holidays. Next it is a 'form of insurance coverage with no policy to sign', and 'an employment agency' that allows children to inherit their parents' professions: two-fifths of Italy's dentists and half of its engineers have simply taken over from their fathers.[49] So long as the children are qualified, this may not matter, but nepotism is a problem in universities and medical schools when supposedly open competitions are regularly won by relatives of senior figures in the departments; in 2008, at the University of Palermo, 230 teachers were relatives of other teachers.[50] Some of the benefits traditionally offered by the family have been eroded by modernity and contemporary life. It was easier, as Severgnini pointed out, for the family to be a residential care home in a farmhouse than in a city flat, although many Italians still manage to live very near their parents. The family also used to be a restaurant 'where you didn't have to reserve a table' but, now that mamma no longer spends seven hours a day in the kitchen (as she did in 1950), 'it's a sort of snack bar where you can always get something to eat'. Yet it remains 'a dormitory when you're at university (average age at graduation – twenty-eight) and a bachelor pad for those between relationships'. Half of Italy's parents still live with adult children.[51]

The social strength of Italy is based not only on the family but also on communal loyalties and a network of charities and aid associations that have been set up to campaign for social, cultural and political goals. Between 4 and 5 million Italians work as volunteers – for society rather than the state – in nearly 40,000 organizations established by individuals to improve the health and civic life of the nation; in recent years it has been difficult to cross a piazza without encountering reformed addicts who firmly but politely urge you to support the fight against drugs. Yet Italians campaign for the good things of the earth as well as attempt to remedy the bad ones. One of the most typical and successful is the Slow Food Movement, set up in 1986 after McDonald's had committed the ultimate sacrilege of selling burgers in Rome's Piazza di Spagna. The organization offered a programme, since imitated in many other countries, that emphasizes the relationship between man and nature and promoted regional cuisine based on local, natural and healthy ingredients. Slow Food owed its success to the receptiveness of a people who abhor frozen food, who have far fewer supermarkets than the French and many times as many food shops as the Germans, a people who treat food with such seriousness that they even establish confraternities in Bologna to safeguard the quality of the city's *tortellini* and in Genoa to protect the purity of pesto sauce.*[52]

Essential Italy remains the Italy of its communes, as it was in the Middle Ages. *Campanilismo* – parochialism or loyalty to the municipal bell-tower – has always been strong, so strong perhaps that, as Giordano Bruno Guerri has suggested, it has helped make Italians a 'non-people with a non-state'.[53] *Campanilismo* is by definition limiting and has thus been mocked, as Lampedusa mocked it, as a breeder of narrow minds. The prince once recalled how, on reaching Palermo's Porta Felice after an absence of two days, one of his friends crossed herself, thanked God for allowing her to see her native city

---

*Pesto is not in fact a purely Genoese sauce. While the basil and the olive oil may come from Liguria, the cheese it contains is parmesan from Emilia-Romagna and pecorino usually from Lazio.

once more and quoted words from Verdi's *I vespri siciliani*, 'O tu, Palermo, terra adorata'. Such a country, argued Lampedusa, could never produce a writer like Joseph Conrad, who found subjects for his novels by roaming the oceans, or Rudyard Kipling, who distilled the Indian experience of living in the Victorian empire.[54]

Yet provincialism in Italy is less parochial than in any other country I know. How many nations have towns like Modena, with a population of 180,000, that can hold a festival of philosophy attended by thousands of its citizens, many hundreds of them sitting for hours in the Piazza Grande to watch a television screen broadcasting lectures delivered to another audience in a different part of the city?

Campanilismo is not like loyalty to a football club, which is a form of tribal loyalty. It is fidelity to an historical and essentially self-contained form of society designed many centuries ago to cater to the needs of its citizens. The well-preserved condition of the city-centres is testament not to the provincialism of their inhabitants but to their pride and sense of responsibility. It is not provincial for the Lucchesi to prefer their nineteenth-century cafés and shop fronts to rows of modern chain-stores: these older places belong to a living heritage that citizens want to protect not because they are good for tourism but because they are part of their identity. Nor are people being provincial if they stroll regularly to their main square, where they find their friends and favourite cafés as well as their cathedral and their bank, their theatre, town council, law courts and police headquarters. *Campanilismo* brings reassurance and a sense of identity to a society which perceives the state to be hostile or indifferent. Local administration regulates an urban life as civilized as any on the planet in scores of towns such as Trento and Bergamo, Pistoia and Arezzo, Mantua and Verona, Lecce and Bressanone. Cremona in Lombardy is a fine example: a lovely city of pinks and duns, of yellows and ochres, a place of slow rhythms and old, unhurried cyclists, of clean streets and well-kept museums, of small workshops where master craftsmen still fashion exquisite violins. So agreeable and well run is the town that its children want to live there, remain there and die there. If you looked at the marriage register in the town hall at the beginning of the twenty-first century, you would have found that nearly all the weddings were still between boys and girls born in Cremona; the closest the town got to a 'mixed marriage' in one season was that between a local man and a girl from Naples.

Even for a 'refounded' communist like the Apulian Nichi Vendola, *campanilismo* is a vital ingredient in Italian life. From an early age, he remarks, children used to derive an identity from the piazza, the cathedral, the priests and the town walls; now they have little to hold on to because they are brought up in the *periferìa*, where they have neither piazza nor city walls, pray in no cathedral and seldom see priests.[55] Beppe Severgnini, a liberal journalist, has a similar view: Italians, he says, traditionally have three 'lines of defence', their home, their piazza and their city walls. He is a travelling Lombard who lived for years in London and Washington, who has reported on war in Lebanon and sport in Beijing, and who is also the honorary president of a football club in Kabul. Yet he returned to Crema, a town near Milan with only 33,000 inhabitants, where he lives in the house he was born in, works in an office near the cathedral and is married to a woman brought up a hundred yards away. An Italian who combines provincialism and internationalism (without much nationalism in between), he has explained why he returned to Crema and what he likes about living there.

> In a small town, we don't just want a congenial barber and a well-stocked news-stand. We want professionally made coffee and a proper pizza. We want a couple of streets to stroll down, an avenue to jog along, a pool to swim in and a cinema for a bit of entertainment. We want a functioning courthouse, a reassuring hospital, a consoling church and an unintimidating cemetery. We want a new university and an old theatre house. We want football fields and town councillors we can pester in the bar. We want to see the mountains beyond the level crossing when the weather's good and the air is clear. We want footsteps on cobbled streets in the night, yellow lights to tinge the mist and bell towers we can recognize from a distance. We want doctors and lawyers who can translate abstract concepts into our dialect – my father can – and people with a kind word and a smile for everyone . . . We want all these things and in Crema we have them.[56]

It is hard not to see this as the real Italy, the one trampled on by the Risorgimento: the communal Italy, result of a millennium of natural evolution, not the nationalist Italy, product of a drastic and insensitive imposition. In its three periods of cultural and economic affluence – the Middle Ages, the Renaissance and the half-century after Mussolini – Italy was either divided or effectively de-nationalized. It was the peninsula's misfortune that in the nineteenth century a victorious national movement tried to make its inhabitants less Italian and more like other peoples, to turn them into conquerors and colonialists, men to be feared and respected by their adversaries. For eight decades Italy's leaders followed the same policy, leading their new and fragile nation on a mistaken journey to poverty, colonial disaster, the fascist experiment and the humiliation of the Second World War. It was not until the 1940s that numbers of people began to wonder whether Italy had abandoned its vocation.

Geography and the vicissitudes of history made certain countries, including France and Britain, more important than the sum of their parts might have indicated. In Italy the opposite was true. The parts are so stupendous that a single region – either Tuscany or the Veneto – would rival every other country in the world in the quality of its art and the civilization of its past. But the parts have not added up to a coherent or identifiable whole. United Italy never became the nation its founders had hoped for because its making had been flawed both in conception and in execution, because it had been truly what Fortunato was told by his father, 'a sin against history and geography'.* It was thus predestined to be a disappointment, to be what Luigi Barzini regretfully recognized many years ago, a country that 'has never been as good as the sum of all her people.'[57] Those people have created much of the world's greatest art, architecture and music, and have produced one of its finest cuisines, some of its most beautiful landscapes and many of its most stylish manufactures. Yet the millennia of their past and the vulnerability of their placement have made it impossible for them to create a successful nation-state.

*See p. 251.

List of Books Used
and Cited in the Text

The years given refer not to the time of original publication but to the date of the edition consulted.

David Abulafia, *Frederick II*, Allen Lane, London, 1988.

David Abulafia (ed.), *Italy in the Central Middle Ages*, Oxford University Press, 2004.

Harold Acton, *The Bourbons of Naples*, Methuen, London, 1974.

Harold Acton, *The Last Bourbons of Naples*, Methuen, London, 1961.

Harold Acton, *The Last Medici*, Faber and Faber, London, 1932.

Harold Acton, *The Pazzi Conspiracy*, Thames and Hudson, London, 1979.

P. A. Allaun, *Politics and Society in Post-War Naples*, Cambridge University Press, 1973.

Robert Alter, *A Lion for Love: A Critical Biography of Stendhal*, Harvard University Press, Cambridge, Mass., 1986.

Grant Amyot, *The Italian Communist Party*, Croom Helm, London, 1981.

Geoff Andrews, *Not a Normal Country: Italy after Berlusconi*, Pluto Press, London, 2005.

Anon, 'The Poisoned Fruits of the Risorgimento', *Times Literary Supplement*, 16 June 1972.

Pino Arlacchi, *Mafia Business*, Verso, London, 1986.

Girolamo Arnaldi, *Italy and Its Invaders*, Harvard University Press, Cambridge, Mass., 2005.

Mario Ascheri, *Le città-Stato*, Mulino, Bologna, 2006.

Albert Russell Ascoli and Krystyna von Henneberg (eds.), *Making and Remaking Italy*, Berg, Oxford, 2001.

Corrado Augias, *The Secrets of Rome*, Rizzoli, New York, 2007.

Massimo d'Azeglio, *Things I Remember*, Oxford University Press, 1966.

Edward Banfield, *The Moral Basis of a Backward Society*, Free Press, New York, 1958.

Alberto Mario Banti, *La nazione del Risorgimento*, Einaudi, Turin, 2000.

Alberto Mario Banti, *Il Risorgimento italiano*, Laterza, Bari, 2006.

Zygmunt G. Barański and Rebecca J. West (eds.), *Modern Italian Culture*, Cambridge University Press, 2005.

Vernon Bartlett, *Tuscan Harvest*, Chatto and Windus, London, 1971.

Vernon Bartlett, *Tuscan Retreat*, Chatto and Windus, London, 1965.

Luigi Barzini, *From Caesar to the Mafia*, Hamish Hamilton, London, 1971.

Luigi Barzini, *The Italians*, Hamish Hamilton, London, 1964.

Giorgio Bassani, *The Garden of the Finzi-Continis*, Quartet, London, 1989.

Timothy Baycraft and Mark Hewitson (eds.), *What Is a Nation? Europe 1789–1914*, Oxford University Press, 2006.

Derek Beales, *England and Italy 1859–60*, Thomas Nelson, Edinburgh, 1961.

Derek Beales, *Joseph II: Against the World, 1780–1790*, Cambridge University Press, 2009.

Derek Beales and Eugenio F. Biagini, *The Risorgimento and the Unification of Italy*, Pearson, London, 2002.

Gilberto Bedini and Giovanni Fanelli, *Lucca: spazio e tempo dall'Ottocento ad oggi*, Maria Pacini Fazzi, Lucca, 1971.

Kinta Beevor, *A Tuscan Childhood*, Viking, London, 1993.

Giovanni Belardelli, Luciano Cafagna, Ernesto Galli della Loggia, Giovanni Sabbatucci, *Miti e storia dell'Italia unita*, Mulino, Bologna, 1999.

Sandra Berresford, *Italian Memorial Sculpture 1820–1940*, Frances Lincoln, London, 2004.

Robert Blake, *Disraeli*, Methuen, London, 1969.

T. C. W. Blanning and David Cannadine (eds.), *History and Biography*, Cambridge University Press, 1996.

Anton Blok, *The Mafia of a Sicilian Village 1860–1960*, Blackwell, Oxford, 1974.

John Boardman, Jasper Griffin and Oswyn Murray (eds.), *The Oxford History of the Roman World*, Oxford University Press, 2001.

Norberto Bobbio, *Ideological Profile of Twentieth-Century Italy*, Princeton University Press, 1995.

Giorgio Bocca, *Storia dell'Italia Partigiana*, Laterza, Bari, 1966.

Peter Bondanella and Julia Conway Bondanella, *The Macmillan Dictionary of Italian Literature*, Macmillan, London, 1979.

Guido Bonsaver, *Censorship and Literature in Fascist Italy*, University of Toronto Press, 2007.

R. J. B. Bosworth, *Mussolini*, Arnold, London, 2002.

R. J. B. Bosworth, *Mussolini's Italy*, Allen Lane, London, 2005.

Louis Antoine Fauvelet de Bourrienne, *Mémoires de Napoléon*, Chez Colburn et Bentley, Paris, 1931.

William M. Bowsky, *A Medieval Italian Commune: Siena under the Nine 1287–1355*, University of California Press, Berkeley, 1981.

Guy Bradley, Elena Isayev and Corinna Riva (eds.), *Ancient Italy*, University of Exeter Press, 2007.

F. Brancaccio di Carpino, *The Fight for Freedom: Palermo 1860*, Folio, London, 1968.

Peter Brand and Lino Pertile, *The Cambridge History of Italian Literature*, Cambridge University Press, 2004.

Fernand Braudel, *The Mediterranean*, vols. 1 and 2, Collins, London, 1972–3.

Julian Budden, *The Operas of Verdi*, vols. 1 and 2, Clarendon Press, Oxford, 1992.

Julian Budden, *Verdi*, J. M Dent, London, 1993.

Vittorio Bufacchi and Simon Burgess, *Italy since 1989*, Palgrave Macmillan, Basingstoke, 2001.

Martin J. Bull and James L. Newell, *Italian Politics*, Polity, Cambridge, 2005.

Peter Burke, *The Italian Renaissance*, Polity, Cambridge, 2005.

M. Caesar and P. Hainsworth, *Writers and Society in Contemporary Italy*, Berg, Leamington Spa, 1984.

Pier Giorgio Camaiani, *Dallo stato cittadino alla città bianca*, La Nuova Italiana, Florence, 1979.

Giuseppe Campolieti, *Breve storia della città di Napoli*, Oscar Mondadori, Milan, 2004.

Giuseppe Campolieti, *Re Franceschiello*, Oscar Mondadori, Milan, 2005.

Franco Cassano, *Il pensiero meridiano*, Laterza, Bari, 2007.

Franco Cassano, *Paeninsula*, Laterza, Bari, 1998.

Roderick Cavaliero, *Italia Romantica*, I. B. Tauris, London, 2005.

Olympia Parenti Cenami, *Lucca dei Mercanti-Patrizi Lucchesi*, Nardini, Florence, 1977.

Anna Cento Bull and Mark Gilbert, *The Lega Nord and the Northern Question in Italian Politics*, Palgrave Macmillan, Basingstoke, 2001.

D. S. Chambers, *The Imperial Age of Venice*, Thames and Hudson, London, 1970.

David G. Chandler, *The Campaigns of Napoleon*, Weidenfeld and Nicolson, London, 1967.

Charlotte Gower Chapman, *Milocca*, George Allen and Unwin, London, 1973.

Martin Clark, *Modern Italy*, Longman, London, 1984.

Edith Clay (ed.), *Lady Blessington in Naples*, Hamish Hamilton, London, 1979.

Richard Cobb, *Promenades*, Oxford University Press, 1980.

Anna Cornelisen, *Torregreca*, Macmillan, London, 1969.

Santi Correnti (ed.), *Palermo d'Allora*, Longanesi, Milan, 1979.

Santi Correnti, *La Sicilia del Cinquecento*, Mursia, Milan, 1980.

Francesco Cossiga, *Italiani sono sempre gli altri*, Mondadori, Milan, 2007.

Maurizio Cotta and Luca Verzichelli, *Political Institutions in Italy*, Oxford University Press, 2007.

John F. Coverdale, *Italian Intervention in the Spanish Civil War*, Princeton University Press, 1975.

Vincent Cronin, *Napoleon*, Collins, London, 1971.

Giorgio and Maurizio Crovato, *Isole abbandonate della laguna veneziana*, San Marco Press, Teddington, 2008.

Barry Cunliffe, *Europe between the Oceans*, Yale University Press, 2008.

Dante Alighieri, *Monarchy and Three Political Letters*, Weidenfeld and Nicolson, London, 1954.

Alastair Davidson, *The Theory and Practice of Italian Communism*, Merlin, London, 1982.

John A. Davis (ed.), *Italy in the Nineteenth Century*, Oxford University Press, 2006.

John A. Davis, *Naples and Napoleon*, Oxford University Press, 2006.

John A. Davis and Paul Ginsborg (eds.), *Society and Politics in the Age of the Risorgimento*, Cambridge University Press, 1991.

Robert C. Davis and Garry R. Marvin, *Venice: The Tourist Maze*, University of California Press, Berkeley, 2004.

Renzo De Felice, *Mussolini*, 7 vols, Einaudi, Turin, 1965–1992.

Alexander De Grand, *Italian Fascism*, University of Nebraska Press, Lincoln, 1982.

Angelo Del Boca, *Italiani, brava gente?* Neri Pozza, Vicenza, 2006.

Tullio De Mauro, *Storia linguistica dell'Italia unita*, Laterza, Bari 2001.

Emma Dench, *Romulus's Asylum: Roman Identities from the Age of Alexander to the Age of Hadrian*, Oxford University Press, 2005.

John Dickie, *Cosa Nostra*, Hodder, London, 2000.

John Dickie, *Delizia*, Hodder and Stoughton, London, 2007.

Gigi Di Fiore, *I vinti del Risorgimento*, UTET, Turin, 2004.

Benjamin Disraeli, *Sibyl*, Peter Davies, London, 1927.

Danilo Dolci, *The Outlaws of Partinico*, Macgibbon and Kee, London, 1960.

Danilo Dolci, *Sicilian Lives*, Pantheon, New York, 1981.

Norman Douglas, *Old Calabria*, Secker and Warburg, London, 1956.

Nicholas Doumanis, *Italy*, Arnold, London, 2001.

Christopher Duggan, *A Concise History of Italy*, Cambridge University Press, 2002.

Christopher Duggan, *Fascism and the Mafia*, Yale University Press, New Haven, 1989.

Christopher Duggan, *The Force of Destiny*, Allen Lane, London, 2007.

Christopher Duggan, *Francesco Crispi*, Oxford University Press, 2002.

Umberto Eco, *Turning Back the Clock*, Harvill Secker, London, 2007.

Nicholas Farrell, *Mussolini*, Weidenfeld and Nicolson, London, 2003.

Ronnie Ferguson, *A Linguistic History of Venice*, Olschki, Florence, 2008.

M. I. Finley, *The Ancient Greeks*, Pelican, London, 1977.

M. I. Finley, *Ancient Sicily*, Chatto and Windus, London, 1979.

David Forgacs (ed.), *Rethinking Italian Fascism*, Lawrence and Wishart, London, 1986.

R. F. Foster, *Paddy and Mr Punch*, Penguin, London, 1995.

John Fraser, *Italy: Society in Crisis/Society in Transformation*, Routledge, London, 1981.

Matt Frei, *Getting the Boot*, Times Books, New York, 1995.

Giorgio Galli, *I partiti politici italiani (1943–2004)*, RCS, Milan, 2001.

Ernesto Galli della Loggia, *L'identità italiana*, Mulino, Bologna, 1998.

Richard N. Gardner, *Mission Italy: On the Front Lines of the Cold War*, Rowman and Littlefield, Lanham, 2005.

Alexander Gerschenkron, *Economic Backwardness in Historical Perspective*, Harvard University, Cambridge, Mass., 1962.

Roberto Gervaso, *Cagliostro*, Gollancz, London, 1974.

Pieter Geyl, *Napoleon: For and Against*, Penguin, London, 1982.

Edward Gibbon, *The Decline and Fall of the Roman Empire*, Dent, London, 1910.

Henry Gibbs, *Italy on Borrowed Time*, Jarrolds, London, 1953.

David Gilmour, *Curzon*, John Murray, London, 1994.

David Gilmour, *The Last Leopard: A Life of Giuseppe Tomasi di Lampedusa*, Eland, London, 2007.

Paul Ginsborg, *A History of Contemporary Italy*, Penguin, London, 1990.

Paul Ginsborg, *Italy and Its Discontents*, Allen Lane, London, 2001.

Paul Ginsborg, *Silvio Berlusconi*, Verso, London, 2005.

Ralph Glasser, *The Net and the Quest*, Temple Smith, London, 1977.

Piero Gobetti, *On Liberal Revolution*, Yale University Press, New Haven, 2000.

Wolfgang Goethe, *Italian Journey*, Penguin, London, 1982.

Martin Goodman, *Rome and Jerusalem*, Allen Lane, London, 2007.

Anthony Grafton, *Leon Battista Alberti*, Allen Lane, London, 2000.

Andrew Graham-Dixon, *Caravaggio*, Allen Lane, London, 2010.

Antonio Gramsci, *Selections from Prison Notebooks*, Lawrence and Wishart, London, 1982.

Michael Grant, *History of Rome*, Weidenfeld and Nicolson, London, 1978.

Michael Grant, *The World of Rome*, Weidenfeld and Nicolson, London, 1962.

W. E. Greening, 'Verdi and Italian Unity', *Contemporary Review*, vol. 190, October 1956.

A. James Gregor, *Giovanni Gentile: Philosopher of Fascism*, Transaction, New Brunswick, 2001.

A. James Gregor, *Mussolini's Intellectuals*, Princeton University Press, 2005.

Desmond Gregory, *Napoleon's Italy*, Associated University Presses, London, 2001.

Raymond Grew, 'How Success Spoiled the Risorgimento', *Journal of Modern History*, vol. xxxiv, September 1962.

Massimo Grillandi, *Invito alla lettura di Bassani*, Mursia, Milan, 1984.

Francis M. Guercio, *Sicily*, Faber and Faber, London, 1968.

Giordano Bruno Guerri, *Antistoria degli Italiani*, Oscar Mondadori, Milan, 1999.

Francesco Guicciardini, *History of Italy*, Richard Sadler and Brown, London, 1966.

John Hale, *The Civilization of Europe in the Renaissance*, HarperCollins, London, 1993.

John Hale, *Florence and the Medici*, Thames and Hudson, London, 1983.

John Hale, *Renaissance Europe 1480–1520*, Fontana, London, 1982.

Augustus Hare, *The Story of My Life*, vol. 6, George Allen, London, 1900.

Sudhir Hazareesingh, *The Legend of Napoleon*, Granta, London, 2005.

Harry Hearder, *Italy in the Age of the Risorgimento*, Longman, London, 1983.

Grant Heiken, Renato Funiciello and Donatella De Rita, *The Seven Hills of Rome*, Princeton University Press, 2007.

Judith Herrin, *Byzantium*, Allen Lane, London, 2007.

Edward Herring and Kathryn Lomas (eds.), *The Emergence of State Identities in Italy in the First Millennium BC*, University of London, 2000.

Robert Hewison, *Ruskin and Venice*, Thames and Hudson, London, 1978.

Gilbert Highet, *Poets in a Landscape*, New York Review Books, 2010.

E. J. Hobsbawm, *Primitive Rebels*, University of Manchester Press, 1971.

Mary Hollingsworth, *The Cardinal's Hat*, Profile, London, 2005.

Hugh Honour, *Companion Guide to Venice*, Collins, London, 1967.

Andrew Hopkins, *Italian Architecture from Michelangelo to Borromini*, Thames and Hudson, London, 2002.

Peregrine Horden and Nicholas Purcell, *The Corrupting Sea*, Blackwell, Oxford, 2000.

Simon Hornblower and Antony Spawforth (eds.), *The Oxford Classical Dictionary*, Oxford University Press, 1996.

Simon Hornblower and Antony Spawforth (eds.), *The Oxford Companion to Classical Civilization*, Oxford University Press, 1998.

J. K. Hyde, *Society and Politics in Medieval Italy*, Macmillan, London, 1973.

Timothy Hyman, *Sienese Painting*, Thames and Hudson, London, 2003.

Ricardo Illy, *Così perdiamo il Nord*, Mondadori, Milan 2008.

Mario Isenghi (ed.), *I luoghi della memoria*, Laterza, Bari, 1998.

Istituto per la storia del risorgimento italiano, *La Sicilia verso l'unità d'Italia*, U. Manfredi, Palermo, 1960.

Italy, vol. 3, Naval Intelligence Division, 1945.

Henry James, *Italian Hours*, Penguin, London, 1975.

Richard Jenkyns (ed.), *The Legacy of Rome*, Oxford University Press, 1992.

Richard Jenkyns, *Virgil's Experience*, Clarendon Press, Oxford, 1998.

Tobias Jones, *The Dark Heart of Italy*, Faber and Faber, London, 2003.

Philippe Julian, *D'Annunzio*, Pall Mall, London, 1972.

Jonathan Keates, *The Siege of Venice*, Chatto and Windus, London, 2005.

Jonathan Keates, *Stendhal*, Sinclair-Stevenson, London, 1994.

Catherine Keen, *Dante and the City*, Tempus, Stroud, 2003.

Tullio Kezich, *Federico Fellini*, I. B.Tauris, London, 2007.

Ross King, *Brunelleschi's Dome*, Pimlico, London, 2001.

Ross King, *Machiavelli*, Harper Press, London, 2007.

Robert Kolker, *Bernardo Bertolucci*, BFI, London, 1985.

Rosario La Duca, *Cercare Palermo*, La Bottega di Hefesto, Palermo, 1985.

David Lane, *Berlusconi's Shadow*, Allen Lane, London, 2004.

Robin Lane Fox, *The Classical World*, Allen Lane, London, 2005.

John Larner, *Culture and Society in Italy 1290–1420*, Batsford, London, 1971.

John Larner, *Italy in the Age of Dante and Petrarch 1216–1380*, Longman, London, 1980.

Cristina La Rocca (ed.), *Italy in the Early Middle Ages*, Oxford University Press, 2002.

Peter Lauritzen, *Venice: A Thousand Years of Culture and Civilization*, Weidenfeld and Nicolson, London, 1978.

P. Lauritzen and A. Zielcke, *Palaces of Venice*, Phaidon, Oxford, 1978.

David Laven, *Venice and Venetia under the Habsburgs, 1815–1835*, Oxford University Press, 2002.

Mary Laven, *Virgins of Venice*, Allen Lane, London, 2002.

Claudia Lazzaro and Roger J. Crum (eds.), *Donatello among the Blackshirts*, Cornell University Press, Ithaca, 2005.

Michael A. Ledeen, *D'Annunzio*, Transaction, New Brunswick, 2006.

Georges Lefebvre, *Napoleon*, vols. 1 and 2, Routledge and Kegan Paul, London, 1969.

Carlo Levi, *Christ Stopped at Eboli*, Farrar Straus, New York, 1947.

Norman Lewis, *The Honoured Society*, Eland, London, 1984.

Norman Lewis, *Naples '44*, Collins, London, 1978.

LiMes, Esiste l'Italia? L'Espresso, Rome, 2009.

Robert J. Littman, *The Greek Experiment*, Thames and Hudson, London, 1974.

A. Lawrence Lowell, *Governments and Parties in Continental Europe*, Longmans, London, 1896.

Robert Lumley and Jonathan Morris (eds.), *The New History of the Italian South*, University of Exeter Press, 1997.

Sergio Luzzatto, *The Body of Il Duce*, Metropolitan, New York, 2005.

Archibald Lyall, *Rome Sweet Rome*, Putnam, London, 1956.

Adrian Lyttelton (ed.), *Liberal and Fascist Italy*, Oxford University Press, 2002.

Mary McCarthy, *The Stones of Florence and Venice Observed*, Penguin, London, 1986.

Patrick McCarthy, *Italy since 1945*, Oxford University Press, 2000.

Diarmid MacCulloch, *Reformation*, Penguin, London, 2004.

Richard Mackenney, *Renaissances: The Culture of Italy, c.1300–c.1600*, Palgrave Macmillan, Basingstoke, 2005.

Denis Mack Smith, *Cavour*, Weidenfeld and Nicolson, London, 1985.

Denis Mack Smith, *Cavour and Garibaldi 1860*, Cambridge University Press, 1985.

Denis Mack Smith (ed.), *Garibaldi*, Prentice-Hall, Englewood Cliffs, 1969.

Denis Mack Smith, *Italy: A Modern History*, University of Michigan Press, Ann Arbor, 1959.

Denis Mack Smith, *Italy and Its Monarchy*, Yale University Press, New Haven, 1989.

Denis Mack Smith, *The Making of Italy 1796–1870*, Macmillan, London, 1968.

Denis Mack Smith, *Mazzini*, Yale University Press, 1994.

Denis Mack Smith, *Medieval Sicily 800–1713*, Chatto and Windus, London, 1969.

Denis Mack Smith, *Modern Italy*, Yale University Press, 1997.

Denis Mack Smith, *Modern Sicily after 1713*, Chatto and Windus, London, 1969.

Denis Mack Smith, *Mussolini*, Weidenfeld and Nicolson, London, 1981.

Denis Mack Smith, *Mussolini's Roman Empire*, Longman, London, 1976.

Denis Mack Smith, *Victor Emanuel, Cavour and the Risorgimento*, Oxford University Press, 1971.

Louis Madelin, *The Consulate and the Empire*, vols. 1 and 2, Heinemann, London, 1934–6.

Anthony Majanlahti, *The Families Who Made Rome*, Pimlico, London, 2006.

Robert Mallett, *Mussolini and the Origins of the Second World War*, Palgrave Macmillan, Basingstoke, 2003.

Augusto Mancini, *Storia di Lucca*, Maria Pacini Fazzi, Lucca, 1975.

Philip Mansel, *The Eagle in Splendour*, George Philip, London, 1978.

Claudio Marazzini, *Breve storia della lingua italiana*, Mulino, Bologna, 2004.

Umberto Marcelli, *Interpretazioni del Risorgimento*, Pàtron, Bologna, 1970.

Giuseppe Carlo Marino, *L'opposizione mafiosa*, Flaccovio, Palermo, 1986.

John A. Marino (ed.), *Early Modern Italy*, Oxford University Press, 2002.

J. A. R. Marriott, *The Makers of Modern Italy*, Oxford University Press, 1931.

Ronald Marshall, *Massimo d'Azeglio*, Oxford University Press, 1966.

George Martin, *Verdi*, Limelight, New York, 1992.

John Martin and Dennis Romano (eds.), *Venice Reconsidered*, Johns Hopkins University Press, Baltimore, 2000.

John Jeffries Martin, *Venice's Hidden Enemies*, Johns Hopkins University Press, Baltimore, 2004.

Lauro Martines, *Power and Imagination: City-States in Renaissance Italy*, Allen Lane, London, 1980.

Roberto Martucci, *L'invenzione dell'Italia unita*, Sansoni, Milan, 1999.

Roberto Martucci, *Storia costituzionale italiana*, Carocci, Rome, 2006.

Georgina Masson, *Companion Guide to Rome*, Collins, London, 1980.

Walter Maturi, *Interpretazioni del Risorgimento*, Einaudi, Turin, 1962.

Gavin Maxwell, *The Ten Pains of Death*, Alan Sutton, Gloucester, 1986.

Vittorio Mazzonis, *Torino ieri e l'altro ieri*, Ruata, Turin, 1961.

Mario Miccinesi, *Invito alla lettura di Carlo Levi*, Mursia, Milan, 1981.

Nelson Moe, *The View from Vesuvius: Italian Culture and the Southern Question*, University of California Press, Berkeley, 2002.

Franco Molfese, *Storia del brigantaggio dopo l'Unità*, Feltrinelli, 1983, Milan.

John N. Molony, *The Emergence of Political Catholicism in Italy*, Croom Helm, London, 1977.

Arnaldo Momigliano, *Studies in Historiography*, Weidenfeld and Nicolson, London, 1966.

Caroline Moorehead, *Iris Origo*, Godine, Boston, 2002.

Elsa Morante, *History*, Allen Lane, London, 1978.

Jasper More, *The Land of Italy*, Batsford, London, 1953.

James Morris, *The Venetian Empire*, Penguin, London, 1990.

James Morris, *Venice*, Faber and Faber, London, 1974.

Jan Morris, *Trieste and the Meaning of Nowhere*, Faber and Faber, London, 2002.

William Murray, *The Last Italian*, Grafton, London, 1991.

John M. Najemy (ed.), *Italy in the Age of the Renaissance*, Oxford University Press, 2004.

Peter Nichols, *Italia, Italia*, Macmillan, London, 1973.

Pietro Nicolosi, *Palermo Fin de Siècle*, Mursia, Milan, 1979.

John Julius Norwich, *Venice*, vols. 1 and 2, Allen Lane, London, 1977 and 1981.

Patrick Key O'Clery, *The Making of Italy*, Kegan Paul, London, 1892.

Iris Origo, *The Last Attachment*, John Murray, London, 1972.

Iris Origo, *The Merchant of Prato*, Alfred A Knopf, New York, 1957.

Iris Origo, *A Need to Testify*, John Murray, London, 1984.

Charles Osborne, *Complete Operas of Verdi*, Indigo, London, 1997.

Charles Osborne, *Verdi*, Weidenfeld and Nicolson, 1987.

Nicholas Ostler, *Empires of the Word*, HarperCollins, London, 2005.

Didier Ottinger (ed.), *Futurism*, Tate Publishing, London, 2009.

Piero Ottone, *Italia mia*, Longanesi, Milan, 2009.

Sergio Pacifici, *The Modern Italian Novel*, Southern Illinois University Press, Carbondale, 1979.

Michael St John Packe, *The Bombs of Orsini*, Secker and Warburg, London, 1957.

George Painter, *Marcel Proust*, Penguin, London, 1983.

Massimo Pallottino, *A History of Earliest Italy*, Routledge, London, 1991.

Pietro Palumbo, *Storia di Lecce*, Congedo, Martina Franca, 2002.

Roger Parker, *Leonora's Last Act*, Princeton University Press, 1997.

Roger Parker, *Verdi and His Operas*, Oxford University Press, 2007.

Tim Parks, *Italian Neighbours*, Vintage, London, 2001.

Alexander Passerin D'Entrèves, *Reflections on the History of Italy*, Clarendon Press, Oxford, 1947.

Birgit Pauls, *Giuseppe Verdi und das Risorgimento*, Akademie Verlag, Berlin, 1996.

Robert O. Paxton, *The Anatomy of Fascism*, Allen Lane, London, 2004.

Santi Peli, *La Resistenza in Italia*, Einaudi, Turin, 2004.

Clara Petacci, *Mussolini Segreto: Diari 1932–1938*, Rizzoli, Milan, 2010.

Mary Phillips-Matz, *Verdi*, Oxford University Press, 1993.

Daniel Pick, *Rome or Death*, Jonathan Cape, London, 2005.

Thomas Pinney (ed.), *The Letters of Rudyard Kipling*, vol. 4, Macmillan, Basingstoke, 1999.

John Pollard, *Catholicism in Modern Italy: Religion, Society and Politics since 1861*, Routledge, London, 2008.

Anna Pomar, *Donna Franca Florio*, Vallechi, Florence, 1985.

Adrian Poole and Jeremy Maule (eds.), *The Oxford Book of Classical Verse*, Oxford University Press, 1995.

Alessandro Molinari Pradelli, *La Toscana com'era*, Newton Compton, Rome, 1986.

Geoffrey Pridham, *The Nature of the Italian Party System*, Croom Helm, London, 1981.

Giuliano Procacci, *History of the Italian People*, Penguin, London, 1978.

Marcel Proust, *The Captive*, Folio, London, 2001.

Robert Putnam, *Making Democracy Work: Civic Traditions in Modern Italy*, Princeton University Press, 1993.

Giuseppe Quatriglio, *Mille anni in Sicilia*, Ediprint, Palermo, 1985.

Domenico Quirico, *Generali*, Oscar Mondadori, Milan, 2007.

Agatha Ramm, 'The Risorgimento in Sicily', *English Historical Review*, vol. 87, 1972.

Elizabeth Rawson, *Cicero*, Allen Lane, London, 1975.

Lucy Riall, *Garibaldi: Invention of a Hero*, Yale University Press, London, 2007.

Lucy Riall, *Risorgimento: The History of Italy from Napoleon to Nation-State*, Palgrave Macmillan, Basingstoke, 2009.

Joanna Richardson, *Stendhal*, Gollancz, London, 1974.

Jasper Ridley, *Garibaldi*, Constable, London, 1974.

Linda Risso and Monica Boria (eds.), *Politics and Culture in Postwar Italy*, Cambridge Scholar Press, Newcastle, 2006.

Sergio Rizzo and Gian Antonio Stella, *La Casta*, Rizzoli, Milan, 2007 (*see also* Stella and Rizzo).

Graham Robb, *The Discovery of France*, Picador, London, 2007.

Peter Robb, *Midnight in Sicily*, Harvill, London, 1988.

Andrea di Robilant, *A Venetian Affair*, Fourth Estate, London, 2004.

N. A. M. Rodger, *The Safeguard of the Sea*, Penguin, London, 2004.

Rosario Romeo, *Il Risorgimento in Sicilia*, Laterza, Bari, 1982.

John Rosselli, *The Life of Bellini*, Cambridge Univesity Press, 1996.

John Rosselli, *The Life of Verdi*, Cambridge University Press, 2001.

Renzo Rossotti, *Torino: I monumenti raccontano*, Edizioni Servizi, Turin, 2004.

Jean-Jacques Rousseau, *Du contrat social*, Clarendon Press, Oxford, 1972.

Steven Runciman, *A History of the Crusades*, vol. 3, Cambridge University Press, 1955.

Steven Runciman, *The Sicilian Vespers*, Cambridge University Press, 1984.

James Ruscoe, *The Italian Communist Party 1976–81*, Macmillan, London, 1982.

John Ruskin, *The Stones of Venice*, George Allen, London, 1905.

Gaetano Salvemini, *Carlo and Nello Rosselli*, Intellectual Liberty, London, 1937.

Donald Sassoon, *Mussolini and the Rise of Fascism*, HarperCollins, London, 2007.

Roberto Saviano, *Gomorrah: Italy's Other Mafia*, Macmillan, Basingstoke, 2007.

Salvatore Scarpino, *La mala unità*, Effesette, Cosenza, 1985.

Aldo Schiavone, *Italiani senza Italia*, Einaudi, Turin, 1998.

Aldo Schiavone, *L'Italia contesa*, Laterza, Bari, 2009.

Alfonso Scirocco, *Garibaldi*, Princeton University Press, 2007.

Walter Scott, *The Two Drovers and Other Stories*, Oxford University Press, 1987.

Domenico Sella, *Italy in the Seventeenth Century*, Longman, London, 1997.

Christopher Seton-Watson, *Italy from Liberalism to Fascism*, Methuen, London, 1967.

Gaia Servadio, *Rossini*, Constable, London, 2003.

Beppe Severgnini, *Italiani si diventa*, RCS, Milan, 1998.

Beppe Severgnini, *La Bella Figura*, Hodder and Stoughton, London, 2008.

Desmond Seward (ed.), *Naples*, Constable, London, 1984.

Desmond Seward and Susan Mountgarret, *Old Puglia*, Haus, London, 2009.

Carlo Sforza, *Contemporary Italy*, Frederick Muller, London, 1946.

Carlo Sforza, *The Real Italians: A Study in European Psychology*, Columbia University Press, New York, 1942.

Quentin Skinner, *Machiavelli*, Oxford University Press, 2000.

Frank Snowden, *The Conquest of Malaria: Italy 1900–1962*, Yale University Press, New Haven, 2006.

Carlotta Sorba, *Teatri: L'Italia del melodramma nell' età del Risorgimento*, Mulino, Bologna, 2001.

Giovanni Spadolini, *Firenze fra ' 800 e ' 900*, Le Monnier, Florence, 1984.

Giorgio Spini and Antonio Casali, *Firenze*, Laterza, Bari, 1986.

C. J. S. Sprigge, *The Development of Modern Italy*, Duckworth, 1943.

John Steer, *A Concise History of Venetian Painting*, Thames and Hudson, London, 1970.

Gian Antonio Stella and Sergio Rizzo, *La Deriva*, Rizzoli, Milan, 2008 (*see also* Rizzo and Stella).

Stendhal, *The Life of Henry Brulard*, New York Review Books, 2002.

Stendhal, *Memoirs of an Egotist*, Chatto and Windus, London, 1975.

Stendhal, *Rome, Naples and Florence*, John Calder, London, 1959.

Stendhal, *To the Happy Few*, John Lehmann, London, 1952.

Alexander Stille, *Excellent Cadavers*, Pantheon, New York, 1995.

Francesco Tabladini, *Bossi; la grande illusione*, Riuniti, Roma, 2003.

Anne Taylor, *Laurence Oliphant*, Oxford University Press, 1982.

Martin Thom, *Republics, Nations and Tribes*, Verso, New York, 1995.

Mark Thompson, *The White War*, Faber and Faber, London, 2008.

Giuseppe Tomasi di Lampedusa, *The Leopard*, Collins and Harvill, London, 1962.

Giuseppe Tomasi di Lampedusa, *Letteratura inglese*, vols. 1 and 2, Mondadori, Milan 1990–91.

Daniele Tomasini, *Verdi e il Risorgimento*, Farnesiana, Piacenza, 1999.

Claretta Micheletti Tonetti, *Bernardo Bertolucci*, Twayne, New York, 1995.

Mario Toscano, *Alto Adige – South Tyrol*, Johns Hopkins University Press, Baltimore, 1975.

G. M. Trevelyan, *Garibaldi and the Thousand*, Longmans, London, 1948.

Raleigh Trevelyan, *Princes under the Volcano*, Macmillan, London, 1972.

Raleigh Trevelyan, *Rome '44*, Secker and Warburg, London, 1981.

Hugh Trevor-Roper, *History and the Enlightenment*, Yale University Press, New Haven, 2010.

Nino Valeri, *Giolitti*, UTET, Turin, 1971.

Danele Varè, *Laughing Diplomat*, John Murray, London, 1938.

Elio Veltri and Marco Travaglio, *L'odore dei soldi*, Riuiniti, Rome, 2006.

Franco Venturi, *Italy and the Enlightenment*, Longman, London, 1972.

Fulco di Verdura, *The Happy Summer Days*, Weidenfeld and Nicolson, London, 1976.

Bruno Vespa, *Vincitori e vinti*, Oscar Mondadori, Milan, 2006.

Pasquale Villari, *The Liberation of Italy*, Nelson, Appleton, 1959.

Virgil, *The Aeneid*, Penguin, London, 2001.

Andrea Vitello, *Giuseppe Tomasi di Lampedusa*, Sellerio, Palermo, 1987.

David Waley, *The Italian City-Republics*, Longman, London, 1978.

David Waley, *Siena and the Sienese in the Thirteenth Century*, Cambridge University Press, 1991.

D. S. Walker, *A Geography of Italy*, Methuen, London, 1958.

Ernst Wangerman, *From Joseph II to the Jacobin Trials*, Oxford University Press, 1969.

Bryan Ward-Perkins, *The Fall of Rome*, Oxford University Press, 2006.

William Weaver, *The Golden Century of Italian Opera*, Thames and Hudson, London, 1980.

William Weaver and Martin Chusid (eds.), *A Verdi Companion*, Gollancz, London, 1980.

Jonathan White, *Italy: The Enduring Culture*, Leicester University Press, London, 2000.

Arnold Whittall, *Romantic Music*, Thames and Hudson, London, 1987.

Garry Wills, *Venice: Lion City*, Washington Square Press, New York, 2002.

Elizabeth Wiskemann, *Italy since 1945*, Macmillan, London, 1971.

S. J. Woolf, *The Italian Risorgimento*, Longmans, London, 1969.

Stuart Woolf, *Italy 1700–1860*, Methuen, London, 1979.

Guido Zucconi, *Venice*, Arsenale Editrice, Verona, 1993.

Notes

I DIVERSE ITALIES

1 Ottone, 124.
2 *Canzoniere,* cxlvi.
3 Mack Smith [1968], 361; Dolci [1981], 144.
4 Duggan [2007], 102.
5 Origo [1957], 317–22.
6 Horden and Purcell, 190; Braudel, vol. 1, 138–9.
7 Cunliffe, 66–71; Braudel, vol. 1, 139.
8 *La Repubblica,* 5 October 2008; *L'Espresso,* 19 March 2010.
9 Bartlett [1965], 98.
10 *La Repubblica,* 25 September 2009.
11 Cunliffe, 475.
12 Glasser, 46–7.
13 Frei, 158.
14 Banti [2000], 160.
15 Graham Robb, 25; Cobb, 94.
16 Origo [1957], *passim.*
17 Hale [1993], 60–62.
18 Scott, 255.
19 Bobbio, xx–xxi, 81–2.
20 Cenami, 23.
21 Jens Petersen quoted in Barański and West (eds.), 23.
22 Martines, 446–9; Hale [1993], 161–3.
23 Sforza [1942], 37.
24 De Mauro, 43; Marazzini, 185–6.
25 Origo [1972], 287.
26 Mack Smith, *Cavour,* 216; Duggan [2002], 13, 18.
27 Umberto Eco in *L'Espresso,* 28 August 2008.
28 *La Repubblica,* 30 July 2009.

29 *Il Venerdi di Repubblica*, 25 September 2009; *La Repubblica*, 30 July 2009.
30 Roderick Conway-Morris in *The Times Literary Supplement*, 12 September 2008.

2 IMPERIAL ITALIES

1 Lane Fox, 282.
2 Dench, 130.
3 Mark Pobjoy in Herring and Lomas (eds.), 187–205.
4 Jenkyns (ed.) [1992], 16.
5 *Georgic I*, translated by David R. Slavitt, in Poole and Maule (eds.), 276.
6 Jenkyns [1998], 77, 97.
7 Finley [1979], 123.
8 Gibbon, vol. 1, 48.
9 Goodman, 490.
10 Momigliano, 181.
11 Ward-Perkins, 87, 100, 117–18.
12 G. W. Bowersock in the *New York Review of Books*, 25 September 2008.
13 Herrin, 321–3.
14 Libretto by Salvatore Cammarano translated by Julian Budden, Philips Classics Productions, 1978.
15 Procacci, 33.

3 CITIES AND POWERS

1 Although I have seen these frescoes many times myself, I am grateful to Timothy Hyman for his analysis of them in his book *Sienese Painting*.
2 *Purgatorio*, xiii 151–4.
3 Bowsky, 14–15.
4 Bowsky, 295–6; Waley [1991], 11; Hyman, 15.
5 *Purgatorio*, v 134, vi 72–5.
6 *De vulgari eloquentia*, I xii 4 and I xvi 3; Keen, 12, 15, 107–8; Dante, 103–4.
7 Lane Fox, 28.
8 Origo [1957], 44, 333.
9 Guicciardini, 86.
10 Mackenney, 140–43.
11 Hale [1983], 15–19; Najemy (ed.), 186.
12 King [2001], 126–8, and King [2007], 67–72.

13 *Purgatorio*, vi 148–51.
14 Acton [1979], 114, 123; Hale [1983], 61–75.
15 Ascheri, 170.
16 Quoted in Hyman, 13.
17 Henk Van Os quoted in Hyman, 209.
18 Mack Smith, *Modern Sicily*, 284.
19 Guerri, 84.
20 Hale [1983], 186–7.
21 Hale [1983], 192.

4 ADRIATIC VENICE

1 Morris [1974], 318; James, 7.
2 Mackenney, 124.
3 Foster, 156.
4 Rousseau, 213–15.
5 Runciman [1955], vol. 3, 130.
6 Lauritzen and Zielcke, 16–23.
7 Ruskin, vol. 3, 297.
8 Lauritzen and Zielcke, 25.
9 Crovato and Crovato, *passim*.
10 Ascheri, 110.
11 Ascheri, 128–9; Wills, 98.
12 Julius Kirshner in Najemy (ed.), 100–101.
13 Robilant, 15.
14 James Morris [1974], 94.
15 John Jeffries Martin, 51, 69, 73–5, 181–2, 219–23.
16 Act 3, scene iii, 26–31.
17 Lauritzen, 13; Blake, 4–5.
18 Theodore K. Rabb in *The Times Literary Supplement*, 11 July 2008.
19 Robilant, 285.
20 'A Toccata of Galuppi's' (1855).

5 DISPUTED ITALIES

1 Guicciardini, 86.
2 Barzini [1964], 287.
3 Guerri, 119–20.
4 Mackenney, 34.

5 Stendhal [1959], 350.
6 Mack Smith, *Medieval Sicily*, vol. 2, 115.
7 Venturi, 289.
8 Wangerman, 89–95.
9 Woolf [1979], 41, 150–51.
10 Acton [1974], 167–8.
11 Goethe, 199, 207, 317–21.
12 Goethe, 246.
13 Romeo, 12–13, 29, 40–52.
14 Mack Smith, *Modern Sicily*, vol. 2, 263–4, 287–303.
15 Goethe, 117.
16 Gervaso, 190–92.
17 Chandler, 206.
18 Woolf [1979], 163.
19 Chandler, 71–3.
20 Cronin, 138
21 Chandler, 209.
22 Bourrienne, epigraph.
23 Madelin, vol. 1, 311. Lefebvre, vol. 1, 250–51.
24 Mansel, 29, 160.
25 Franco Della Peruta in Davis and Ginsborg (eds.), 39–47.
26 Davis, *Naples and Napoleon*, 261.
27 Mack Smith [1968], 18.
28 Collection in the Casa Mazzini in Genoa.
29 Hazareesingh, 260.
30 Woolf [1969], 39.
31 Duggan [2007], 103.
32 Mack Smith [1968], 110 and [1985], 26.
33 Clay (ed.), 8, 127.
34 Martha Petrusewicz in Lumley and Morris (eds.), 20–23.
35 Banti [2000], 21.
36 Stendhal [1959], 358.
37 Stendhal [2002], 480.
38 Stendhal [1959], 413, 468.
39 Mack Smith, *Cavour*, 32, and [1971], 11.

6 REVOLUTIONARY ITALIES

1 Marshall, 13–14, 38.
2 Azeglio, 110–11, 129.

3 Barzini [1964], 180.

4 Duggan [2007], 100.

5 Ascheri, 13.

6 Woolf [1969], 45.

7 Denis Mack Smith in *The Times Literary Supplement*, 21 January 1955; Mack Smith [1994], 41.

8 Keates [2005], 9.

9 Riall [2007], 30.

10 Ridley, 238.

11 Tomasi di Lampedusa [1990–91], vol. 1, 89–91.

12 Sorba, 26–8.

13 Sorba, 178-9.

14 Phillips-Matz, 230–31.

15 Phillips-Matz, 236–7.

16 Parker [1997], 35–9; Mary Ann Smart in Ascoli and Henneberg (eds.), 107–8.

17 Weaver and Chusid (eds.), 5.

18 Parker [1997], 25.

19 Parker [1997], 33–4.

7 THE MAKING OF ITALY

1 Marshall, 141, 160.

2 Mack Smith, *Cavour*, 112.

3 Ridley, 385; Marshall, 236; Beales [1961], 148.

4 *Gazzetta Piemontese*, 12 January 1856.

5 Mack Smith [Garibaldi], 30.

6 Quoted in Mack Smith [1968], 215.

7 Beales [1961], 21, 51.

8 Martucci [1999], 84–8.

9 Martucci [1999], 91; Mack Smith, *Cavour*, 172–3.

10 O'Clery, 53.

11 Beales [1961], 156.

12 Mack Smith [1968], 302, 355.

13 Taylor, 75–8.

14 Ridley, 435.

15 Ridley, 480–82.

16 Quirico, 32.

17 Di Fiore, 46.

18 Mack Smith, *Cavour and Garibaldi*, 398.

19 Mack Smith, *Cavour and Garibaldi*, 387.

20 Moe, 175–6; Mack Smith, *Cavour and Garibaldi*, 407, 430, and [1968], 328–30.

21 Di Fiore, 199, 202, 262, 340; Proust, 229, 254–5, 300–301; Painter, 567.

22 G. M. Trevelyan, 44.

23 Conversation with Giuseppe Galasso, March 2009.

24 Duggan [2002], 281.

25 Varè, 210.

26 *La Mia Guida Pratica di Treviso* (2006).

27 Pick 155; Riall [2007], 369.

28 Marshall, 291; Azeglio, 180.

8 LEGENDARY ITALY

1 Lowell, 148–9.

2 G. M. Trevelyan, 26–7; Woolf [1969], 72.

3 Woolf [1969], 83.

4 Woolf [1969], 69, 79–80.

5 Mack Smith, *Cavour*, 109, 150–51.

6 Mack Smith, *Cavour*, 197.

7 Mack Smith, *Cavour*, 160–61, 242.

8 Scirocco, 10.

9 Riall [2007], 69.

10 Mack Smith [1994], 212, and [1969], 174.

11 Quoted by David Lowenthal in *The Times Literary Supplement*, 24 June 2005.

12 Ridley, 635–6.

13 Rossotti, 6.

14 Mack Smith [1989], 43, and [1994], 100.

15 Mack Smith, *Cavour*, 82–3, and [1989], 60.

16 Mack Smith [1989], 15, 20, 34, 44, 50–51, 63.

17 Mack Smith [1989], 42.

18 Domenico Zanichelli, quoted by Denis Mack Smith in Blanning and Cannadine (eds.), 185.

19 Marshall, 172.

20 Marshall, 204.

21 Quirico, 88–109; O'Clery, 397–401.

22 Banti [2000], 45–6.

23 Scirocco, 165.

24 Gramsci, 53–9; Maturi, 644–7; Adolfo Omodeo in Woolf [1969], 74, 95–6.

25 Mack Smith [1968], 10–11.

26 Beales and Biagini [2002], 6.

9 MAKING ITALIANS

1 Lane Fox, 36.

2 Moe, 37–8.

3 Moe, 63.

4 See Guercio, 160, on eastern Sicilians.

5 Mack Smith [1968], 330–31; Moe, 176.

6 Woolf [1969], 75.

7 Marshall, 275–89.

8 Mack Smith, *Cavour and Garibaldi*, 429–30.

9 Martucci [1999], 305–6.

10 Martucci [1999], 294; O'Clery, 294.

11 Mack Smith [1968], 379; Romeo, 385.

12 Verdura, 134.

13 Quoted by Gabriella Gribaudi in Lumley and Morris (eds.), 94, 100–101.

14 Arnaldi, 192.

15 Del Boca, 48.

16 Hare, vol. 6, 412–13.

17 Allaun, 69.

18 Duggan [2002], 375–6, 454–5, 718, and [2007], 298.

19 Belardelli et al., 56.

20 Duggan [2002], 447; Denis Mack Smith in Blanning and Cannadine (eds.), 183.

21 Belardelli et al., 65–6.

22 Mack Smith [1959], 78.

23 Duggan [2002], 358, 361, 432.

24 Del Boca, 13; Duggan [2002], 500, 528–30.

25 Del Boca, 75

26 Mack Smith [1989], 93, 113.

27 Sorba, 171.

28 Weaver, 155; Rosselli [2001], 77; Parker [2007], 45; Pauls, 250–55, 323.

29 Martin, 270.

30 Martin, 305.

31 Martin, 312, 317; Phillips-Matz, 429–30.
32 Martin, 250.
33 Tomasini, 85–7; Martin, 379; Duggan [2002], 441; Pauls, 273–5.
34 Duggan [2002], 543.
35 Phillips-Matz, 762–5.

10 NATIONALIST ITALY

1 Disraeli, 77.
2 Belardelli, 52–60.
3 Valeri, 8,
4 Woolf [1969], 80.
5 Bobbio, 94–6.
6 Ottinger (ed.), *passim*; Dickie [2007], 273.
7 Duggan [2007], 384.
8 Del Boca, 106.
9 Isenghi (ed.), 271.
10 Mack Smith [1989], 232.
11 Bobbio, 94.
12 Thompson, 2–3.
13 Pinney (ed.), vol. 4, 457–8, 464.
14 Mack Smith [1989], 230.
15 Duggan [2007], 392.
16 Thompson, 351.
17 Chapman, 154–5.
18 Bosworth [2005], 96–7.
19 Toscano, 8–9.
20 Thompson, 378.
21 Jan Morris, 188.
22 Jan Morris, 3.
23 Origo [1984], 149.
24 Sassoon, 101.
25 Sassoon, 25.
26 Martucci [2006], 106–7.

11 FASCIST ITALY

1 Gerald Silkin in Lazzaro and Crum (eds.), 69.
2 Mack Smith [1981], 114.

3 Bosworth [2005], 233.

4 Bosworth [2002], 259, 314.

5 Duggan [2007], 449.

6 Guerri, 298.

7 Mack Smith [1981], 145.

8 D. Medina Lasansky in Lazzaro and Crum (eds.), 113–31.

9 Ascoli and Henneberg (eds.), 215–16, 260–61.

10 Eugenia Paulicelli in Barański and West (eds.), 253–4.

11 Bonsaver, 9, 62, 156–7, 200.

12 Varè, 166.

13 Bosworth [2005], 419.

14 Grillandi, 99.

15 Quoted by Ian Thomson in *The Times Literary Supplement*, 2 July 2010.

16 Varè, 208.

17 Alberto Mario Banti in *LiMes*, 117.

18 Barzini [1971], 204.

19 Duggan [1989], 141, 177, 183, 208, 225–6, 245–9.

20 Allaun, 84–5.

21 Barzini [1971], 172–4.

22 Levi, 3.

23 *La Voce dei Calanchi*, December 2007.

24 Gilmour [1994], 557; Mack Smith [1981], 59–60.

25 Gilmour [1994], 560–89.

26 Del Boca, 182, 184.

27 Bosworth [2002], 308.

28 Mack Smith [1976], 74–5.

29 Bosworth [2002], 320; Del Boca, 210–14.

30 Del Boca, *passim*; *Observer*, 24 January 1988.

31 Farrell, 281–2.

32 Coverdale, 251.

33 MacGregor Knox in Lyttelton (ed.), 111.

34 See Mallett, 2–15.

35 Denis Mack Smith in Blanning and Cannadine (eds.), 178.

36 Mack Smith [1976], 96, 195.

37 Bosworth [2005], 446; Mack Smith [1976], 178.

38 Mack Smith [1976], 202.

39 Del Boca, 234; *Observer*, 24 January 1988.

40 Duggan [2007], 487; Guerri, 331.

41 Sforza [1942], 27.

12 COLD WAR ITALY

1 Bocca, 261–5; Peli, 74, 119, 134.
2 Peli, 241–4.
3 Raleigh Trevelyan [1981], 102.
4 Luzzatto, 159.
5 Ginsborg [1990], 92.
6 Barzini [1971], 180–81.
7 Pridham, 125.
8 Sforza [1942], the dedication.
9 Ottone, 130.
10 Bobbio, 183.
11 Ginsborg [1990], 198.
12 Amyot, 214.
13 White, 210–15.
14 Tonetti, 148.
15 *Nuovi Argomenti*, May–August 1959; Caesar and Hainsworth, 26.
16 Bonsaver, 142–6; Vitello, 238.
17 Barzini (1971), 203.
18 *Lettres françaises*, 23 December 1959 and 18 February 1960.
19 Vitello, 351–2.
20 Ottone, 13–16.
21 Illy, 32–9; *L'Espresso*, 26 March 2009.
22 Dickie [2007], 17.
23 Saviano, 119–20.

13 MODERN ITALY

1 Rizzo and Stella, 192, 204–5; Paolo Verre in *LiMes*, 187–8.
2 Tabladini, *passim*.
3 Illy, 5, 21, 47, 59–60, 77, 79.
4 *La Repubblica*, 3 October 2008; *Guardian*, 9 March 2008.
5 Saviano, 18.
6 Duggan [2007], 568.
7 *La Repubblica*, 10 April 2002.
8 *La Repubblica*, 18 September 2008.
9 *Economist*, 26 April 2001.
10 Eco, 153; Jones, 235.
11 *Spectator*, 6 and 13 September 2003.

12 *La Repubblica*, 16 September 2008.

13 Veltri and Travaglio, 7.

14 Eco, 124.

15 Christopher Wagstaff in Barański and West (eds.), 249.

16 *Foreign Policy*, 1 May 2009.

17 Interview in *Il Venerdi di Repubblica*, 11 September 2009.

18 John Hooper in the *Guardian Weekend*, 31 October 2009.

19 Alexander Stille in the *New York Review of Books*, 25 May 2006.

20 Alexander Stille in the *New York Review of Books*, 8 April 2010.

21 *Spectator*, 6 and 13 September 2003.

22 Paolo Verre in *LiMes*, 184; *Guardian*, 2 October 2009.

23 Jones, 214; Dickie [2007], 439.

24 Antonio Golini in *LiMes*, 83; Severgnini [2008], 171.

25 Agence France-Presse, 25 June 2010.

26 Paolo Verre in *LiMes*, 183–4; Stella and Rizzo, 19–21.

27 Information from Legambiente Lombardia, March 2010; *La Repubblica*, 5 October 2008; *L'Espresso*, 19 March 2009; *Liberazione*, 16 July 2009.

28 Bull and Newell, 112.

29 Saviano, 64, 160, 185, 234, 283–97, 300.

30 Ginsborg [2001], 217; Illy, 96.

31 Mack Smith [1997], 494; Ottone, 52; Severgnini [2008], 15; Illy, 10.

32 Ottone, 39, 46, 76.

33 Severgnini [2008], 159.

34 Barzini [1971], 254–5; *La Repubblica*, 18 March 2008; Rizzo and Stella, 13, 27–34, 59–60.

35 Bull and Newell, 213.

36 *L'Espresso*, 12 February 2009.

37 Ilvo Diamanti in *LiMes*, 29.

38 *LiMes*, 9; John Dickie in Barański and West (eds.), 29.

39 Ottone, 51, 185.

40 John Dickie in Barański and West (eds.), 29.

41 Massimo Nicolazzi in *LiMes*, 173–6.

42 Schiavone [1998], 111.

43 *La Repubblica*, 26 July 2009.

44 *La Repubblica*, 19 September 2009.

45 Barzini [1964], 190; Ginsborg [2001], xiii.

46 See for example the *Guardian* and the *Independent* of 6 April 2002.

47 Banfield, 10, 83.

48 Frei, 111.

49 Severgnini, [2008] 65.
50 Alexander Stille in the *New York Review of Books*, 4 December 2008;
    the *Economist* 15 November 2008.
51 Severgnini [2008], 66–8.
52 Dickie [2007], 328, 331.
53 Guerri, 69.
54 Tomasi di Lampedusa [1991], vol. 2, 372.
55 Conversation with the author, March 2008.
56 Severgnini [2008], 219.
57 Barzini [1964], 327.

Index